Food, Environment, and Climate Change

Food, Environment, and Climate Change

Justice at the Intersections

Edited by
Erinn Gilson and Sarah Kenehan

ROWMAN & LITTLEFIELD
INTERNATIONAL

Lanham • Boulder • New York • London

Published by Rowman & Littlefield International Ltd
6 Tinworth Street, London SE11 5AL
www.rowmaninternational.com

Rowman & Littlefield International Ltd. is an affiliate of Rowman & Littlefield
4501 Forbes Boulevard, Suite 200, Lanham, Maryland 20706, USA
With additional offices in Boulder, New York, Toronto (Canada), and Plymouth (UK)
www.rowman.com

British Library Cataloguing in Publication Data
A catalogue record for this book is available from the British Library

ISBN: HB 978-1-7866-0923-6

Library of Congress Cataloging-in-Publication Data Is Available

ISBN 978-1-78660-923-6 (cloth : alk. paper)
ISBN 978-1-5381-5298-0 (pbk : alk. paper)
ISBN 978-1-78660-924-3 (electronic)

♾️™ The paper used in this publication meets the minimum requirements of American
National Standard for Information Sciences—Permanence of Paper for Printed Library
Materials, ANSI/NISO Z39.48-1992.

Printed in the United States of America

Contents

Introduction

Erinn Gilson and Sarah Kenehan

In San Pedro de Gallo, in the state of Durango in Mexico, drought has produced arid, unproductive land, destroying farmers' livelihoods and starving cattle who no longer have pasture on which to graze. Climate change not only has devastated agriculture in the region but has induced migration. Over the course of two years, the population of the town has fallen from 4,800 to 1,600 (The Climate Reality Project 2013). Farmer Jose Angel Ochoa speculates that "at the rate we are going, we will be a ghost town" (ibid.). These kinds of environmental effects of climate change are widespread and more complex than might initially be assumed. Fatoumata Diallo, a researcher studying climate change and energy in Mali, comments not only on how climate change impacts the environment and thus agriculture in Mali but also on how the need for food and energy leads to environmental problems that exacerbate the effects of climate change:

> The demand for food by a growing population in combination with a large demand for firewood and charcoal contributes to a reduction in vegetative land, which is cleared for these purposes. ... Climate change is shifting the precipitation patterns in Mali. ... Thus, soil degradation, the clearing of land, and changing precipitation patterns are causing increased desertification, or the spread of dry areas. (Climate Stories Project 2018)

Diallo's concerns highlight the complex interconnections between patterns of land and resource use, environmental problems, climate change, and the need for and the production of food. Yet, like many, she also believes that the connections between them hold the potential for solutions. If the production of food contributes to greenhouse gas (GHG) emissions and causes environmental damage that is detrimental and is then further exacerbated by a destabilized climate, food and agricultural practices can likewise ameliorate these conditions. Similarly, we might respond to climate change by amending environmental and agricultural practices not only with the aim of reducing emissions and mitigating the effects of climate change but also with the aim of generating more sustainable and just—that is, democratic—food systems. As these cases show, it is impossible to ignore the links between climate change, agriculture, and environmental health.

Food and agriculture increasingly have become topics of widespread popular and academic interest. This interest is spurred by the growing sense that what we eat, how we produce it, and the effects that our food has on the environment and on us is of greater significance than we might have realized. In particular, food and agriculture are now recognized as matters of *ethical and political* significance. As awareness of basic issues with the dominant systems of food production—such as the environmental impact of conventional methods of agriculture, the treatment of animals used for food, the working conditions in agriculture and food industries, and the effects of many common food products on the health of eaters—has grown, this awareness has extended further to critique of many common features of food and agricultural systems: of what it means to treat food as a market commodity, of the ensuing unequal access to healthful food, and of the impact that a global market in food has on food security, food sovereignty, the living and working conditions for farmers and food workers around the world, and the sustainability of agriculture and food production. The connections between food and agriculture, climate change, and environmental health lie at the heart of each of these concerns.

Thus, this volume addresses that central but underrepresented topic in the growing discussions of food and agriculture: the multifaceted connections between food and agricultural systems, the environment, and global climate change (GCC). Most discussion of this relationship has focused on the impact that the food we eat has on carbon emissions, encapsulated in the notion of "food miles." Yet, as the examples above indicate, the connections between food and agricultural systems, environmental conditions and effects, and GCC are more complex than the food miles focus suggests. The ways in which food and agricultural production, its environmental consequences, and climate change affect and are affected by other problems are likewise complex. We aim to capture some of the facets of these interrelationships.

I. BACKGROUND

In this section, we provide empirical and historical background in order to explain the problems addressed in the volume and contextualize the normative issues these problems raise. Specifically, we highlight some of the major features of food and agricultural systems and the nature and impact of GCC.

1. Agriculture and Food Production

Much of the concern about the ethical and political implications of food and agricultural practices stems from a range of relatively recent changes in these practices. How food is produced, consumed, distributed, and marketed changed dramatically over the latter half of the twentieth century. In the domain of food production, both the scale and the nature of production have changed. These changes are often summed up as the "industrialization" of agriculture and food. In this context, industrialization refers to the increased use of technology of various sorts (mechanical, electrical, chemical, and biological), to the accompanying mechanization in agriculture and food production, and to the mass production of food thus made possible. Changes in plant agriculture have included shifting to large-scale mono-cropping along with devoting a greater proportion of cropland to commodity crops such as corn, wheat, and soy. This kind of farming involves the increased use of agricultural chemicals in the form of fertilizers, insecticides, pesticides, and fungicides. In animal agriculture, industrialization has meant intensive confinement practices that require significant inputs in the form of antibiotics to prevent disease and hormones to stimulate rapid growth; both the techniques of animal husbandry and the animals themselves have been significantly altered to increase production.

These processes are also now undertaken on a global scale. Food and agriculture have long been global undertakings, central to European projects of colonization, for example. Yet the fact that food and agriculture are globalized means that the global distribution of food and agricultural products has expanded and intensified to such an extent as to be commonplace. For instance, the United States imports Chinese-grown garlic and exports U.S.-grown garlic to Canada. Together, Brazil and the United States export 80 percent of the world's soybeans, and China imports 60 percent of all globally traded soybeans (Gu and Thukral 2018). The WH Group, based in Hong Kong, owns U.S.-based Smithfield Foods, the largest pig producer and processor in the United States. Restaurant chains have long been multinational enterprises: based in Louisville, Kentucky, multinational Yum! Brands operates fast-food chains Taco Bell, Pizza Hut, and KFC everywhere from India to the West Bank. Grocery retailers are joining them as multinationals, such as U.S.-based Walmart and French Carrefour, have expanded. These instances of globalization are also examples of one of the major structural changes in food and agriculture: market consolidation in which (usually larger) companies grow by subsuming smaller ones in the same industry.

These structural changes include not only the aforementioned industrial techniques and the market consolidation to which they have given rise but also vertical integration among sectors (e.g., poultry producers now often own the chickens, operate the hatcheries and the processing plants/slaughterhouses, and sell the chicken under their label), which results in an increase in subcontracting within consolidated industries (e.g., farmers are "growers" who are contracted to raise chickens for major poultry producers) and the accompanying escalation of food advertising. These features of the structure of the global food system have a few implications: First, there is greater physical distance between those who make decisions about how food is produced and the places and people involved in the work of producing food, who bear the repercussions of those decisions the most. Second, agricultural crops, animals raised for food, and foodstuffs are regarded first and foremost as commodities; they are part of a complex global economy. The development of enormous markets not just in food products but in the whole apparatus of the food system—agricultural machinery, fertilizers, seeds, pesticides, food packaging and storage, animal feed and infrastructure, transportation, and so on—makes each dimension of that system a site for profit. Third, and relatedly, dramatic increases in agricultural productivity have led to concomitant increases in marketing and advertising: because food is plentiful and food is a commodity, it needs to be marketed as such to encourage consumption. Fourth, consequently and perhaps most significantly, the current global, industrial system of food production allows for the continual externalization of costs. Such a far-reaching system produces numerous costs that are not integrated into the market economy and thus not paid for as part of the cost of production, such as the pollution of air and water by confinement animal agriculture (Pew 2008). These costs, however, are borne by others, such as the individuals, communities, and ecosystems affected by them, as in the case of higher rates of asthma among children who live near confinement facilities (Pew 2008, 17). Such costs can be readily externalized in part because decision-makers operate at a distance from those who bear the brunt of their decisions. Costs are also externalized because externalized costs are, generally, integral to profit. Indeed, even when mechanisms exist to hold food corporations accountable for externalized costs—such as regulation that stipulates fines for excessive pollution—they frequently incorporate these fines as simply part of the cost of doing business rather than alter their production practices. For instance, in 1997 Smithfield Foods was issued the highest fine ever for water pollution for violating the U.S. Clean Water Act and yet has continued its same waste disposal practices to the present (Foer 2009, 91).[1] Also included in these costs are the emissions that contribute to

GCC: together, food production and consumption (fertilizer manufacturing, agriculture, processing, transportation, retail, household food management and waste disposal) are estimated to contribute 19 to 29 percent of all anthropogenic GHG emissions (Vermeulen, Campbell, and Ingram 2012).

2. Global Climate Change

In *Climate Change 2014* the Intergovernmental Panel on Climate Change (IPCC) reported, "Human influence on the climate system is clear, and recent anthropogenic emissions of green-house gases are the highest in history. Recent climate changes have had widespread impacts on human and natural systems" (Working Groups I, II, and III 2015, 2). In particular, increased quantities of carbon dioxide, methane, and nitrous oxide are being released into the earth's atmosphere, jointly acting as a blanket by trapping heat on the earth's surface. Human activities like the production of energy, transportation, land development, and the production and distribution of food (for instance) all contribute to GHG emissions and together have "led to atmospheric concentrations of carbon dioxide, methane and nitrous oxide that are unprecedented in at least the last 800,000 years" (ibid., 2). In short, human activities have changed the way the earth's natural heating and cooling system works.

One of the most obvious and important ways the climate is changing is through an increased average global land and surface temperature: an increase of 0.85 degrees C from 1880 to 2012, with the last three decades likely being the warmest period in the Northern Hemisphere in the last 1,400 years (ibid., 2). Although some may be tempted to classify this increase as inconsequential in the grand scheme of things, the human impact on the climate system has been anything but: the ocean is rising, its temperature is warming, and the water is becoming more acidic; the Greenland and Antarctic ice sheets have been losing mass at alarming rates; and Arctic sea ice is likewise decreasing, to name just a few of the symptoms of a warming planet (ibid.). Such changes have consequences for the ways in which the climate system functions. For instance, the number of cold days and nights have decreased and warm days and nights have increased, regional patterns of precipitation are rapidly changing, and climate-related weather events like heat waves, droughts, floods, cyclones, and wildfires have increased in incidence and intensity (ibid.). Together, these changes force species extinction and migration, make it difficult for many people to secure potable water, increase the incidence of vector- and water-borne disease, change the places and ways in which we can grow food, increase weather-related human morbidity and mortality rates, and will catalyze mass human migration from weather-battered areas of the globe (Working Group II 2014). Moreover, the human populations that are most vulnerable to these effects are the ones that are already stricken with poverty, food insecurity, and economic and political instability (ibid.).

Even though serious coordinated efforts to combat climate change have been happening since at least 1992, the year the first global treaty (the United Nations Framework Convention on Climate Change) was signed, global GHG emissions have nonetheless been rising steadily (United Nations Framework Convention on Climate Change n.d.a; Working Group III). As a result, subsequent treaties have focused both on mitigation of climate change and adaptation to climate change, since, given historical global emissions, a certain amount of warming is now inevitable. The Paris Agreement, implemented on November 4, 2016, is the most recent and aggressive treaty. It aims to "strengthen the global response to the threat of climate change by keeping a global temperature rise this century well below 2 degrees Celsius above preindustrial levels and to pursue efforts to limit the temperature increase even further to 1.5 degrees Celsius. Additionally, the agreement aims to strengthen the ability of countries to deal with the impacts of climate change" (United Nations Framework Convention on Climate Change n.d.b). But, as important an instrument as they are, these efforts are rife with problems, not the least of which is that a nation's commitment to these aims can wane with shifts in political will, most recently illustrated when the United States (historically, one of the world's largest GHG contributors [Working Group III]) withdrew from the treaty under the leadership of the Trump administration, thus potentially threatening the overall efficacy of the agreement.

3. The Relation between Global Climate Change and Agriculture and Food Production

Agriculture not only contributes a significant amount of GHG emissions, just under one-quarter of global anthropogenic GHG emissions (Working Group II 2014, 816), but food systems as a whole have been estimated to produce up to 29 percent of such emissions (Vermeulen, Campbell, and Ingram 2012). Animal agriculture alone is estimated to produce 14.5 percent of anthropogenic GHG emissions (Gerber et al. 2013). But the relationship between agriculture and food production is bidirectional: as climate change becomes a reality rather than just a feature of a speculative future, its considerable effects on agricultural and food production are recognized more and more. Other environmental problems, including those generated by agriculture and food production techniques, are also exacerbated by climate change. For instance, desertification, sometimes following agriculture-induced deforestation, worsens with a greater number of hotter days and decreasing precipitation. Likewise, eutrophication, which leads to oxygen-depleted "dead zones" and fish kills—and is a common effect of runoff of fertilizer and animal waste into rivers, lakes, estuaries, and oceans—is likely intensified by rising temperatures (Paerl and Huisman 2008). Impaired ecosystems are also less resilient and able to withstand the effects of climate change. For example, the earth's oceans have thus far absorbed 25 to 30 percent of all human-generated GHG emissions; however, their capacity to operate as carbon sinks is expected to decline, given warming water and slower upwelling of deep oceanic waters (Doney 2010).

Thus, reinforcing feedback loops characterize the relationship between climate change, the environment, and food and agriculture practices. Yet because agriculture is a domain in which land and resource management occurs, it also has the potential to be a prime site for more sustainable ways of relating to our environment and thus for climate change mitigation and adaption. By transforming our techniques, habits, and ways of thinking about food, agriculture, and the ecosystems upon which we rely, we can address the harmful effects of climate change and prepare for the ones that are now inevitable.

II. THEORETICAL FRAMEWORKS

In this section, we discuss some of the theoretical frameworks that are applied to address the problems surrounding food, agriculture, the environment, and climate change. These problems are recognized as ones of ethical and political concern, that is, as ones that raise questions about rightness or wrongness, goodness and badness, justice, equality, fairness, and virtue. We consider first general philosophical theories of justice and then turn to how justice is theorized with respect to each of the three main domains that are the subjects of this volume: food, environment, and climate.

1. Theories of Justice

Although there are many different theories of justice and types of justice (a variety of which are discussed by Robaey and Timmermann in chapter 11), for the purposes of this volume a few key theories and concepts are of particular interest: liberal political theory, global justice, distributive justice, and structural justice and injustice.

When it comes to problems of food and agriculture, climate change, and environmental health, one of the most important and often utilized ideas of justice is that of distributive justice. The concept of distributive justice is concerned with the fair distribution of the benefits and burdens of social cooperation. Benefits might include healthy food, clean air and water, and green spaces, whereas burdens might include pollution, unstable and deteriorating environments, and difficulty accessing decent food. Contemporary liberal theorizing about distributive justice is greatly indebted to John Rawls, who argued that liberal political justice requires that the basic structures of society adhere to and reflect two principles of justice. The first principle demands that every citizen has an equal right to the greatest scheme of basic liberties, and the second principle dictates fair equality of opportunity and stipulates that social and economic inequalities are only just if they work to the greatest advantage of the least well-off (Rawls 1999, 53).

Liberal political theory is a broad school of thought, and certainly extends beyond Rawlsian principles and methods. But despite the diversity of views, liberal political theorists are generally concerned with individual freedom and autonomy and to what extent state policies that limit freedom and autonomy can be justified. As the aim is to think about how best to achieve individual moral and political autonomy, core values of this position typically include tolerance, pluralism, and equality, though theorists disagree about how to define these values and when and to what degree they matter. Even as liberals agree that individuals should have the opportunity to exercise their autonomy, they disagree about whether those opportunities should be created by the state and thus about the role of government and whether it is necessary or even permissible for the state to intervene for the purposes of redistributing goods, wealth, and opportunities (e.g., Nozick 1974; Cohen 2008). And still others argue that the borders of the nation state are morally arbitrary and that considerations of justice should extend beyond concern for our fellow citizens (e.g., Caney 2006; Nussbaum 2000). Thinking about the nature of our obligations to distant others and how we balance these obligations (if they exist) against the domestic demands of justice are issues that concern global justice theorists.

In the context of global climate change, and given the global nature of our food system, it's not a risky assumption to presume that we do have some sort of obligation to noncompatriots, even if we don't yet know what that obligation specifically demands. As such, there are two general theories of global justice that are deserving of our attention, as they create space for substantive international obligations. First, some thinkers argue that we should apply principles of equality at home and principles of sufficiency abroad, a position known as sufficientarianiam (e.g., Blake 2002; Miller 2007; Rawls 2002). Specifically, sufficientarian thinkers argue that, as a matter of justice, all people/groups should be brought to the level of a morally important threshold, which can be defined in terms of human rights, subsistence, conditions for individual moral autonomy, democratic stability, and the like. Falling below the threshold generates a positive duty of justice to move individuals above the threshold. So, to the extent that global climate change or food insecurity threatens the ability to maintain the relevant standard, theorists would argue that the international community has an obligation to help nations in need—be it via climate change mitigation/adaptation, food aid, technology exchanges, or other assistance—to achieve and maintain the standard.

Other theorists argue that there are no morally important differences between citizens and noncitizens, and so all should be owed the same considerations of justice. This general position is called cosmopolitan liberalism (e.g., Beitz 1973; Caney 2006; Nussbaum 2000; Singer 1972). Cosmopolitan liberalism, arguing that citizenship is morally arbitrary in the same way that gender, race, and the like are, goes further than sufficientarianism and seeks to extend liberal principles of justice worldwide. That is, as a matter of consistency, liberalism must be applied on a global level. This means, for example, that we might enforce human rights standards worldwide or we might demand that each nation stick to a fairly devised quota system that permits nations or individuals to emit a certain amount of GHG in the context of GCC. But, some theorists in this camp diverge from a strictly egalitarian position to give priority to those who are the worst off globally. They argue that famine and underdevelopment cannot be justified within the context of liberal theory, which leads to the conclusion that the conditions that create famine and the like ought to be changed (e.g., Singer 1972). From this point of view, all things being equal, our obligations to nonnationals are the same as our obligations to compatriots, but our obligations to those suffering from famine or extreme poverty are more urgent and so should be tended to first. Applying this lens to examine the intersections of food, climate, and environmental justice would mean that we prioritize the needs of the communities most vulnerable to climate change and food insecurity.

Insofar as we are concerned with justice, especially distributive and global justice, we are concerned with structures and with justice as a matter pertaining to structures. Indeed, Rawls takes the "basic structures of society," those fundamental social and political institutions that are arranged so as to distribute the benefits and burdens of shared life, to be the subject of justice (Rawls 1999, 6). This approach, known as ideal theory, offers an account of what is required for a society to be completely just, often assuming idealized social conditions, including these basic structures, and articulating principles to guide action under these fully just conditions. In contrast, nonideal theory begins from a description of actual, frequently unjust conditions and seeks to understand how social-structural processes operate to produce injustice (e.g., Mills 2005; Sen 2006; Tessman 2010; Zack 2017).[2] The aim is to understand fully the injustices so as to begin "dismantling presently operating structures of oppression" and repairing wrongs (Tessman 2010, 809).

From this perspective, structures are not static but are "social-structural processes" that function as they do only because of the actions of those operating within them (Young 2011, 53). They are composed of various social rules, including those of institutions, and the concrete shape the material world has taken, both of which provide a context for the exercise of individual and group agency. Thus, structures are forms of organization that produce social positions and roles, channeling action, and, accordingly, circumscribing the possibilities that are open to, accessible by, or closed for people. Social-structural processes both constrain and enable in a patterned manner and often affect people differently by virtue of their social group membership. In light of this understanding of social-structural processes, the concept of "structural injustice" has emerged to name a particular kind of wrong: one that is not attributable solely to an individual or institution but rather stems from the confluence of the actions of many different parties, both individuals and institutions, who are acting in accordance with the prevailing rules and norms of the social-structural processes in which they are situated to achieve their desired goals. As Iris Young defines it, structural injustice occurs when "social processes put large groups of persons under systematic threat of domination or deprivation of the means to develop and exercise their capacities, at the same time that these processes enable others to dominate or to have a wide range of opportunities for developing and exercising capacities available to them" (2011, 52).

Food and agricultural practices are enmeshed in myriad structural processes (political, economic, social, and cultural) in different intertwined domains (regional, national, international). To the extent that dominant food and agricultural practices are systemic rather than localized, they have a significant impact on the environment and contribute to climate change; in other words, the harms that amount to structural injustices are the consequences of the system-wide processes and structures through which food is produced, distributed, marketed, accessed, eaten, and regulated. Particular structural features of food systems, such as those identified above (market consolidation, vertical integration, subcontracting, increased distance between decision-makers and those who bear the brunt of their decisions, and the externalization of costs), are implicated in environmental and climate injustice. Moreover, structures that overlap in their contributions to food, climate, and environmental injustice, such as global economic structures that conduce to worldwide import-export markets in food, shape how food, agriculture, the environment, and climate change impact one another. Accordingly, many activists and theorists take a structural approach to food and agriculture, the environment, climate change, and the relations among them, as in chapter 2 where Teea Kortetmäki analyzes the food and climate nexus as a structural injustice.

More generally, when it comes to the food, agriculture, environment, and climate nexus, there are at least two focal points for critical analysis of social-structural processes and the injustices emerging from them. First, there are the normal background conditions on the basis of which people, institutions, and other actors operate. These normal conditions include the taken-for-granted activities and roles that social-structural processes call for, and the symbolic systems of meaning, norms, and ideologies on which they rest. Examples of the latter include the assumption that humans ought to dominate and control nature, including nonhuman animals. Along these lines, we might ask how this assumption has buttressed the processes of an ecologically unsustainable food system, as Wendy Lee examines in chapter 6. Second, there is the relationship between historical structural processes and current ones, which includes analyzing how features of past processes are preserved even as they are transformed. We might ask, for instance, what impact the processes of colonization have had on current global politico-economic policies or that racist housing policies have had on food access. This kind of analysis is taken up by Joan McGregor, Mary Rawlinson, Gabriela Arguedas-Ramírez, and Deborah Adelman and Shamili Ajgaonkar, in chapters 1, 5, 7, and 8, respectively.

Concern for justice and injustice—whether distributive, participatory, or structural—draws attention to the different levels on which action is taken in ways that contribute to injustice or determine responsibility to avoid or ameliorate it: individual, social group, institutional, national, and international. From the perspective of justice, these levels are interconnected. Individuals within institutions must act so as to enable the institution to take responsibility for reducing its emissions, for example. National governments, composed of individuals and groups, must coordinate with one another and with NGOs on international policy. In these instances, individuals have responsibilities by virtue of their position or role in institutions, and we also regularly hold institutions responsible as collective agents.[3]

Yet individuals also seek to take transformative action apart from such positions, in their personal and interpersonal lives. They seek to make ethical decisions and undertake ethical action in relation to these problems. In many ways individual ethical responsibility is inseparable from changes in policy, law, and culture that aim at justice: individuals may decide to eat in what they determine is a more ethically sound manner, as John Nolt and Annette Mendola explore in chapter 13, but individuals also may decide to express their ethical concerns through political involvement. Indeed, we should also consider the manner in which we frame our ethical and political concerns and responsibilities, for instance, as those of ethically responsible consumers or as those of engaged, reflective citizens, as Rachel Ankeny debates in chapter 14. Many questions arise about the nature and extent of individual responsibility, and the effect that individual action can have on systemic, structural injustices, as well as about the specific responsibilities of individuals, collectives, institutions, and governments and how they can best undertake them. For instance, it may be that, given the severity of the externalized costs of raising animals for food in the context of a warming world, we have reasons of political justice to restrict the choice of animal proteins in citizens' diets, as Kenehan maintains in chapter 12. Or we may believe, as argued by Robaey and Timmermann in chapter 11, that agricultural researchers have special obligations to act in ways that are transparent and participatory and that ultimately empower farmers to meet the needs of their communities sustainably in a warming world.

2. Food Justice

Food justice is often considered synonymous with the burgeoning alternative food movements, which encourage growing and consuming more local and organic food and criticize the dominance of agribusiness and corporate interest in food policy and production. It has also been linked to concerns about food security and the need to feed the world, especially in the context of anticipated population growth and ecological devastation.[4] Generally, food justice can be defined "as seeking to transform where, what, and how food is grown, produced, transported, accessed, and eaten" (Gottlieb and Joshi 2010, 5). It is oriented toward changing the food system *as a whole* instead of merely addressing isolated problems, and toward seeking the causes of injustices and paths to justice in social-structural processes, not solely in individual actions or socioenvironmental conditions. Further, as scholars and activists increasingly collaborate, a more robust understanding of food justice appears. On this understanding, food justice centers on the connections between food issues and other social justice issues (such as poverty, immigrants' rights, and racial justice), and thus on seeking equity in power and control of resources and decision-making. Indeed, Agyeman and McEntee note that food justice "as a social movement arose largely from urban-located social justice groups that explicitly addressed food inequalities based on race and/or socioeconomics ... [and] is significantly influenced by historical anti-oppression undertakings and ideology, including those of racial injustice and civil rights" (2014, 212).

Thus, when food justice is understood simply as a matter of ensuring that all people have access to an adequate amount of healthful food, it is conceived as a matter of distributive justice.[5] From a more transformative perspective, the distributive framework for food justice encompasses fair distribution not only of the benefits of healthful food but also of the myriad burdens and benefits of all food systems processes: growing, producing, transporting, marketing, and accessing food (Gottlieb and Joshi 2010, 6). Taking into account how injustices pertaining to food are connected to other social injustices, however, requires moving beyond the distributive paradigm to frameworks for justice that encompass how relations among people are structured. Accordingly, food justice is also a matter of procedural and participatory justice, as Clement Loo argues in chapter 3.[6] This perspective is expressed clearly in the definition of food sovereignty offered by the organizations pursuing food sovereignty at the World Forum for Food Sovereignty:

> Food sovereignty is the right of peoples to healthy and culturally appropriate food produced through ecologically sound and sustainable methods, and their right to define their own food and agriculture systems … It ensures that the rights to use and manage lands, territories, waters, seeds, livestock and bio-diversity are in the hands of those of us who produce food. Food sovereignty implies new social relations free of oppression and inequality between men and women, peoples, racial groups, social and economic classes and generations. (Declaration of Nyéléni 2007)

Food justice, therefore, concerns not just an adequate supply of and access to decent food but also community autonomy and self-determination and thus community control over their own food resources and practices. Hence, what food and the practices concerning it—eating, growing, preparing, and storing—mean is also more robust: food is not merely instrumental in sustaining biological life and health but rather is integral to social and cultural life. As a matter of systems, food is linked not only to ecological systems—waterways, soil, air, flora, and fauna—but to sociocultural ones, to people's history and identities.[7]

3. Environmental Justice

Thus we can see how this robust sense of food justice emerged, in part, from the environmental justice (EJ) movement that originated in the 1980s, with the activism of communities of color in response to structural environmental racism, that is, "the disproportionate impact of environmental hazards on people of color" (EJNET). Robert Bullard's (1990) research revealing that garbage dumps were disproportionately located in communities of color is often regarded as the foundation of the movement. More broadly, EJ exposes and contests the unequal burden of environmental harms born by communities of color, indigenous, and working-class communities. Thus it can be understood as both an extension of and a radical departure from traditional environmentalism, which was oriented primarily toward conservation. In particular, rather than distinguish *the environment* as the natural world apart from humans, EJ starts from the assumption that "the environment is every-thing: where we live, work, play, go to school, as well as the physical and natural world" (Bullard 1999). As such, EJ links concerns for social justice with concerns for the natural world by regarding them as inextricably tied.

Environmental justice brings into view some of the limitations of the distributive framework for justice: although the response of the U.S. federal government to environmental justice activism in the 1990s was a call for "environmental equity" (Environmental Equity Workgroup 1992)—a call to distribute the risk of environmental harms more fairly—justice demands not merely a fairer redistribution of burdens but a reduction in such harms altogether. Additionally, to move beyond contesting such inequalities, a more expansive sense of justice is needed, one that conceives justice as a matter of the quality of relationships among different beings and thus of power and equity in relationships. David Pellow suggests that critical EJ might focus on "the concept of *ecological justice*, which centers on the relationship of human beings to the broader nonhuman world" (2016, 13). He notes: "By the term ecological justice, I mean to suggest a more respectful and egalitarian relationship of human beings to one another and to the greater more-than-human world" (ibid.). On this view, environmental concerns, especially those linked to agriculture and food,[8] are not just about the impact that human action has on the environment—the harms we do to ecosystems and nonhuman animals, and the unsustainability of our use of the resources of the natural world, which harms us now and in the future—but are also about our habitual ways of relating to the natural world, animals, and each other. In seeking ecological justice, we are seeking to alter those established patterns of relationships, especially those relationships in which we take for granted the plants, animals, soil, water, and air, not to mention human others, that share the world with us. To use ecofeminist Val Plumwood's concept, we should aim to move from relationships of denied dependency, in which we take the other's service(s) for granted while "denying the importance of the other's contribution" or very being (1993, 48), to ones of acknowledged dependency (MacIntyre 1999) or even "indispensability," in which we affirm "that excluded, marginalized, and othered populations, beings, and things—both human and more-than-human—must be viewed not as expendable but rather as indispensable to our collective futures" (Pellow 2016, 11).[9] For instance, given the recognition that aspects of the natural world can have meaning or value beyond the human purpose, then we must also acknowledge that our relationships to land, animals, ecosystems, and the like will be characterized by conflicting aims and values. For instance, we may have to choose between promoting agricultural production and food security or cultivating environmental resilience, a tension addressed by Noll in chapter 9.

4. Climate Justice

Conceiving of the natural world as an unlimited resource to serve human purposes has contributed greatly to the problem of global climate change. It is this attitude that has allowed us to treat the atmosphere as an infinite global emissions dump and thus has catalyzed the warming of the planet. Peter Singer elaborates on this problem:

> All of this forces us to think differently about our ethics. Our value system evolved in circumstances in which the atmosphere, like the oceans, seemed an unlimited resource, and responsibilities and harms were generally clear and well defined. ... Now the twin problem of the ozone hole and climate change have revealed bizarre new ways of killing people. ... By driving your car, you could be releasing carbon dioxide that is part of a causal chain leading to lethal floods in Bangladesh. How can we adjust our ethics to take account of this new situation? (Singer 2002, 19–20)

In recognition of the previously underappreciated way that humans are connected to the natural world and so to one another, we must ask: What should be done about global climate change, and who is responsible for doing it? This question is inordinately difficult to answer, since the problem is one that spans both generations and nations. In addition, the problem is not just one of finding an alternative to, for instance, fossil fuels but rather one caused by large, complex, and interconnected economic, trade, political, and legal structures and processes, and is simultaneously a problem of individual and social/cultural values. For all of these reasons, GCC challenges our current conceptions of justice and threatens to stretch our political institutions beyond their limits. It is, as Stephen Gardiner puts it, "the perfect moral storm" (2010).

In response to these concerns, scholars have proposed some ways to think about justice in the context of GCC. Indeed there are several principles that might be applicable in this case, including the following three core principles:

- Polluter Pays Principle (PPP). This principle states that whoever caused the problem is responsible for the costs of fixing it (e.g., Gosseries 2004; Meyer and Roser 2010; Shue 2010a; Singer 2002).
- Beneficiaries Pay Principle (BPP). Caney explains this principle in the following way: "Where A has been made better off by a policy pursued by others, and the pursuit by others of that policy has contributed to the imposition of adverse effects on third parties, then A has an obligation not to pursue the policy itself (mitigation) and/or an obligation to address the harmful effects suffered by the third parties (adaptation)" (2010, 128; see also Page 2012; Shue 2010a).

- Ability to Pay Principle (APP). Shue describes this principle in the following way: "Among the number of parties, all of whom are bound to contribute to some common endeavor, the parties who have the most resources normally should contribute the most to the endeavor" (2010a, 105; see also Caney 2010; Margolioth 2012).

Though it's likely that each of these principles will converge on a similar group of responsible parties—namely, the wealthy nations that have contributed the most to climate change—the justifications that each principle offers for attributing those responsibilities will differ. Thus the viability of the principles in a real-world context will be a function of the both the moral positions and the political and socioeconomic circumstances of the parties involved.

Instead of identifying specific responsibilities of particular agents, such as polluters, beneficiaries, or the most able to pay, other theorists have focused on identifying those groups to whom special moral attention should be paid as a result of the impacts of GCC. In particular, they identify the groups most at risk to suffer the consequences of GCC, and then they argue that measures should be taken to protect those groups, the idea being that our moral priorities should align with the protection of those who have the most to lose. Importantly, this perspective may operate as an independent framework or it may complement the principles described above. In the case of GCC, two groups are often cited as being the most vulnerable: future generations (e.g., Shue 2010b; Gardiner 2006) and the global poor (e.g., Caney 2010; Shue 2010c). Both groups are situated such that they lack agency or they experience diminished agency: future generations don't have agency in this moment because they don't yet exist, and the poor are lacking the conditions that would enable them to exercise agency. These groups are at a severe disadvantage with regard to the ability to advocate for their interests, as future generations are temporally disadvantaged and the poor are often politically and economically marginalized.

Finally, we may want to think about responsibility for GCC with regard to corporations and industries, or even individuals. Some attention has been paid to the transportation and energy industries in this context, and special responsibilities have been attributed to them based on their historical contribution to the problem, especially because of the failure of the market (and so, perhaps, policies) to control the externalities that contribute to climate change (Arnold and Bustos 2007). Other thinkers have focused on individual obligations to reduce contributions to climate change by showing that these contributions are both non-negligible and harmful (see, for instance, Nolt 2011).

In the end, whatever method or combination of methods that we use to attribute responsibility for the costs associated with GCC will have to be applied in a real-world context where there are differing needs, histories, environments, and sociopolitical circumstances. Thus, among other things, care must be taken to ensure that the global environmental costs of food production are adequately accounted for and mitigated. Likewise, attention needs to be paid to those who are already food insecure (a condition that will likely worsen with the influence of GCC) or those who will become food insecure as a result of GCC, and to those groups who are already socially, politically, and economically marginalized and so are likely to be victims of environmental racism and classism. This may require that food producers work to alleviate their contribution to global change or that food researchers focus their efforts on meeting the difficulties of growing food in a warming world. Or it may require that governments, communities, and individuals work to localize and democratize food systems in efforts to make them less environmentally harmful and to empower the local growers and consumers of food. In short, we cannot think about climate justice and obligations of climate change mitigation and adaptation without also thinking about what and how we eat.

III. THEMATIC OVERVIEW

This volume seeks to address the wide range of questions and concerns pertaining to the connections between food and agriculture, the environment, and climate change. In particular, the following chapters work to bridge the theoretical and the practical. They analyze the myriad problems in these interconnected domains; assess existing policies, practices, and frameworks employed to respond to these problems; and propose alternative ones.

The chapters that compose part I of the book provide insight into how best to understand the injustices related to food and agriculture, the environment, and climate change. They explore in detail how these domains are connected, as in Joan McGregor's chapter 1. In her analysis of the systemic interconnections among food and agriculture, environmental problems, and climate change, McGregor calls attention to how the injustices in these domains systemically harm the same vulnerable groups of people: those who are impoverished worldwide and those who are marginalized on the basis of racial group membership. Harms such as poor health due to lack of access to healthy food, continual exposure to pesticides, and forced migration due to a changing climate are disproportionately experienced by these groups because of structural background conditions that include inequality in decision-making power and spatial segregation. Injustice is only perpetuated when vulnerability to these harms is attributed to individual choice, conceived merely as the result of market forces. This simplified lens on complex interactions not only ignores the structuring conditions that give rise to those (constrained) choices in the first place but likewise ignores that justice demands that we treat access to adequate healthy food, a decent environment, and a stable climate as human rights. The view that food and climate injustice are *structural* injustices is developed in further detail by Teea Kortetmäki in chapter 2. Kortetmäki applies Iris Young's (2011) account of structural injustice to the food and climate nexus, demonstrating how both are paradigmatic instances of structural injustice. This kind of account illuminates the two-way relationship between the global food system and climate change—wherein food and agricultural production contributes to climate change yet climate change also impacts food and agricultural production—by showing them to be part of interconnected systems. The implication of both chapters is that justice in one domain cannot be sought at the expense of justice in the other domains. In particular, Kortetmäki elaborates four policies and practices that need to be reconsidered in light of the food-climate connection: the food justice focus on the "local," which is actually far from the most emissions-reducing practice; charity-based food aid that relies on food "waste," legitimizing waste; using crops for biofuel, which may be in service of climate justice but undermines food justice; and potential climate (geo)engineering, which will have diverse and complex effects on food production.

As the focus on the concept of structural injustice indicates, the chapters in part I also investigate which theoretical resources—concepts, theories, and frameworks—are best poised to address the complex relationships between global food systems, environmental problems, and climate change, perhaps remedying oversights or providing new perspectives. Both Kortetmäki and McGregor suggest that more robust participation in decision-making, and thus the lens of participatory justice, is central to food-environmental-climate justice. Clement Loo elaborates this suggestion in chapter 3, arguing for the salience and centrality of a participative justice framework to supplement the dominant distributive justice framework. In order to develop a robust sense of what it means to seek participative justice with respect to food and climate, he explicates the core components of participative equity: recognition and autonomy. Equitable participation entails fostering the autonomy of participants and recognizing both their equal dignity and their difference. Thus, taking a participative approach also requires greater, more dialogic collaboration between scholars and advocates and the people of the communities they study or for whom they advocate. Participative justice demands ensuring that underrepresented stakeholders are involved but also that the broad range of perspectives and values all stakeholders bring are admitted to the decision-making table. Building on the critique of the myopic focus on individual choice regarding food that McGregor raises, Jennifer Szende draws on feminist relational theory to explore the food "desert" as both a concrete injustice and a metaphor for that injustice. Feminist relational theory directs attention to our existence within a web of relationships and thus, as Szende expresses in her chapter 4, "reminds us that large, complex public health problems such as those raised by food deserts are socially embedded phenomena." The "desert" metaphor is typically used to identify an area lacking in robust, healthy food options; however, critiques of this metaphor tend to draw on a limited range of meanings: the desert is empty and natural, and desertification is nearly irreversible. Situating the phenomenon and the metaphor of food deserts in their complex web of social, economic, and ecological relationships—including relationships with climate change and environmental conditions such as desertification—however, leads to a richer set of meanings and thus to a better understanding of the nature of the problem and the potential solutions.

Part II turns to critical analysis of current practices and policies concerning food and agriculture, the environment, and climate change. These chapters weigh the drawbacks and problems with dominant agricultural and food production practices, common ways of thinking about food and the environment, and the prevailing narratives about food and agriculture. Many of these contributions address the role that structures of oppression and domination— such as coloniality, globalization, and geopolitical maneuvering in general— play in creating and perpetuating injustice in these domains. They explore how varied epistemic, cultural, political, and ethical claims intersect and overlap when it comes to food, the environment, and climate, and consider whose knowledge, concerns, and voices are, and should be, valued in making global climate policy and agricultural and food policy. In the face of long-standing and persistent inequities in participation in decision-making, each of the chapters in part II argues in some way for the importance of diverse forms of knowledge about food justice and injustice. Therefore, many also advocate for alternative approaches to address food-environmental-climate injustices.

In chapter 5, Mary Rawlinson delves into the relationship between truth and justice by exploring the role of deception in enabling injustice. The failure to comprehend the truth—for instance, the scientific consensus about the realities of climate change—undermines the potential for justice. On Rawlinson's analysis, deception and manipulation are both abiding strategies of the food industry as well as mechanisms in the service of two central ideologies about food: the fallacy of choice and the free market, and the fallacy of necessity and progress. These fallacies, promulgated by agribusiness as well as by international organizations, characterize how we think about food and agriculture and thus shape the solutions to food injustices that are developed and employed. Such fallacies prevent both recognition of and reckoning with the structural conditions for food-climate-environmental injustices. Indeed, the deceptive and manipulative practices amount to structural injustices. Thus, for Rawlinson, as for Szende, truth lies instead in recognizing that food is

an instantiation of a web of relationships, "a *culture of possibilities.*" The
relationship between dominant ideology and structures of inequality is also
a focal point of Wendy Lynne Lee's chapter 6, which critiques the status
of animals *as food* in food aid, assistance, and security practices and discourse. Lee begins from the ecofeminist assumption that the oppression and
exploitation of women, people of color, working-class people, indigenous
people, and nonhuman animals are interconnected. On her analysis, ecological devastation, impending climate catastrophes, and food insecurity are
precipitated by the prevailing logic of commodification, a logic that treats all
oppressed group members as exploitable and consumable, albeit in different
ways. Continuing to treat nonhuman animals merely *as food*—for instance,
in food aid and assistance policies and practices—only reinforces the logic
of commodification. As long as food aid and assistance programs remain
caught up in markets in food and so complicit with agribusiness, including
industrial animal agribusiness, such efforts will contribute to food and climate injustices rather than genuinely mitigating them. In chapter 7, Gabriela
Arguedas-Ramírez likewise employs the framework of feminist food justice
to offer an "ethical-political and epistemological reflection on the problem
of hunger." Her analysis explores the intersection of food security, environmental degradation, and the impacts of climate change from the perspective
of contemporary Central America. In particular, she analyzes how historical
legacies of colonialism and their corollaries in contemporary neoliberal geopolitics have contributed to hunger and climate change, especially through
land acquisitions that have displaced and further marginalized poor and indigenous people. High levels of violence against women, indigenous people,
environmentalists, and journalists also accompany and are reinforced by the
extractivist ideologies and practices that neoliberal geopolitics promotes.
Consonant with Rawlinson, Arguedas-Ramírez argues that the human right
to food should be understood as one stemming from community interdepend-
ence rather than one that can be fulfilled through existing politico-economic
frameworks that render food a commodity. Thus, this right "requires action
to prevent both land dispossession and accumulation, and not just plain acts
of charity in cases of emergency and starvation."

Deborah Adelman and Shamili Ajgaonkar's chapter 8 provides another
lens on the relationship between the global economy and food, climate, and
environmental justice in the Americas. Framing their work through Native
American writer Anita Endrezze's poem "Corn Mother," they trace the history and evolution of corn production from its beginnings as a subsistence
crop in pre-Columbian Mesoamerica to its current globalized and commodified form. They argue that the changes in the way that corn is cultivated
and used have contributed to the myriad social and environmental injustices
experienced by indigenous communities. Because the dominant system of

agricultural production that is exemplified by corn farming is not only unjust but unsustainable, especially in light of the challenges of global climate change, a more democratic model for food and agriculture is needed. By employing the methods and lens of ecocriticism, Adelman and Ajgaonkar illustrate the power of the narrative to shed light on injustice and advocate for new imaginative frameworks for a more just future. The issue of sustainable agriculture and land use is also central to Samantha Noll's argument in chapter 9. Noll investigates how to balance the apparent tension between concerns for ecological resilience and concerns for food security. This tension is illustrated by the problem of climate-induced migration for both human and nonhuman populations; violent conflict and the slow onset of the effects of climate change (such as desertification and rising sea levels) push people to migrate, thus exacerbating food insecurity. Similarly, nonhuman animals respond to the pressures of their changing environments by migrating, and such migrations are correlated with species loss, extinction, and a decrease in biodiversity. Since these changes impact agricultural and food production, ecological resilience and food security are fundamentally intertwined. Thus, Noll argues that, in a warming world, both concerns are deserving of special attention, yet our traditional ethical frameworks seem unequipped to offer substantive guidance in resolving the conflict between the two. As such, she draws on the contemporary food sovereignty movements that, in their ethically pluralist decision-making, "challenge agricultural paradigms and provide a blueprint for cultivating ecological resilience, as well as food-crops, in the age of the Anthropocene."

Part III focuses specifically on responsibility and social change, and the chapters therein investigate the nature of ethical and political decision-making. In general, they ask: What are the ethical and political responsibilities of various parties in relation to this nexus of problems? What should different parties—individuals, communities, government, and so on—do and what is the best way to motivate appropriate action? How can individuals make ethical decisions about food choices and what are the best frames through which to understand responsible food choices?

The first two chapters examine the role of technology in pursuing sustainable, productive agriculture and achieving food security in the face of the threats posed by a changing climate. In particular, the oft lauded and oft maligned practice of genetic engineering has the potential to enable the adaptation of key crops to changing climatic conditions and thus contribute to food security, but it also poses risks, especially because in the United States it is generally unregulated. In chapter 10, Paul Thompson seeks to strike a middle path between full-fledged skepticism that is resistant to any unknown risks of food technology, on the one hand, and full-fledged trust in science that breeds unyielding confidence in both technology and the rationality of risk assessment processes, on the other. Although Thompson is disinclined to credit concerns about the environmental and food safety risks of agricultural technologies, of more concern are the inequalities involved in their use in both agricultural production and food consumption: if risks are present in any way, those who are already disadvantaged by virtue of race, class, gender, or other features are likely to bear the risks disproportionately. Thompson thus concludes that it is far better to approach food technologies "through deliberative democracy and discourse ethics ... than leaving things up to scientized regulatory agencies and the vagaries of the market." Yet, given the contentious and often distorted nature of the debate, more work needs to be done "building the institutional setting for reflective discourse on our technological future," which entails greater intellectual responsibility on the part of both philosophers and scientists. The question of how best to assess innovations in agricultural technology is also the subject of Zoë Robaey and Cristian Timmermann's contribution in chapter 11. Given that a warming world will no doubt force changes to our current food system, there will be an ever-increasing need to find ways to meet the needs of the world's hungry through agricultural innovation. In this context, Robaey and Timmermann identify the different paths of agricultural innovation and then argue that, in the age of GCC, each of these paths needs to take fairness into account in each of the stages of innovation (goal setting, research and development, and empowerment strategies). As a measure of fairness, the authors propose a hybrid ethical assessment tool that combines insights from "responsible research and innovation" and theories of justice. They argue that particular emphasis should be placed on empowering the user of technology to continue assessing and innovating. In this way, their framework addresses the social challenges that arise in agricultural innovation in the context of climate change, and identifies the shortcomings of each innovation stream in light of this ethical assessment. The guidelines they propose "aim to redress the unequal balances in access to knowledge, participation in innovation decisions, and the governance of these innovations."

A consideration of the responsibilities of government is the subject of chapter 12, in which Sarah Kenehan explores the tension between liberal political justice and limiting food choice. This tension is starkly illustrated by the choice to eat meat (especially factory-farmed meat) in a dangerously warming world, where the practice of raising animals for food is a major contributor to local and global environmental harms, including GCC. After showing that these harms disproportionately affect the poor (globally and nationally), Kenehan argues this unequal distribution of burdens is necessarily the purview of political justice, as these burdens threaten the equal status of citizens at home and the democratic stability of nations abroad and then gives substance to these claims through the application of Rawls's theory of justice. She concludes that there are strong reasons of justice to limit food choice in liberal societies and in particular that the U.S. government has at minimum a responsibility to curtail subsidies and other support for the animal agriculture industry.

The final two chapters in the volume analyze individuals' responsibilities to address the injustices related to food and agriculture, environmental ills, and climate change. John Nolt and Annette Mendola consider the issue of food choice from the perspective of the ethically minded consumer in chapter 13. When we make food choices, we are often trying to weigh several values and considerations: healthfulness, taste, price, environmental impact, contribution to GCC, and human and animal welfare, among others. Such calculations have taken on greater urgency given that individual choice does matter, for instance, when thinking about our responsibilities with regard to climate change, but these calculations can, nevertheless, be both exhausting and frustrating. With the aim of making practical sense of these sorts of decisions, Nolt and Mendola argue that these values are not, in fact, comparable and that we will never be situated so as to have all the information we need to make fully informed decisions about the food we eat. Yet these obstacles of incomparability and ignorance should not paralyze us in our choices or lead us to inaction. Rather, they suggest that we should orient our decision-making around the principle of non-harm and seek to develop an array of virtuous habits that reflect our myriad values; cultivating virtuous habits will not only make it easier to take ethical action but also enable us to integrate these practices and values into our characters and lives. In chapter 14, Rachel Ankeny questions the model of ethical consumerism and analyzes some of the problems involved in this model for environmentally responsible food choice. Such problems include the conceptual and practical difficulties pertaining to common concepts—namely, "food miles," "local," and "green"—used to express the ethical impact of food, especially its impact on the environment and its contribution to GHG emissions. These concepts are often conceptually ambiguous and may be misleading (as in the idea that eating "local" food is the best way to reduce GHG emissions); moreover, Ankeny argues that their ambiguity can disincentivize ethically conscious consumer choices. As an alternative to the ethical food consumerism model, she explores the merits of food citizenship. The citizenship model refrains from locating responsibility primarily with the individual and the individual's privatized consumer behavior and instead requires consideration of the collective good and of shared values. Additionally, because food citizenship entails a range of different kinds of ethical decisions and actions (in contrast with ethical consumption), it enables a better grasp of the impact that one, in conjunction with others, can have on local, regional, national, and global levels; likewise, the impact on the environment of, say, policy decisions for which food citizens advocate is clearer than individual consumer-oriented decisions.

The perspectives and topics encompassed in this volume are far-ranging, addressing technology, policy, metaphors and myths, geopolitics, narratives and theoretical frameworks, activist work, and scholarly collaboration, among other issues. On the whole, the chapters offer critical and directive analyses of the many issues of justice that arise at the intersections of food systems, the environment, and climate. They are all simultaneously critical and diagnostic *and* constructive, pointing to ways to move toward more just relationships, social structures, policies, and a more just world as a whole. There are areas of scholarly consensus, for instance, with respect to the disastrous harms caused by industrialized animal agriculture and the pressing need for more democratic, participatory means of making decisions about food, agricultural, environmental, and climate-related issues. Yet there are also points of difference, for instance, concerning the risks posed by genetic engineering, the value of traditional ethical frameworks, and the most productive ways for individuals to take responsibility for their food choices. Such tensions highlight the complexity of the issues at stake and, ideally, can spur further critical reflection on that complexity. As the intersection of food, environment, and climate is an area of research that, as of yet, has been given little substantive attention, we hope that this collection will catalyze a larger conversation among researchers and students alike, so that the problems that are identified within can be explored further, addressed, and eventually ameliorated.

NOTES

1. For evidence of the continuation of Smithfield's standard practices, see June 8, 2018, EPA citation of Smithfield in Nebraska (https://www.epa.gov/ne/smithfield-fresh-meats-corp-clean-water-act-public-notice), Yaggi 2017, and AP 2018.

2. Also see Robeyns 2008 and Valentini 2012 for discussion of some of the nuances of the distinctions between ideal and nonideal theory.

3. For an overview of the substantial philosophical discussion about collective responsibility, see Smiley 2017.

4. For a critical analysis of these two uses of the term "food justice," see Cadieux and Slocum 2015; and for critical analysis of how the alternative food movement works within market structures, see Agyeman and McEntee 2014.

5. For elaboration of the distributive paradigm for food justice, see Dieterle 2015a, 2015b; and Szende 2015.

6. Also see Werkheiser, Tyler, and Thompson 2015.

7. For another perspective on food's cultural significance, see feminist food theorists such as Allen and Sachs 2007.

8. For an overview of the impact of agriculture on the environment, see Tanentzap et al. 2015.

9. For an elaboration of this view, see Gilson 2015.

Part I

THEORIZING INJUSTICES
Key Concepts and Frameworks

Chapter 1

The Intersection of Environmental, Climate, and Food Justice

Joan McGregor

The current food system is harming the most vulnerable people in our society. If you are poor and minority, you have a much higher chance of being obese, having diabetes, and the diseases related to it. African Americans are nearly 1.5 times as likely to be obese as whites are, and African American children are at even higher risk of obesity than white children are. With Latino and Native American children, the rates of obesity and diabetes are even higher (GAIN n.d.). Many of these same people have high rates of food insecurity, namely, lack of regular access to sufficient nutritious food; these people include farm workers, who have the highest levels of food insecurity in the nation (Grauel and Chambers 2014). "Food deserts," areas without reasonably close access to grocery stores with fresh foods, are also most prevalent either in inner cities with high concentrations of low-income and minority populations or in rural areas, such as agricultural areas and tribal nations. Many workers in the food system, such as farm workers, meat processors, and restaurant workers, are minorities and women, subject to low wages and often dangerous working conditions, such as exposure to high levels of chemicals in fields or dangerous equipment in the meat industry. The current system of industrial food production not only results in environmental harms such as soil depletion, chemical runoffs in streams and other waterways, and the subsequent loss of biodiversity but also has detrimental health effects on the surrounding human communities because of its intense chemical burden (Nicolopoulou-Stamati et al. 2016). That same industrial agriculture system that is causing harm to vulnerable humans' health has a substantial impact on the amount of global greenhouse gases, constituting somewhere between 30 and 40 percent of the total amount (Gilbert 2012). Excessive carbon in the atmosphere will harm future generations but is already having effects on current populations, often the most vulnerable ones. Climate change is harming the food systems of vulnerable communities now; for instance, with seas rising and permafrost melting, the Inuit people are forced to relocate, inevitably to places where they cannot access their traditional foods (Tsosie 2007).

Until recently, the food system was not recognized as a locus of social justice problems. Its effects on the environment and the climate were mostly ignored as well. Largely fueled by popular writers and filmmakers Eric Schlosser (*Fast Food Nation*, 2001), Michael Pollan (*The Omnivore's Dilemma*, 2007), and Marion Nestle (*Food Politics*, 2007), food is now on the radar for many more people. These popular writers exposed the problems with the growth and ubiquity of "big-ag" with its monocultures cheapening the price and the quality of food, leading to an abundance of low-quality food and in turn causing a burgeoning health crisis of obesity, cancer, and heart disease. Additionally, they exposed industrial agricultures' reliance on artificial fertilizers and pesticides, resulting in devastating effects on the environment. Out of this attention to the health and environmental problems of the food system grew a robust nationwide food movement focused on healthy, organic foods that are good for people and the planet. Michelle Obama even got into the spotlight, growing a garden at the White House and making "Let's Move," a healthy eating and fitness campaign for children, a centerpiece of her mission as First Lady. This food movement is largely populated, however, by the white upper middle class who have the resources and the ability to access healthy, environmentally friendly alternatives. With it, we have witnessed an explosion of farmers' markets, Community Supported Agriculture (CSAs), community gardens, and farm to table restaurants. The organic food industry is the largest growth area in the food system (Organic Trade Association 2017). While this movement is bringing needed attention to the food system, its concentration has not been on the social inequities in and around the food system and the barriers faced by low-income and minority communities that prevent them from participating in the food movement's proposed solutions. Much of the food movement has been focused on changing people's behavior, namely, calling them to make better choices, and has not acknowledged the structural and interrelated problems that make individual choices and market solutions very difficult or not viable at all in many communities. For members of low-income and minority communities, the proposed solutions, such as Pollan's "Eat mostly plants, especially leaves" (2009) are not necessarily possible, since many of those communities are food deserts with no access to full-service markets with fresh vegetables. Furthermore, the income of the poor has been steadily declining since the 1970s (Pew Research Center 2015) and, ironically, if the inner city poor have access to fresh vegetables in their neighborhoods, the vegetables tend to be cost-prohibitive, even more expensive than in predominately white, suburban neighborhoods (Treuhaft and Karpyn 2010).

Another food movement, the food justice movement, has been emerging as well, led by grassroots organizations focused on the inequities in the food system. "Food justice" is defined as "communities exercising their right to grow, sell, and eat [food that is] fresh, nutritious, affordable, culturally appropriate, and grown locally with care for the well-being of the land, workers, and animals" (Alkon and Agyeman 2011, 2). This movement's attention is to issues of affordability, access, and participation and thereby is concerned with how people are differently affected by food injustices by virtue of their social position/identity/group. These dimensions of social position/identity/group are also a basis for collective resistance to injustice. At the global level, for example, La Via Campesina is championing the rights of peasant farmers to sustainably grow foods for their own communities and resisting the corporate global markets in food (La Via Campesina n.d.).

What is missing from both these food movements is recognition that the food system sits at a unique intersection of problems of justice: the trifecta of food justice (focused on a right to access healthy, nutritious, culturally appropriate food and rights to participation in the decision-making about the food system), environmental justice (focused on exposing and rectifying the differential impact of our industrialized system on marginalized communities, mostly poor and minority communities, and the procedural exclusion of those groups from the decision-making that resulted in those impacts), and climate justice (focused on the distributional inequalities of the effects of greenhouse gases on the planet). Tackling the injustices of the food system requires attention to all the interactions and interdependencies of these domains and, in turn, solutions to the injustices of food should have positive impacts on environmental and climate justice and on sustainability generally.

In this chapter, I will investigate the intersection of these domains of justice and how the same populations share vulnerabilities to distributional and participatory injustices. I will argue that we need to take responsibility for the structural injustices that limit the opportunities and perpetuate unfair outcomes for the poor and minorities both in the United States and globally. Furthermore, governments need to acknowledge the right to a decent environment (including one that is not detrimentally impacted by climate change) and the right to food as basic human rights, and it is our responsibility, as citizens of democratic societies and moral agents, particularly those with privilege and access to political power, to ensure the social and institutional structures to guarantee those rights are respected. The harms addressed by the food, environment, and climate justice movements are interrelated injustices. They are perpetrated by government policies and practices and are consequences of, as Iris Marion Young argues, the background social structure in which "many individuals and institutions [act] to pursue their own particular goals and interests, for the most part within the limits of accepted rules and norms"

(2011, 52). The social structure includes the background conditions, rules, policies, practices, and norms that govern individuals' actions, collectives' actions, and government actions. When the social structure unfairly constrains or limits some people's opportunities, including inflicting upon them more of the burdens of collective practices—like fossil fuel use—and those same processes increase others' opportunities and powers, the social structure creates structural injustices. Many of the actions of individuals and even governments are not aimed at limiting opportunities or harming particular groups, such as the poor, women, and minorities; instead, they are working within the practices and norms of that structure. This is one of the reasons that it is not possible necessarily to point out specific intentions to be racist, for example, when heavy concentrations of pollutants end up in minority communities. The actors involved may well act within the particular guidelines laid out for the processes of picking a waste site, for instance, which are *de jure* race neutral. Understanding these background conditions and how they result in injustice particularly around food, the environment, and climate and how we can take responsibility to change them is the subject of this chapter.

I. FOOD [IN]JUSTICE

The contemporary food system has led to the so-called obesity epidemic in developed and developing nations (Thompson 2014), particularly among the poor and minority populations. Many of these people are undernourished because the foods they eat have little or no nutritional value. Soaring rates of cancer, heart disease, and other lifestyle diseases are also products of our current food practices (Cleveland Clinic 2017). The major killers in the world are no longer infectious diseases; rather they are heart disease, cancers, lung disease, and diabetes, as reported by the World Health Organization. Industrial bioengineered plants and animals, and animals raised in concentrated feeding operations (referred to as CAFOs) have produced more food, but at what cost to human health, animal welfare, and the welfare of the planet? At the same time, malnourishment and starvation remain rampant in less developed nations where wholesale loss of cultural food practices has occurred due to increases in agricultural trade and resulting crop choices. As the Food and Agriculture Organization's 2017 report, *The Future of Food and Agriculture*, stated, the "'triple burden' of malnutrition weighing on most countries consists of undernutrition, micronutrient deficiencies, and overweight and obesity" (FAO 2017).

The "obesity epidemic" and health disparities in poor and minority communities in the United States are met with concern but not as injustices perpetrated by individuals, corporate actors, or the state. More often than not, the conditions of the poor and minorities are discussed as consequences of individual choices and not as the product of government or other actors' decision-making and control. This view ignores the background conditions within which people act and how we got to this place in the transformed food system. Further, it does not account for the government's agency in creating and sustaining the background circumstances generating the harms, nor does it acknowledge the complexity of other background conditions, social rules, and norms that limit individuals' choices—for example, the direct, aggressive marketing of unhealthy food to children and the lack of access to other food options in low-income and minority communities. The assumption that the circumstances of the poor and minorities are not injustices to be rectified relies on the idea that we are all free actors, voluntarily making informed choices in markets free from social structures that constrain our options. This conception of the circumstances of individuals is belied by the facts in which we act, particularly with regard to food.

Twenty-three and one-half million Americans currently live in food deserts. Food deserts occur when there is no access or very limited access to healthy and affordable food. They can occur in urban and rural communities (USDA 2017). Lack of access to fresh, healthy foods leaves individuals in those communities with few options except to purchase fast unhealthy foods. Fast-food outlets or mini-marts are often prevalent in poor urban neighborhoods. For example,

> West Oakland, California, a neighborhood of 30,000 people populated primarily by African Americans and Latinos, has one supermarket and thirty-six liquor and convenience stores. The supermarket is not accessible on foot to most of the area's residents. The convenience stores charge twice as much as grocery stores for identical items. Fast food restaurants selling cheap and hot food appear on almost every corner. (Freeman 2007, 2221)

Why people live where they do is not, as is sometimes suggested, merely a product of individual choices and impartial market forces. Segregated urban communities developed in the 1940s when the government, the Federal Housing Administration, and Veterans' Affairs in particular, provided white middle-class families with home loans enabling them to move to the suburbs of cities. Richard Rothstein in *The Color of Law* (2017) details how the FHA subsidized builders creating suburbs with the requirement that no houses be sold to African Americans. With white movement to the suburbs, many businesses followed, and the development of supermarkets grew in the suburbs, leaving the urban areas without investments and reliable sources of affordable, healthy foods. As a consequence of these government programs and the businesses following suit, "African American families were unable to access the same low-interest home loans as white families due to government sanctioned redlining, restrictive housing covenants, and discrimination, and were left stranded in the cities" (Barker et al. 2012). By 1970 the demographics of the country had drastically changed, and the typical northern African American was "more likely to live with other blacks than with whites" (ibid.). In the 1980s cities continued to lose grocery stores, but there was continued growth of supermarkets in the suburbs. It is important to highlight that "segregated living patterns are not a natural consequence of private choices ... but have been significantly influenced by government policies" (ibid.).

Governmental policies in the housing area demonstrates that these housing patterns are a result of historical institutional racism and not the result of a few "racist" actors. The production of food in minority communities has been affected further by institutional racism. The USDA for decades discriminated against African American and Native American farmers as well as other minority farmers by not providing farm loans to them (Thompson 2010). Those practices led to a sharp decline in the number of minority farmers and illustrates one of the many institutional practices that affected access to capital for minority farmers. Furthermore, fewer minority farmers means less production of foods that connect communities to their cultural food ways, eroding the sustainability of those communities. Native communities lost many of their traditional food ways with dislocation to reservations, the government's prohibition on Native people hunting or fishing off reservation, the provisions of surplus foods not part of Native people's cultural traditions and diet, and from lack of support from the USDA farm loan programs.

Extending the government's role in the current food situation, in the 1930s the government started subsidizing commodity crops like corn and soy. The subsidies resulted in price reductions and surpluses of those foods. Those subsidies continue and are given mostly to large-scale farmers (Imhoff 2012). With the prices down, the food industry created new markets for foods loaded with corn syrup and fat, engineering them to be "irresistible" (Kessler 2009). The food industry spends millions more selling the public on these foods, including direct advertising of unhealthy foods to children, building lifelong tastes for food that is unhealthy.

When prescriptions for the problems of the food system are framed as making better-informed food choices and "voting with your fork" (Gilson 2014), food problems are conceived as occurring within a background that is just and neutral, where individuals control the range of choices. In turn, that framing leads to calls for holding people responsible for their bad food choices and the outcomes of those choices. In fact, the harms resulting from the food system are the consequence of a complex network of government policies and practices and of individuals and groups advancing their own goals within the social rules and norms of society (Kortetmäki, this volume). Consequently, the harms of the food system, for instance, the harms caused by urban minority communities' lack of access to fresh foods, are not necessarily traceable to specific wrong actions or policies. The food industry's practices, for example, are a mix of merely acting within the rules of society, generating profits for their industry; there are not necessarily traceable wrongs in their practices. Are food retailers wronging the poor by failing to build grocery stores in low-income neighborhoods, and are agri-businesses wrong in buying up smaller farms, creating conglomerates that grow subsidized commodity crops? Indeed there are, nevertheless, practices of the government and individuals or corporate actors that are clear moral wrongs: redlining by the government, for example, or the food industry's funding researchers to exonerate their products from blame for the obesity epidemic and other health problems (Domonoske 2016). But just looking for traceable wrongs for the distributional disparities of the food system will not provide a full explanation of those unjust outcomes. To be clear, there are governmental policies that if different would make significant differences in outcomes pertaining to food in poor and minority neighborhoods. The point is, rather, that there are many factors at work causing these wrongs, not all of which are blameworthy.

II. ENVIRONMENTAL [IN]JUSTICE

Another domain where there has been significant attention to distributional disparities is in exposure to environmental hazards. The environmental justice (EJ) movement started in the 1980s as a grassroots movement to champion the cause of low-income, mostly minority communities that were being disproportionately burdened by environmental pollutants (Bullard 1990). These environmental hazards result in harms to the community in the form of health disparities, early mortality rates, and property value declines. Since statistically so many of these inequitable burdens are heaped upon minority communities, the name "environmental racism" was given to these practices (Newkirk 2018). The EJ movement expanded the notion of "environment" beyond the mainstream environmental movement's attention to wilderness protection. EJ focused on everyday hazards people face in the communities where they "live, work and play," urban, suburban, and rural. EJ combined notions of environmental sustainability with demands for social justice. The food system is a major contributor to environmental hazards for minorities, for example, the concentration of CAFOs in largely African American communities such as in North Carolina. The CAFOs result not only in noxious smells and "mucosal irritation and respiratory ailments in nearby residents but also decreased quality of life, mental stress, and elevated blood pressure" (Nicole 2013, 183). Another major environmental hazard generated by the contemporary food system comes from the chemical pesticides and herbicides that subject farm workers and their families to toxins. Allegations of environmental injustice were met with skepticism about whether in fact these were intentional instances of discrimination in which minority neighborhoods were targeted as sites for dumping toxins or farm workers were subject to undue pollutants from agriculture. Opponents argued that seating waste sites in particular communities, for instance, was not a product of racism but rather market forces. Individuals are free actors in the market, they said, and can choose to live, work, and play as they see fit. The market argument went on: Individuals are responsible for the conditions in which they find themselves. Consequently, the fact of the differential burdens is not an injustice that needs to be rectified nor is there a need to change practices of disposing or using environmental hazards.

To ignore the background conditions under which individuals make choices, the reasons that people live and work where they do, the processes of decision-making for environmental regulation, is to miss the government, corporate actors, and other individuals' actions, practices, and policies that put and keep people into the current situation. Suggesting that people simply "choose" to live in a certain neighborhood fails to recognize the systemic, structural, and historical facts and injustices that got and keep people there. Environmental justice is not about equity issues alone but about how injustice is constructed, why those already exposed to other forms of disadvantage are also subject to environmental burdens.

III. CLIMATE [IN]JUSTICE

The consequences of greenhouse gases growing exponentially in the atmosphere are having and will continue to have distributional disparities detrimentally affecting low-income people and minorities, nationally and internationally. The accumulation is driven by emissions from fossil fuel consumption, coal fire burning, and other activities such as deforestation, animal husbandry, and other industrial agriculture practices, the latter contributing one-third of all greenhouse gases to the atmosphere (Gilbert 2012). Because of anthropogenic-induced change to the atmosphere, the planet is getting warmer. Over the twentieth century the temperature went up 1.69 degrees Fahrenheit. That warming of the planet is melting polar ice, shrinking glaciers, and raising sea levels. The weather is changing as well. There have been many more climate-related disasters, three times as many since the 1980s. These include heat waves and drought, hurricanes, and floods. Climate change will affect most people in the world but will most seriously affect less developed nations and vulnerable communities in the United States. To see these effects of climate change, witness the devastation of the African American community in New Orleans after Hurricane Katrina (Brunsma, Overfelt, Picou 2007), or consider the effects on indigenous communities, such as the Navajo, of the extended drought in the Southwest (Garfin et al. 2014). Climate change is going to harm many people; millions will be displaced and their ability to grow food significantly damaged (Working Groups I, II, and III 2015). The victims of climate change, however, are not necessarily the people who created or benefited from the causes of the changes. Industrialized societies, for instance, have benefited from their industrialization, but the higher CO_2 levels causing climate change are an ongoing externality of that process. The least industrialized societies, particularly those with coastlines that will be flooded, displacing millions, were not the major contributors to the greenhouse gases in the atmosphere. Even in this country where we find vulnerable communities such as Native communities being affected by climate change, most of them were not the direct beneficiaries of industrialization; for example, consider that 32 percent of Navajo homes are without electricity (Landry 2015).

Concerns for the harms perpetrated by climate change developed a research area known as "climate justice" that considers where the burdens of climate change are falling, who is responsible for creating those dangerous levels of greenhouse gases, and who should take responsibility for mitigation in the future. Inevitably, accounts of responsibility for the levels of greenhouse gases in the atmosphere, and prescriptions for the future haven't been met with agreement. Simple principles such as "polluter pays" have not received widespread acceptance, especially in the United States (Moellendorf 2014). It is even harder to decide where to lay responsibility for historical emissions. For instance, in 1997 the Brail Proposal, which argued for the polluters to pay for historical emissions, was rejected by the United Nations Framework Convention on Climate Change. Meanwhile, the harms of climate change are occurring and already affecting the most vulnerable in the United States and globally. Furthermore, unless collective action is taken quickly, the effects of dangerous climate change will catastrophically affect future generations' capacities to live quality lives and especially affect food production (Myers et al. 2017). Again, the reasons that the impact of climate change will be greater in some communities both domestically and globally, particularly poor and minority communities, has to do with the same background conditions that lead to the other injustices of the food system and environmental pollutants.

IV. INTERSECTIONALITY OF FOOD, ENVIRONMENTAL, AND CLIMATE JUSTICE

These three domains and the movements they sprouted have not been allying with one another theoretically or practically even though there are important intersections of concerns about the distributional disparities of the products of industrial society and who is most vulnerable to the burdens (Gottlieb and Fisher 2000; Schlosberg and Collins 2014; Robaey and Timmerman, this volume). The industrial food system subsidized by the U.S. government uses more chemicals, second only to China, in the production of food (World Atlas 2017), which detrimentally affects farm workers' health and the neighborhoods of the poor (Alavanja 2009). Government subsidies for commodity crops, which involve the use of large quantities of chemicals, lead to cheap abundance of unhealthy foods, which the poor consume (because it is what they have access to, can afford, and are heavily marketed to by the food industry), leading to disastrous health outcomes in those populations. In addition, that same food system is generating record amounts of greenhouse gases, with little regulation, that will cause even more harm to vulnerable communities, near and far, geographically and in time. Finally, vulnerable populations are most likely to be impacted by climate disturbances if not for any other reason than lack of participation in the process of mitigation due to, for example, lack of funds to mitigate and adapt to those changes, including moving to different places, shopping for alternative foods, or creating or purchasing technologies to adapt to climate changes.

It would be mistaken to merely focus on the unequal distributional burdens, that is, seeing these harms solely as an issue of distributional justice. That framing misses the social structure and institutional contexts (which include epistemic injustices and epistemologies of ignorance [Fricker 2007]) within which these harms occur. Understanding the problem of these unjust outcomes as the result of structural injustices that exist and perpetuate patterns of unequal distribution results in different prescriptions for change. As discussed earlier, the social structure includes the background conditions, the rules, policies, practices, and norms that govern individuals' actions, collectives' actions, and government actions. Structural injustices are created when the background conditions unfairly constrain or limit some people's opportunities, and conversely those same processes increase power and opportunities for others. The social structure is the largely invisible framework in which we act. Quoting Iris Young:

> Social structures do not constrain in the form of direct coercion of some individuals over others; they constrain more indirectly and cumulatively as blocking possibilities. Part of the difficulty of seeing structure, moreover, is that we do

not experience particular institutions, particular material facts, or particular rules as themselves sources of constraint; the constraint occurs through the joint action of individuals within institutions and given physical conditions as they affect our possibilities. (2011, 55)

The reasons for the obesity problem in low-income and minority communities is not caused by any one bad actor; neither is it true that individuals are "coerced" into making certain food choices. Rather, there is a confluence of background conditions, including reasons why minority families have less wealth and thereby have limited opportunities about where they work and live. Some of the conditions, no doubt, are created by government, some by individuals, and some by corporate actors blocking opportunities and encouraging certain behaviors. But just focusing on one policy—for instance, government subsidies of commodity crops—will miss out on other important factors, such as the norm of efficiency pertaining to food driving those policies. Attention needs to be paid not to the specific distributional inequalities alone but to the social structures that produce those outcomes; otherwise we will just re-create the unjust outcomes. It is important to notice that these structures do not eliminate the freedom of actors within them; rather, they put barriers and limits on individuals' opportunities.

Questions about the fairness of the allocations of the burdens and benefits of society are significant ones; nevertheless, we should also recognize that a consequence of the social structure is the distributional disparities in participation in the decision-making processes about these allocations. A centerpiece of the EJ movement is the importance of participation in the processes where decisions are made and of exposing the unequal levels of participation from members of the most vulnerable communities (Loo, this volume). For instance, decisions about climate change policy inevitably do not have consultation or representation from poor and minority communities. Their exclusion is often a product of their lack of political power. The redlining that caused the underinvestment in minority communities, leading to food deserts and the reduction of property values, undoubtedly was not a product of minority communities' participation. Even the zoning and permitting that allow multiple liquor stores and fast-food outlets in communities are the result of decisions made by government boards or commissions without representation from the affected communities. The food sovereignty movement, La Via Campesina, has put sovereignty, the agency of the actors, at the forefront in their calls for justice. Having a voice, participating in the process, having agency, is central to treating persons with respect and as critical as the justice of the substantive distribution. Historically marginalized groups have not been at the table, or not in enough numbers, to participate in the process of making regulations or constructing policies. The intersections of food, environment, and climate and their effects on poor and minority groups mean that the latter need to be part of the conversation and decision-making for policies going forward. That includes what chemicals are used in the food system and what levels of hazardous pollutants are acceptable for surrounding communities. Participatory justice, the right to participate in the process of decision-making, is as important as distributional justice in all the domains of food, environment, and climate justice. Both participatory and distributional disparities are consequences of the social structure and hence represent structural injustices.

One more aspect of justice and a unique type of harm represented in these three domains is the harm of misrecognition. Marginal groups want to be "recognized" for their unique cultural identities as opposed to being treated as "universal persons." Justice requires, as Charles Taylor reminds us, that we recognize the "person's understanding of who they are, of their fundamental characteristics as human being" (Taylor 1994, 25). Recognition is a "vital human need" and, consequently, misrecognitions can be a grievous harm to persons (Fraser 1997). An example of a misrecognition that leads to a cultural harm is inducing Native Americans to eat surplus commodity food provided by the government. The imposition of those foods on Native people does not recognize their traditional foods and food ways; and the government's providing these culturally inappropriate foods creates dependency and devalues their identities as unique peoples with their own practices and values around food. Social structures purporting to "treat everyone the same" miss the importance of being recognized for one's cultural identity as a dimension of respect for persons. Providing Native Americans with surplus commodity food when they were prevented from preserving their traditional food ways satisfied the distributional requirement of providing Native people with food but failed to recognize their unique identities and therefore perpetuated a harm upon them. Analogously, as a result of climate change, Inuit people are losing their land due to warming and the suggestion that the government will merely relocate them fails to recognize their unique identity as indigenous people with ties to the land.

Solving the problems of injustice from the food system, environmental contaminants, and climate change requires that we change the background conditions that structure the relationships in society and not focus merely on individual bad actions. Changing the social structure so it does not produce unfair outcomes in one domain will have effects in others. The social justice problems of the modern food system are multiple and complex; some that we have discussed are lack of access to healthy food, the marketing of fast unhealthy foods, and the failure to give government loans to minority farmers. What are some of the background conditions that could be changed? Changing the policies and incentives around where grocery stores are located—favorable zoning and taxation, for example—changing the government's policies about what foods it subsidizes, what chemicals can be used in agriculture, what foods it provides in school lunch programs; changing the rules around marketing unhealthy foods, particularly to children, are some of the possible changes to the social structure particularly with regard to the government's role. For example, changing what foods get government subsidies would have outcomes in all these domains. The government's food subsidies focused on human and environmental health would change what food gets produced, how it is produced, and how affordable it is. Those policy changes would have the effect of slowing the process of climate change as well. There are formal and informal social rules around food that may be more difficult to change. Beliefs about what foods are healthy and tasty, for example, are difficult to change. Nevertheless, changing the marketing practices of food would blunt the worst effects of the current system. And there is historical precedent for successful change in social norms—for example, around tobacco use.

Changing the norms around food production and consumption would have substantial effects as well. For example, changing the goal of the food system from efficiency or lowest cost to quality and protection of the workers, consumers, and the planet would create a radical change in practices, as would, generally, changing how we view food as a market commodity to a public good. We do not, for instance, view education as a commodity to be produced at the lowest cost but rather as a public good where the quality of the process and the outcome matter. Changing society's conception of the food system to one focused on the welfare of individuals, animals, communities, and planet would permeate the policies, practices, and norms affecting food.

V. RIGHTS AND RESPONSIBILITY: WHAT DO WE OWE EACH OTHER?

There are wrongful harms from the food system and other aspects of our industrialized society that disproportionately impact the poor and minorities. The food system is causing harm to the health and welfare of those groups in its production, transportation, consumption, and waste. It does so in direct and indirect fashions. For instance, low nutrient/high caloric foods are heavily consumed by members of those groups, causing health problems, and the production of the food causes environmental hazards including those that lead to climate change, which in turn has deleterious effects on the poor and minority communities. There is an intersection of harms from the current food system on low-income and minority communities. Acknowledging these harms as wrongful, as matters of justice, is to identify them as violations of what people are owed, what they deserve. People deserve equal concern and respect, meaning among other things that they deserve opportunities equal to those of others in society for developing their capabilities to live good lives and not to be constrained by multiple social forces. We have focused to a large extent on the background conditions that limit people's opportunities and abilities, resulting in these wrongful differential impacts. We have argued that these harms are not all the result of bad actors, racists trying to perpetrate harm on certain populations, for instance. Rather, many—maybe most—are products of agents within processes of the social structure who are advancing their own interests. Indeed, some of those who unwittingly perpetrate harms are acting within systems that are products of historical structural injustices in society that cause populations to be vulnerable to these abuses. The actors themselves didn't create those particular injustices.

Claims of injustice are linked with calls for responsibility: who owes the debt or remedying treatment to another. If we acknowledge that the current patterns of distribution of burdens, opportunities, and powers are unfair, who is responsible for ensuring that the wrongful harms are not perpetrated going forward? Because structural injustices are not products of individual action, attributions of responsibility are resisted. There isn't necessarily someone or one transparently morally wrong government policy at fault for the unfair treatment of the poor and minorities. Traditionally, theories of responsibility have focused on the particular guilty party who caused the harm or is liable for harm. This theory of responsibility is used as a deflection of responsibility for the harms to future generations of climate change, since it is argued that our individual actions or omissions are not the "cause" of the harm (Jamieson 2014). It is the collective action or omissions of many of us, millions of us in a complex network that cause the harm to the future. Any one of us changing what we do isn't going to have a causal effect on the climate. Consequently, though we might feel bad about those unlucky future people since they will have a degraded world, we have no responsibility to change our lifestyle because of the harm to them (see Nolt 2011 and Hiller 2011 for contrary arguments).

Accounts of responsibility are often backward-looking, assigning blame based on fault or liability to harm. But we also talk about "taking responsibility" for the future to ensure that harm or injustices do not occur. That theory of responsibility is what Young calls a "social connection model" and Darrel Moellendorf calls "social responsibility": both require us to collectively assume responsibility for changing the social structures that produce and reproduce these unjust outcomes. This is a shared responsibility of citizens (nationally and globally) to make these changes. As a start on those changes, we should recognize that (healthy) food and a decent environment are not the same types of goods as other goods. They are not commodities that we might or might not have, nor are they fungible goods that could be traded off for other goods. They are preconditions to the exercise of other capacities, such as health, political participation, or education. Not having enough decent food or living in an unhealthy environment undermines the exercise of these other capacities. Hence, healthy food and a decent environment are necessary conditions for exercising the capacities to live any life. Conceiving healthy food and environment as basic human rights acknowledges that people cannot do or be anything without adequate (and healthy)[1] food and a decent environment, including a stable climate.

A right to food has been rejected by some since it is assumed that the right to food means a right to be fed, the right of others to give you food thereby imposing on all of us a duty to feed people. That is not the only construction of the right to food, however. The right to food is a right to feed oneself, to produce food, to have access to healthy food at affordable prices, and to have agency over food. The Right to Food as the UN Special Rapporteur has stated is "the right to have regular, permanent and unrestricted access, either directly or by means of financial purchases, to quantitatively and qualitatively adequate and sufficient food corresponding to the cultural traditions of the people to which the consumer belongs, and which ensure a physical and mental, individual and collective, fulfilling and dignified life free of fear" (OHCHR). Human rights are claims against coercive social institutions, governments, international bodies such as WTO, and those who uphold and support those institutions. The background structures, the institutional arrangements, laws, rules, practices and procedures, and the people in charge of ensuring they are functioning properly can support or violate peoples' human rights, including the right to food. Governmental policies and practices can undermine or place barriers in the way of people's exercise of their human rights.

The right to food can be promoted or violated through agricultural practices and policies of governments, for example, subsidizing certain crops (healthy ones versus unhealthy ones, commodity corn rather than fresh vegetables), creating policies about food required in school lunch programs that are focused on the health and nutrition of children rather than corporate financial interests, enacting zoning policies and other regulations that either provide for access to healthy foods or discourage unhealthy ones, mandating agricultural and distribution practices that do not contribute to GHG emissions, and encouraging ones that capture carbon. This conception of the right to food aims at not only access to nutritious food but also the sustainability of the food supply, and that can be advanced or thwarted by agricultural, environmental, and climate policies, both nationally and internationally. "This right," Sandra Raponi reminds us, "also acknowledges the communal and cultural importance of food," supporting the notion of the recognition of wrongs possible by violations of the right to food (2017, 102). The right to food is one that is exercised with others in a community, hence the emerging importance of the notion of food sovereignty as an essential part of the right to food. Food sovereignty speaks to the importance of participatory justice, the right to have a say in your food and food system, particularly attending to the cultural significance of food. Food, like water and energy, is critical to human existence. Yet what makes tackling the problems of the food system more difficult is that it has deeper layers of meaning derived from the significant role food plays in human life and culture. More than necessary for survival, food forms a significant part of individuals' and groups' identities and acquires and provides deep meaning in peoples' lives. Culture and the rituals that are derived from cultural understandings are infused with traditions about food.

The right to adequate food also includes protecting sustainable food security in the future. This concern can be addressed by government restrictions on agricultural practices and products that contribute to soil erosion or reduce the ability to grow important food crops in the future. Climate policies too will have a significant effect on food products, and common methods of food production are prime contributors to climate change. Attention to both is necessary. Governments might prohibit or restrict the use of certain pesticides, mono-cropping, and certain GMOs. The right to food is a right to produce food, and this right can be violated by policies and practices of governments to exclude minority and small-scale farmers from farm loan programs. These practices and many more undermine the capacity for low-income minority communities to exercise their right to food, to have agency in their food system. States have a positive duty to protect the right to food, which means ensuring that people can exercise their rights, and we collectively have the responsibility to ensure that the background conditions in the form of policies that violate peoples' right to food are altered.

Having a decent environment, at minimum free from hazardous pollution or the dangerous effects of climate change, is also fundamental to anything else that human beings want to do or be. As we have seen, the evidence of the concentrations of environmental toxins and pollution in some communities, particularly poor and minority communities, leaves those communities having to contend with the unfairness of experiencing those harms that result from the hazards, particularly since they are shouldering the disadvantages that others, more privileged, are not. This should be recognized as a distributional injustice, a violation of a basic human right to a decent environment. Again, there are multiple actions, policies, and decisions that produce these unjust outcomes. Taking collective responsibility to change the structural processes that produce these unjust outcomes will be multifaceted. One place to start is reconstructing the processes whereby the decisions about the use of chemicals in agriculture get made. Doing so involves not only changing the composition of the decision-making bodies but requiring that decisions not be made on market values; since basic human rights to food and a decent environment are involved, the criteria for decision-making should reflect and protect those values for consumers, community members, workers, and future generations. The damaging effects of meat production are well known, for example; not only do CAFOs have devastating effects on the nearby communities and the animals but the greenhouse gases they produce will harm future generations' food security and environments.

Recognizing a decent environment, including one that is not harmed by climate change, and a healthy food system as instrumental for individuals living flourishing lives, whatever they look like, is grounds for the claim that they are basic human rights. In other words, recognizing food and environment (including climate) as basic human rights necessitates that we stop leaving their quality and character up to the background conditions of the marketplace and instead consider closely the institutional structures that up to this point have produced outcomes that are unjust for all, but especially low-income and minority groups. Acknowledging that a decent environment with a stable climate and a safe healthy food system is a human right puts the regulation of food, environment, and climate into the domain of public deliberation for the public good. Also, the awareness that these are not discreet domains but have overlapping and interdependent effects on one another is critical. How we best ensure an environment that meets the standards of safety and quality that everyone should enjoy, not based on who you are or what community you live in, should to a large extent be controlled by democratic deliberative bodies (not influenced by corporate actors) protecting the welfare of peoples' human right to a decent environment and stable climate. These standards need to be ensured for each community. The food system should provide healthy, culturally appropriate foods, and the regulation of food should be based on the needs of people's health and well-being and not left to market principles alone, focused on efficiency and food as commodity. The U.S. food system has been driven by the profit interests of corporate agriculture and not the interests of health, nutrition, and the environment (Nestle 2002). Environmental, climate, and food vulnerabilities are symptoms of social inequities, but they also represent a relationship between humans and the natural world that creates social injustice and environmental destruction. Changing how we structure our food system, the system of distribution of environmental burdens, climate change policies, who has a say over these matters, and designing for long-term sustainability would go a long way to protecting the earth for future generations.

VI. CONCLUSION: PUTTING IT ALL TOGETHER

There is an intersection of concerns with food justice, environmental justice, and climate justice: it involves who is disadvantaged, what the causes of differential impacts are, who is responsible, what an appropriate response to particular groups' harms is, and who gets to decide. Achieving social justice at this intersection means addressing the background social structures that produce and reproduce unjust outcomes. The poor and minorities are the most vulnerable to the harms of the food system, industrial wastes, and climate change. These harms are often produced not by particular unjust actions but by a network of processes and actions that are permitted by the social structure, which includes laws and regulations but also social rules and norms. It is often difficult to single out a particular bad actor to blame for the wrongful harm. We need to recognize the larger set of background conditions that limit and constrain some groups' behavior and lives and expand and empower other groups' opportunities. We need to stop seeing the inequitable burdens on vulnerable communities as merely the result of market forces, "where people choose to live or what they choose to eat," and begin to see them as systemic and structural problems of social injustice. We collectively need to take responsibility for changing the background circumstances within which people act. Some of this collective change will be done by reconceiving healthy food and decent environment, including a stable climate, as not merely commodities to be purchased in the marketplace but human rights that individuals are due. Collectively it is our responsibility to ensure that everyone has the capacity to exercise those rights. Protecting the environment, including ameliorating the effects of climate change, and ensuring a safe, secure food system are issues of the public good and should be addressed by public deliberation, for the public good, through decision-making by communities.

NOTE

1. There is limited space to argue for the claim that the right to food is a right to "healthy [and culturally appropriate] food" and not just any food. If current food injustices show us anything, it is that unhealthy calories are detrimental to the capacity to live a flourishing life.

Chapter 2

Nobody's Fault?

Structural Injustice, Food, and Climate Change

Teea Kortetmäki

Due to the industrialization and globalization of food systems, food system activities from field to fork (or to waste) and their connections have become more complex, less locally governable, and harder to understand. This makes it difficult to point out and name food system–related responsibilities by using conventional theoretical approaches. Yet there is a pressing need to address inequalities in the global food systems in a way that also considers the relationship between the global food system and climate change. Neglecting their interconnectedness creates a risk that promoting justice in one domain creates injustices in another.

Structural injustice is a term that shows promise for examining the complex relations that are characteristic of the food-climate nexus. The term signifies situations where various social processes or structures systematically create inequalities in ways that cannot be traced back to the blameful action of particular agents. Activities that contribute to structural injustices may well comply with the existing norms, yet together they maintain and reproduce injustices and undesirable consequences. The main question of this chapter is: How does the notion of structural injustice help understand global food injustices in relation to climate change? Answering this question requires clarifying the notion of structural food injustice and showing how it is interconnected with structural climate injustice. For practical purposes, the approach must also address the question of who should do what to alleviate structural global food injustices.

In this chapter, I am concerned with social justice: the equality of people with regard to the distribution of benefits and harms, rights and obligations, and opportunities for equal participation in the society and social life.[1] I also maintain, in line with most justice theories, that justice relates primarily to the structures of a society: social processes, relations, and institutional arrangements. Justice denotes, roughly speaking, *the fairness of the society* (wherein society may be something else than a nation-state) in how it treats its members. This chapter considers two particular domains of justice: food and climate matters. Both have become distinct yet overlapping arenas of justice discourse and theorizing. Food justice involves issues that relate to how, where, what, and by whom food is produced, processed, sold, and consumed. Climate justice is concerned with the distribution of burdens and risks that result from climate change or climate policies.

Justice theorizing has a long tradition in political theory and philosophy. Contemporary problems have challenged the applicability of the conventional notions of that literature. The "standard cases of injustice" (discussed thoroughly in the canonical justice literature) can often be traced back to particular institutional arrangements like certain laws or regulations. In these standard cases, those actors or practices can be judged as culpable for creating inequalities: consider the lack of political or social rights, unequal rights to have property, or regressive income taxation. These cases have also been typically state-territorial, happening within a particular nation-state.

Iris Marion Young argued that a new form of inequality, structural injustice, challenges the conventional assumptions about what inequality is and how it comes about. Structural injustice "exists when social processes put large groups of persons under systematic threat of domination or deprivation of the means to develop and exercise their capacities, at the same time that these processes enable others to dominate or to have a wide range of opportunities for developing and exercising capacities available to them" (Young 2011, 51). Sweatshops exemplify a paradigmatic case of this form of injustice. Even if there are instances of clear wrongdoings by malevolent individuals within the factories, the overall plight of sweatshop workers results from a combination of social-structural factors (policies, institutions, and market relations) more than from intentionally harmful actions (Young 2006; Calder 2010). It is impossible to point out a particular actor or institutional arrangement that would account for the existence of sweatshops or that could eradicate them.

The idea that injustices may be of a systemic nature is not new as such. Karl Marx already made a similar point, and it has been noted by several political philosophers and theorists since then. Structural injustice, as coined by Young, has distinct features that make it a particular species of systemic injustice (Young 2011, 44–63):

1. Structural injustice is not traceable to individual harms or certain policies or practices exercised by institutional actors: there are always multiple actors and relations involved.
2. It results from complex interactions and processes: it is hard to say where the injustice begins.

3. It results from the events over a long term: it is hard to say when the injustice begins. It is also an ongoing process rather than a terminal outcome.

4. It usually happens as an accumulated outcome of uncoordinated[2] actions that in themselves are considered normal and not particularly blameworthy or unjust.

Climate change is an epitome of structural injustice. Climate-related harms are produced through (mostly uncoordinated) practices that are largely considered nonblameworthy and "normal" (Eckersley 2016, 346–47). Emissions are a by-product of everyday human activities that are not intended to cause emissions. No single agent or group of agents can be held liable for climate change. Even the global North, often identified as the major instigator of historical emissions, involves a large and heterogeneous area where the emissions have resulted from a bunch of uncoordinated activities and within which there are great variations in regional and individual emissions.[3] Christopher Kutz (2007) makes a similar point by calling climate change an unstructured collective harm (though he grounds related responsibilities differently from Young's approach). Emissions arise in a complex web of interactions between individuals, collectives, enterprises, and institutions that are embedded in ways that make it impossible to say exactly who is responsible for emissions.[4] Climate change creates and manifests social inequalities that are pertinent to structural injustices and determine the opportunities available for different social groups. The marginal position of the least developed communities in the global order puts them in a weak position to reduce vulnerability to climate change (Eckersley 2016, 347) even though they have not benefited much from the infliction of earlier emissions.

I. THE GLOBAL FOOD SYSTEM AND STRUCTURAL INJUSTICE

Food systems are networks of activities that relate to food production, processing and packaging, distribution and retail, and consumption, involving the different social, economic, and environmental dimensions of these activities (Ericksen 2008, 234). Food systems are best understood as broad systems that include both food handling activities (the chain from farm to fork) as well as other relations with the environment and the society that essentially shape and influence food activities. Public policies, global institutions, and trade agreements are of particular importance among the factors that shape the food global food system in indirect ways.

Food injustice refers to a broad set of concerns that relate to the patterns of inequality or domination in relation to the food system activities. Such concerns include (but are not limited to) the lack of food security[5]; injustices in agricultural production and food industry; the unequal distribution of harms resulting from the unsustainability of the food system; and the lack of democratic control over food system activities (Dieterle 2015b, ix). Many injustices in the food system are "ordinary" rather than structural: it is possible to identify culpable actors (or a single actor) who would be able to prevent the injustice had they acted in nonblameworthy ways. For example, companies who put people in the United States to work in slavery-like conditions (Gottlieb and Joshi 2010, 13–21) are more than likely culpable and liable for what they have done.[6] Structural injustices are more complex. A paradigmatic example could be the income distribution structure in various global food supply chains, like the coffee chain. Regardless of annual variations, the coffee producers' share of the retail price is remarkably low, has been declining over the years, and in poor years may be less than 10 percent (Talbot 1997). The global coffee trade produces inequalities that result from its structures (Valkila and Nygren 2009). The skewed profit distribution results from structural processes (including market mechanisms, institutional rules, trade regulations, and asymmetry in the capacities of actors to make choices) rather than from the intentional actions of particular agents. Actors in the supply chain operate in given circumstances regarding competition and like matters, and they need to retain profitability (see Calder 2010 for a similar point on sweatshops). Even the fair trade schemes that guarantee producers a minimum price may fail to improve the fairness of profit distribution (while they may have other benefits): the "responsibility surplus value" harvested by other supply chain actors leave fair trade producers with a smaller share of the retail price than in the case of conventional coffee. Due to structures, farmers may also receive a higher price in the mainstream market during the periods of high coffee prices (Valkila and Nygren 2009).

The global coffee trade is but one case of the structural inequalities in the global food system. Inequalities are manifested, more generally, in how consumers in wealthy countries benefit from the existing global inequalities that allow them to import products from, and conduct food processing in, poor countries with notably low prices. This dynamic maintains inequalities in the household food expenditures, which are less than 15 percent in wealthy countries but over 40 percent in the poorest countries.[7] This difference reproduces other inequalities since it leaves people in poor countries with no economic buffer for investing in their future or children. Structural factors also establish legal yet indecent working conditions in the food system and reinforce power inequalities in business-to-business negotiations (Gottlieb and Joshi 2010). Inequalities are maintained and reproduced in global agreements and negotiations where negotiators possess divergent political and economic capacities, and processes tend to strengthen rather than alleviate these inequalities.

The aforementioned injustices fit the earlier four-point characterization of structural injustices. They are not traceable to individual harms, a particular policy, or a particular action; they involve multiple actors. They result from complex global interactions and from complex, long-term developments in trade globalization, agricultural reforms, and political changes. Further, they are an outcome of a set of uncoordinated actions (of trade and consumption) that are usually not blameworthy as such. Food companies comply with the regulations and "just mind their businesses." For a single enterprise, choosing a heroic strategy and taking supererogatory actions to improve fairness in food chains involves a risk of significant economic losses. Changing the rules of the game would require a majority of the companies to change practices simultaneously, and even this may fail if the "lower-standard production" merely moves to the hands of other actors that operate in regions with loose or nonexistent regulations.[8] Structural factors also make improvements difficult. Due to price formation structures, many improvements in sustainability or fairness raise consumer prices more than the cost of the improvement. This is a competitive disadvantage for any improvement. States cannot change the situation easily either unless (almost) all of them cooperate:[9] the corporatization of the food system and the free trade paradigm has reduced their power to govern the food systems. International trade agreements prevent states from restricting the imports of unfairly or unsustainably produced food unless the production process can be shown to alter the final product in a way that is harmful to the consumer (Oosterveer and Sonnenfeld 2012, 68–69). International trade regulations also restrict the provision of tax benefits for more sustainable alternatives. Injustices in the international order, for one, hinder the possibilities for fair bargaining between countries on these matters.

II. THE FOOD-CLIMATE NEXUS: CONNECTIONS BETWEEN STRUCTURAL INJUSTICES

There is a two-way relationship between the global food system and climate change. Climate change influences global food production and food system activities especially by threatening food production and yielding security due to rising temperatures and precipitation changes. On the other hand, food system activities account for 25 to 30 percent of total human-made emissions and are among the most significant emission sources (Working Group III 2014). I will next discuss the food-climate linkages to illustrate the interconnectedness of related structural injustices. Like climate injustices, structural injustices in the global food system are part of the broader context of globally unequal ecological exchange of resources and energy, where the global North extracts resources cheaply from the global South while shifting the environmental burdens of extractive activities to developing countries (Parks and Roberts 2010).

The Impact of Climate Change on Food System Activities

Climate change causes twofold injustices in the global food system through causal effects that emerge from complex multiactor relations and are by-products of everyday (not particularly blameworthy) practices. Although climate change will likely harm food production everywhere, it hits first and hardest the poor countries who already face the greatest difficulties in promoting food security, which in turn relates to injustices in the global food system and the plight of the farmers in the global South. Because unequal access to food is worsened by harms that originate from both food system activities and climate change, correcting its causes within the food system does not sufficiently fix the problems in the future. Tackling food insecurity requires action on both food and climate policies.

Agriculture and food exports (especially unprocessed primary products) are also an important source of income for many developing, climate-vulnerable countries.[10] When climate change damages their agricultural production, food producers and workers who already suffer from injustices (unfairly low and unreliable income, poor working conditions) are likely to end up in a worse position because they lack the adaptive capacity to respond to climate change and to the changing conditions in the global markets. They likewise lack capacities to secure livelihoods with investments or alternative sources of income—to increase their competitiveness in global markets—as well as capacities to ensure fair agreements in global trade. Moreover, many developing countries have a narrow income base, and failures in one major constituent of the GDP are detrimental for the whole community.

Within the global food system, the social structural position of farmers deserves special attention.[11] Farmers are often in the weakest position in supply chains when it comes to profitability, labor rights, and negotiation power. This is particularly true for small family farms characteristic of many countries, since they are very small operators, unlike large food industry and trade enterprises, and farmers' unions tend to lack sufficient capacities to truly stand for their members. Farmers are also exceptionally vulnerable to climate change. Their income depends heavily on annual weather conditions and they often lack satisfactory economic and social safety networks for weather-related disasters. Cash crops are particularly vulnerable to market fluctuations and weather extremes. Contrary to other food business operators, farming lacks flexibility: fields cannot be moved to conditions that are more favorable. Overall, farmers face a heavy burden of structural harms that originate from both climate change and food system activities. Yet it would be extremely difficult to identify a culpable instigator of these harms, which instead result from a complex network of regulations, environmental conditions, and relations between multiple actors who try to keep their own business running or protect their own national interests for the good of fellow citizens.

The connection between food insecurity and climate change extends beyond production, too. A major difference between the well-off countries and those in a weaker social structural position is in the resilience of their food systems.[12] Despite often monocultural (and hence less resilient) farming practices, the developed countries have better capacities for utilizing alternative procurement channels and emergency stockpiles if the primary supply chains fail. They are also capable of safeguarding the profitability of domestic production in hard times and paying higher prices for food. These factors increase their resilience in the face of climate-related challenges. Wealthy countries are also better equipped for climate-related abnormalities like weather extremes and disease risks.

The Impact of Food System Activities on Climate Change

The global food system significantly contributes to climate change as the aggregate result of uncoordinated (or very loosely coordinated) food system activities from farm to plate (or to waste). The global food system is hence a central contributor to structural climate injustices. This is not intentional: the initial purpose of the food system is to provide food security and satisfy vital human needs, and GHG emissions are merely a by-product of that. It is tragic that the satisfaction of basic needs contributes to a phenomenon that threatens the satisfaction of the same (and other) basic needs.

It is impossible to single out particular actors as liable for food-related emissions, even if the physical origin of emissions could be identified. Primary production, the main origin of GHG emissions in the food system, is shaped by consumer demands, public and private policies, and economic structures. Prevailing circumstances often leave only little room for (the already hard-pressed) farmers to make decisions about farming if they wish to retain their profitability. For example, changing the production sector often requires big investments they cannot afford. Consumers cannot make all the difference either: the aggregate food demand results from uncoordinated individual decisions that are influenced by personal assets, structural factors (including product availability, prices, available information, and store locations), and sociocultural issues. This "choice architecture" enables, restricts, encourages, and discourages various individual choices. What about food system actors between the farm and fork, then? The problem is that food industry and retailers consider themselves, perhaps plausibly, merely "neutral mediators" of preferences expressed in markets. Yet these actors often possess the greatest economic and political power in the food system; the public sector, in contrast, has lost much of its command over the global food trade and food system activities.

Overall, the attribution of liability for food system emissions is like the "chicken or the egg" dilemma. The chicken and the egg are in dynamic movement, though structural injustices emerge and exist only in action (Young 2011, 61–62), and the existing institutions and shared social practices support them, tending to create a vicious cycle. An important theme for future research would be to identify mechanisms through which actors (often unconsciously) reproduce the patterns of structural food and climate injustice. In that vein, I tentatively suggest some mechanisms that relate to meat supply chains, which are a significant source of climate emissions.[13]

First, mainstream Western dietary patterns and cultural values support carbon-intensive diets. Average Western diets include high amounts of animal protein, whose production is the most significant source of food-related emissions (Steinfeld et al. 2006). Dietary patterns are strongly habitual, and daily meat consumption is considered normal (perhaps even necessary) rather than blameworthy, though recent discussions have begun to challenge its normality.[14] In addition to this "normalization," dietary patterns are supported by the prevalent food valuations that are difficult and slow to transform. Meat is highly valued in many cultures: it represents the core of a satisfactory meal (consider the proverbial "Where's the beef?"), provides vitality, and signifies wealth (Adams 2015). The high social status of meat is not peculiar to the Western world only. In China, for example, meat consumption and production has expanded rapidly from the mid-1970s ("the Pork miracle"), hand in hand with economic growth (Schneider and Sharma 2014).

Second, the globalized trade structures partly "hide" the carbon-intensiveness of food production. This especially concerns products like beef, which has the highest carbon footprint among the common protein sources (Nijdam, Rood, and Westhoek 2012). A great deal of global beef production takes place in four South American countries: Uruguay, Argentina, Brazil, and Paraguay. The same countries (except for Uruguay) also produce nearly half of the feed soy for meat production elsewhere.[15] Market structures "relocate" the carbon footprint of wealthy beef (or feed) importers to South America as a result of price optimization. This distorts the national emission accounting by transferring the carbon footprint of wealthier countries to poorer areas and makes the products appear in the wealthy countries much cheaper than they "should" be, since they are produced in countries with lower wage and input costs. The low price, in turn, supports high beef consumption.

The above-described problem is structural. Though food system actors usually comply with existing regulations and norms, the aggregate effect of their interactions is that wealthy countries benefit from the economic disadvantage of poorer areas that can produce food or input resources cheaply. The wealthiest countries benefit most from the opportunity to relocate production, which transfers the carbon footprint of primary production elsewhere while retaining control over the supply chain and profits largely in their own hands. This mechanism links structural food and climate inequalities. It has emerged from several factors, including market structures, background inequalities,[16] and differences in agricultural conditions. Yet everyone seems to be "just doing their business" or "just feeding one's family and oneself" like everyone else, and markets appear as a neutral mediator of actor preferences.

Implications of the Food-Climate Nexus

Due to their interconnected features, structural food and climate injustices should be examined in parallel for two reasons. First, we lack resources to correct all the wrongs in the world and it is unlikely that all responsibilities could ever be fully discharged. Hence, identifying synergies helps maximize global justice in this imperfect situation. Second, the food-climate nexus may also cause highly counterproductive effects: some ways to fight climate change actually worsen food injustice and vice versa. I illustrate these points with four examples.

1. Increasing local food democracy or promoting local food production without climate awareness might improve food justice yet hamper climate action. There are common misconceptions about the relative environmental impacts of food system activities. For example, "local" is often perceived as synonymous for "low-carbon," which may lead to supporting local production whatever it involves (McWilliams 2009). Yet the perception is incorrect, and dietary shift (reducing meat consumption) is more important for climate mitigation than the locality of food (Weber and Matthews 2008). Food democracy should hence be coupled with effective climate education and the provision of research knowledge; if successful, this coupling may advance achieving synergies in promoting climate and food justice (see Loo in this volume for a more comprehensive discussion on participatory food justice and climate change).

2. Charity-based food aid that relies on food "waste" (edible foodstuff that would not be purchased by consumers in primary markets any longer) is sometimes viewed as a win-win strategy that promotes food justice,

provides help for those in need, and reduces climate emissions related to food waste. Yet such aid actually legitimizes and supports structures that maintain inequality and ecological unsustainability: waste-based food aid makes the production of food waste a lesser concern since it can be used to help people and legitimizes a practice of discarding edible products by wealthy consumers, supporting a "wasteful" culture (Kortetmäki and Silvasti 2017).

3. Biofuel policies may promote climate justice but undermine food justice. While some advanced biofuel crops may contribute to climate mitigation and provide income for poor areas, they threaten the global availability of food. Raised energy prices (a likely result of climate policies) also create a risk that biofuel production will replace traditional crops or that food crops are sold to energy use. Therefore, the biofuel industry should focus on the utilization of waste streams whose potential is promising. This would also help reduce emissions in the global food system.

4. Climate (geo)engineering, by, for example, solar radiation management, has been brought up as a strategy that may efficiently prevent dangerous climate change even if mitigation attempts remain modest, as they have been. The most effective forms of climate engineering significantly threaten food justice because they may influence precipitation in large and vulnerable cultivation areas (especially in Asia), and these methods cannot be reliably tested on a small scale (Kortetmäki and Oksanen 2016). On the other hand, "soft" climate engineering such as carbon capture to fields may actually support soil health and improve yields. "Soft" methods warrant further research due to the potential for synergy in improving food security (especially in arid, poor areas) and climate justice.

III. ATTRIBUTING RESPONSIBILITIES FOR GLOBAL FOOD JUSTICE

Conventional legal and moral discourses have usually grounded responsibilities in liability (and beyond that, accountability): harms are traced back to particular agents who are liable for bringing about the situation and hence responsible for correcting it. Young (2006) calls this liability model of responsibility a backward-looking approach, because it looks back to identify the culpable actors. While the approach fits addressing "ordinary injustice," Young argues that structural injustice requires a forward-looking approach to responsibility. Since structural injustices result from complex processes and actions that are often not blameworthy as such, emphasis should be shifted from the moral, blame-oriented ("whose fault was it?") to the political aspects of responsibility ("who should do what?"). Forward-looking responsibility does not involve the attribution of guilt or fault, yet it evokes responsibility for remedying injustice.

If no one is to blame, how can one determine who is responsible for alleviating structural injustices? Young (2006; 2011) advocates a social connection model where the responsibility for justice is shared among all actors who participate in structural processes that create or maintain structural injustices as the aggregate outcome of those actions. People who participate in those processes are socially connected to each other and responsible for the outcomes of the processes they participate in, even if the outcomes are unintentional. The emphasis on looking forward might help avoid the rhetorical and practical limitations of the backward-looking, blame-oriented models and "culprit-victim" dichotomies in political discourse (Young 2011, 113–20).

Perhaps surprisingly, the model also (logically) entails that many of the victims of injustice also share the responsibility for change (Young 2006, 123) since they are connected to the very same processes that contribute to structural injustices. This idea challenges climate discourse that has emphasized the historical culpability for emissions and the attribution of responsibility to developed countries (Eckersley 2016, 348–50). In relation to this point, the social connection model has been criticized for looking too strictly forward: focusing merely on the future would mean that agents cannot be blamed for not discharging their responsibility for justice in the past (Neuhäuser 2014). However, the social connection model does not necessitate full ignorance about the historical responsibility for the past harm (Young 2011, 108). The model can also integrate both forward- and backward-looking concerns (Eckersley 2016) and is not to be taken as a strict (or the only relevant) viewpoint. It is possible to hold certain agents culpable, not as *definitive* causes of the injustice but as exceptionally significant contributors to it, and simultaneously maintain that some other agents are not culpable but share the responsibility for improving the situation, alongside with the culpable actors (Neuhäuser 2014, 245–46).

The social connection model views responsibility as shared responsibility between individuals: this differs from collective responsibility that can be borne by organized collectives like corporations (Young 2006, 122–23).[17] Because individuals lack capacities to change structures on their own, they share responsibility for collective action: the engagement with others to organize social relations and coordinate actions in a way that would make the outcome more just (Young 2006, 123; 2011, 111–12). Political responsibility may relate to public policies or state activities or take place through other arenas like civil society organizations. Essentially, this means that the responsibility for remedying structural food injustice is not an issue of responsible consumerism even if that may be important for other reasons (though see also Gilson 2014). Consumption choices are made privately, and consumption is an uncoordinated practice (except regarding price optimization) in the liberal economic system. Making consumption matter for structural justice would involve politicizing it. This idea is akin to food citizenship that would transform us from consumers to citizens in the food system (which should be understood to involve much more than "voting with one's fork" or the unification of citizen and consumer roles) (Wilkins 2005; see also Ankeny in this volume).

Christian Neuhäuser (2014) has questioned the attribution of responsibility solely to individuals in the social connection model. He points out that Young actually embraces the distribution of certain forward-looking responsibilities to corporate agents. Moreover, it has been argued that even states can be held responsible for structural injustices (Parekh 2011). I view it as plausible that at least some collective actors can be held responsible in a forward-looking way and in relation to structural food injustice. To avoid complicating matters too far here, I will restrict my focus to the role of individuals as actors in the social connection model while acknowledging that the issue of collective responsibility for remedying structural injustices requires further examination.

In the global food system, almost every human shares the responsibility for food justice. Everyone eats food, and very few produce and consume it on a fully self-sustaining[18] basis: participation in global food system activities is nearly unavoidable. Yet it would be unconvincing to claim that everyone, whether a poor family farmer or an affluent epicurean in the wealthy world, should do the same things in the name of responsibility. Young (2011, 123) argues that in the model of shared responsibility, everyone is *equally responsible* for changing things yet there are differences in the degrees and kinds of *discharging the responsibility*. Consequently, she proposes four parameters for determining how persons in different positions can remedy injustice. The parameters are: (1) the power or capacity to influence structures, (2) privilege (privileged persons and institutions are greater beneficiaries of the prevailing situation), (3) interests, and (4) collective abilities (Young 2011, 142–46). For example, the privileged groups who benefit from present structures are more capable of influencing structures whereas students are often well equipped to organize collective organizational action to promote justice.

Young proposes that the above "parameters of reasoning" help decision-making about how (through which duties) each one could most reasonably discharge one's responsibility. Young's suggestion is pragmatic yet open to serious criticism (Neuhäuser 2014). It does not propose any criteria for the distribution of concrete responsibilities, which might postpone action since there is no common point of reference about the fair distribution of tasks. The model also lacks discussion about how the joint action (whose promotion is our responsibility) should take place and how one should act if others neglect or fail to discharge their responsibilities. In the rest of this chapter, I propose a preliminary strategy for addressing the distribution of responsibilities regarding food justice. My proposal builds on the remark that forward-looking responsibilities are common regarding everyday roles people adopt: they have responsibilities *as* parents, *as* workers in an influential position, *as* pet owners, and so forth. The role determines the corresponding capacities, duties, and the degree of responsibility. Duties to discharge the responsibility for food justice can be determined likewise, according to different (though overlapping) roles people have in relation to the global food system.

Policymakers have the greatest capacity to change structures. Hence, they have special duties regarding the transformation of the institutional regulations and norms that contribute to injustices. Yet it should be acknowledged that public policymakers deal with an exhaustive set of issues. They cannot be expected to dig for all information about what should be changed and how; they need support in this, and it is a duty of *researchers* and *organizations* to provide such information. *Big food business operators,* in turn, possess economic power and answer for a great deal of activities in the food trade. When the existing structures prevent fair trade outcomes within the limits of competition and profitability, business operators have a duty to communicate these problems to policymakers and urge support for critical policy efforts. Corporations also may have a duty for collective action between corporations, in a way exemplified by (for example) the Corporate Climate Alliance and The Climate Reality Project (that reaches beyond corporations).

Victims of injustice are closely connected to processes that create injustices and are in the best position to express the interests and worries of the subordinated, yet they have the least capacity to change things. They have a duty to get organized to increase mutual solidarity and empowerment and to make claims for justice together, like the international peasant movement La Via Campesina has done. This same movement has also participated in climate change discourse (McKeon 2015), demonstrating integration of the two concerns I have discussed in this chapter. Weaker actors also need external support: other civil society organizations and persons who design participatory structures for planning processes are also responsible for helping weaker actors' voices get heard, promoting their participation, and showing support for their claims.

What about the role of ordinary *citizen-consumers*? We participate daily in the global food trade, and our related duties could arise from the remark that we are, as consumers, "forced" to contribute to injustices because we cannot break from structural processes if we are to eat. Citizen-consumers have at least some resources that enable various ways to discharge responsibility: participating in public discourse, joining NGO action or supporting campaigns, or establishing joint action to influence the policymakers and corporations. We may even aim at adopting more powerful roles to promote change. Those who feel too busy with their well-paid jobs can contribute monetary resources for collective action. We are also connected to actors with other roles: experts and the victims of injustice can provide us information about what to do, and cooperative projects between various collectives help increase their influence over the food system processes. In the social connection model, we are not alone with our responsibilities.

NOTES

1. The more precise contents of the justice ("the equality of what?") and the criteria for fair distribution ("equality in which terms?") vary in different philosophical accounts on justice, but the argument of this chapter does not require committing to any particular account.

2. "Uncoordinated" means here that the actors cannot significantly affect each other though they can take the actions of others into account when planning their own behavior. Something might also be coordinated in one respect yet not in others. Free markets are coordinated with regard to achieving price optimums but not with regard to sharing the benefits and burdens of trade optimally.

3. Even within the global North, the emissions of different social groups vary greatly, and there are individuals and elite groups in the global South whose emissions significantly exceed that of the average person in the global North.

4. Although production emissions emerge in the producing factory, the reason for the existence of that production is in the markets. Laws and market mechanisms in turn influence significantly how the factory can operate.

5. Food security, roughly put, means the situation in which all people have access to sufficient, nutritious, and culturally acceptable food to enable an active human life.

6. I take that the companies in wealthy states are in a position to change their operations more easily than "sweatshop companies," which makes this issue different from the sweatshop case used by Young and Calder.

7. Admittedly, there are great intranational variations, and even in wealthy countries the low-income households may spend up to 50 percent of their income on food. Information received from https://www.weforum.org/agenda/2016/12/this-map-shows-how-much-each-country-spends-on-food/.

8. A multinational company could purchase the food products from (or conduct the processing in) a country with better working conditions and wages, but the poorer country may continue its business with another company without making improvements (to avoid the loss of export-dependent jobs and income).

9. Some of the most powerful economies together could make an exception, but even they are unlikely to be able to change the situation alone if others refuse to comply with the new rules.

10. The share of the food exports of all merchandise exports is highest (more than one-third of total exports) in Paraguay, New Zealand, Antigua and Barbuda, Zimbabwe, Iceland, Georgia, Brazil, Senegal, Armenia, and Barbados (World Bank data 2017). Among the countries where agriculture comprises more than one-third of the GDP, developing countries in Africa clearly dominate the list (World Factbook 2015).

11. These problems concern the position of small farmers in many wealthy countries as well.

12. "Resilience" is the ability of a given system to withstand different disturbances without a collapse.

13. See Gilson 2014 for some related points on the industrialized meat production.

14. These discussions concern animal welfare and the climate impacts of the industrial meat sector. From the philosophical viewpoint, it should also be noted that the normality (commonness) of some activity does not actually mean that it would not be blameworthy.

15. https://atlas.media.mit.edu/en/profile/hs92/1201/. In total, these three countries account for around half of the world's soybean trade.

16. "Background inequality" means inequality between different countries that already existed before the emergence of the global food trade regime (e.g., as a result of colonialization).

17. The relationship between collective and individual responsibilities is a complex matter that cannot be explored in detail here, since such details are not essential for the argumentation of this chapter.

18. Domestic production is almost never separate from the global food system either. Input resources, agricultural machinery, and fuels are just some examples of how production often links to the global system. Also, buying products often must be done in a way that is connected to mainstream food system processes.

Chapter 3

Participation and Food Justice in Light of Global Climate Change

Clement Loo

The primary objective of this chapter is to build upon existing food justice literature by examining scholarships concerned with participative justice to identify how it would be useful for guiding both academic and practical work relevant to food justice and climate change. More specifically, I decompose the concept of participative justice into its constituent elements—autonomy and recognition—and suggest that each of those two elements reveals a number of objectives that should inform the work of those concerned with food justice given the impacts of climate change.

Before I examine how autonomy and recognition would be useful for better understanding participative food justice, I will first take a moment to discuss why I believe that food justice is an important consideration in conversations about climate change. I will also take some time to explain why I believe that food justice should be understood in participative terms.

I. CLIMATE CHANGE AS A FOOD JUSTICE PROBLEM

Climate change has a number of impacts on food systems that are best understood as justice problems. These impacts include disparities with regard to reductions in crop yields due to heat stress, drought, and loss of arable land to flooding (Challinor et al. 2014, 287; Lobell et al. 2011, 616, 620; Parry et al. 2004, 54); uneven impacts of rising food costs (Schmidhuber and Tubiello 2007, 19705); differing capacity to dictate the strategies for adapting agricultural regimes (Vanloqueren and Baret 2009, 976); and unequal responsibility to pay the costs associated with sustainable development (Gruen and Loo 2014, 183–87).

The full list of disparities associated with climate change's expected effects on food systems is so long that it would not be possible to review it in its full breadth within this chapter. I also do not believe that such a comprehensive accounting of disparities would be required for my argument. As such, I will only discuss two disparities that I believe are particularly vicious: the uneven effect of climate change on crop productivity between temperate and tropical countries, and the uneven distribution of harm associated with expected increases in food prices due to climate change. I believe that these two disparities on their own are sufficient to indicate that climate change is a problem relevant to conversations about food justice.

According to Working Group I to the IPCC (2013), if we as a global community are unable to substantially curtail our greenhouse gas (GHG) emissions in relatively short order, we should expect to experience a number of environmental changes. We have already experienced roughly a 0.85° C increase in average global atmospheric temperature since the end of the nineteenth century (ibid., 5). Depending on how effectively we reduce emissions of carbon dioxide, methane, and other greenhouse gases, we should expect to see further warming—perhaps as much as 4.8° C by 2100 (ibid., 20). We are virtually certain to encounter a greater number of warm and hot days (and fewer cool and cold days) throughout much of the world and are very likely to experience a far greater number of heat waves (ibid., 7, 20). Such shifts in temperature will have cascading effects on climate, substantively changing precipitation patterns and storm activity. We are very likely to encounter far more heavy precipitation events in the mid-latitudes, will likely experience a greater number of droughts across the world, and will more likely than not see increases in tropical cyclone activity (ibid., 7). Higher average temperatures will also very likely result in large-scale shrinking of the world's glaciers and this, in combination with thermal expansion, will very likely result in sea level rise and an increase in numbers of extreme high sea level events (ibid., 7, 25–26). This will result in flooding in a number of coastal and island communities.

All of the effects associated with climate change listed above will have impacts on global food production (Challinor et al. 2014, 287; Lobell et al. 2011, 617–19; Parry et al. 2004, 55, 58–62). Meta-analysis of 1,700 published projections of the effects of climate change on crop yields reveals that the midrange projection of average yield decreases of all crops across the world is somewhere between 25 to 50 percent by the 2100s (relative to the present day) (Challinor et al. 2014, 288–90). However, changes in crop yields will not occur evenly across the globe (Challinor et al. 2014, 288; Lobell et al. 2011, 619; Parry et al. 2004, 58–61).

For example, under every emissions scenario considered, crop yields will decrease to a greater extent in South America, Africa, and Central Asia when compared to North America and Western Europe (Parry et al. 2004, 58–61). Challinor et al. found that the consensus across projections is that, with appropriate adaptation, climate change may result in a small increase in yields of wheat in temperate areas (even with as much as 5° C of warming) (2014, 289–90). In contrast, even with our best efforts at adapting to climate change, we can expect no better outcome than a 20 percent decrease in wheat yields in tropical areas if average air temperature increases 5° C (Challinor et al. 2014, 288–89). Fischer et al. suggest that while lower- and middle-income countries will experience substantive decreases in their GDP due to lost agricultural yields attributable to climate change, a number of higher-income countries will in fact experience economic gains within their agricultural sectors due to climate change (2002, 109).

Such disparity with regard to the impact of climate change on regional crop yields suggests that equity and fairness—and, thus, justice—are topics that those concerned about food systems ought to consider when they think about climate change. Such is particularly evident when one recognizes which countries have been responsible for the greatest cumulative GHG emissions since the beginning of the Industrial Revolution (see Gruen and Loo 2014 for more details on this topic). The aptness of justice as a lens becomes yet even more apparent when one considers the second impact of climate change that I will discuss below: the expected effect of climate change on food prices and risk of hunger.

Decreases in agricultural productivity, because they will not be even across countries, on their own suggest that social justice is an appropriate framework for conversations about climate change and its effects upon food systems. Moreover, they will also create second-order disparities. Most important of these is that more anemic global agricultural productivity will result in increasing food commodity prices (Fischer et al. 2002, 109; Schmidhuber and Tubiello 2007, 19705). According to Fischer et al., the effect of climate change on cropland production, when combined with the effect of a growing world population, will result in approximately between a 2 and 19.5 percent increase in world cereal prices (2002, 108).[1]

Such increase in food price is expected to result in substantial increases in hunger, particularly within lower-income countries (Fischer et al. 2002, 111–15). If the worst case scenarios obtain, we can expect an additional 175 million undernourished people across the globe relative to baseline projections of hunger that do not include the impact of climate change (ibid.). Even given best-case scenarios with minimal warming, we can expect an additional 35 million people who are likely to have difficulty accessing adequate nutrition (ibid.). Again, the impacts will not be evenly distributed. Across all scenarios and projections, the majority of those who will be at risk of hunger due to climate change will be persons living in lower- and middle-income countries in Africa and Asia (ibid.).

The impact of climate change on crop productivity, food prices, and hunger clearly indicates that climate change is a food justice problem. It is likely true that climate change will be bad for everyone, but it will be far worse for some in comparison to others. It is exceedingly clear that climate change will particularly threaten the ability of those living in lower- and middle-income countries within the global South to access diets supportive of good health. Such pronounced disparity suggests that food, particularly in the context of climate change, should be thought of in terms of justice as well as security. That is, the unevenness when it comes to the potential harms to food systems associated with climate change suggests that we should be attentive to equity when developing global strategies for addressing the impact of anthropogenic greenhouse gases. Because those living in lower- and middle-income countries will be particularly subject to harm, global discourse about how we collectively respond to climate change must robustly include and be informed by the perspectives of those living in such countries.

Given the above, for the remainder of this chapter I will examine what might be required to develop a robust conversation about food justice in the context of climate change. More specifically, I will argue that appropriately adapting to climate change—vis-à-vis food systems—requires that we critically examine systems of governance with recognition and autonomy in mind.

II. PARTICIPATION AND FOOD JUSTICE

In the past, scholarship and advocacy about food justice have tended to emphasize fair distribution with regard to the benefits and costs associated with the food system (Loo 2014). Authors tend to consider questions about who should be the net contributor of resources and who should be the net recipient of resources and the justifications for such redistribution.

However, there is a growing recognition that food justice, particularly as it is relevant to climate change, must also be considered in terms of participation. For example, Bradley and Galt argue for the importance of self-determination vis-à-vis food justice, by stating that "food justice embraces a variety of ways of valuing food system work, including self-improvement and community improvement.... Self-determination—at the organisational and individual levels—and respect for others are crucial to food justice practice" (2014, 176). Similar themes are found in Passidomo's (2014) and Moragues-Faus's (2017, 104) work, both of whom argue that food justice involves communities mobilizing to improve their capacity to determine the nature of their food systems.

A key element of the work of all the authors listed above is the recognition that food justice involves more than ensuring that all segments of the population have food available to them. It is clear that who participates in making decisions about the production, distribution, and use of food is essential for food justice as well. All of the authors above suggest that redressing disparities within the food system first requires redressing disparities regarding capacity to directly influence decisions affecting the nature of the food system.

However, while there is growing recognition that participation and participative equity are important topics for conversations about food justice, it is not entirely clear what it would mean in practice to better integrate participative justice into food justice work (Slocum and Cadieux 2015, 28–29). The objective of this chapter then is to examine what it might mean to better integrate participative justice in the context of promoting food justice as a response to some of the harms associated with climate change.

To tackle the issue of integrating participation with food justice, it will be helpful to examine theories of participative justice to identify elements that are generally considered to be constitutive of participative justice. Once those components are identified, the next step will be to determine how those components could be translated to practical advice for those engaged in food justice scholarship and advocacy.

III. BUILDING PARTICIPATIVE EQUITY

While it would be impossible in a chapter-length work to provide a comprehensive review of the literature concerned with participative justice, one can perhaps develop a working understanding of the topic through review of a handful of seminal works. And, indeed, much of the literature concerned with the relationship between participation and justice—particularly within the realm of food and the environment—refers to the work of several authors. Those authors include David Schlosberg (2007, 2004), Kristin Shrader-Frechette (2002), Nancy Fraser (2001, 2000, 1998), Iris Marion Young (1990), and Michael Walzer (1983).

Therefore, I suspect that if one were to review the work of the above-listed authors, one would likely gain a foothold for understanding how participative equity is generally defined within the environmental and food justice literature and, thus, perhaps gain some insight that might be informative for practice. To wit, considering the work of Schlosberg, Shrader-Frechette, Fraser, Young, and Walzer suggests that participative justice is often conceived of as including at least two components: (1) recognition and (2) autonomy.

Recognition, according to Schlosberg, is essential for participative justice 3 because recognition—or the lack thereof—is a key factor determining whether resources are distributed in an equitable and fair manner (2004, 103). Recognition also features prominently in the work of Young (1990), who appeals to recognition as a means of undermining colonialism and other forms of oppression. Young contends that addressing oppression requires that we acknowledge and embrace that there is heterogeneity between (and within) communities (1990, 184). In doing that, we better respond to the likelihood that different individuals and communities have diverse and possibly diverging interests and perspectives, which is an essential step in promoting participative equity.

An argument for the importance of autonomy for participative justice can be found in Shrader-Frechette's (2002, 57, 108–9, 144–46, 157–62) work. Shrader-Frechette (2002, 57) suggests that if we are not appropriately concerned and attentive to preserving autonomy, it becomes easy to fail to identify instances where those in marginalized communities are subject to duress, coercion, or other forms of interference limiting their capacity to pursue their interests. Such duress or coercion would make it impossible for individuals or communities to enter into voluntary transactions with others, which would be a barrier for participative equity.

Given the arguments presented by Schlosberg, Shrader-Frechette, and Young, it seems understanding participative justice and how it might be applied as a framework for thinking about food justice in light of climate change would require analysis of recognition and autonomy. I will offer my contribution to this task below.

Recognition and Food Justice

I will begin with recognition. Recognition includes two components: (1) equal dignity and (2) the politics of difference (Schlosberg 2004, 102). The first of these components, equal dignity, according to Schlosberg is a requirement for a basic respect for all persons (2004, 102). To appropriately recognize a person requires one to acknowledge that the person has value and is deserving of equal rights and consideration as oneself. While the equal dignity component identifies a manner that all should be treated similarly, the politics of difference suggests a manner in which we should be treated distinctly. According to Young, the politics of difference holds that, though we all are deserving of common respect and consideration, we are distinct from one another and should be understood as such (1986, 22). That is, across any sufficiently large population of humans there will be substantive differences in perspectives, interests, goals, and so on. Appropriate recognition thus would require appreciating and embracing distinctness rather than demanding or assuming similarity.

If we understand recognition as a two-element relationship involving equal dignity and the politics of difference, we should aim toward several objectives if we wish to build more participatively equitable food systems. Equal dignity makes it clear that a fair food system is a system where all participants are treated as valuable and worthy of equal consideration. Achieving more just and fair food systems, particularly in light of climate change, requires responding to the political and economic hierarchies affecting discourse. It requires improving institutions and procedures in a manner that is informed by the acknowledgment that all perspectives are worthy of consideration. Our ways of political decision-making must facilitate the fair weighing of the views of all interested parties, particularly those from marginalized communities. Further, our public and political discourse should never dismiss perspectives out of hand without substantive reasons.

If the literature regarding the politics of difference is correct then for any given case of political discourse, one should not expect to be able to identify a unique most fair outcome that would best serve the varied interests of all parties (Young 1990, 184). Rather, one should expect that the evaluation of the value or disvalue of the different potential options would be weighed based on criteria that differ between different parties. Different parties can be expected to hold incompatible values or to prioritize values in substantively different ways. And, because of these differing values or rankings of values, different parties may hold different goals or prefer different outcomes with regard to a given set of conditions. Failure to acknowledge such diversity of perspectives or failure to accept the legitimacy of views different from one's own leads to obscuring of perspectives that should be considered if one is interested in an equitable result.

Attempts at impartiality therefore may instead result in reification of dominant perspectives and the marginalization of others (Young 1990, 185). If one's primary goal while adjudicating between disagreements about which outcomes should be pursued in a given case is to try to identify the unique most fair endpoint, one may instead be led astray by one's biases—biases that often reflect those of the dominant culture within one's society. Thus, fair recognition suggests that interlocutors should grant that there are multiple legitimate ways to frame the topic of discourse. The objective of democratic deliberation should be a matter of encouraging the interlocutors to best advocate for their positions and to negotiate mutually acceptable compromise.

More practically, in the realm of food, the above suggests that those working toward fairer food systems must be aware that what would count as a just food system is context-dependent. Different parties may very well have substantially differing conceptions of what should be valued or disvalued with regard to outcomes associated with the structure of their food systems. Similarly, different groups may be concerned with the fair distribution of different goods. Different communities may also hold different views about how to most fairly engage in collective decision-making. Importantly, this list of items is far from being comprehensive: there are likely many other ways that various parties may disagree about the characteristics of a fair and just food system.

It is essential then that those of us interested in promoting food justice in light of climate change must be careful not to make unwarranted assumptions about what sorts of goals should be pursued through our interventions. Those of us who are scholars and advocates working toward food justice should endeavor to collaborate with members of the communities subject to food injustices to better ensure that their perspectives are informing our scholarship and/or practice. I would assert that much of the current academic and policy discourse about food seems to revolve around fairly narrow understandings of health and economics.

Such is particularly true of how we conceive of problems associated with the impact of climate change upon food systems. Review of the literature (see, e.g., Brown and Funk 2008, Fischer et al. 2002, Lobell et al. 2011, Parry et al. 2004, and Schmidhuber and Tubiello 2007) suggests that scholarship regarding climate change and food often focuses on three factors: agricultural yields, food prices, and hunger. To be clear, I do not wish to suggest that the aforementioned three factors are not important. However, they are not comprehensive in regards to capturing the full range of values that are associated with food. Thus, to gain a fuller appreciation of how communities might subjectively experience the impact of climate change on their food systems requires a richer understanding of what communities in fact value.

However, there is a broad range of values that are likely relevant to food systems. Taste, tradition, history, familial and community relationships, ritual, and religion are all considerations often associated with food. That such considerations often are not considered by scholars, advocates, and other professionals concerned with food justice suggests that the manners in which we think about food are far too narrow and could benefit from input from those holding a broader range of perspectives.

Acknowledging that a broader range of values is relevant to food systems, that social context affects which values are salient, and not presuming that dominant values prima facie ought to be preferred to values espoused by marginalized populations would be an important step in better incorporating fair recognition into food justice. By better including a broader range of values in consideration, we would move toward adopting the sort of politics of difference endorsed by Young (1990, 156–91). And, by being more careful to not dismiss differing perspectives without robust reasons, we would better incorporate Schlosberg's notion of equal dignity into our scholarship and practice.

Autonomy and Food Justice

As I noted earlier, participative justice is commonly understood to also include autonomy in addition to recognition. So, examining autonomy and what is required to ensure that communities and individuals are able to participate in public discourse and decision-making in an autonomous manner will also be useful for considering how to promote food justice.

Autonomy, as it is defined by Shrader-Frechette (2002) and Walzer (1983), includes three elements: (1) self-definition, (2) self-organization, and (3) self-advocacy. Essentially, the autonomy component of participative justice suggests that fair participation in democratic deliberation requires that parties are able to determine their own positions based upon self-determined internal decision-making processes and that they are able to directly engage in inter-party discourse to promote their positions without uninvited external intervention. Practically, concern for autonomy suggests that scholars and activists should work with stakeholders to develop resources that promote the ability of those stakeholders to identify how their self-identified interests and objectives may be best achieved and that contribute to the capacity of stakeholders to more effectively argue for their positions. Drawing from Shrader-Frechette (2002) and others engaging in similar scholarship (such as Elliott 2011), academics and other experts may contribute to the autonomy of stakeholders in at least three ways.

The first of these is by facilitating access to information. Those with research expertise should collaborate with the public to identify the sort of information that would be desired by stakeholders to identify how various activities or interventions may affect the interests and concerns that they find most salient. Researchers should then collaborate with members of the public to gather such information and disseminate it through media and in vernacular that are commonly used. Practically, this suggests that those engaged in research aimed at identifying strategies to adapt agricultural and food systems to better resist the effects of climate change should be partnering with climate-vulnerable communities to frame potential problems and identify research questions that address the concerns and interests of the members of those communities. Such collaborations could also be a mechanism to ensure that the results are disseminated in manners to promote accessibility.

Second, experts should endeavor to work with members of stakeholder communities and the broader public to develop local and independent capacities to analyze available information and to use institutions and governance processes to advocate for their interests. Such may be accomplished through working with community organizers to offer trainings and workshops for those interested in engaging in advocacy. Another manner of promoting independent capacity might be through collaborations intended to build institutions that facilitate community-based research and/or engagement in political processes.

At present much of the research capacity within agricultural science resides within the United States and a handful of higher-income countries (in particular Japan and Germany). This is evident when one considers that the vast majority of agricultural patents are issued in one of three countries (in order, they are the United States, Japan, and Germany) (OECD 2016). And, indeed, well more than half of such patents are issued within one country (the United States) (OECD 2016). Given that traditional diets, growing conditions, concepts of land ownership, and agricultural practices vary substantially across countries, it is imperative that efforts are taken to more equitably distribute research capacity. Research capacity that is more equitably distributed to include those living within lower- and middle-income countries would allow many currently marginalized communities to better identify and argue for interventions and adaptations informed by and suited to their concerns and contexts.

Finally, we should refrain from exerting the influence associated with our "roles, authority, or power" in manners that undermine the ability of others to make decisions based upon the pursuit of their self-identified interests relevant to the issue of interest (Shrader-Frechette 2002, 56–63). This last requirement warrants concern, given the disparities associated with climate change and its effects on food access.

More specifically, as has been discussed earlier in this chapter, there are disparities with regard to agricultural productivity. Additionally there are disparities in access to capital and technology that affects capacity to adapt agricultural and food systems to the impacts of climate change. Also as discussed earlier in this chapter, we can expect that climate change will continue to exacerbate the previously listed disparities.

The above three factors, particularly when they are acting in conjunction, result in uneven capacity to respond to the effects of climate. Those of us who live in Canada, the United States, and Western Europe will find ourselves in a position where we can, in a relatively unilateral manner, dictate who has access to food and who has access to the resources and technologies that would possibly be useful for resisting some of the deleterious effects of changing conditions on agriculture. This will result in imbalances in power, which we must attend carefully to in order to avoid limiting the capacity of those who live within more equatorial latitudes to make decisions about the nature of their food systems.

In the past there has been a tendency for those of us living in higher-income countries (particularly those of us working within agricultural science) to argue that those of us living in lower- and middle-income countries should move away from traditional agriculture and food systems and adopt practices more akin to those found in countries that participated in the Green Revolution (see, e.g., Brown and Funk 2008; Evans 1998; and Godfray et al. 2010; also see Vanloqueren and Baret 2009 for further discussion on this topic). However, before we pursue implementing such a radical shift in land use, technology, and markets, we should be careful to ensure that decisions affecting how communities grow, harvest, distribute, and use their food in fact involve members of said communities.

Developing strategies for agricultural adaptation should involve robust collaborations with farmers, food processors, vendors, and eaters to identify and consider the full range of their interests with regard to their food systems (rather than narrowly focusing on outcomes such as productivity or profit margins). Considering a broader set of perspectives, and thus a broader set of values, will provide a broader range of options (and options that are developed with local perspectives in mind) for those living in climate-vulnerable communities. Additionally, attention should be paid to indigenous knowledges and indigenous technologies; researchers and professionals should not simply assume that solutions are exclusively to be found through the particular set of technologies that have contributed to the agricultural productivity of higher-income industrial nations. They should be willing to consider the potential roles of technologies and practices traditional to a given region in contributing to efforts to promote the capacity of food systems to be more resilient to the impacts of climate change.[2]

To summarize, respecting autonomy involves promoting the capacity to self-define, organize, and advocate. In the context of scholars and advocates concerned with food justice in light of climate change, this largely involves helping communities to be better able to independently obtain and analyze information. Independent capacity to gather and review data would allow communities to be better able to identify how both potential threats and interventions would affect the interests and objectives that they find most salient. Such capacity would also allow communities to better collectively make decisions about what actions they should take to address threats posed by climate change to local food systems and thus promote the ability to self-organize and advocate. Promoting the capacity of communities, particularly marginalized communities, to self-organize and advocate also requires those with greater unilateral capacity to influence the course of development of food systems to refrain from unilaterally acting and embrace more collaborative approaches to addressing climate change.

CONCLUSION

Reflecting upon the components of participative justice—recognition and autonomy—suggests a number of practical objectives for those working on promoting and protecting food justice in response to climate change. First, such reflection indicates that we must be careful to be attentive and inclusive of a broad range of perspectives and values when engaged in tasks such as identifying the salient risks associated with climate change as well as identifying objectives for agricultural and food system adaptation. Second, we should take care to ensure that underrepresented stakeholders are participating in discourse and decision-making in a robust manner. Such, in turn, suggests that efforts must be made to support the capacity of historically marginalized communities to independently analyze information, engage in internal decision-making in a manner that is independent of external interference, and advocate for their self-identified positions in the global context.

Accomplishing such tasks involves collaboration between those who have historically been acknowledged as experts and representatives of communities to ensure that research concerned with the impacts of climate on food addresses questions that are relevant to and framed in terms of the interests and concerns most salient to climate vulnerable communities. It also requires taking care to ensure that the results of such research are published in vernacular and through media that is broadly accessible and commonly accessed to ensure broad access.

Attending to the capacity of marginalized communities to participate more effectively in promoting and protecting their access to food in light of climate change also highlights the need for collaborative efforts to offer education and to use institutions to promote the ability of communities to organize and strengthen their capacity to participate in discourse that they may have previously been excluded from. Finally, attending to participation makes clear that experts and others who historically have been more centrally influential in collective decision-making must be intentional in avoiding undue interference with the capacity of more marginalized parties to identify and pursue their interests independently.

There has been a historical tendency for countries in the global North to insist that more food-vulnerable countries in the global South adopt Green Revolution technologies and practices as bulwarks to protect food security. This approach undermines the autonomy of many of those living in the most climate-vulnerable countries and, as such, a more inclusive approach to identifying, developing, and implementing interventions to adapt food systems to climate change should be adopted. Such an approach would be better informed by the perspectives of communities regarding their preferences and values relevant to the sorts of technologies they wish to use and would also be informed by indigenous and traditional knowledges and technologies.

NOTES

1. If the HadCM3 climate projections obtain, then, depending on the model, we should experience between 2 and 19.5 percent increases in cereal prices. If the CSIRO projections obtain, we should expect cereal prices to increase between 4 and 10 percent (Fischer et al. 2002, 108).

2. An example of such more inclusive research can be found in the United Nations Development Programme's Community-Based Adaptation to Climate Change through Coastal Afforestation project. For more details about this project, please refer to Rawlani and Sovacool 2011.

Chapter 4

Thriving in the Desert

Theorizing Food, Justice, and Climate Change

Jennifer Szende

Who wants to live in a food desert? The label invokes an inhospitable environment, with sparse food availability in some sense. When used as a technical term, "food desert" implies that some population has difficulty accessing food with high nutritional content within a geographic area or region (LeClair and Aksan 2014, 537). The terminology furthermore implies few food retailers within the geographic area or region and may imply the existence of physical or economic barriers to accessing food with high nutritional content (Hill 2017, 230). However, both this definition and the very terminology of a food desert are contentious along a number of vectors (LeClair and Aksan 2014; Walker, Keane, and Burke 2010; Hendrickson, Smith, and Eikenberry 2006; Szende 2015; Hill 2017). The rhetorical implications of the terminology of a food desert are complex.

Food deserts are defined differently by different scholars, and there is certainly a lack of consensus on how the term should be defined or measured (Walker, Keane, and Burke 2010). The food desert terminology has been used to pick out urban and rural communities in Canada, the United States, and the United Kingdom, and frequently refers to circumstances experienced by African American, Latinx, immigrant, minority, or otherwise socially marginalized groups (LeClair and Aksan 2014, 539; Walker, Keane, and Burke 2010). The terminology is often used in conjunction with discussions of social justice activism around food, including "food justice" and "food sovereignty" (Werkheiser, Tyler, and Thompson 2015; Sbicca 2012). But despite the lack of consensus regarding the precise meaning of the term "food desert," it continues to have negative connotations and remains an undesirable feature to be overcome or resisted by those who experience it.

For these and other reasons, the food desert can be an active locus of political engagement within food justice, environmental justice, and food security movements (Werkheiser, Tyler, and Thompson 2015; Sbicca 2012). Identifying and labeling a food desert can have a mobilizing effect. Yet both the concept and the terminology of the food desert remain contested (LeClair and Aksan 2014; Hill 2017). This chapter unpacks the implications of the terminology by parsing three implications of the language of a food desert in order to illuminate several dimensions of the underlying phenomenon and thereby to suggest ways to respond to and combat food deserts.

First, the food desert metaphor invokes the "emptiness" of a desert. Deserts are, it is implied, empty and unable to support human life in particular. The problem with this implication is that actual food deserts are often socially vibrant communities that may suffer from difficulty of access to highly nutritional and culturally appropriate food but almost never suffer from a total absence of food. Food deserts are typically identified by the absence of supermarkets but not by the absence of food altogether. Food deserts may in fact be replete with bodegas, convenience stores, and fast-food outlets. So the problem flagged by the presence of a food desert is not lack of food altogether but rather a lack of choice, lack of access to nutritious food, high prices, or difficulty of access to whatever forms of food are present.

Second, the vocabulary of the food desert carries an implication of being a natural and perhaps unavoidable phenomenon. Deserts are sites of natural beauty, and the metaphor evokes pristine wilderness. The terminology can evoke "natural" and therefore beautiful, or "natural" and therefore unavoidable. Food deserts, on the other hand, are human-caused sites of oppression resulting from a confluence of human and institutional factors. Some food justice activists therefore suggest that more accurate terminology would highlight "food apartheid" or "food racism." The problem with the desert metaphor from this perspective is that it elides the agency and oppressive institutional structures at the heart of food injustice. Furthermore, it may reify the injustice.

In light of the agency and causal factors that are highlighted when we examine the "natural phenomenon" implication of food desert terminology, a third problematic implication of the desert metaphor emerges. Desertification, considered with reference to climate change, is a human-caused and difficult-to-reverse process. Food desertification, by analogy, may seem like an irreversible process. But both have human causes—some proximate and some more distant in a long causal chain. And both can be reversed or made less problematic with the right types of careful interventions. Food deserts considered as such rhetorically imply a lost cause because desertification is seemingly irreversible. The third worry that is hidden in the metaphor of a food desert is that once a food desert is established, it may be impossible to reverse the process.

But, this chapter argues, there is hope. Real deserts support much more life and, indeed, biodiversity than the "empty" interpretation of the metaphor suggests. Desert ecosystems may remain dormant for long periods of time but nonetheless support important plant and animal life. Humans, too, have learned to survive in the desert and have developed civilizations and resilient cultures in regions with limited rainfall. And desertification is not irreversible, although interventions must be carefully considered and contextually appropriate. Accordingly, desert science, desert culture, and desert politics may therefore provide resources for combating the hopelessness implied by the terminology of the food desert.

This chapter examines how this powerful language of food desert, contextualized in relation with food justice, environmental justice, and climate change, can lead to better conceptualizations of both the problem and possible solutions. The chapter employs the tools of feminist relational theory to contextualize this discussion in relation to complex human and social factors. Feminist relational theory reminds us to situate "choice" institutionally and socially and to look both backward and forward in order to understand a causal nexus related to food injustice. Many existing objections to the terminology and framing of food deserts draw on an impoverished set of connotations, so this chapter explores a richer and expanded set of connotations.[1]

I. EMPTY DESERTS

Historically, the metaphor of a desert implies an empty or sparsely populated place, often perceived to be uninhabitable even in principle (Hill 2017, 231). But "food desert" has not generally been taken to imply sparse population although it does rhetorically carry the inhospitable implication. Rather, food deserts often arise in densely populated urban areas, in which case the "emptiness" reference is to a sparse distribution of a certain type of food retail option. It carries an implication of an inequitable distribution of accessible food options, which is taken to make the neighborhood or city an undesirable place to live. Or, to tell a different causal story, the neighborhood or city in question may be undervalued, and this may give rise to the lack of retail options in places labeled as food deserts in the first place (Hill 2017; Szende 2015). The emptiness implication of the metaphor ahistorically abstracts from the context in which choices—retail or otherwise—arise. The term "food deserts" defined solely in terms of correlated distributions of retail food options and people abstracts from the causes of the distribution and the conditions that structure inequality (Szende 2015; Sherwin and Stockdale 2017; Young 1990).

The terminology of a food desert may have its origin with a resident of a Scottish housing estate, "who used it in the early 1990s to capture the experience of what it was like to live in a deprived neighborhood where food was expensive and relatively unavailable" (Cummins and Macintyre 2002, 2115). Early use of the terminology of a food desert invoked "disadvantaged consumers" defined with reference to low income and restricted mobility and their constrained food choices (Wrigley 2002; Whelan et al. 2002). Early use tended to focus on the retail environment and examine the factors that led supermarkets and other large retailers to be located in places that were inaccessible to certain already disadvantaged populations (Wrigley 2002).

Food deserts are often defined primarily with reference to sparse distribution of supermarkets and correlated social or economic deprivation or marginalization (Smoyer-Tomic, Spence, and Amrhein 2006; Black et al. 2012; Dieterle 2015a). Food sold in supermarkets is expected to be cheaper than food sold in smaller stores, in part because of economies of scale. The increasing likelihood that supermarkets will be located outside of city centers implies an increasing likelihood that food in city centers will be expensive, and that consumers without independent transport will not be in a position to choose between cheaper suburban supermarkets and expensive and limited central options (Wrigley 2002, 2031). Food deserts in this context were defined in terms of poor access to nutritious or healthy food, and were taken to exemplify spatial inequalities (Cummins and Macintyre 2002, 2116).

In isolated communities labeled "food deserts," such as those in remote regions of Canada, food insecurity may be heightened in a context where supermarkets are prohibitively expensive, colonialism and relocation have led to the loss of traditional hunting knowledge, and climate change may exacerbate both (Ford 2009; Moore 2013, 218). Industrialization may likewise lead to a loss of traditional agricultural knowledge or to the loss of its relevance, which, in turn, can make marginalized groups more dependent and less resilient. Labeling these rural or isolated communities as food deserts highlights the significance of barriers to accessing nutritious or culturally appropriate food in defining food deserts. What highly populated urban food deserts share with sparsely populated rural or remote food deserts is barriers to access rather than emptiness of either population or food sources.

The more recent social scientific definitions of food desert have become much more nuanced. As Leclair and Aksan point out, "In the more recent literature, the existence of a food desert does not imply lack of access to food per se, but rather the inability to easily acquire food with high nutritional content" (LeClair and Aksan 2014, 537). This means that while food deserts may have plenty of high-calorie, high-fat, and salty food options, they nonetheless have relatively few fruit or vegetable options (Weatherspoon et al. 2013).

A complicating factor is that language has the effect of minimizing the human presence, and, indeed, human causes of food deserts (Hill 2017). Given that food deserts are typically associated with racialized or otherwise oppressed groups, Hill points out that the emptiness implied by the desert metaphor may have undertones of racism, ableism, xenophobia, or generalized bias against the Other. For example, in the example of the perception of the majority African American city of Detroit as a food desert, "the assumption that Detroit is empty cannot exist without also assuming that black people don't matter" (Hill 2017, 236).

In these ways, food deserts have come to be understood as often having plentiful food options but nonetheless constrained food choice. Choices may be constrained by high prices of available food, by distance to affordable food, by limited selection, or by a combination of all of the above. But the problem singled out by the term "food desert" is not a problem of emptiness. Rather, the problem is a lack of a certain range of retail options and the resultant limitations on residents' ability to choose.

II. FOOD DESERTS AS NATURAL PHENOMENA

The second concern considered by this chapter is with the implication that deserts are natural and perhaps pristine sites of beauty. The concern is raised, in particular, within the food justice and food sovereignty literature, where a preference for the language of "food apartheid" or "food racism" framings is sometimes expressed (Sbicca 2012, 461). This objection can be parsed into two related components.

Deserts understood as natural phenomena are not uniquely attached to a disvalue. Or, to the extent that they are value laden, their value can exhibit more than one moral valence when considered contextually. In other words, deserts are both good and bad, whereas food deserts have been burdened by the rhetorical implication that deserts are unequivocally a bad thing. Deserts certainly have positive value, at least when considered aesthetically and biologically. Deserts can be beautiful. Deserts are unique ecosystems, which are home to unique plant and animal forms that thrive with limited water. Desert ecosystems have led to interesting and unique adaptations and to unique forms of resilience. Deserts around the world have been inhabited for millennia and have spawned unique cultures, some of them nomadic. Deserts inspire art, photography, poetry, and literature. Deserts are not necessarily or inherently bad, whereas food deserts are rhetorically taken to be fundamentally bad. Reframing the problem under discussion as food apartheid or food racism would remove this value ambiguity.

In addition, the natural implication of a desert metaphor can hide an implication that food deserts *arise* naturally. The idea of a food desert may in this way elide agency or systems of oppression that structure agricultural and retail practices. As in the emptiness implication of the metaphor, the natural implication can minimize the fact that food deserts are a human phenomenon. But whereas the emptiness implication arises by ignoring or minimizing the people living—and eating—in food deserts, the natural implication also hides the agricultural, political, and social systems that intersect to cause and sustain food deserts. Reframing the problem in terms of food apartheid or food racism can foreground these concerns and open up discussions of the intersecting oppressive systems of which food deserts are only a symptom.

A food justice framing and food justice movements do not have a universally agreed-upon definition, but they generally imply pursuit of a "liberatory principle focusing on the right of historically disenfranchised communities to have healthy, culturally appropriate food, which is also justly and sustainably grown" (Sbicca 2012, 456). Food justice activists inherited their framings from, among others, the black power movement and the environmental justice movement (Sbicca 2012, 457). That is, they are deeply committed to identifying food injustice in social justice terms. Moreover, they build on social justice movements that examine and work to overthrow harmful social structures, including those exemplified by food deserts.

A related food sovereignty framing offers another option for highlighting and examining oppressive and marginalizing structures related to food. While a food sovereignty framing can likewise be ambiguous or contested, it generally invokes the idea that "one of the most important ways in which communities are subjected to injustices is through the lack of participation in decisionmaking about their food systems" (Werkheiser, Tyler, and Thompson 2015, 72). This framing further foregrounds the powerlessness encountered by residents of food deserts in relation to intersecting food and social systems.

Food justice concerns, including some uses of the food desert metaphor, emerged from within an active environmental justice framing. Environmental justice concerns the unfair distribution of environmental benefits and burdens, and the ways in which these distributions correlate with various social and interpersonal forms of privilege, on the one hand, and oppression or domination, on the other hand. So, for example, access to clean water, parks, trees, or pristine wilderness is correlated with other forms of social privilege, whereas sites of environmental burden including toxic waste, chemical hazards, and other forms of pollution are correlated with social and economic marginalization and disadvantage. The "injustice" of "environmental injustice" is identified through this unfair correlation. A food justice framing draws on related correlations between food access and privilege and, conversely, lack of food access with oppression and domination. Food access within the food justice movement can be seen as functioning in a way that is parallel to access to environmental benefits within the environmental justice movement.

So this second critique that the food desert metaphor falsely implies a natural phenomenon, and the implication that food desert terminology ought to be replaced by food apartheid or food racism framings, functions in parallel with an ongoing discussion about the effect of highlighting "environmental justice" as opposed to "environmental racism." Framing these issues in terms of environmental injustices, and, indeed, "food injustices," may have the effect of concealing important sociocultural dimensions of the injustice as well as obscuring important justification for activism to effectively combat the injustice (Hanafi 2017). An environmental racism framing highlights the roles that systemic racism—including structural and cultural components of racist ideology—play in structuring physical racial-spatial practices such as segregation (Hanafi 2017, 398). Similarly, a food racism framing foregrounds the role of racist ideology and domination in the emergence of segregated spaces and ghettoization. Hanafi argues:

> The long process of spatial confinement and racial subordination of the black population dating back to colonial America with the introduction of slavery, along with the cultural meanings, representations, and images notoriously attached to black space, have jointly coalesced to form geographies of racism that have constantly relegated blacks to inferior, polluted, and risky locations. (Hanafi 2017, 399)

In the context of food deserts, these inferior, polluted, or risky locations entail the absence or limited occurrence of fresh, nutritious, or affordable foods. Supermarkets choose to locate elsewhere, ostensibly for fear of theft or the impossibility of turning a profit. Farms—even urban farms—are unable to fill the gap because the soil, air, or water is unsafe. The perception of a space as unsafe may be a self-fulfilling prophecy, or the perception may indicate and recognize some unsafe features of the space. In either case, the food injustice that is labeled "food desert" highlights human and social features of the space, not natural ones.

On the other hand, the move away from food racism and environmental racism and toward a "justice" framing allows for the possibility of an intersectional approach. The types of social marginalizations and oppressive constructs that constitute food injustice are not limited to racism and racialization. Instead, a wide variety of social constructs and forms of oppression work together to create food and environmental injustices. Marginalized gender identity, class identity, age, or disability is also a predictor of environmental marginalization including difficulty accessing safe and culturally appropriate foods. So while the language of food apartheid and food racism may have desirable mobilizing effects and may avoid the natural phenomenon implication of the food desert metaphor, the shift in language simultaneously has a potential silencing effect with respect to other dimensions of oppression and domination.

Against the backdrop of competing and intersecting forms of oppression, the food desert framing has an obscuring effect: it obscures myriad social and oppressive phenomena that intersect to structure the experience of having difficulty accessing nutritious, safe, and culturally appropriate foods. It hides contested but important human dimensions of the injustice in question behind the veneer of a "natural" occurrence.

III. DESERTIFICATION AS A PROCESS OF DEGRADATION

The United Nations Convention to Combat Desertification (UNCCD) defines desertification as "land degradation in arid, semi-arid, and dry sub-humid areas resulting from various factors, including climatic variations and human activities" (UNCCD 1994). "Desertification" is rhetorically understood to be a process by which fertile land becomes infertile desert, often as a result of anthropogenic climate change but sometimes much more directly as a result of specific human practices. Slash and burn agricultural practices, for example, may change the water retention properties of the soil, cause erosion of topsoil, and also change the agricultural and socioeconomic properties of a piece of land. That is, the land may cease to support historically viable types of plant and animal life and thereby lose much of its value to people who have historically depended on it. In the present context it is worth highlighting that the loss of value may, in particular, include loss of food production value. The process of desertification is generally thought to have ecological, meteorological, and socioeconomic (human) dimensions, and these dimensions function together (Geist 2017). Desertification is a process, and according to the UNCCD, "it is caused by complex interactions among physical, biological, political, social, cultural, and economic factors" (UNCCD 1994). The idea and language of food desertification inherits many of these connotations.

Given that desertification is defined in terms of "degradation" and as a process, it carries a rhetorical implication that the process is characterized by a permanent or difficult to reverse loss of value. Indeed, the aim of the UNCCD is to "combat" desertification, which is further explained in terms of "improve[ing] productivity of land," and "rehabilitation, conservation, and sustainable management of land and water resources, leading to improved living conditions, particularly at the community level" (UNCCD 1994).

Food desertification also inherits the rhetorical implication of permanence, even though there is no reason to assume in advance that food accessibility is inherently difficult to improve. Food deserts can be saved, and the process can be reversed (Hill 2017). After all, on occasions when they are defined solely with reference to distribution of supermarkets, the mere opening of a supermarket would seemingly go a long way toward resolving the identified problem. But when food deserts are defined more broadly and in a more nuanced fashion, the obvious and attainable remedy remains an increase in retail options. That is, food desertification can, like desertification *tout court*, be reversed, and "combating" food desertification remains an option, albeit a difficult one.

Desertification is linked to climate change, and it is often seen as one of the most serious environmental problems confronting the world (Geist 2017; UNCCD 1994). Food desertification may likewise be seen as one of the most serious examples of food injustice, although many have argued that it is merely one among many serious examples of food insecurity (Werkheiser, Tyler, and Thompson 2015; Sbicca 2012; Szende 2015; Scoville 2015). But the links to climate change are significant. As climate change increases and accelerates land degradation in various parts of the world, the global capacity for food production is expected to decrease (Reiheld 2016). The UNCCD includes food security among its concerns and explicitly links desertification to food security (UNCCD 1994).

Desertification and climate change have a direct impact on food security, vulnerability related to food, and food deserts (Reiheld 2016, 201). As land becomes more arid, it ceases to support existing forms of agriculture and food production (Reiheld 2016, 202). Desertification can cause or generate food deserts to the extent that it contributes to both global and local loss of food production. So desertification can make nutritious or culturally appropriate food more difficult to access on a global scale as well as locally or for specific populations. As Reiheld argues, "the complicated system of agricultural production and distribution has already made some people vulnerable and, when disrupted by climate change, may exacerbate existing vulnerabilities and create new ones" (Reiheld 2016, 202).

Examining the desertification implications of the food desert metaphor highlights an important intersection between food deserts and climate change: namely, as climate change occurs, agricultural features and capacities will change. Some traditional and low-tech forms of agriculture may cease to be effective. Climate change therefore predictably increases the prevalence of food deserts, food insecurity, and food vulnerability (Ford 2009).

But the language of degradation also helps to explain some of the negative connotations of labeling some population as living in a food desert. The language connotes lost or missing value. Whether a food desert is identified by comparison with other regions or populations, or whether it is identified through comparison with historic availability of food, it is identified by virtue of missing value: the value of nutritious and culturally appropriate food, the value of choice, the value of a sustainable and rich community. Food desertification is not inevitable, but addressing it is more complex than some common framings suggest. Holistic and contextual examination of missing values will go a long way toward illuminating the problem and making appropriate responses possible.

CONCLUSION

This chapter has examined how the injustice of the food desert is best conceptualized. This concluding section offers some reflections on how we might respond to food deserts in light of the expanded conceptualization of a "food desert" developed here. The conceptualization of the phenomenon of a food desert has an impact on the normative responses available. Armed with a richer set of connotations, I explore a richer set of responses and solutions.

Feminist relational theory provides us with both diagnostic and programmatic tools for explaining food deserts and their solutions. It reminds us that large, complex public health problems such as those raised by food deserts are socially embedded phenomena. They may be the product of ongoing oppressive relationships between governments, institutions, and individuals (Sherwin and Stockdale 2017). Feminist relational theory reminds us to examine food deserts contextually and to look forward as well as backward in our explanations as well as our responses.

Feminist relational theory understands individuals as "essentially relational beings who exist and develop within a web of relationships" (Sherwin and Stockdale 2017, 9). Helping these individuals requires examining these relationships in both our analysis and our proposed solutions. Furthermore, a feminist relational approach demands intersectional analysis of these relationships and pays particular attention to "relationships structured by systematic patterns of privilege or disadvantage, dominance or oppression, and relative power or powerlessness" (Sherwin and Stockdale 2017, 9). Multiple forms of oppression or multiple systems of disadvantage may intersect to limit food choice and to make nutritious food inaccessible. But also, systems of privilege and systems of oppression may intersect, and the resulting pattern of access to food can falsely appear individual and idiosyncratic rather than systematic. Feminist relational analysis reminds us to examine the patterns and systems that structure individual choice and individual situations.

When examining food deserts, we therefore ought to consider how climate change affects their prevalence. Changes in migratory patterns, extinction of species, and desertification all imply change in food availability or access. Wherever climate change affects availability of a food item or range of items, the change will affect each population differently. The injustice implied by the presence of a food desert involves barriers to accessing highly nutritional or culturally appropriate foods. These barriers may arise because of, or be exacerbated by, climate change. Where crops fail because of changes in rainfall or a shift in migratory patterns, in response to changes in weather patterns, or extreme weather that redraws the contours of the map, not all populations will experience an acute loss. But in the face of these types of changes, and as global food availability becomes increasingly limited, the unequal distribution of food will increasingly be associated with deprivation for some. Food deserts may become more common, and our ability to respond to unjust distributions of culturally and nutritionally appropriate food may become more limited.

Important lessons can be drawn from a contextually informed examination of the food desert metaphor and its uses. Several rhetorical implications of the metaphor are factually inaccurate and mischaracterize the underlying phenomenon. Food deserts are not empty, nor natural, nor are they characterized by unidirectional degradation. They may be thriving communities, and their populations deserve respect and a proper understanding of what factors are functioning to limit their food choices or food access. Food deserts are, in addition, a social phenomenon. They are influenced by social, political, and economic pressures. To the extent that they arise in ways that are beyond individual agential control, they nonetheless remain a human phenomenon. Food deserts arise through a process, and that process has a history. Looking at food deserts ahistorically misunderstands the phenomenon.

First, food deserts remain an embedded social problem. Food deserts can be a spatial and physical manifestation of a wide variety of injustices related to lack of choice. Labeling the problem is just a first step. An easy response is, of course, improving access to and choice of nutritious and culturally appropriate food. But given the social background within which food deserts arise, responses focused exclusively on provision of food miss the point. Rather, the maldistribution of food is only part of the problem highlighted by the label "food desert." The problem also includes powerlessness, lack of representation, and procedural injustices. That is, the lack of choice indicated by the label "food desert" includes a lack of real and effective choice but also lack of power and an absence of a fair procedure for restoring choice. Hence, food deserts can and should continue to be a focus of social justice movements, which aim for empowerment along with increased food access.

Second, food deserts remain an environmental issue. Discussions of food deserts emerged within a food justice and food sovereignty framing, and both of these social movements borrow heavily from environmental justice movements and environmental justice framings. It is worth highlighting that the food availability aspects of a space or region *are* features of its geography and its environment. This is true even in urban spaces or regions. In these senses, food deserts are simply one measure of, and one example of, environmental injustice.

Third, food deserts may be sites of great beauty, but the food desert phenomenon is not the beautiful aspect. Food deserts may be sites of great value, but the food desert phenomenon would not thereby become a valuable feature worthy of preservation. The food desert is not valuable in itself, even if it coexists with, inspires, or otherwise causes great value. In this context, an appropriate response to the identification of a food desert is to seek to produce or add value. The missing values that identify an area as a food desert help indicate appropriate responses: increase the presence of nutritious and culturally appropriate food, increase choice, and develop a sustainable and rich community.

Finally, food deserts—and deserts unmodified—are places where plants, animals, and cultures adapt. Thriving in the desert is possible. After all, a desert is defined by its arid climate, but it is not necessarily without water. And food deserts, likewise, are defined by their lack of food choice or limitations on certain types of food availability, but they are not without food. They are characterized by adaptation in spite of limited choice, and activism in an attempt to achieve greater food justice and food sovereignty. Identifying a food desert or labeling some space a food desert may, in this sense, be a positive first step in motivating activism, advocacy, and ally-ship. The act of labeling itself may thereby lead to positive change.

In the context of examining food deserts, we are reminded to look at the interaction between social, economic, and food systems. These systems can function together to limit food availability and food choice. But given the structural nature of these systems, the same systems can be difficult to perceive and extremely difficult to dismantle or change. Food justice and food sovereignty movements retain both types of aims in their activism by simultaneously making food-related oppressions visible and working toward participatory solutions. To the extent that the "food desert" label calls attention to systematic social, economic, and food related injustices, it helps motivate the difficult work of counteracting these injustices.

NOTE

1. For helpful feedback on this chapter at various stages, I would like to thank Erinn Gilson, Sarah Kenehan, Barrett Emerick, Alison Reiheld, Annaleigh E. Curtis, and Susan Helwig.

Part II

CRITIQUE AND CONSTRUCTION

Beyond Dominant Frameworks

Chapter 5

The Climate of Food

Justice, Truth, and Structural Change

Mary C. Rawlinson

In 1778 Frederick the Great of Prussia proposed an essay competition on the question of whether or not it would be permissible for a sovereign to willfully delude his people. Famous for his absolutist style of government, Frederick appeared to believe, with Plato, that circumstances might require a ruler to lie to his subjects in order to preserve his authority, secure public order, or enhance the efficient functioning of the state apparatus, and that such lying would be in the best interests of the people.[1] In commenting on the proposed competition, however, Hegel insists that, while the people might be duped in particular, isolated cases—enticed to accept counterfeit money, for example, or convinced that a military loss was actually a victory—it would be impossible to make deception part of the structure of governance, for the state provides the locus of identity and the condition of each particular individual's self-certainty and agency. The individual can only be realized in the political community of the state, and the state can only succeed to the extent that it provides the infrastructure for that self-realization. Thus, in Hegel's account, the idea that the state could undertake any long-term or pervasive deception of its citizens proves untenable (Hegel [1807] 1977, 550).

In fact, a strong connection between truth and justice comes rather late in Anglo-European jurisprudence, and it remains fragile today around the globe. Only with the establishment of the Sûreté in Paris in 1812, under Eugène François Vidocq, and the formation, led by Sir Robert Peel, of the Metropolitan Police Service (Scotland Yard) in 1829 did Anglo-European justice found itself on principles of truth and scientific evidence. Prior to the creation of these institutions, judgment and punishment regularly depended less on evidence and truth than on torture and confession or on the force and prerogatives of economic and political power. Only with the emergence of modern police forces and the development of forensic science was an essential link between truth and justice established.[2] The Enlightenment emphasis on scientific method and procedures of truth laid the foundation for modern juridical proceedings and penal codes (Foucault [1975] 1995, 11).

Unfortunately, in our own time, the use of torture and force to extract confessions has not disappeared, undermining the link between justice and truth. In some countries, like China or Saudi Arabia, confessions are regularly extracted through physical abuse (Amnesty International 2015; UNCAT 2016). In the United States under George W. Bush, the use of torture and other forms of physical humiliation and harassment became government policy for dealing with defendants charged with responsibility for or complicity in the events of 9/11 (Fontas 2010). More troubling still in the U.S. context is the evidence of pervasive use of coercion and intimidation to extract confessions from vulnerable defendants, leading to unjust imprisonments based on false confessions.[3] Even in our time the link between justice and truth remains fragile.

In the case of climate science, the fragility of this connection between truth and justice and the public's lack of trust in both science and government prove to be severe impediments in attempts to address the deleterious effects of climate change on infrastructures of life. In 2016 the Pew Research Center conducted an extensive survey of the American public's views on climate science and the capacity of public and private institutions to formulate policies adequate to ameliorate the negative consequences of climate change (Funk and Kennedy 2016). The results of the survey reveal a widespread willingness to disbelieve scientific evidence and an equally widespread distrust of the institutions of government and the media. In spite of Hegel's argument that disinformation has no place in statecraft or in the public institutions that sustain the state, a significant portion of the American public believes it is being duped about climate change, not only by the institutions of government but also by the scientific community as well as the press, which is widely regarded as anything but honest and free of coercive influences.

Based on the survey results, less than half of the public believed that climate change results from human activity, while 20 percent believed that there is no evidence of climate change at all. Less than 45 percent of respondents believed that climate change will affect biodiversity (43 percent), make storms and droughts more severe (42 percent), or cause rising seas and erode shorelines (41 percent). They held these views in spite of widespread reporting on the loss of species and the loss of land mass in coastal regions.[4] The survey indicates that 35 percent of the public believed that the media exaggerate the effects of climate change, while 40 percent believed that the media give too little attention to climate change skeptics. Only 7 percent of the respondents strongly believed that they are receiving accurate information from the media about climate change, while only 4 percent believed strongly that the public is accurately informed by elected officials on this issue.

The Intergovernmental Panel on Climate Change (IPCC) claims a 95 percent certainty that human activity is the dominant cause of climate change since 1950, and 93 percent of American Academy of Science members holding a PhD in earth sciences report that Earth is warming because of human activity. Yet, only 28 percent of the public believed that climate scientists understand very well the causes of climate change, and only 27 percent believed that almost all climate scientists share a consensus on climate change.[5] Only 19 percent believed that climate scientists understand very well the best way to address climate change.[6]

When asked who should make policy on climate change, respondents favored climate scientists (67 percent) over elected officials (44 percent), but 56 percent of the respondents thought that the general public should have a major role in making policy, clearly indicating a disregard for expertise, and 53 percent thought that energy industry leaders should play a major role, clearly disregarding conflicts of interest. At the same time, the respondents indicated a substantial lack of trust in science. Only 39 percent trusted science a lot, and only 32 percent believed that scientists based their findings on the best available evidence. Most respondents expressed the belief that scientific research reflected the scientists' own self-interest rather than truth. Of the respondents, 36 percent attributed the claims of scientific research to the scientists' desire to advance their own careers, 27 percent thought scientists' claims were influenced by their political views, and 26 percent believed scientists were trying to help industry.

In sum, the survey reveals widespread public disbelief in climate change, its origin in human activity, and its negative effects, in spite of overwhelming consensus in the scientific community. The survey indicates a pervasive lack of trust in both science and government, as well as a deep suspicion about the motives of climate scientists. In the wider contemporary climate of "fake news," climate change and climate science seem to have been singled out in particular by the public for a suspicion and disbelief that will make achieving any solidarity or collective action around policies to address the harms of climate change very difficult if not all but impossible.

Unfortunately, the authors of the survey exhibit a tendency within debates about climate science to focus on energy usage as the only causal element in climate change. Aside from scientists, government, and the press, the only other constituency cited in their questions about trust and authority are "energy industry leaders." Thus, the survey itself covers over an important truth of climate change: the role of industrialized agriculture in the degradation of climate, the environment, and biodiversity. This omission is particularly egregious given that this industry regularly perverts and hides the truth, not only by deceiving the public about agriculture's role in climate change and environmental degradation but also by misrepresenting products clearly linked to obesity and obesity-related diseases as healthy while at the same time pursuing schemes to addict consumers. Secrecy, disinformation, and the abuse of public trust prove to be strategies essential to and well integrated into the business models of industrial agriculture.

I. THE UNTRUTH OF AGRIBUSINESS

International agencies estimate that agriculture contributes 20 to 30 percent of global greenhouse gas emissions (GGGEs; Vermeulen, Campbell, and Ingram 2012).[7] Its dependence on fossil fuels, on the clearing of vast tracts of land for plantation farms, and on long-distance transportation makes agribusiness a primary source of massive increases in GGGEs and a major factor in climate change. Earth and all living beings are pervasively and profoundly affected by how humans eat. In the United States and much of the developed world, however, agribusiness[8] works to obscure the origin and itinerary of the food for sale in grocery stores, in order to avoid its responsibility not only for the serious health crises precipitated by the widespread consumption of soda and processed foods but also for the deleterious effects of livestock production and commodity farming on the climate and environment.

So-called ag-gag laws are perhaps the most blatant example of agribusiness's opposition to truth.[9] These laws prevent whistleblowers from exposing the cruelty and suffering regularly inflicted upon animals in industrialized meat production. Insofar as they make it a crime to enter a facility "under false pretenses," these laws effectively criminalize undercover investigation or reporting. Most of the laws specifically criminalize any kind of photographic documentation as well as the procurement of other kinds of documentary evidence. Clearly, the industry believes that the truth is dangerous and that, if Americans knew what lay behind the shrink-wrapped meat in the super-market, the economic order would be threatened.

Certainly, *The Jungle*, Upton Sinclair's famous exposé of the meat produc-tion industry in Chicago, had a radical effect. In 1904, Sinclair worked for six months in a Chicago slaughterhouse, where he discovered not only cruelty to animals but also dangerous and abusive working conditions as well as the butchering for sale of diseased animals, a practice that posed a public health threat. His fictionalized account of his experience created a public furor that led to the passage of the Federal Meat Inspection Act of 1906 and the Pure Food and Drug Act of 1906, as well as to the establishment in the same year of the precursor to the U.S. Food and Drug Administration. Sinclair's description of the "Beef Trust" emphasizes the collusion of government and industry in duping the public:

> It was the incarnation of blind and insensate Greed ... it was the Great Butcher—it was the spirit of Capitalism made flesh. ... Bribery and corruption were its everyday methods. In Chicago the city government was simply one of its branch offices; it stole billions of gallons of city water openly; it dictated to the courts the sentences of disorderly strikers; it forbade the mayor to enforce the building laws against it. In the national capital it had the power to prevent the inspection of its product and to falsify government reports. (Sinclair [1906] 2016, 258)

Sinclair details the way in which the same vertical integration currently pursued by modern agribusiness led to a monopoly power that threatened other agricultural producers. The meatpacking industry drove the price of beef so low that the industry was able to take over ranchers' enterprises. Given its monopoly over refrigerator cars, the industry was able to "levy an enormous tribute upon all poultry and eggs and fruit and vegetables" (Sinclair [1906] 2016, 258), thus gaining power over these agricultural sectors, while setting prices for the consumer.

Sinclair demonstrates the way in which this power depended not only on graft and political influence but also on secrecy and deception—on duping the public: "The people of Chicago saw the government inspectors in Packingtown, and they all took that to mean that they were protected from diseased meat ... they did not understand that these hundred and sixty-three inspectors had been appointed at the request of the packers" (Sinclair [1906] 2016, 78).[10] When a load of tubercular steers containing "deadly poisons" was found to have been butchered and sold in the city, the packers induced the mayor to abolish inspections altogether "so that there was no longer even a pretense of any interference with the graft.... There was said to be two thousand dollars a week in hush money from the tubercular steers alone" (Sinclair [1906] 2016, 79).

Ag-gag laws and contemporary collusion between industry and the political sector similarly allow the increasingly consolidated and globalized meat industry to hide its conditions of production and their effects on animals, human health, and climate change.[11] The industry spends significantly on advertising in an effort to control the social narrative and amplify the virtues of eating meat while erasing threats to public health and the contribution of industrialized meat to climate change (Broad 2016). The more ignorant the public is of these consequences, the more likely that the industry will be able to continue its current, highly profitable practices. Controlling the public narrative about food proves essential to securing public trust and to manipulating the public to serve the industry's profit.

While some public awareness has developed around the costs to health and animal welfare in the industrialized meat industry, even the whistleblowers who have exposed these costs fail to make evident the complicity of this sector of agribusiness in the deleterious effects of climate change. The responsibility of this industry for climate and environmental degradation remains almost invisible.

> Last year, three of the world's largest meat companies—JBS, Cargill, and Tyson Foods—emitted more greenhouse gases than France, and nearly as much as some big oil companies. And yet, while energy giants like Exxon and Shell have drawn fire for their role in fueling climate change, the corporate meat and dairy industries have largely avoided scrutiny.... To bring attention to this issue, the Institute for Agriculture and Trade Policy, GRAIN, and Germany's Heinrich Böll Foundation recently teamed up to study the "supersized climate footprint" of the global livestock trade. What we found was shocking. In 2016, the world's 20 largest meat and dairy companies emitted more greenhouse gases than Germany. If these companies were a country, they would be the world's seventh-largest emitter. (Sharma 2017)

In critiques of industrialized meat production, animal rights may immediately engage human empathy, while issues of individual and public health spark human self-interest. Yet, despite the fact that it concerns the sustainability of life on the planet, the issue of climate change remains virtually invisible or a target for suspicion and skepticism.

The continued hegemony of agribusiness in global food production depends on practices of deception and manipulation that sustain this obscurity, ensuring the invisibility of the costs of industrialized food to animal welfare, human health, and the sustainability of the environment and its biodiversity. The industry's untruth rests largely on the promulgation of two fallacies: the fallacy of choice, or the "free" market, and the fallacy of necessity and progress. In each case the denial or erasure of the connection between industrialized food production and climate change proves to be a key element.

II. THE FALLACY OF CHOICE OR THE "FREE" MARKET

Debates about food ethics, food justice, and public health often hinge on the distinction between food as a *commodity* and food as a *right*. Both approaches tend to focus on individual choice and obscure not only the reality of food as an infrastructure of life but also the deception and manipulation that are intrinsic to the success of industrial food, as well as its complicity in climate change, environmental degradation, and the food insecurity of vulnerable populations.

Food as a Commodity

Global agribusiness and industrialized food producers, governments, and international agencies such as the World Trade Organization (WTO) or the Organization for Economic Cooperation and Development (OECD) tend to treat food as a commodity that is best regulated by market forces. From this perspective, profits and a focus on increased production and processing tend to trump all other values.

> The pervasive treatment of food first as a tradable commodity, and second as a subject of cultural, social, and political interest, has given rise to institutions that favour commercial interests and that shift power to commercial actors. The concentration of control of production technology and distribution systems in the hands of relatively few companies has led to circumstances in which scarce resources are allocated on the basis of where profits and commercial opportunities are the greatest, rather than where needs and rights related to food are acute. (Eakin et al. 2010, 252)

Lengthy, globalized food chains give rise to the idea that food can be treated as a global commodity for which there is uniform demand across all markets: "wheat is wheat" (Eakin et al. 2010, 253). Globalized agribusiness or commodity agriculture aims to maximize and secure production through the use of advanced technologies and synthetic inputs to overcome limitations imposed by the natural environment (Eakin et al. 2010, 254). The near-monopoly status of a handful of global firms controlling food production, processing, and distribution encourages government policies that support industrialized farming and its reliance on chemical inputs and petrochemicals, both for the production of fertilizer and for its distribution systems (Cannon 1987).[12]

This approach to food emerged in the United States in the 1930s and expanded to the United Kingdom and Western Europe with post–World War II reconstruction and the Marshall Plan. Since the 1970s, it has rapidly expanded in developing countries in Asia and the global South. The hegemony of this capital- and fossil-fuel-intensive model has been coupled with "expanding markets for agro-industrial inputs, such as farm equipment, seeds, and agri-chemicals, and ensured low-cost supplies for downstream processing industries and food distributors" (Goodman and Redclift 1991, 102). The cheap food produced by industrialized agriculture also freed capital that could then be spent on other mass-produced goods, like clothing and automobiles; so agribusiness played a crucial role in the success of post–World War II capitalism and its global dominance of economies, goods, and services (Goodman and Redclift 1991, 88). Thus, the development of industrialized agriculture proved to be a key element in the global triumph of neoliberal capitalism.

This model has been promoted and sustained not only by the arguments that it is the most efficient and economical strategy for producing food for a growing world population (the fallacy of necessity) and that it represents the superiority of science and technological expertise over primitive, indigenous methods (the fallacy of progress) but also by the argument that it results from free and open markets and promotes consumer choice. In fact, the control of food manufacturers over the type and quality of food available has reproduced the same brands of processed foods and the same fast-food outlets from one end of the globe to the other. Whole, unprocessed foods have become increasingly marginalized in this system. Indeed, "agriculture is no longer the primary income generating (or labour employing) activity in food supply chains globally and in many developed countries" (Ericksen, Stewart, Dixon et al. 2010, 26). Processing, packaging, distribution, and retailing activities now claim a greater economic importance than the actual production of food itself. This trend is directly related to climate change: for example, 40 percent of the GHG emissions from the United States derive from food processing, distribution, or waste disposal (Liverman and Kapadia 2010, 11).[13]

Extensive advertising, often involving systematic misrepresentation of the quality of this global food, has been essential to the establishment and maintenance of the hegemony of industrialized agriculture and food production (Cannon 1987).[14] Women's magazines in the United States beginning in the 1950s relied on food advertising that encouraged women to buy and serve processed foods. Sometimes the ads emphasized scientific precision and consistency: Betty Crocker's cake mix advertisements guaranteed "a perfect cake every time you bake." Sometimes the appeal was for convenience and saving time: a woman in a suit promotes vegetables wrapped in DuPont cellophane by reporting that she "never has to wait for a clerk" and can "shop in a jiffy."[15] Some ads link processed food with the new medium of television and promote a new, "modern" way of eating: an ad for Swanson's TV Dinners depicting a family eating around the television set addresses "Mom" and informs her "how to catch the early, early show with an easy, easy dinner." Many ads attempt to conflate the processed food with whole foods. An ad for Heinz ketchup features a scale topped by a pyramid of tomatoes, with the promise that "you and Heinz Ketchup put 24 pounds of tomatoes on the table at every meal." No mention is made of the sugar and other additives in the ketchup. Even more disingenuous is an advertisement for Bird's Eye frozen corn that shows a farmer with two stalks of corn standing behind a frozen food container into which a woman is reaching to remove a package of frozen corn. The caption reads, "How to pick corn—real farm-fresh CORN—during Lent!"—that is, outside of the season for fresh corn. An ad for Domino sugar anticipates contemporary ads marketing "low-fat" foods that are nonetheless high in sugars and other additives. The ad juxtaposes two photographs: on the left are three teaspoons of sugar, on the right, a single apple. Above the photos the caption reads, "Which is LESS FATTENING?" Beneath the photos the ad states, "Three Teaspoons of Pure Domino Sugar Contain Fewer Calories than one medium Apple!"[16] Along with the themes of modernity, saving time, purity, and reliability that dominate food advertisements in the 1950s and 1960s, the deceptive elision of the difference between whole and processed foods or the substitution of the latter for the former, as if nothing has been lost, proves to be a key strategy in promoting processed food.

Beginning in the 1970s, in response to changing demographics and consumer interests, food advertisements emphasize "eating well" and consumer choice, and they present processed foods as "natural." An ad for filled potatoes offers thirty different fillings, all processed, with the promise of "Fast Food that Isn't Junk." Kraft marketed its packaged macaroni and cheese dinner with the slogan, "How to eat well in spite of it all," while Buc Wheats cereal asked, "Want to feel like a million Bucks?" Burger King urged the consumer, "Have it your way!" while McDonald's reported that "Jimmy's mother knows that McDonald's hamburgers are 100% beef." All of these ads target women's desire to feed their families healthy, nourishing food that is also "modern." All of these foods contained high levels of sugar, fat, and chemical inputs meant to enhance "flavor."

In the intervening decades, processed-food manufacturers have amplified their efforts to represent their products as healthy and natural, at the same time that they have continued to rely on addictive ingredients like sugar and sugar substitutes, high levels of salt, and processed fats. "As the food we consume has become more processed, it has been presented as more natural by the food industry" (Goodman and Redclift 1991, 250). Indeed, the industry has invested considerable sums in research on how to produce addiction (Moss 2015). Food addiction is not an accident or an effect of individual weakness of will, but the result of a "conscious effort" on the part of agribusiness and the processed food industry to produce consumer addiction to foods that are convenient and inexpensive (Moss 2015, 131).[17]

The diet imposed by global agribusiness through its deceptive advertising and monopolistic practices has produced a global obesity crisis. The U.S. Center for Disease Control estimates, based on data collected in 2013–2014, that nearly 38 percent of U.S. adults over 20 are obese. The statistics for younger people are equally alarming: 20.6 percent of U.S. youths between 12 and 19 are obese, while 17.4 percent of children between six and eleven and 9.4 percent of young children between two and five exhibit obesity. As global food has infiltrated markets in the developing world, rates of obesity have begun to spike in those countries as well (Gortmacher et al. 2011; see also Swinburn et al. 2011). The WHO estimates that, by the year 2020, 70 percent of diet-related diseases will occur in low- and middle-income countries (World Health Organization 2017).

Thus the treatment of food as a commodity has resulted in monopolistic practices that severely limit the variety of foods available while promoting patterns of eating that have precipitated a global obesity crisis. This public-health crisis has been well recognized in the last decade and receives frequent attention in the media; yet the connection between this crisis and climate change remains obscure. The fact that the commodification of food produces *both* the obesity epidemic *and* the degradation of climate and the environment receives little public attention. Critics of commodified food may focus on its effects on human health or animal welfare, but they rarely make the connection to climate change and environmental degradation. Yet installing and sustaining this model of food production required an eightfold increase in the global use of nitrogen fertilizers between 1961 and 2002 and a three-fold increase in the use of phosphorus fertilizers between 1961 and 1980. Fertilizer runoff produces eutrophication resulting in huge marine dead zones (Liverman and Kapadia 2010, 10).[18] The Millennium Ecosystem Assessment estimates that fertilizer runoff is largely responsible for the loss of 20 percent of coral reefs and 35 percent of mangrove area globally, producing significant decreases in biodiversity (Liverman and Kapadia 2010, 8).

Similarly, the role of industrialized agriculture and the commodification of food in contributing to climate change through deforestation remains underreported and largely unrecognized in public discussions, which, like the Pew Survey, tend to focus on energy use and engine emissions. Extensive deforestation in Latin America in recent decades to make way for beef cattle production is directly linked to the growth of fast-food merchandising in the United States (Pelto and Pelto 1983, 325). The development of the beef industry in Central America in the 1970s, through vertical integration with fast-food chains in the United States, resulted in the clearing of nearly two-thirds of the region's lowland and lower montane forests (Goodman and Redclift 1991, 160–61). Indeed, deforestation has been a key element of the expansion of industrialized agriculture and commodity food since the creation of massive sugar plantations in the nineteenth century (Braudel 1981, 225–26). Though the link between deforestation and climate change is well documented, not only does this effect of commodified food on climate degradation remain almost invisible in public discourse but land use is rarely taken into account in measuring the contribution of industrialized agriculture and commodified food to GGGEs.

Food as a Right

Opposition to the commodification of food regularly takes the form of the assertion of a *right to food*. Article 25 of the United Nations 1948 Universal Declaration of Human Rights invokes a right to food (UN General Assembly 1948), as does the United Nations Human Rights Commission's International Covenant on Economic, Social, and Cultural Rights, proposed in 1966 and adopted in 1976 (UN General Assembly 1966, Article 11). These documents list the right to food alongside the rights to other conditions of well-being, including clothing and housing.

In 2000, the United Nations appointed a Special Rapporteur on the right to food and gave a more detailed articulation of this right:

A human right, inherent in all people, to have regular, permanent and unrestricted access, either directly or by means of financial purchases, to quantitatively and qualitatively adequate and sufficient food corresponding to the cultural traditions of people to which the consumer belongs, and which ensures a physical and mental, individual and collective fulfilling and dignified life free of fear. (OHCHR 2000)

This strategy of attempting to counter the commodification of food and the maldistribution of access to food through the articulation of a right to food proves both conceptually and empirically flawed. Conceptually, rights are modeled on the right to property, and the articulation of a right to food continues the understanding of food as a form of property to be regulated by market forces. In addition, declarations such as this one install rights that are sufficiently abstract to forestall any engagement with real inequity and injustice, at times even providing cover for the beneficiaries of inequity and injustice.[19] Empirically, these articulations of abstract rights have little, if any, effect on reducing "persistent and increasing social inequality" (Eakin et al. 2010, 253). Moreover, these declarations of a right to food are complicit with industrialized agriculture in emphasizing the "improvement" of methods of production and distribution through "scientific and technological knowledge," clearly favoring the developed world and its economies over the local knowledges and successful methods of indigenous agricultures.[20] The lack of robust mechanisms for enforcing these rights generally means that they provide moral cover for the reigning economic and political powers, while failing to ameliorate the inequities and injustices they were meant to address (Cf. Eakin et al. 2010, 260).

Food as a Culture of Possibilities: The Fiction of Choice

An adequate phenomenology of food reveals that it is neither a commodity nor a right but a *culture of possibilities*. Food is not only, as Montanari argues, "an extraordinary vehicle of self-representation ... [and] the first way of entering into contact with a different culture" (Montanari 2006, 133). How we eat also shapes our experience of time and space, our relations with other humans—particularly across genders and generations—and our relations with other animals, as well as our relation to Earth and to the temporalities of nature. It would be hard to name an aspect of human experience not imbricated with food.[21] Commodity agriculture gained hegemony with the institution of its own culture: the giant fast-food empires emerged in the 1950s along with the proliferation of the automobile and suburban housing tracts (Goodman and Redclift 1991, 101).

Agency depends on a culture of possibilities, and what a human being eats depends upon the culture of possibilities in which she or he is situated. A wealthy Parisian has a far greater range of choices available than an impoverished working parent living in one of the "food deserts" that exist in many urban areas of the United States, where processed foods and fast food may be the only options. When eating is framed as a matter of personal choice, as it is by agribusiness, and obesity is medicalized as a disorder of individual willpower, there is scant attention given to structural change. As Marion Nestle argues,

> The emphasis on individual choice serves the interests of the food industry for one critical reason: if diet is a matter of individual free will, then the only appropriate remedy for poor diets is education, and nutritionists should be off teaching people to take personal responsibility for their own diet and health—not how to institute societal changes that might make it easier for everyone to do so. (Nestle 2002, 360)

Nestle does not deny the role of "personal responsibility" in diet, but she also demonstrates how its exercise depends on "the environment of food choice." A critical phenomenology of food must look beyond a thin notion of individual liberty to the food culture or environment.

The dichotomy between individual choice and state paternalism on which food policy debates often turn proves doubly misleading. On the one hand, the focus on individual choice or responsibility operates under a fiction of liberty. In low- and middle-income countries, food alternatives are often severely constricted by poverty and lack of infrastructure, while in high-income countries, vast machineries of production manipulate land and water, harvest animals, and promote poor food options directly related to the epidemic of obesity and obesity-related diseases.

On the other hand, not only are isolated state bans on certain products unlikely to remake the culture of possibilities that determines how people eat but these bans do not represent a new, paternalistic intrusion of the state into the domain of food. States like the United States already collude with agribusiness through decades of policies favoring industrial agriculture and the economics of big farming over local sustainable farming.[22] Many states have long been complicit with agribusiness in shaping culinary practices and norms to favor global food.

Industrialized agriculture and the processed-food industry, increasingly unified as a monolith, promulgate an ideology of consumer choice, which not only deflects their responsibility for the obesity epidemic but also covers over the role of agribusiness in climate change and environmental degradation. This strategy obscures the active role of agribusiness in creating addiction, thereby constraining consumer choice. The design and construction of retail space, packaging, branding, and marketing manipulate behavior to produce profitable outcomes.[23] The corporations of agribusiness specifically target schools and young children to create brand loyalty from an early age. Given the success of these practices on a global scale and the addictive quality of foods high in sugar, salt, and fat, individual choice proves too thin to support personal responsibility. Given the scale of the system, it is unlikely that isolated policies limiting portions or sugar will have much effect in changing the culture of possibilities in which human agency is actually deployed. And, beyond the question of health, a reliance on personal responsibility in matters of food will certainly do little to address the role of agribusiness in climate change.

The claim that the markets in which agribusiness and the processed-food industry[24] operate are "free" proves just as fallacious as the claim that com- modified food represents a response to individual choice. The hegemony of agribusiness and processed food in global markets depends on more than sixty years of industry collusion with national governments and infrastructures of global capital, such as the WTO (formerly the General Agreement on Tariffs and Trade) and the International Monetary Fund (IMF), both established under U.S. leadership after World War II. Global food policies after the war favored excess food production in industrialized countries and encouraged a reliance on food imports and food aid in developing countries. Prejudices in favor of industrialized agriculture and against indigenous farming methods led to the view that food aid was the best means of preventing famine and malnutrition in the developing world. Governments in developing coun- tries were discouraged from investing in research on local agricultures or in improving local agricultural infrastructures. What investments were funded followed the model of industrialized agriculture, focusing on the use of nonrenewable inputs such as genetically modified seeds, fertilizers, and pesticides (Boserup 1983, 205–207). The developed nations and supra-national institutions of global capital that approach food as a commodity insist that markets "are the most efficient means of addressing food security and adequate distribution of food globally." At the same time, "government policy has often tended toward nationalistic goals of protecting consumer and producer markets, particularly in industrialized nations" (Eakin et al. 2010, 256).[25] The world is not flat, and the markets are not free; nor is it evident either that agribusiness is necessary to food security or that it represents pro-gress over indigenous methods. The erasure of its contributions to climate change and environmental degradation proves essential to maintaining the fallacy of its necessity and progress.

III. THE FALLACY OF NECESSITY AND PROGRESS

The governments of developed nations and the supranational institutions of global capital regularly assert, as did the UNCHR in articulating a right to food, that global food security necessarily depends on increased pro-duction and the dissemination of scientific knowledge and technological interventions. In fact, as Amartya Sen argued in his classic study *Poverty and Famine: An Essay on Entitlement and Deprivation*, "starvation is a function of entitlements and not of food availability" (Sen 1981, 7).[26] The question is not "what *exists*" but "who can *command* what exists" (Sen 1981, 8). As Liverman and Kapadia (2010, 8) demonstrate, "the overall availability of food is rarely a cause of food insecurity: 78% of all malnourished children under five in developing countries live in countries with food surpluses." Food insecurity in developing countries results not from poor production methods but from war and conflict, inequitable access, and, increasingly, cataclysmic weather events related to global climate change.

While developed countries and supranational actors like the United Nations, WTO, and IMF regularly act as if the improvement of quality of life in developing countries depends on the importation of science, technology, and economic models, the importation of these models often produces sub-stantial harm both because of their deleterious effect on the local environment and because of their displacement of indigenous systems and knowledges.

> At a time when chronic hunger, dispossession of food providers and workers, commodity and land speculation, and global warming are on the rise, governments, multilateral agencies and financial institutions are offering proposals that will only deepen these crises. ... Actions by some governments and top UN leadership ... constitute an assault on small-scale food providers

(among whom women are in the forefront) and the natural commons. (Eakin et al. 2010, 246)

Through the first half of the twentieth century, "delocalization"—the dissemination of uniform practices of food varieties, production methods, and consumption patterns—was associated in the industrialized world with a diversification and improvement of diet widely shared across social classes. At the same time, in the nonindustrialized world, this dissemination had the opposite effect, diminishing dietary quality for all but the elites by promoting reliance on one or two cash crops as well as by causing a loss of local control over distribution systems. "Thus, world-wide food distribution and food-use transformations have occurred at the expense of economically marginal populations" (Pelto and Pelto 1983, 310). Thus, far from improving food security in developing nations, the hegemony of agribusiness and the processed-food industry has contributed substantially to those nations' vulnerability and lack of food sovereignty.[27]

This impact is not contingent but structural. The export of food abroad as "foreign aid" has compensated for the overproduction of food in developed countries, thus sustaining prices at home. This practice is justified by representing the developing nation as food insecure and its indigenous agricultural practices as inadequate and primitive. The U.S. Food for Peace Act (PL 480), originally passed in 1954 and renewed in various forms in 1966, 1990, and 2008, created a program that protected U.S. farmers from overproduction while undermining local agricultures and creating dependency in the developing world. The substantial agricultural subsidies paid to farmers in the United States produced excessive production of basic commodity crops. PL 480 and its descendants have allowed the United States to convert this excess production into food aid, sustaining prices for American farmers, "albeit at considerable cost both in terms of food shipments and associated environmental externalities, and in terms of the effects on the receiving country's domestic production and food import markets" (Eakin et al. 2010, 258; see also Director International Affairs and Trade 2007). Thus, far from enhancing food security in developing nations, the hegemony of agribusiness clearly undermines both food security and food sovereignty at the same time that it imposes unnecessary environmental costs related to chemical inputs and transportation.[28] As Liverman and Kapadia (2010, 9) note, the massive changes in agriculture that have occurred since World War II led to food security only in the global North, while undermining local food security in the global South and contributing significantly to environmental degradation and climate change. In addition, land-use policies in the developing world regularly result in the displacement of small farmers in favor of global agribusiness and commodity crops. The forced migration of formerly independent farmers to urban areas not only contributes to food insecurity but also produces deleterious effects on climate and environment through increased transportation costs and waste-management challenges.

The valorization of Western scientific methods and technological intervention by developed nations as well as supranational actors like UNESCO and the WTO exhibits a disrespect for local knowledges and practices that sustains the economic advantage of the developed nations at the same time that it undermines local autonomy and enhances vulnerabilities in the developing world—particularly vulnerability to climate change. The intrusion of industrialized, commodity agriculture into developing markets regularly results in a reduction of access to land for subsistence farming as well as a reduction of demand for farm labor, thus increasing migration from rural to urban areas. National and global policies require formerly independent agricultural communities to yield "local community control to the regional and national food-processing systems" (Pelto and Pelto 1983, 323). This shift involves "a number of major cost increases," including processing, packaging, advertising, transportation, and distribution, as well as the profits extracted at each point in the global food chain (Pelto and Pelto 1983, 329). Agribusiness conflates progress with processing and tries to insert as many steps as possible between the origin of the food and the moment that it is eaten in order to extract profit at every point along the way. These cost increases exacerbate local social and economic inequities, while the poor, who cannot afford these additional costs, "are reduced to a narrower selection of the cheaper foods" (329). Globalized agriculture also results in "the reduction of local autonomy of energy resources, due to dependence on gasoline-driven equipment for transportation, local industry, and other essential processes" (312). Equally pernicious are the structural effects on future autonomy and economic independence. The importation of food and food technologies from the developed to the developing world discourages investments in local agricultures, creating dependency and enhancing the risk of future food crises. Moreover, economic development has historically depended on financing from a robust food export sector (see Boserup 1983, 207). Thus, global food policy and food policy in industrialized nations, particularly the United States, produced a lack of agricultural autonomy in poorer developing countries. As a result, these communities are especially vulnerable to climate change events and their effect on local and global food markets. At the same time, these policies function as a subtle colonialism. The countries' lack of food sovereignty structurally disadvantages them in possibilities for the future even as it perpetuates dependence and undermines health.

This dual strategy—on the one hand, economic policies that create dependency in developing nations on overproduction of commodity crops in developed nations and, on the other, the valorization of industrialized

agricultural against indigenous knowledges and practices—is directly responsible for the decline of small-scale family farms and the independence and
self-sufficiency that they provided. "As a result, once agriculturally self-
sufficient areas now experience rising levels of malnutrition, underemploy-
ment, and poverty" (Goodman and Redclift 1991, 140). Prior to World
War II, Latin America, Africa, and Asia were largely self-sufficient in the
cereals and grains that formed the bulk of the local diet. This self-sufficiency
was sacrificed in the 1950s to cheap food policies, consumer subsidies,
and strongly discriminatory agricultural modernization policies, as well as
American domination of the world grain trade and low world prices resulting
from American farm policies (Goodman and Redclift 1991, 153).[29]

> Within a single generation, self-sufficiency in food grains had been squandered,
> at an incalculable cost to the nutrition and well-being of future generations.
> Moreover, import dependence effectively transfers control over natural resources
> to international markets and agri-food complexes dominated by a handful
> of powerful corporations. Agricultural sectors are mortgaged to earn foreign
> exchange and service external debt accumulated, in part, to pay for imports of
> basic foods. (Goodman and Redclift 1991, 165)

The collusion of agribusiness, developed nations, and the institutions of
global capital depends on fallacious arguments about progress and necessity. These political and economic forces created food insecurities in order
to create markets for their overproduction of commodity crops. Their policies have ignored the real efficacy of indigenous practices and knowledges,
forestalling local development while creating dependencies that constrain
across generations.

Moreover, these policies facilitated the globalization of food and the extension of American habits of consumption around the world, leading not only
to a global obesity epidemic but also to a food system globally dependent on
the devastating effects of industrialized agriculture, including habitat destruction, the reduction of biodiversity through the reliance on monocultures, the
pollution of water sources, and, through a reliance on fossil fuels and chemical inputs, a major role in the increased frequency and severity of cataclysmic
climate events (see Goodman and Redclift 1991, 89, 123). As Vandana Shiva
argues, "industrial food is cheap not because it is efficient—either in terms of
resource or energy efficiency—but because it is supported by subsidies and
externalizes all costs—the wars, the diseases, the environmental destruction,
the cultural decay, the social disintegration" (2006, 164). When the costs to
the environment and climate, public health, and indigenous social forms and
practices are taken into account, agribusiness and its industrial food prove
neither necessary nor progressive but unsustainable. So, far from addressing

food insecurity, industrialized agriculture is complicit in creating it, both through national and supranational policies that favor industrialized agriculture and the developed world and through the devastating, unsustainable effects of this agriculture on the environment and climate.

Consider an example. From the 1950s to the 1970s, the demand for bananas in North America led many small farmers in Jamaica to shift from diversified farming to monoculture, a shift encouraged by government policies focused on producing foreign capital. This created a dependence on imported food from the United States to meet local dietary needs. The oil crisis in the 1970s caused food prices to soar, while the price the farmers received for their bananas did not increase. Ironically, this crisis improved child nutrition as compared to the decade before, because it spurred a resurgence of diversified farming and a reliance on homegrown rather than imported foods. Nutrition improved with a shift back to local produce from imported, processed foods (Pelto and Pelto 1983, 324). So, far from being necessary and leading to progress, the intrusion of industrialized agriculture produced economic vulnerability, food insecurity, and a threat to public health, as well as environmental degradation.[30]

The fallacies of necessity and progress on which agribusiness relies to justify its intrusions into the developing world and to obscure the truth of its devastating economic, social, and environmental effects are nowhere more apparent than in sub-Saharan Africa. Michael Mortimore has demonstrated "the long tradition of successful adaptation by smallholder farmers in sub-Saharan Africa in the face of challenging climatic and environmental conditions" (Mortimore 2005; cited in Ericksen, Stewart, Eriksen et al. 2010, 119). He chronicles traditional practices of seed exchange and food-sharing that effectively address periods of food insecurity. Some of these practices have historically addressed immediate food crises, such as a period in 2005 when excessive rainfalls into the harvesting season affected the yield of millet and groundnuts, the main staple and cash crops. "Other exchanges represented longer-term, strategic investments so as to fortify existing social capital in anticipation of future shocks and vulnerabilities" (Ericksen, Stewart, Eriksen et al. 2010, 119–20). Far from being "primitive," the agricultural practices in these communities are supported by complex technical and social infrastructures, and they exhibit long-term resilience in the face of severe conditions.

Much has been written about the vulnerability of sub-Saharan Africa *to* climate change in the future, but less attention has been given to the truth that the region currently suffers extreme fragility *because of* human-induced climate change that derives to a large extent from industrialized agriculture. Scientists and development professionals, repeating the fallacies of necessity and progress, approach the region ready to dispense their technological and economic solutions while generally ignoring the historical resilience of its agriculture and husbandry in the face of severe weather events.[31] Drought has always been a feature of life for indigenous peoples of the region, and they have historically developed strategies and practices for coping. Drought cycles every five years allowed farmers to reestablish herds, but the increasing frequency of periods of drought prevents them from rebuilding in this way. Polly Ericksen and her coauthors observe that "the adaptive capacity of pastoralists to manage during droughts has been slowly eroded through a gradual loss of assets (livestock) with recurrent droughts from which they cannot recover. Their social networks are stretched too thin, and food aid relief is insufficient ... social thresholds have been breached" (Ericksen, Stewart, Eriksen et al. 2010, 127–28). Government and NGO responses to this crisis have proved inadequate because of two related failures. First, those responses have failed to recognize the way in which national and supranational policies that favor global producers have exacerbated the stresses inflicted by climate change. Second, they have failed to focus on long-term structural change that would maximize local resiliencies rather than relying on food aid, which creates dependency and provides a "response of last resort that is more focused on saving lives than livelihoods" (Ericksen, Stewart, Eriksen et al. 2010, 129). These global agencies tend to aim to "transform the 'inappropriate' local practices," rather than "aim[ing] to build on local experience" (Mortimore 2005; cited in Ericksen, Stewart, Ericksen et al. 2010, 119). A just approach to food insecurity both in developed and developing countries requires respect for the integrity and agency of insecure communities as well as a rejection of the falsehood that this insecurity derives from a failure of local knowledges and practices.

While food insecurity in the global South results from policies that favor global agribusiness and consumer demand in the North at the expense of local agricultures and local food sharing or distribution systems, it is exacerbated by climate change, particularly in areas where the insecurity is already greatest. "The industrialization and globalization of our food systems is dividing us: North–South, producer–consumer, rich–poor" (Shiva 2006, 162). Thus, food justice will require more than food aid: it will require the admission of hard truths about the complicity of global agribusiness in the production of both food insecurity and climate change. Policies are needed that repudiate agricultural colonialism and promote local food sovereignty.

IV. INTERGENERATIONAL ETHICS: POSSIBILITIES
FOR STRUCTURAL CHANGE

Climate Change Justice (2010), by Eric Posner and David Weisbach, is perhaps the most influential book of the last decade on the ethical dimensions of climate change, but it has almost nothing to say about the connection between industrialized agriculture, food insecurity, and climate change.[32] The authors do not mention agricultural reform in their discussion of "policy instruments" (Posner and Weisbach 2010, 41–58). Unfortunately, this failure to connect food justice with climate justice characterizes the literature on both topics.

Posner and Weisbach recognize that poorer countries in the global South will suffer more from climate change than the developed North while having fewer resources and capacities to cope with its adverse effects. At the same time, the authors argue that, while, "by any measure, many poor countries, particular[ly] those in Africa, emit very little, and almost all rich countries have high or very high emissions," by most measures the list of top emitters includes both wealthy and poor countries (2010, 12). Successfully addressing climate change will require "substantial cuts in emissions by all nations," including poorer countries in the developing world (2010, 33). The authors argue for a pragmatic, future-oriented approach to climate change, rather than a "corrective justice" approach that would seek to identify those responsible and assign the costs of amelioration to them. It is no doubt true that "the number of culpable contributors to the climate problem who are alive today is a modest fraction of all contributors" (2010, 102).

While I too would focus ethics and justice on the future, the authors must be criticized for their failure to assign responsibility to current political leaders in the developed world and to the leaders of industrialized agribusiness. Like the mid-century leaders of the automotive industry, government officials in the United States who laid down the policies that produced agribusiness may not have known how their activities would lead to cataclysmic climate change; however, *today's leaders in government, supranational agencies, and agribusiness do know*. These contemporary leaders avoid making structural changes only by purveying untruth about the role of agribusiness in climate change and perpetuating fallacious arguments of individual choice, free markets, necessity, and progress. They can and ought to be held responsible, not only because the role of agribusiness in climate change and the apocalyptic effects of that change are facts that can be disputed only by a will to untruth but also because these leaders have the power and resources to address the problem. The chairman of Monsanto or Archer Daniels Midland is more responsible and more culpable than the farmer in India burning coal or cutting trees for fuel because of the scale of his agency and the levers of power at his hand. As Posner and Weisbach argue, "whenever people engage in activities that emit carbon, such as heating, cooling, transportation, or the use of metals, paper, cement, chemicals or meat, they deplete the resource but *do not pay a price for the harm they impose on others*" (2010, 43, emphasis mine). The harms of cataclysmic climate change, food insecurity, and public health crises related to processed foods do not derive merely from the accumulated effects of individual consumption: they derive from the structural injustice perpetrated by national and supranational actors in collusion with global capital. Subsidies and tariffs that favor industrialized agriculture, the use of developing countries to compensate for overproduction in developed countries, the privileging of food aid to address food insecurity over building local capacity and food sovereignty, the disrespect of local knowledges and practices of sustainable farming in favor of industrialized inputs and technological interventions, and the failure to count the actual costs of industrialized agriculture to public health and the environment in computing its purported efficiency—these all constitute structural injustices that can only be addressed by structural reforms in what we eat and how that food is produced and distributed.

Moreover, these structural injustices are only maintained through concerted practices of disinformation and strategic efforts to obscure or hide the real costs of global agribusiness. The failure in analyzing the ethics of climate change to connect it directly to global agribusiness only further obscures the truth of what is really going on and what will be required to work toward climate justice. There will be no climate justice without food justice.

Posner and Weisbach rightly argue that justice includes an obligation to take seriously the interests of future generations. They insist on "intergenerational neutrality" and claim that "the citizens of later generations are entitled to the same weight as those of the current generation" (2010, 154, 191). Unfortunately, they offer no robust philosophical grounding for this claim and, hence, undertake a purely calculative approach, weighing costs to future generations against costs to current populations: "Climate change abatement helps the *future* poor, not today's poor, who may even be made worse off by interventions to reduce emissions" (2010, 26–27). This approach undermines rather than strengthens ethical commitments across generations. Because everyone is born of the body of another and everyone has been fed by another before one is able to feed oneself, individual humans are always already situated within transgenerational relations that make ethical claims. This intergenerational generativity makes possible and sustains any individual agency so that each and every human being is always already claimed by the generative relations in which the human finds himself or herself situated. Relations of parent and child, teacher and student, doctor and patient, boss and employee—that is, relations in which one has the opportunity to promote the agency of the other—install ethical claims prior to any contract or articulation of abstract rights.[33] Justice requires not merely intergenerational "neutrality" but a recognition of the ways in which intergenerational generativity sustains and claims each one of us.

Only because they fail to connect climate change with food justice can Posner and Weisbach claim that climate change abatement will not help today's poor. Changing food policies and practices to favor sustainable farming over industrialized agribusiness would immediately address the injustices imposed on today's poor by unfair subsidies and tariffs, land-use policies that favor commodity farming, the management of surpluses as food aid, the undermining of local resiliencies, and the health crises now being imposed on developing nations through the intrusion of processed foods, at the same time that it would address a major contributor to cataclysmic climate change.

Currently, agribusiness and the processed-food industry, in collusion with the U.S. government, are engaged in a massive effort to prevent developing countries from adopting a warning-label system pioneered by Chile that effectively deters the consumption of processed foods and sodas (Ahmed, Richtel, and Jacobs 2018; see also Perlroth 2017). Government and industry groups have mounted an aggressive campaign to prevent countries like Mexico, Brazil, Indonesia, Ecuador, Peru, and Thailand—all countries with spiking rates of obesity and obesity-related diseases—from following Chile's lead. Contradicting the overwhelming evidence—well recognized by the World Health Organization—of the link between processed food and obesity-related disease, industry lobbyists insist that their opposition is based on "science" and "evidence." Even more alarming, the United States Trade Representative is seeking to include in a renegotiated North American Free Trade Agreement (NAFTA) a provision that prohibits any warning label that "inappropriately denotes that a hazard exists from consumption of the food or nonalcoholic beverages," in an effort not only to preserve foreign markets but also to stymie any robust effort for domestic regulation. A spokesperson for the Representative states that "the United States supports science-based labeling that is truthful and not misleading," but this is clearly just the latest installment in the use of disinformation, secrecy, and lies to sustain industrialized agribusiness and the processed-food industry at the expense of public health and the environment (Ahmed, Richtel, and Jacobs 2018). The industry's aggressive campaign is a reaction to the success of Chile's labeling program in reducing the consumption of processed foods and sugary beverages to improve individual and public health. Here is a concrete example of policies that can be enacted *today* to improve the welfare not only of the poor in developing countries but of the citizens of the developed world who are no less at the mercy of this collusion of interests. At the same time, reductions in the markets for processed foods would improve global health and the welfare of future generations by reducing the agricultural and production practices that are at the heart of cataclysmic climate change. As the example of Chile demonstrates, when the public knows the truth about the health effects of these products, its behavior changes; hence, these industries must continue to rely on lies, misinformation, and secrecy. Neither food justice nor climate justice can be achieved while the truth is systematically perverted and hidden.

New solidarities will be required to successfully counter the collusion of interests that continues to sustain agribusiness and the processed-food industry. The communities of scholars and activists engaged in environmental ethics and climate justice, on the one hand, and those engaged in promoting food justice and food sovereignty, on the other, need to join with each other and with those forces promoting individual and public health in exposing and combating the complex of structural injustices currently embodied in what we eat and how that food is produced. Scientists, scholars, and NGOs need to learn to appreciate local knowledges and practices, to listen to the farmers across the globe who endeavor to feed their families healthy and pleasurable food, in spite of the constraints placed on their choices by agribusiness or limited economic resources.[34] These intellectual and activist communities also need to recognize the special role that women can play as drivers of change, not only because they form the majority of small farmers and remain overwhelmingly responsible for feeding their families but also because the education and empowerment of women significantly reduce population growth and food insecurity.[35] These constituencies need to join forces around the recognition that there will be no climate justice or environmental justice without food justice, gender justice, labor justice, and economic justice.

Writing in 1987, Geoffrey Cannon chronicled in detail the collusion between agribusiness, the processed-food industry, chemical manufacturers, and the U.K. government in employing disinformation and perverting the truth in order to obscure the health risks of food additives and processed foods high in sugar, fat, and salt. Yet, Cannon ends his analysis with a remarkably hopeful call that remains commanding today:

> A national policy designed to encourage whole, fresh food, and to discourage processed fats, sugars, salt, and chemical additives will change the shape of British farming and food manufacture. Such a policy will vigorously support the small farmer and the small manufacturer. Overall it will be good for business, creating new jobs and more wealth. We need new priorities: support for small farms and for vegetable and fruit farmers, for the cultivation of low-input and organic produce, and for the fishing fleet. (1987, 384)

Cannon makes the connections between public health, labor justice, and economic justice that are essential to address public health and food insecurity. Implicit in his call lies the necessity of linking these aims to efforts to address cataclysmic climate change. These new solidarities can only flourish if the public refuses any longer to be duped and demands the truth, both about the food that it eats and about the effect of the production of that food on the climate and future generations. Justice in every arena depends on new solidarities and narratives of truth.

NOTES

1. The question, posed in French, was *"Est-il utile au Peuple d'être trompé, soit qu'on l'induise dans de nouvelles erreurs, ou qu'on l'entretienne dans celles où il est?"* [Is it useful for the people to be deceived, either by leading them to new errors, or by maintaining them in those they currently hold?]

2. See Symonds ([1972] 1992, chapter 2) for a discussion of the transformation in jurisprudence, as well as the cultural effects, ushered in by the establishment of public police forces.

3. A particularly notable example was the 1989 conviction of five teenaged boys of color, based on coerced confessions in the rape case of the "Central Park jogger." The case resurfaced in the news due to Donald Trump's involvement. Trump avidly advocated for the boys' execution (Laughland 2016; see also The Innocence Project n.d.; and Gross 2015).

4. See, for example, AP (2010) and Rice (2018).

5. In the IPCC's (2013) analysis of peer-reviewed scientific articles published in 2013–2014, 99.8 percent of the authors recognized human-caused climate change (Working Group I 2013). See also Powell (2015).

6. A slightly more recent poll by the Yale Program on Climate Change Communication reports that just over half of Americans believe that climate change is caused by human activity (54 percent), while the percentage of respondents who believe that it derives from natural causes is nearly identical to the Pew Research Center Poll (33 percent). A substantially smaller percentage of respondents in the Yale poll believe that climate scientists agree on the reality of human-caused climate change (15 percent versus 27 percent in the Pew survey; Leiserowitz et al. 2017). See also Saad (2015), reporting on a Gallup poll from March 2015 that "although climate scientists have been in the news describing this winter as a strong signal that global warming is producing more extreme weather, Americans are no more likely today (55%) than in the past two years to believe the effects of global warming are occurring."

7. The U.S. Environmental Protection Agency puts the estimate at 24 percent (EPA n.d.). The Consultative Group on International Agricultural Research finds that food production contributes up to 33 percent of all GGGEs, which is perhaps the

most reliable estimate, including all aspects of agricultural production and land use (Gilbert 2012).

8. By "agribusiness" or "industrialized agriculture," I refer to the complete array of processes and activities involved in global food production, from field to mouth, including not only agriculture per se but also the production of fertilizer, processing and packaging, advertising, and transportation, as well as the conversion of prairies, grasslands, forests, and diversified farms into the monocultures that serve commodity production. Since 1950 agribusiness has pursued a strategy of "vertical integration," whereby a few global firms control food production from field to mouth (Kilmer 1986).

9. The term "ag-gag" is widely credited to Mark Bitmann (2011), who employed it in a *New York Times* opinion piece, "Who Protects the Animals?"; however, it was employed in the early 1960s to describe USDA policies limiting the release of information to the public. Though most ag-gag laws have been passed since 2010, Montana passed a law in 1991 criminalizing entry into an "animal facility" with the intent to take photographs or video or to otherwise expose the facility to "defamation." Alabama passed a law in 2002 making it illegal to enter property "under false pretenses.

10. Today's consumers are no less trusting. They trust their water, though it has proven unsafe in many communities. They trust their food producers without clearly understanding how the food is produced or the degree to which producers aim at addiction. They trust restaurants without knowing if the cooks are sick or how wholesome the food is. Just how risky is eating in our time?

11. In 2017 the combined agricultural sectors of meat and meat production, livestock, and eggs and poultry spent $10,181,383 on lobbying. In 2016 these sectors contributed $8,842,733 to congressional campaigns (CRP 2016; see also Fiber-Ostrow and Lovell 2016; and Wrock 2016).

12. In the intervening thirty years since Cannon's analysis, the reach of global agriculture and industrialized food production has penetrated virtually every corner of Earth.

13. The authors report that processed food now accounts for 75 percent of total world food sales (Liverman and Kapadia 2010, 6).

14. Cannon emphasizes the efforts of agribusiness to misrepresent the quality of processed foods and to obscure its negative effects on health.

15. This ad also reveals the tendency of agribusiness and the processed food industry to eliminate human labor (the clerk) in favor of processing and packaging.

16. These ads can all be viewed online through an image search for 1950s food advertising.

17. See also Brownell and Warner (2009). Big Food seems to be following the playbook of Big Tobacco in at least three ways: purveying an ideology of consumer choice and personal responsibility, pursuing explicit strategies to addict consumers, and obscuring or denying the harmful effects of their products.

18. Fertilizer runoff in the Gulf of Mexico has produced the world's largest marine dead zone. On the link between industrialized agriculture and eutrophication, see also Goodman and Redclift (1991, 212).

19. For example, in Saudi Arabia women have little political or economic independence; yet, Saudi Arabia is a signatory to the United Nation's Convention on the Elimination of All Forms of Discrimination Against Women (CEDAW). For an analysis of how all rights are modeled on the right to property, as well as the way in which these articulations of abstract rights actually forestall genuine engagement with social inequity and injustice, see Rawlinson (2016a, part I: "Critique of Rights").

20. For a discussion of the deleterious effects of this failure to respect the local knowledges of the developing world, see Korthals (2012).

21. For a discussion of the pervasive role of food in human experience, including its intellectual aspect, see Rawlinson (2016a, chapter 5). For a detailed discussion of how certain foodstuffs have determined landscapes, such as wheat in France or rice in China, and ways of life, such as tea in England, coffee in France, or fish in Japan, see Braudel (1981, 211–60). An important aspect of Braudel's analysis for food justice and climate change is his demonstration of the association of meat with power and status: "The few eat meat and the many eat vegetables and grains" (Braudel 1981, 106). Increased wealth in the developing world is associated with an increased demand for meat (Misselhorn et al. 2010, 101). Liverman and Kapadia (2010, 3) also write: "The growing size and complexity of food systems have ... transformed the landscapes that humans inhabit."

22. See Pollan's (2007, 48–53) discussion of the history of policies in the United States favoring bigger farms.

23. Nestle (2002, 369) reports that more is spent to advertise a single candy bar or soda "by a factor of 50 to 100" than is spent in a year by the educational program of the National Cancer Institute's "5 A Day" partnership with industry to promote consumption of five servings of fruits and vegetables daily. See also Nestle's discussion of the strategies used by industry to capture school age children as a market (2002, 175–96).

24. I continue to refer to "agribusiness and the processed food industry" not because they are distinct, but only to remind the reader that, thanks to vertical integration, the two are continuous. Agriculture in the developed world can no longer be distinguished from commodified, processed food.

25. The authors cite the duplicity of the WTO in requiring developing nations to reduce tariffs and nontariff barriers to trade, while allowing the United States to retain and increase agricultural subsidies on export crops such as maize. See also Gonzalez (2004).

26. See also Ericksen, Stewart, Dixon et al. (2010, 25), which shows how food security depends not only on production, but also on access: "Historical famines have occurred where supply was not the issue, but rather poverty, conflicts or an inadequate social contract to protect people from hunger."

27. Korthals (2012) offers two telling examples. He quotes a Dutch aid worker to demonstrate how U.N. intervention produces food crises: "White people like me were flying in to save little children, as if the local inhabitants of Niger aren't able to do this themselves." The aid worker reports on a competent local physician who instructed mothers in traditional cooking and food education, using local products, to improve their diets. This doctor was compelled to stop his efforts because UNICEF

required that even lightly undernourished children be fed with the Unimix food from abroad, although such an intervention normally would be necessary only for severely undernourished children (105–106). In a second example, taken from Hubert Sauper's 2014 documentary *Darwin's Nightmare*, Korthals reports on how the introduction of the export-oriented monoculture production of Victoria perch in Tanzania's Victoria Lake virtually destroyed the culture of the indigenous inhabitants. Local people were forced to live on the refuse of fish production; experienced the destruction of families, the neglect of children and the abuse of women; and suffered under the collusion of the fish transport industry with illegal arms trafficking. "The Sukumas, the region's original inhabitants, traditionally lived from cattle and some crops, but because of the total destruction of their habitat they are compelled to eat fish remains. The way these remains are stored and processed mirrors the total disrespect that the Sukumas encounter" (115).

28. Indeed, the negative impact of agribusiness on food security is also evident in developed countries. "In some countries where private sector interests are particularly well organized, agriculture and food policies may also favour protecting commercial interests at the expense of domestic food security and public health. This has been illustrated in the debates surrounding food policy in the USA and UK, in which some have argued that policy tends to support the production of foods that do little to enhance the dietary health of the population, or which create 'food deserts' where poor populations have no easy access to healthy produce and food products" (Eakin et al. 2010, 253; see also Sen 1981, 166, on food insecurity in the United States in the midst of plenty).

29. See also Pelto and Pelto (1983, 325–26): "In the developing world, delocalization results in a loss of food resources and flexibility as productive agricultural land is put to use for cash crops in competition with land use for local food production, and national food systems become increasingly dependent on the developed nations for shipments of grain and other basic foods."

30. Terry Marsden's (1997) analysis of the effects of agribusiness and the "interpenetration of foreign capital" in Barbados provides another example of the way in which the intrusion of Northern food manufacturers and retailers into the Caribbean region marginalizes small producers, creates economic vulnerability and food insecurity, exacerbates local inequities, and subordinates environmental integrity to the interest of global capital.

31. Even authors who suggest a reliance on local practices or who recognize the resiliencies inherent in local practices approach African farmers as objects of study or a population to be managed rather than as sources of knowledge or partners in addressing food insecurity and climate change.

32. Posner and Weisbach do note that most calculations of responsibility for climate change focus only on emissions. When land use is considered, developing nations such as Brazil, Indonesia, or Malaysia make the list of top emitters.

33. For a fuller account of this ethics of intergenerational generativity, see Rawlinson (2016a, part II, chapter 4, and part IV).

34. The rise in the consumption of processed foods is directly related to women working outside the home and the concomitant reduction in home cooking. Women

remain overwhelmingly responsible for feeding their families yet dramatically underrepresented in the councils that determine the future. For a discussion of how this responsibility for food reflects the gender division of labor and power differentials within the family and the state, as well as greater demands on women's time, labor, psychic freedom, and security, see Charles and Kerr (1988). For a discussion of the importance of valorizing women's labor in efforts to achieve food sovereignty, improve public health, and mitigate climate change, see Rawlinson (2016b).

35. Discussions of the relationship between population growth, poverty, and food insecurity rarely make this link to the practical strategy of educating and empowering women, nor do they make a connection to the importance of accessible contraception and reproductive rights. See, for example, Misselhorn et al. (2010, 100).

Chapter 6

Eating Our Own

Food Insecurity and the Commodity Logic of As Food in the Age of Climate Change

Wendy Lynne Lee

While the majority of scholarly as well as public discourse concerning food security makes its primary focus human welfare, questions about whether nonhuman animals figure into that discourse in any significant way beyond the implications of animal agriculture for human health and atmospheric stability remain undertheorized. I'll argue that nonhuman animals should matter greatly to anyone who works at the thorny intersections of structural inequality and environmental justice, especially feminists and antiracism theorists, activists, and policymakers. Why?

- The very ways in which we conceive nonhuman animal bodies *as food* reinforces a social and economic order whereby the commodifiability of sex, gender, race, and class is made possible. Nonhuman animals are not invisible in this order, but they are also not visible as living creatures capable of pleasure and suffering. This state of affairs advantages the beneficiaries of capitalism, themselves disproportionately white, Western(ized) men, and cannot be corrected without taking every intersection—sex, gender, race, indigenous status, species, and ecology—into account.
- *As food* sets the precedent for the conversion of living sentient entities into commodifiable exchange value, thereby reinforcing a structural inequality not only heteropatriarchal and racialized, but essentially *human chauvinistic*. On this view, human beings are presumed to be the arbiter of all value, and some human beings, namely some men, determine not only social place but also existential condition. *As food* means *as instrument, consumable, disposable* according to a hierarchically ordered worldview that systemically privileges a very few at the expense of the very many.
- While the causes of food insecurity include natural events like drought, flood, and disease, its primary (though often elided) cause is structural

119

inequality operationalized via a *logic of commodification* for which the *as food* status of nonhuman animal bodies functions as a baseline justificatory narrative.

- The same dynamics that contribute to inequality are also at the root of climate change. A logic capable of transforming everything into a potential commodity, and for which the ends are profits (not the planet and not its living species) not only presupposes endless resources but also that its atmosphere can function as an inexhaustible receptacle for waste.

In short, there will be no way to effectively address food insecurity for human populations without at the same time addressing the commodification of nonhuman animals *as food*. And, there will be no way to address climate change without addressing the inequalities that produce food insecurity; these issues are intimately and inseparably connected. The logic responsible for human hunger structures the world so as to maintain the status quo not only for the most privileged but for a future of consumers entitled as a function of sex, gender, race—and species. Whether what's consumed are women's (and some men's) bodies in acts of rape, the lives of African American men in cases of police brutality, the laboring bodies of those condemned to wage slavery, the futures of either the recruits or the victims of terrorism, or animal bodies in the course of meat-eating, commodity logic doesn't discriminate on the basis of any criteria other than exchange value, that is, what can be bought or sold.

The problem with this conception of the world is that in addition to the sheer quotient of suffering, the logic of commodification generates a view of the planet—the capitalist's *world*—that is and has always been no more than a fantasy. The planet required to support this world's beneficiaries is necessarily conceived of as an inexhaustible storehouse of extractible resources, its atmosphere an endless repository for pollutants and greenhouse gases, its land masses indefatigably fertile, its oceans a bottomless landfill for human waste. What commodity logic requires is a commitment not only to consumption but to a *myth* of endless resources, since the planet is, in fact, none of these things (Daly 1996, 11). The problem, then, is that myths can have consequences. We exhaust our limited resources and, in the bargain, pollute our water and air. In so doing we can alter the very conditions of the planet and its atmosphere to support life. The same logic that invites us to conceive of nonhuman animals as meat, forests as timber, water as drilling solvent, women as sexual disposables, African American men as cash cows for private prisons, and the indigenous peoples of the developing world as obstacles or labor pools now invites us to ignore the greatest environmental peril we've ever faced, the ultimate by-product of commodification: *climate change*.

Many of us work hard to encourage awareness of the fact that climate change is real, that its root cause is human chauvinism instantiated as capitalist enterprise. At the intersection of environmentalism and human health, for example, we recognize the relationship between animal agriculture and greenhouse gas (GHG) emissions; we understand the link between land use, grain consumption, and the health hazards posed by large-scale factory farms. At the border of global feminism and the struggles of indigenous peoples, we know that food security in both the developed and the developing world is intimately tethered not only to global North consumption but to environmental and labor exploitation at home and in the global South. We among the Marxists/socialists know that the hard currency necessary to sustain the myth of endless resources—the hydrocarbons, sugars, potable water sources, animal bodies, as well as human and nonhuman labor—is not an inexhaustible tender. And we know the denial of these facts is essential for maintaining a social and economic order whose primary beneficiaries remain mostly white, Western(ized) men whose corporate portfolios depend on this extractivist worldview. And we know, though many work tirelessly to ignore it, that climate change can bring it all down.

Since the early 1990s feminist theorists like Kimberlé Crenshaw have argued that the structural inequalities that support a racialized heteropatriarchal social and economic order intersect across boundaries of ethnicity, sex, gender, and class. While violence against black women is the primary focus of Crenshaw's analyses of these intersections, the role that food security plays is clear. She argues, for example, that the physical and psychic abuse that compels some black women to shelters is the consequence not only of male domination but of poverty, lack of job skills, and responsibility for child care—all intimately connected to food (Crenshaw 1991, 1245). While what counts or ought to count *as food* remains largely taken for granted in her account, heteropatriarchal relationships pockmarked by violence and economic vulnerability are also affected by food insecurity. What's vital to see is that Crenshaw's view of intersectionality sheds light on power and privilege and hence to the constitutive role food insecurity plays in their maintenance. That Crenshaw doesn't specifically theorize food in her account suggests only that feminists may overlook the issue as much as other theorists, and this isn't surprising. Nonetheless, Crenshaw's view of the intersection of sex, gender, race, and economic vulnerability invites us to think more seriously about the concept *as food* as a crucial component in the maintenance of intersectional structural inequality. It's only a short step from the relationship of food insecurity and, for instance, domestic violence to the *as food* status of nonhuman animals in factory farms.

Among the reasons, however, that animal bodies per se may not figure into discussions of food security, at least directly, is because *as food* is not necessarily *as meat* but—as is especially the case of emergency food aid in the developing world—appears as powdered milk or in ready-to-use food supplements like Plumpy'Sup (see, e.g., World Food Program USA n.d.). Because animal body proteins can appear in many forms, such as powdered milk and eggs, they are more likely to be treated as a supplement for nursing mothers and not as an instantiation of the structural inequality that helps to reproduce the conditions of food insecurity in the first place, since these products are so far removed from the animal. When animal bodies are included in the food aid mix, the potential concerns that might arise are more likely to be about whether cow's milk can replace breast milk in the context of HIV infection, conflicts sometimes inflected by the role that culture and tradition play in food preparation (Shah 2007).

To emphasize this extension of Crenshaw's insight concerning intersectionality in another way, it is possible to think about the symbolic use of nonhuman animals in reinforcing structural inequality. I have argued that the animalizing of black women in slavery discourse provides one such instance (Lee 2010, 203–12), the hypermasculine depiction deployed to justify killing zoo animals like the lowland gorilla, Harambe, another (Lee 2016, 48–49). But more work needs to be done concerning the role that nonhuman animals play *as food* in reinforcing structural inequality: if our goal is social and economic justice, we must attend to the moral considerability of nonhuman animals and not just to what their mass manufacture contributes to pollution, land use, and climate change. They cannot be visible to us only as commodities. Hence our arguments must be about more than environmental justice. Until we come to see that eating nonhuman animals (and wearing their fur, holding them captive in zoos, performing medical and other forms of experimentation on them, etc.) contributes to the very logic whereby everything constitutes a potential commodity, we'll fail to meaningfully address food insecurity even as we insist otherwise. Commodity logic undermines the existential conditions of life on the planet. Such is the *meaning* of climate change: the food insecurity with which we're now confronted is not about food; it is about what counts *as food* because it is about what counts as *value* in the face of potential catastrophe and about whether what we can do about it is genuinely sustainable or amounts merely to triage.

I. THE COMMODITY LOGIC OF *AS FOOD*

While writers like Carol Adams introduce us to the intersection of gender, race, and species in ways that offer an invaluable voice to the suffering of human beings and nonhuman animals in terms of their cultural production as meat, her focus is less about food per se and more about the conceptual intersection of the dominated, demeaned, and disposable. In *Neither Man nor Beast* (1995), Adams argues that women and nonhuman animals are similarly cast as commodities, replete with a reinforcing vocabulary of divisible body parts, and she asks the tough question: Given a logic that casts women and nonhuman animals as consumables, ought nonhuman animals count *as food*? Can we continue to consume nonhuman animal bodies and not reinforce the vocabulary of meat? The answer for Adams is clearly no, a view she develops in *The Sexual Politics of Meat: A Feminist Vegetarian Critical Theory* (2015). Here she argues that the concept of meat takes the place of the *absent referent,* the living creature disappears *as* living in consumption, but reappears *as* an inert commodity. Similarly, sexual violence against women is authorized through the objectification of the female body, reducing it to parts and erasing the woman whose body is violated all the while hypersexualizing the object for consumption.

Adams's conclusion that veganism is an essential feminist commitment is, I think, compelling. Nevertheless, part of its force derives from the assumption of the availability of food; that is, Adams regards veganism as a credible, even morally essential, alternative because it is an available one. The trouble, of course, is that adequately nutritious vegan alternatives are not necessarily readily available or, even if so, affordable, especially (as Crenshaw intimates) under conditions of the kind of extreme economic vulnerability that could compel a woman to remain with a batterer. For Adams, nonhuman animals *cannot* count *as food*, but this is at least in part because food *insecurity* does not figure into her analysis. For Crenshaw, nonhuman animals might count *as food*, and this is because food security does figure into her analysis. Moreover, vegetarian perspectives on food security have tended to be framed in terms of distribution and/or reallocation of grains to human populations as opposed to feed for livestock (see, e.g., Singer 1972). Much of this discourse, though focused on hunger in the developing world, has also been largely immune to feminist arguments concerning the structural inequalities that determine that distribution on the basis of race, sex, and gender. Climate change complicates this picture even further since, according to the Intergovernmental Panel on Climate Change (IPCC), its implications for a warming planet affect the capacity of land to support crops, the incidence of insects, the possibility of wildfires, disease, catastrophic weather events, and human migration (Working Group II 2014).

How, then, should feminism respond to these exigencies? According to ecofeminist Greta Gaard, in her essay "Feminism and Environmental Justice,"

transnational feminist and gender studies scholars have largely neglected both environment and species as analytical categories for research, focusing their attentions on human issues of gender, race, class, sexuality, age, and to a lesser extent, ability. While the still-radical concept of intersectionality articulated by Black feminists [such as Crenshaw] ... co-occurred with the rise of the environmental justice movement, it simultaneously excluded environments from its analysis. (2017, 1)

Gaard contends that the crucial role the environment plays at every level of the social and economic order makes its debut with ecological feminism and that insofar as ecofeminist philosophers have developed "intersectional analyses" that "centered race and gender along with species, sexuality, and colonialism," they became better able to focus "on the material conditions of women's lives and women's marginalized participation in policy, government, and economic systems that affect their lives" (2017, 2).

In "Ecofeminism and Climate Change," Gaard further develops this theme, arguing that because climate change is the product of "first world overconsumption" and "masculinist ideology," it is unlikely to be solved, or even mitigated, via the same "free market" strategies that assume the myth of endless resources and depend on structural inequality for labor. "[S]tructural barriers of gender," writes Gaard, "put women—and children—among the world's poorest people, situated on the front lines of climate change" (2015, 49). What's important to see, however, is that the structural barriers to which Gaard refers operate according to the same commodity logic Crenshaw and Adams articulate in their analyses. The addition made by Gaard is to explicitly incorporate the environment altered and compromised by climate change. We can then see that the ligature connecting race, sex, gender, species, and environment within the ideological universe of structural inequality is not only chauvinistic but the material translation of human chauvinism as *capitalism*. We're better equipped to see, for example, why the mechanisms of capital conquest responsible for sustaining the economic order become ever-more rigidly institutionalized as corporate and/or government policy. We can see that the causes of climate change are not only human self-interest, but self-interest incorporated as profit-generating enterprise.

The hydrocarbon extraction industry epitomizes Gaard's point with respect to both the structural inequalities integral to its business model and its contribution to climate change. Facilitated by government (de)regulation or, alternately, government policy intended to bolster profit making, oil and gas corporations are sustained by a logic that supports their environmentally destructive activities *despite* the fact of diminishing resources, environmental crisis, and their associated potential for human catastrophe. President Trump's environmental policies exemplify this relationship: one million acres of Bears Ears National Monument was made available to gas and oil companies (Phippen 2018) despite its importance to paleontology (D'Angelo 2018), and its cultural, historical, and spiritual value to Native American tribes such as the Navajo, Ute, Hopi, and Zuni (Tribes Uniting to Protect Bears Ears n.d.). As Gaard argues, the developing world is not necessarily defined by geography but by economic status, racial and/or gender discrimination, or, as in the case of the indigenous peoples of the Americas, the expropriation of land, culture, and access to resources. The primary beneficiaries of government decisions are rarely native indigenous peoples; instead they're those whose relationships with and within government are defined by corporate profitability, leverage within relevant agencies (the Bureau of Land Management or the Environmental Protection Agency), or access to election financing. Yet while this is certainly condemnable as human chauvinism, it's only through the lens of capitalist exploitation that we can see its objective: money and the maintenance of a racist heteropatriarchal status quo.

Let's then narrow our focus to several specific but critically *antecedent* issues that, once recognized, raise serious questions about how discourse concerning food security has come to be framed and therefore whether we, as ecofeminists, need to undertake an equally serious review of the assumptions governing that discourse. I'll argue that this review is, in fact, crucial to our understanding of the *very way we think* as feminists about food security, and that as a philosophical, moral, and practical matter, we stand little chance of articulating any vision of justice, particularly in the face of climate change, until we address these questions:

- What role does our conception of nonhuman animals *as food* play in feminist and nonfeminist discourse concerning the causes of food insecurity for human beings? Which count *as food*? Why some species and not others?
- Does our conception of nonhuman animals *as food* bear on *how* we conceive the *necessary conditions* of food security for human beings? If we decide that nonhuman animal suffering is morally considerable, is this overridden by the *practical* necessities associated with preventing human starvation? If animal agriculture can provide a higher volume of food distributed as food aid, does that absolve its contribution to nonhuman animal suffering?
- Insofar as we can predict that the quotient of human suffering is likely to rise via climate change, ought we to consider *timeliness* an important factor in human food security discourse? Is the moral considerability of nonhuman animals a luxury of less volatile times?

Although each of these questions touches on an important aspect of *as food*, we can see that each is really an aspect of one central problem: the causes of human food insecurity are essentially the same as those that entitle some human beings to conceive and value all living things, including other human beings, as commodities. Indeed, they're the same causes that, by helping to accelerate climate change, ultimately endanger the integrity of the planet's capacity to support living things. We'll gain no ground addressing human food insecurity until we begin to take seriously not merely what we count *as food*, but a *for whom* whose beneficiaries, as Crenshaw and Adams show, are not generic human beings but rather the men *for whom* animal bodies, women's bodies, brown bodies, children's bodies, bodies of water, and bodies of land function *as* food, *as* labor, *as* entertainment, *as* a slake to thirst, and *as* property. In short, *for whom* is the men for whom the planet itself is not habitat but property. There's no defensible segregation of the bodies of animals as an exception to the logic of commodification; *as instrumental* functions as a *for whom* that defines them all. If we want to end human food insecurity, we must take seriously the logic whereby *as food* counts not only as justification to objectify but to commodify across the board: human beings, nonhuman animals, ecosystems, the planet, and its atmosphere.

Taking seriously what we count *as food* is also not another iteration of the worn appeal to an indirect duty to avoid cruelty to nonhuman animals for the sake of setting a good example for human agents. It's not simply a plea to shutter factory farms in light of their massive contribution to GHG emissions (though this is plainly critical to mitigating against the effects of climate change). We can now see that the way we *conceive* what counts *as food* contributes directly and indirectly to perpetuating the conditions of human oppression and nonhuman exploitation—human and nonhuman suffering. We claim to care about suffering, but the logic of commodification effectively renders everyone and everything a potential resource, disposable, or obstacle; it preempts any principled way to assess value other than as exchange value. Hence, we cannot address human suffering without addressing nonhuman suffering; both are part and parcel of the same antecedent presuppositions that are the root cause of food insecurity. By gaining a clearer view of the extent to which the beneficiaries of this logic depend on our *failure* to examine our presuppositions, we gain a clearer view of the work that needs to be done in ecofeminist theory and practice to address food insecurity *and* nonhuman animal suffering as simply two aspects of the same problem: the capital commodification of *everything*.

II. *AS FOOD* AND THE ROLE OF FOOD AID AND ASSISTANCE IN THE GLOBAL CIRCULATION OF CAPITAL

The United States Agency for International Development (USAID) defines "fit for purpose" food aid in terms of access to food by nutritionally vulnerable people, the reduction of child malnutrition (wasting), and addressing micro-nutrient deficiencies, that is, deficiencies in the nutrients required in small, but nonetheless essential, quantities to prevent malnutrition and promote growth and/or overall health (Webb, Caiafa, and Walton 2017). Despite the availability of basic foodstuffs to meet these goals, the wider the gap grows between the world's wealthy and its poor, the more food insecurity itself widens. Why is this the case? To answer this question, we need first to dis-tinguish between food aid programs like USAID and food assistance more commonly associated with agricultural corporations. Although only the latter are specifically identified as for-profit enterprises, both participate in a cap-italist system that depends on the capacity of food to be monetized. Hence, because the food most readily available either via aid or assistance tends to have a quantifiable value as charity or surplus, it seems reasonable to adopt an inclusive definition of food aid that captures both aid and assistance and that focuses on *purpose*—to prevent starvation for nutritionally vulnerable people—rather than focusing on differences in origin. Given, moreover, deteriorating environmental conditions that will negatively impact the pro-duction and distribution of aid regardless of the motives of its producers, combined with the likelihood that aid of all kinds is to become monetized in the interest of advancing other corporate and/or national interests, the less likely nonhuman animals are to be counted as morally considerable. Moreover, because the operative logic is the same, it may not matter whether we're referring to well-intentioned relief agencies and their patrons or to cor-porate interests whose range of distribution is determined as much by shelf life, spoilage, and advertising opportunity as by nutritional need. Both food aid and food assistance operate according to the logic of commodification. Hence, it's not surprising that neither interrogate the status of nonhuman animals *as food*.

Many agencies concerned with food security in the developing world—for instance, USAID—work tirelessly to divorce food aid programs from the profit motives of potential donors. They strive to be sensitive to particularities of culture and religion, and they place premium value on nutritional impact. Yet few (if any) question the *as food* commodity status of nonhuman animal bodies or whether that status reflects anything more systemic with respect to the structural inequalities facilitating the commodification of human beings. In essence, the *as food* status of nonhuman animals functions as an *invita-tion* not only to the commodification of human bodies and labor but also to the development of large-scale animal agriculture. In other words, the same structural inequalities that obtain in global corporate operations, especially but not only in the developing world, apply to the ways in which we con-ceive food aid, and for the same reasons: once we're committed to the *as food* status of nonhuman animals we've already effectively embarked on a course that "justifies" the continuing exploitation of vulnerable human beings. And once we chart that course, we cannot fail to continue the *as food* status of nonhuman animals; insofar as we've seeded the ground for the continuation of human hunger, we've guaranteed the commitment of food aid agencies to address it—*in any way they can*. Such is how commodity logic reproduces the hunger that supplies cheap labor to multinational corporate enterprise. Charitable food aid organizations aim to prevent hunger, but in their urgency to prevent that suffering, they're compelled to ignore the fact that the very way they address it contributes to the production of its future incidents. They ignore the fact that the industries whose food assistance includes animal proteins, even elided as dried milk or eggs, contribute directly through land expropriation, waste lagoons, and their GHG emissions to future hunger crises.

Given the contribution of food aid programs to producing future crises of food insecurity, it's not surprising that such programs are only modestly (or even marginally) successful (Shah 2007). What commodity logic insures are the economic conditions that generate the urgency that then require us to see nonhuman animal bodies *as food, and* that in so doing we reproduce not only an axis of the myth of endless resources, that is, animal bodies, but the structural inequality that authorizes multinational corporate concerns to profit from human and nonhuman animal suffering. As long as commodity logic is allowed to seed the conditions of human starvation, nonhuman animal body products will remain on the menu—and animal agriculture (including factory dairies) will continue to turn a profit, the beneficiaries of which are advantaged by the structural inequalities that necessitate food aid and so make CEOs momentary saviors. Consider a typical example of an approach to food aid that packages itself as progressive but in fact reproduces the very conditions that make for food insecurity, the statement by the Global Policy Forum (GPF) on challenges in the developing world. Katerina Wahlberg observes that:

> After decades of providing food aid, donor countries have not succeeded in eradicating hunger in poor countries. Therefore, some critics conclude that food aid is a waste of money. But, those critics ignore the fact that food aid is not always primarily aimed at reducing hunger. Donor countries often use food aid to promote their own commercial and national strategic interests. Under such circumstances, food aid is not likely to reduce hunger, and can even harm food security in recipient countries. Donor countries have a responsibility to ensure that food aid favors the needs of the poor and hungry. They should provide more timely and predictable funding and increase quantities for neglected hunger crises. They should abolish program food aid and monetization, provide all food aid as un-conditional grants, and purchase food aid locally and regionally.

And, they should "target" the aid at the ones who need it most and abstain from donating potentially harmful GM crops. (2008)

Wahlberg is rightly critical of food aid programs harnessed to national and commercial interests whose primary aims may not be food security. She's right to advocate for unconditional grants, and she's right to be skeptical of GMOs. Earlier in the piece she addresses the importance of respect for regional food preferences as well as for cultural considerations about what counts *as food*. But as clearly focused on "the needs of the poor and hungry" as are the GPF assessment and its recommendations, as sensitive to issues concerning the potential benefits and harms attendant on food aid, Wahlberg remains silent on the issue of whether nonhuman animal bodies ought to count *as food*. Put differently, except *as food*, nonhuman animals remain an absent referent even to progressive arguments for food aid, potentially even to many feminist arguments rightly seeking an end to human hunger, but unable to see, as Adams puts it, the animal in the aid equation.

At least two things are troubling about this instantiation of the absent referent, and both undermine the claim to be "progressive": First, insofar as the beneficiaries of commodity logic are defined in terms of sex, gender, race, and class in addition to species, the unexamined assumption that the suffering of the poor and hungry counts more than the suffering of factory-farmed animals is speciesist. If we're to take seriously the fact of suffering—if that is to be the focus of what we mean by "progressive"—we must include all those species likely to be capable of it. Any other criteria are either aimed at insuring a particular set of beneficiaries or they're simply arbitrary. Both likely reinforce the logic of commodification because both maintain the status of living things capable of suffering *as food*. Where commercial interests are at stake, food aid isn't about food or aid; it's about markets and products. Preventing starvation functions as an advertising strategy for corporations like Smithfield Foods who can compassion-wash the image of the factory farm with that of feeding a hungry child. In the globalized economy of "North" and "South," moreover, food insecurity ensures the provision of labor through the vulnerability created by wage slavery, and we needn't look to the developing world to find examples of how food aid broadly construed functions to reinforce this aspect of commodity logic. Consider Smithfield's Virginia "Helping Hungry Homes" tour, January 2018:

Yesterday, Smithfield Foods, Inc. joined forces with Farm Fresh to donate nearly 120,000 pounds of protein, benefiting thousands facing food insecurity throughout Virginia. The donation launched the 2018 Helping Hungry Homes® tour, Smithfield's company-wide initiative focused on alleviating hunger and helping Americans become more food secure. In celebration of the program's

10-year anniversary, a kickoff donation event was held at the company's
headquarters in Smithfield, Virginia. "At Smithfield, we're passionate about
feeding people and helping communities in need," said Kenneth M. Sullivan,
president and chief executive officer for Smithfield Foods. "We are committed
to improving food security and ending hunger by donating high-quality, nutritious food and providing financial support to hunger-relief organizations, and
we're thrilled to begin the 10th year of our Helping Hungry Homes initiative
in Virginia, the community we call home." At the event, Smithfield and Farm
Fresh presented the donation, equivalent to more than 475,000 servings of protein, a staple of a well-balanced meal, to the Foodbank of Southeastern Virginia
and the Eastern Shore, FeedMore, and the Virginia Peninsula Foodbank.
(Smithfield Foods 2018)

However generous the Helping Hungry Homes program may appear, it's
hard to deny its advertising potential for Smithfield Foods and Farm Fresh.
Perhaps we don't begrudge them this. But perhaps we do, once we examine
the facts in light of its commodity logic.

    Consider Warsaw, North Carolina. Here residents have filed civil lawsuits
on the grounds that when Smithfield Foods waste lagoons are full, the company sprays the overload onto local fields, exposing people unfortunate
enough to live near the concentrated animal feeding operation, or CAFO,
to toxic fumes. Moreover, according to the environmental watchdog group,
Waterkeeper Alliance, this constitutes environmental racism because the state
permits CAFOs "disproportionately near minority communities" (Jernigan
2015). Unsurprisingly, Smithfield denies the accusation of racism, but that's
beside the point: CAFOs are built and operated according to a logic whereby
everything that is not a direct beneficiary of a business plan functions as a
commodity, regulatory obstacle, or disposable in the execution of that plan.
Food assistance recipients are tools in the creation of civic-minded window
dressing for a company that poisons its factory farm neighbors. African
American neighbors whose class status makes them unlikely complainants,
especially those who do double duty as cheap labor for Smithfield, insure
against both regulatory enforcement and lawsuit. Insofar, then, as economic
vulnerability provides Smithfield the very thing it needs to appear generous—the poor and hungry—Helping Hungry Homes can only reinforce
the systemic commodification of precisely that which guarantees its corporate objectives: as wide a profit margin as possible with little investment
of capital.

    The second troubling issue with the way in which nonhuman animals are
conceived *as food* in food programs like Smithfield's follows directly from the
first: Smithfield knows that few people, especially food assistance recipients,
are likely to question the types of proteins in a Helping Hungry Homes's
gift. They'll assume, right along with their Smithfield Foods benefactors,

that the suffering of the poor counts for more than that of these proteins. Indeed, proteins function to erase the animal from *as food*; living, breathing, experiencing, hungry, thirsty, crying, calving, nursing, screaming, suffering aren't merely elided in this gift, they're *preempted* by proteins. The way in which the ceremonial gift-giving is structured forecloses any such question as at least bad-mannered if not ungrateful. After all, the heteropatriarchs of Smithfield (whose current leadership consists of seven men and no women) are handing out not merely free stuff but *food*; the role of the recipient is to be humble about their circumstance and acquiescent to authority and certainly not to sue the gifter for exposure to airborne toxins. But this logic is perverse: the consumption of nonhuman animal bodies *as food*—as food *security*—serves to reinforce the structural inequality that reminds us that this *other* is not us. Nonhuman animals function as referents whose absence as living, suffering creatures reinforces an "us" whose own superior place in the social and economic hierarchy is supported by our license to consume that other *as food*. In so doing, we reinforce our own status as the always vulnerable potential recipients of food, and we provide the labor necessary to preserve the structural inequality that commodity logic requires as fuel for its capitalist ventures.

III. CLIMATE CHANGE, DISPOSABLE BODIES, AND FOOD SECURITY: MORE THAN UTILITY

Even as we turn our attention toward mitigating the consequences of climate change, it becomes clear that preventing human starvation has itself little to do with compassion, and more to do with ensuring the labor and consumption necessary to future capitalist conquests. Nonhuman animal bodies are vital to these ventures. We discount them as morally considerable not because they don't exist for us but because we need them as commodity value. Images of cows, pigs, lambs, and chickens grace billboards and magazine ads, TV commercials, and internet pop-ups. They're systemically discounted as animals because they exist for us *as food*. We're indemnified from cradle to grave against the possibility they could be anything else: "Beef! It's what's for dinner" and "Pork! The other white meat." These slogans and imagery reinforce our assumptions so seamlessly that, as Kip Anderson and Keagan Kuhn show in their documentary *Cowspiracy*, when Big Green environmental organizations like the Sierra Club or the Environmental Defense Fund are confronted with the question of why their focus on GHG emissions excludes animal agriculture, they struggle to evade the issue (Anderson and Kuhn 2015). They're willing to criticize corporations with respect to fueling our cars and trucks, but we must not get too close to talking about food.

One's about "mere" transportation; the other is about eating. Yet even this, of course, isn't true unless you're fortunate enough to be a citizen of a global North society. After all, if you're walking miles every day to secure firewood, transportation *is* food.

It's also not surprising that on a global scale, *as food* is likely to be reinforced by the sheer magnitude of human desperation in the face of soil exhaustion, seed piracies and monopolies, polluted waterways and wells, increasingly virulent disease vectors, crisis migration, human overpopulation, droughts, floods, and fires, all of which are accelerated by climate change (Working Group II 2014). Yet it's precisely that desperation that's a boon to corporations like Smithfield, both because it offers an opportunity to pretend to be charitable and beneficent and because the greater the desperation, the less likely we are to disrupt a food distribution system that promises at least modest alleviation of hunger. The latter motive might be counted as particularly ironic and perverse, given two facts: one, only CAFOs are likely to have the capacity to process sufficient numbers of animal bodies *as food* to actually address food insecurity; and two, CAFOs are major contributors to climate change and are thus at least partly responsible as environmental drivers of human migration and its consequent food insecurity, which is itself among the causes of migration particularly in light of drought, flood, and crop failure (see Noll, this volume). Thus, a catch-22: insofar as we remain committed to the *as food* status of nonhuman animal bodies in the service of food security, we remain committed to their factory-scale production; yet, it's precisely this factory-scale production that contributes mightily to climate change in the form of waste lagoons that produce methane emissions, deforestation in the construction of CAFO-sized operations, and the greenhouse gases emitted on a massive scale by the animals themselves. Climate change will help to generate conditions—flooding, fire, species loss, and desertification—that make crop production less possible and less sustaining, and as farming becomes less productive (at whatever scale), the resort to animal proteins will become more common even as stressed environmental conditions accelerate human migration (Koneswaran and Nierenberg 2008).

And on it goes. The only way to break this nihilistic cycle is to exclude nonhuman animal bodies from *as food*, both because the practical consequences of animal agriculture are self-defeating and because conceiving nonhuman animal bodies as disposable only reinforces the antecedent that so too are some human bodies, that is, that they can be commodified as labor put to the service of the very production and consumption that brought us climate change. Insofar as our focus remains not the animal but on the agriculture, and not on the future of a planet upon which we all depend but on whether we can sustain our level of consumption (we can't), we're destined to reproduce precisely the conditions that have engendered these crises. To the extent that we treat nonhuman animals *as food*, whether the crop produced is cows or corn, chickens or chickpeas, even arguments like Peter Singer's, namely, that grains consumed by livestock should be redirected to people to prevent starvation, fall short because they're directed not at the intimate relationships that tether human bodies to nonhuman animals, especially in the fragile age of climate change, but primarily to human welfare (1972, 229–43). Presumably, if we could arrange animal agriculture in some other way, without using up so much arable land or making so much waste, Singer would approve it. But this, in fact, runs contrary to Singer's own view of the moral equality of suffering. Once we determine that what's wrong with factory farming is limited to its deleterious effects for human populations, we have already conceded the very thing critical to the disruption of the commodity logic that creates the conditions of human destitution and thus cheap labor markets. Put simply, it's the way we conceive *bodies*—some as labor, others *as food*—that sets into motion a system in which suffering is not a salient category of moral considerability. Once the suffering animal is excluded from solutions to food insecurity, so too does all suffering become subject to comparison against the commodity value of the sufferer. Commodity logic, in other words, must be confronted at every level and intersection of structural inequality, not merely those that impact human welfare.

IV. *AS FOOD* IS EATING OUR OWN

Some of what most endangers the futures of many vulnerable peoples—for example, the peoples of the flooding Kiribati Islands in the Central Pacific—are the implications of climate change and the instability that accompanies forced migration. Some of what endangers the vulnerable, particularly, as Gaard argues, women and children, are the exploitations of corporations who take advantage of already well-established, structural inequalities to compassion-wash a poor company image, dump agribusiness excess, conduct unregulated hydrocarbon extraction, or effectively utilize arable land as a bio-technology laboratory. But what each has in common is the failure to examine how the inequalities privileging human beings over nonhuman animals and nonhuman nature cast the die in favor of reproducing the conditions that all but guarantee food insecurity, and all of the catastrophes that foreshadow its occurrence or follow in its wake. What each has in common, in other words, is the failure to recognize the logic that informs the transformation of living things and their ecologies into commodities. Things may be even worse: the *as food* status of nonhuman animals may not merely be a consequence of the commodity logic but essential to its maintenance.

As Singer (1972) shows, one of the major causes of food insecurity is the sheer volume of land put to the manufacture of animal bodies, land that can no longer be put to growing food crops, land whose soil and water sources are polluted beyond reclamation for decades. This state of affairs is a boon to the capitalist in need of cheap labor; it's a primary cause and effect of externalizing costs and internalizing profits. It's commodity logic taking advantage of structural inequality at work: whatever renders a people economically vulnerable to low wages and unregulated working conditions is good for capital. Many things may help to facilitate this, but few are likely more effective than industrial animal agriculture, both by virtue of the volume of land it appropriates and because it so effectively reinforces the presupposition that some exist to serve others, with their bodies or even their lives. The moral is clear even in the case—perhaps especially in the case—where society is confronted with a still higher value, namely, the future of life on the planet: so long as the value of nonhuman animals is assessed not in terms of characteristics they share in common with human beings, like sentience or the capacity for suffering, but *as food*, the justification for their industrial manufacture will not only remain secure but it will be reinforced by the very development programs with whom the multinational shares the operational premise, *as food*. So long as that justification is secure, it contributes to the conditions of human food insecurity through its domination of resources and a conceptual tyranny that, in its conversion of sentient creatures to commodities, reinforces the structural inequalities upon which industrial enterprises depend for cheap labor. Commodity logic is not conspiratorial; it simply facilitates the necessary machinations of capital conquest whose beneficiaries rely on the inequalities that provide laboring bodies—human and nonhuman—to their profit endeavors.

And, as Naomi Klein puts it, "*climate change changes everything*" (Klein 2014). Insofar as the concept *as food* reinforces a logic whereby the value of sentient living things can be commodified regardless of race, sex, gender, or species, it will continue to be deployed at a level of industrial manufacture whose GHG emissions accelerate climate change. As science makes clearer by the hour, the consequences are potentially catastrophic. Climate change has no geographical or geopolitical borders. Some human communities will be better provisioned to protect themselves from its consequences in the short term. Others will face ever-greater food insecurity and the prospect of becoming refugees from untenable environmental conditions, civil war, and terrorism. Still others, like the Sumatran elephant, among the planet's vulnerable species, will be driven to extinction. We can choose to agitate for policies aimed at mitigating the effects of global warming, or we can choose to believe that *as food* still offers something essential to food security. But the latter is false, despite our capacity for the denial of both climate change and nonhuman animal suffering. It may already be too late to mitigate meaningfully against a warming planet. I don't know. This much, however, is surely true: we can no longer afford to think only about ourselves if what we want to save is our future. For it's the same logic—human self-interest pathologized in its value of profits over moral progress—that will be the undoing of even the most privileged. Chickens, pigs, cows, and dogs; fish, fowl, forest dweller—these are not food. They're our opportunity to recuperate the possibility of a future fit for all.

Chapter 7

A Feminist Food Justice Reflection on the Politics of Food, Land, and Agriculture in Central America

Gabriela Arguedas-Ramírez

The purpose of this chapter is to contribute to the discussion about climate change and food justice, emphasizing the structural (cultural, political, economic, and historical) causes of hunger and climate vulnerability in the global South. The analysis will focus on Central America and the ongoing violence exerted against indigenous and peasants' communities, women, and environmental and social justice activists as an instrument to perpetuate the structures of injustice that produce hunger and other types of vulnerability.

In this sociohistoric context, I want to offer an ethical-political and epistemological reflection on the problem of hunger as fundamentally related to justice and to the material basis of human existence. I stress the point that a

Figure 7.1: "With hunger there is no peace" (Con hambre no hay paz)
Photograph taken by the author, Cartago Province, Costa Rica.

rigorous analysis about food justice, climate change, and state policies needs to be grounded in history and the specific context of geopolitical locations. In order to do that, I engage in a dialogue with the concept of feminist food justice, a concept still in construction (Sachs and Patel-Campillo 2014, 404), which emphasizes the political dimensions of the production of hunger and climate change (Shiva 2006, 65).

Hunger is a violation of human rights to which the international community has not been able to respond in a consistent way. It has been widely demonstrated that hunger and the various forms of food insecurity are not the result of insufficient food production in the world but of an unfair redistribution of material and symbolic resources and possibilities. Food insecurity is also the result of the accumulated damage produced by the historical oppression and discrimination of many, which is linked to the historical accumulation of wealth in the hands of few. From this perspective, climate change is one of those accumulated damages which, even though it affects all ecosystems, does not affect all human beings in the same way because some human beings enjoy certain protective privileges. For the purposes of this chapter, it is of special interest to emphasize the negative effect of climate change on social inequality, food security, and violence related to conflicts for land access and impoverishment (Santelices-Spikin and Rojas-Hernández 2016, 6; Reyer et al. 2015, 1620).

Climate change aggravates conflicts over land ownership and use, causing an increase in violence in peasant and indigenous areas of a region, which also accentuates food insecurity. This is why it is relevant to analyze the problems of food insecurity and climate change, taking into account the consequences of colonialism and imperialism. As Murphy affirms:

> This is the signature process of imperialism. Today it is widespread in relation to food production where poorer countries increasingly provide food for rich consumers in Europe, North America and elsewhere. Climate change and the world's response is another example. As the richest countries fail to act because *real politik* makes it impossible to question the profligate lifestyles of their citizens they undermine the environments of poorer countries and life-chances of poorer people. At the same time, strategies adopted to "solve the problem of climate change" might burden the marginalized disproportionately, raising the specter of ecological imperialism. (2009, 24)

In addition, the neoliberal conceptualization of the problem of hunger and climate vulnerability dismisses this perspective and naturalizes the consequences of colonialism and imperialism. The standard neoliberal response to hunger and to the effects of climate change in impoverished countries is charitable aid (including mainstream international cooperation), which elides ethical reflections about the burden of responsibility that individuals, specific groups, and states have for the destruction of ways of life and the perpetuation of power relations that violate fundamental rights. Nagel considered that charity should be rejected as a solution because it implies a refusal to challenge the system of political and economic institutions that reproduces radical economic inequalities (1977, 57). Likewise, I maintain that charity also obscures the history behind current inequalities between global North and global South, thus rebuffing recognition and reparation of the damage produced by colonialism.

Central America is marked by profound internal economic, social, political, and cultural inequalities (Rodas 2015), which determine the distribution of and access to the material and symbolic resources needed to survive daily life. While being able to access food and water in sufficient quantity and quality is a taken for granted fact of life for people in upper socioeconomic sectors, for others meeting this basic need is much more difficult. For these people, accessing food and water can be an extremely stressful and anxious task, one that may require violent negotiations related to commercial sexual exploitation, selling drugs, or participating in fundamentalist religious groups.

Moreover, given the extreme vulnerability of this region to climate change effects, those daily life activities—getting water and food—will become even more difficult for the people who are already in conditions of marginalization. The impacts of climate change on agriculture, biodiversity, and the availability of clean water are well documented and are producing severe damage. Social conflicts related to land access will worsen because there will be less soil apt for agriculture. Fundamental crops for food security in the region, such as beans, rice, and maize, are very sensitive to changes in rain patterns, high temperatures, and drought (Imbach et al. 2017, 6).

Also, Central America is one of the most violent regions in the world, above all when it comes to violence against women (Honduras, Guatemala, and El Salvador have the highest rates of femicide in the world), LGBTQ people, children, and journalists. By observing these expressions of violence through an intersectional feminist lens, the ideological connections between the oppression of these specific groups and the politics that foster extractive activities that damage the environment and exacerbate climate change become visible. Additionally, the political power of fundamentalist religious groups is growing, in alliance with right-wing sectors. Right-wing political groups, in turn, have promoted extractivist exploitation projects such as open pit mining, monoculture single-crop farming that is extremely damaging for the ecosystem (for example, the planting of fruit crops for export, especially bananas and pineapples), and the development of hydroelectric projects in environmentally protected areas or zones populated by indigenous people. In these ways, fundamentalist political groups are strategic allies of powerful business elites that reject public policy that is oriented toward environmental protection and adaptation to climate change. Equally important to notice is that Central America is just beginning to recuperate after the dictatorships, genocides, and guerrilla wars that typified the second half of the twentieth century.

I. FEMINIST FOOD JUSTICE: THINKING ABOUT HUNGER AND CLIMATE CHANGE FROM CENTRAL AMERICA

The concept of feminist food justice (Sachs and Patel-Campillo 2014, 404) is based on food sovereignty and food security philosophies while also integrating an intersectional feminist perspective like that proposed by Kimberlé Crenshaw (1991, 1243). Production of food is recognized, in this context, as taking place on a number of scales. The hegemonic food regime occurs on the largest, most macro scale, in which the strongest corporate and political interests coincide. However, the majority of the food that is consumed by the most vulnerable sectors relies on smallholder agriculture, which is much more susceptible to the voracious buying and selling of land. On this more micro scale, it is usually poor women with little education and, often, immigrants who are in charge of the production and preparation of food. Here, the seeds, methods, and types of food are very different, biologically and culturally, from those products that arrive on the market from the hegemonic food regime.

Understanding these details is fundamental when making an ethical and political proposal for ending hunger and vulnerability due to climate change, or as Sassen calls it, "the production of dead land and dead water" (2014, 97). Vandana Shiva has also demonstrated that, for the majority of women in the world, "involvement in the environmental movement has started with their lives and the severe threat to the health of their families" (1994, 2). For these women, the environment is not some external or distant category; rather, it is the place where life itself occurs. As Shiva affirms, "environmental problems become health problems because there is a continuity between the earth and the human body through the processes that maintain life" (1994, 3). UN Special Rapporteur on Right to Food Hilal Elver has repeatedly shown, for example, the importance of agroecology to feed people in an effective and just manner. As understood by Elver, "agroecology ensures food and nutrition security without compromising the economic, social and environmental needs of future generation; it focuses on maintaining productive agriculture that sustains yields and optimizes the use of local resources while minimizing the negative environmental and socioeconomic impacts of modern technologies" (2016, 22).

For these authors, a serious discussion about how to eradicate hunger means taking into account and addressing the long and violent history throughout which transnational political and economic elites have stolen and accumulated lands. National and international legal policies that are used to stimulate direct foreign investment and to concentrate land among only a few big owners should also be critically observed and analyzed.

Accordingly, the ethical demands of critical thinking imply a duty to debunk neoliberal narratives on food production. As Sachs and Patel-Campillo make clear, "a feminist food justice approach would demystify and disembed dominant discourses and ideologies that allow such constructs and practices (such as the need to pay low wages in order to be competitive in the global food market) to take hold" (2014, 408). Elver has also emphasized how much we need to question big agrobusiness myths and recognize what constitutes the political economy of hunger (2016, 8). The political economy of hunger can be understood, on the basis of the paradigmatic work of Drèze and Sen (1990, 2) and the human rights perspective developed by the prior Special Rapporteur on the human right to food, Olivier de Schutter (2009, 3), as the interconnected political, social, and cultural factors that determine complex economic problems. If those complexities are not identified and understood, it is not possible to comprehend the causation of hunger or implement suitable corrective actions.

Central American governments, however, are going in the opposite direction to what the Special Rapporteur recommends. The amount of land dedicated to monocultures for export has only increased, forcing thousands of indigenous and peasant families from their homes and livelihoods. This forced displacement is accomplished through violent means, including the use of private security forces that work for large agrobusiness corporations. Since these security teams also work under the protection of whichever government is in power, impunity is the norm (Takeuchi 2014, 12; Terminski 2015, 49).

II. HUNGER AND CLIMATE VULNERABILITY IN CONTEXT

The current conditions in the region are due, in part, to the history of violent conquest and colonization, the resistance and survival of indigenous groups, the mixture of ethnic groups (including African workers who were brought, mostly from Jamaica, to build railroads, among other things; and migrants from other areas of the globe who coexisted while forging diverse nations), and this region's relations with its larger and stronger neighbors to the north.

The region's contemporary history has been marked by tensions between oligarchies and the large swaths of the population that have been systematically dispossessed. In addition to these conflicts, there are also those related to U.S. geopolitical interests, often characterized by diverse analysts as *imperialist* in nature (Faber 1992, 17; Schoonover and Schoonover 1991, 77). Armed conflict and guerrilla warfare, in which the United States has intervened under various guises (from humanitarian aid to neopentacostal Evangelicalism and, even, to direct military intervention), have left deep wounds in Central American societies. The consequences of this continuum of political and armed conflicts are reflected in institutional instability, co-opted democracies, and growing inequality. This scenario has become even more complicated by drug trafficking from the South (producer) to the North/United States (consumer), which has intensified the region's violence, as well as the continued U.S. intervention in several countries of the region.[1]

In addition, murder rates continue to be very high. In 2016 four of the region's seven countries registered, on average, more than 30 homicides for every 100,000 inhabitants (Estado de la Región 2018). El Salvador and Honduras have, respectively, the second and the third highest femicide rates in the world (Sabatini and Galindo 2017). Furthermore, femicide rates are increasing as a result of transnational, organized human trafficking, according to the Regional Representative of the United Nations Office on Drugs and Crime (Yagoub 2016).

Central American environmental conditions also continue to deteriorate. Forest coverage has decreased and CO_2 emissions have increased. These changes lead to greater vulnerability to natural disasters (Estado de la Región 2018). At the same time, the region continues to be overwhelmed by low economic growth and the inability to adequately collect tax revenue and correct fiscal imbalances, which together lead to debt. Remittances, that is, money sent from a country's citizens working abroad, have increased, accounting for 17 percent of the GDP in El Salvador and Honduras in 2016. The poverty rate is 47 percent, far above the Latin American average, and Guatemala, Honduras, and Nicaragua are among the continent's five poorest countries (FAO 2013, 6).

Regarding the vulnerability to climate change and its impact on food security, recent Intergovernmental Panel on Climate Change (IPCC) reports show a number of emerging risks that are related to links between food security, soil and ecosystem degradation, poisoned or disappearing groundwater, and reduced health and malnourishment. Soil degradation often reduces the efficiency of water and energy use, and these interactions can compromise food security (CDKN and ODI 2014, 5). Projected climate change could severely affect the poorest members of the population, especially with regard to their food security, increasing current levels of chronic malnutrition.[2] Currently, Guatemala is the country with the greatest rate of food insecurity (30.4 percent) and this problem has only worsened over the last few years. Climatic instability and climate change pose a great challenge to the region due to the consequences already occurring in agriculture and access to water. For instance, 1.4 million people in Guatemala, El Salvador, Honduras, and Nicaragua owe their livelihoods to coffee production, which is very susceptible to climate change (Magrin et al. 2014, 1530; Estado de la Región 2015, 11). Changing climactic conditions have made it such that new plant diseases and plagues—like coffee rust (*roya*), which in 2012–2013 affected almost 600,000 hectares of land—could survive and thrive (Agencia AFP 2017).

III. MARKETS, LAND, AND FOOD

Two recent episodes demonstrate how geopolitics determine important food security conditions and environmental protection in Central America: the Central America Free Trade Agreement (CAFTA), between Central America, the Dominican Republic, and the United States, and the 2009 coup d'état in Honduras.

CAFTA

CAFTA, which is an example of neoliberal policy executed through bilateral agreements on more imbalanced conditions than the ones established in multilateral trade forums, limits participating states' abilities to protect their agricultural production according to their food needs by eliminating tariffs on food importation. This restriction can weaken, or even destroy, local food production, making countries dependent on food imports. While, in some cases, this policy could improve the availability of foodstuffs in a given country, at certain times it also means that countries run the risk of being at the mercy of fluctuating market prices and the ever-changing whims of international trade.

The majority of the region's countries are net importers of basic grains (corn, beans, and rice), as well as cooking oils, dairy products, and meat. Over the last two decades importation of these foodstuffs has increased gradually, so that now Guatemala, Honduras, and Nicaragua must dedicate more than 5 percent of their gross domestic product to food imports (FAO 2013, 6).

One of the major problems of this severe dependence on food imports is that food prices on the world market have been increasing over the last decade. The fact that access to food is mediated by purchasing power has gravely affected rural and indigenous communities, which have to spend a higher percentage of their earnings on buying food (Estado de la Región

2015, 10). A poor family that has some land can be food secure, even though it does not have very much money. However, as Saskia Sassen has demonstrated, land is what large global capital firms require and what is central to the economic dynamics of free trade (Sassen 2014, 80). Without access to land, families—mainly rural families, but also, to some extent, urban families—lose any possibility of producing at least a small part of what they eat. They also miss out on the opportunity to create networks of community support, which can also ensure people's access to food whether or not they are members of a distinct family unit.

In relation to the new global land market, Sassen points to two significant factors that have contributed to a sharp increase in land acquisition: First, there is a growing demand for industrial crops (palm plantations for biofuels but also the farming of foodstuffs). And, second, the considerable rise in global food prices in the 2000s made land a desired investment. More and more capital was invested in land as a means of acquiring a broad range of products (food, industrial crops, rare minerals, water) (Sassen 2014, 96–97).

Massive land acquisitions produce an enormous number of microexpulsions[3] as well as generating water and air toxicity, which leads to a loss of biodiversity and consequent soil degradation. After a few decades the land becomes infertile, a situation common to the oldest Central American plantation zones: "As a result, there has been hunger in areas where there wasn't before, even though its inhabitants were poor: soy beans have replaced black beans, which were a source of income and food for poor farmers. Many of them end up forced to move to the poorest neighborhoods of big cities" (Sassen 2014, 97).

Likewise, Sassen warns that these land acquisitions are transforming sovereign state territories: this instrumentalization of land, even indirectly, degrades the quality of the governments that sell or rent it (2014, 81). As Sassen explains, the purchase of foreign lands is not an isolated event. It is linked to a vast global land market that involves the development of a far-reaching and intricate service infrastructure to allow sales and acquisitions, to secure property rights, to develop appropriate legal instruments, and to demand the creation of new laws that are more conducive to this type of business transactions. This is an infrastructure that goes far beyond supporting the ordinary act of buying. It not only facilitates but also encourages new foreign acquisitions of land.

In fact, large-scale foreign land acquisition has been made possible by International Monetary Fund (IMF) and World Bank debt restructuring programs, implemented in the majority of the global South during the 1980s. These were strengthened by measures taken by the World Trade Organization (WTO) in the 1990s, such as lifting export and import barriers in the name of free trade. Since then, free trade agreements have been questioned, as they are mechanisms that help to avoid implementing concrete and effective environmental protection measures, adapting and alleviating climate change, and promoting food security policies (Lilliston 2016, 2; von Braun 2007, 5; Brecha 2016). According to Ilana Solomon (2016) more than 700 cases against the policies of more than 100 governments have been launched through the system known as "investor-state dispute settlement." This system is based on rules, included in trade agreements, that enable multinational corporations to challenge government policies in private tribunals, where they can force governments to pay large reimbursements if a new climate policy generates obstacles for their business. The UN Special Rapporteur on Right to Food has denounced the negative effects on nutrition and access to adequate food caused by trade liberalization and the unregulated commercialization of foodstuffs, which are hallmarks of neoliberalism. Trade liberalization and direct foreign investment by transnational companies in the processed foods industry has provoked an increase in the availability of ultraprocessed foods. The elimination of policies that protect national markets has thus led to a rise in the production of unhealthy, cheap foods (Elver 2016, 7). Ultraprocessed food (mostly imported) is cheap because it can last longer on the shelves, but at a high cost for the health of consumers. People living in poverty and marginalization usually don't have any other option but to consume that kind of food. The situation is even more complicated if local food systems are destroyed as a consequence of food imports and extended monocultures for exportation (Thow and Hawkes 2009, 13).

Orford (2015, 61), tracing the ideological origins of contemporary international trade law and its relation to food production and commercialization, explains that in 1958 the General Agreement on Tariffs and Trade (GATT) committee published the report "Trends in International Trade," which reflected positions developed by influential liberal economists who were worried that postcolonial states were becoming vehicles for agrarian reform, redistribution of land or wealth, industrialization, and economic growth. The strategy to counteract this possible trend of emancipation in the South promoted an extractivist model for the global South and also fostered authoritarianism. From that moment on, liberal economics has promoted the idea that state agricultural subsidies, the fall in food prices, and an excess of food supply should all be seen as problems. However, if seen from the lens of redistributive justice, low food prices and excess world food supply can be viewed as a shared resource. It is only through the "free market" perspective that these effects are seen as market "distortions."

The Honduran Coup d'État

On June 28, 2009, political and military forces executed a coup in Honduras. President Barack Obama and Secretary of State Hillary Clinton contributed to the ousting of President Manuel Zelaya of Honduras by supporting the de facto government, which was widely rejected by Hondurans and by most of the members of the Organization of American States (OAS). Following the coup, an aggressive privatization campaign was initiated in Honduras, wherein concessions were granted for the exploitation of mining, forestry, and hydroelectric opportunities. This campaign served the financial interests of groups with economic power in Honduras, including the United States, China, and Canada. As a result, violence increased, especially against environmentalists and opposition journalists, placing Honduras at the top of the list of the most dangerous countries for environmental activists and journalists (Main 2010, 18; Amnesty International 2017, 9; Cohen 2017, 2)

One important plan of the post-coup Honduran government (backed by the World Bank) was the Agua Zarca hydroelectric dam project on the Gualcarque River. The Civic Council of Popular and Indigenous Honduran Organizations (COPINH), under the leadership of the Lenca indigenous woman, Berta Cáceres, demonstrated that this project would have a disastrous socioenvironmental impact. Besides, it had been initiated through the theft of indigenous lands, permitted by a corrupt government. Berta Cáceres was recognized internationally for her activism, but she also received several death threats against herself and her family. Even though she was formally under the protection of the Inter-American Commission on Human Rights, Berta was murdered in her home on March 3, 2016 (OXFAM 2017, 16; Interamerican Commission on Human Rights 2016).

Like CAFTA before it, the economic and political changes in Honduras after the coup produced a series of state, judicial, and economic transformations that benefited those elite groups linked to large transnational corporations while punishing large sectors of Honduran society, among them, small farmers and women. The government's decision to promote "clean" energy, using hydroelectric dams, and to produce single-crop exports, like those used for the production of biodiesel (e.g., African palm) resulted in the displacement of indigenous and rural communities, an increase in food insecurity in the most vulnerable socioeconomic sectors, and a subsequent upswing in violence and expulsions. This tendency toward consolidation of the neoliberal economic model deepened inequality, favored accumulation by dispossession (Harvey 2004, 64), and worsened the challenges posed by climate change in the region.

It could be assumed that the Honduran situation is due to a weak democracy, that Honduras is a failed state, incapable of facing the challenges posed by its vulnerability to climate change and its serious problem of food and nutritional security. Using the term "failed" or "weak" in reference to states that are "at high risk" when considering the implementation of public policy on climate change is common. Foreign Policy & the Fund for Peace asserts that "the types of places where climate-induced changes in livelihoods are a risk factor for violent conflict include those in which the state is weak as it could be indicated in the Failed States Index" (quoted in Barnett and Adger 2007, 649). In this way, they are assuming that a causal relationship between "failed states," food insecurity, and climate vulnerability exists. However, those terms have been called into question. Sassen explains, "The language of failed States, which is the most common way of describing those nation-States that are weakened, or, even, devastated, ignores many of the negative effects that key actors in international governance, principally the IMF and the WTO, have had on those countries that had to follow their policies. This language represents State breakdown as something endogenous, a function of its own weaknesses and corruption" (2014, 101).

In this sense, and following Chayes (2017, 76), Honduras exemplifies the new form of political hegemony in the twenty-first century and demonstrates how it promotes climate change, inequality, and social conflict. Corruption organizes complex networks that link the public and private sectors with criminals and even murderers, whose main objective is to maximize benefits for network members (Lakhani 2017). Bribery is integrated into the institutional functioning of countries like Honduras and its transnational kleptocratic networks, which are able to cross international borders, exchanging favors and even receiving international aid funding.

The Truth Commission Report on the Honduran coup d'état,[4] published in 2012, backs up much of the analysis done by Sassen and Chayes. In Honduras and more generally throughout Central America, high levels of social conflict have been maintained through land concentration. Since 1992, when the Norton Law was approved in Honduras, a large quantity of land that was going to be redistributed through agrarian reform ended up being used in order to pay political favors. From 2008 on, then president Zelaya showed important political support for agrarian reform, promoting laws and programs in order to fix these problems. However, this whole process was reversed once the coup d'état took place,[5] which immediately meant more repression for rural communities (Edelman and León 2014, 211).

There are numerous court cases that have been brought by the state and private interests against the defenders of human rights, land, and the environment in those communities. According to one Amnesty International Report,[6] based on evidence presented by the Committee of Family Members of the Detained and Disappeared in Honduras (COFADEH), it is estimated that around 3,000 peasants were criminally accused and tried for no reason,

700 of them from Bajo Aguán, the region in which the planned Agua Zarca hydroelectric dam project was to be built (Amnesty International 2017, 13).

IV. WHAT CAN BE LEARNED FROM BERTA CÁCERES'S MURDER

From the perspective of feminist food justice, it is clear that in Central America, access to land lies at the very core of the dispute between neoliberal policies for economic growth and preservation of agroecological and ancestral ways of life. The notion of body-land territory is useful to understand the vital force of women in the resistance movements for food sovereignty and the defense of indigenous and peasants' territories. As Lorena Cabnal, a feminist intellectual of the Maya and Xinka ethnic groups, has explained, the statement "our body-land territory is not sold, it is recovered and defended" began to be used as a political slogan in the territorial defense of the mountain of Xalapán within the framework of the fight against both sexual violence and mining (2015, 3). Later, it became a political phrase for communitarian feminism in Guatemala. It defines a way of posing and feeling the body as a living and historical territory, not in the Western geographical conception of a map but, rather, referring to a cosmogonic and political interpretation of how bodies have a relationship in the web of life.

The body-land territory, along with the feminist food justice framework, makes visible certain practices of social belonging that are embedded and embodied in the continuum of life in ecosystems. Women's bodies are also a territory threatened by colonization and exploitation. The strategies for defending those sites of material and symbolic existence are possible only through the community of bodies interdependent with each other and with the land and the nonhuman life that surrounds them. Without land there is no community and, therefore, there can be no collective organization for the defense of human life. In this ethical and epistemological framework, the production and preparation of food and the protection of the environment that enables crops, access to water, seeds, and knowledge for the use of all—these common goods—are the vital axis of the political resistance and defense of the environment.

Cáceres's murder has been commented upon as just one more case that shows how the state has failed to protect human rights and environmental activists. Nevertheless, this crime has also been interpreted as a necessary act, taken in order to protect the economic interests linked to the Desarrollos Energéticos SA (DESA) hydroelectric dam project. Cáceres's fight for land and water, as well as her struggle to protect traditional Honduran indigenous subsistence farming, revealed that the Honduran state was much more invested in the protection of private enterprises—crucial for national and foreign elites—than in the survival of its rural and indigenous communities. Cáceres's murder was tied up with power politics and corporate interests and for that reason this crime can be held up to show the embodied complexities of the fight for land, water, ecosystems, and life in Central America (*New York Times* 2018). It is crucial to make visible the embodied individual and collective forms of oppression and hierarchy in order to understand the economic, political, environmental, and cultural processes that produce hunger in Central America, and the structural and historical barriers faced in the fight for food and climate justice. The decision to position Berta Cáceres's murder in the center of this analysis is an ethical and epistemological attempt to make that exercise of "making visible" more concrete. Doing so is also necessary to prevent the reproduction of narratives that excuse individual and collective actors from responsibility, letting political organizations and global financial entities off the hook.

In Central America, narratives that criticize environmental, rural, and indigenous activism continue to be related to anticommunism. This tactic is known as the "watermelon syndrome." For those in favor of neoliberalism, environmental activists are called "watermelons": green on the outside and red on the inside, referring to the colors historically associated with environmental activism (green) and the traditional, Marxist left (red). This metaphor, which associates color with political positioning and has its roots in traditional, oligarchic politics, is part of a political discourse that constructs all of its opposition as *communist enemies.* Under this label, many people were disparaged and persecuted, and even killed, if they opposed their governments' repressive actions during the period of guerrilla warfare in Central America, roughly considered to be from the 1960s to the early 1990s (Mowforth 2014, 180).

Consequently, using the slur "watermelon" against those that organize and fight to end contamination, open-pit mining, illegal land seizures, and the irrational expansion of monocultures sets up a discourse in which the "enemies" are those who defend the earth, their communities, and the environment. This same discourse is used to justify the persecution, repression, and use of violence against these people, their families, and their organizations.[7] As Mowforth reminds us, and as those of us who live in this region already know, death squads are just as active against the "watermelons" today as they were against the communists in the past.[8]

In general, crimes committed against environmental activists and community leaders go unpunished, producing two primary effects: (1) the normalization of violence, including murder, against people who oppose a given development model; and, (2) social demobilization, as families, friends, and fellow group members of the organizations of slain activists face intimidation and enormous difficulties just to survive. This situation also weakens community action and the collaborative work between institutions and social organizations that is indispensable to preserve food and nutritional security, alleviate or adapt to climate change, protect the environment, and generate a counterweight to economic and transnational powers.

Furthermore, international human rights law and its institutions have been weakened by growing criticisms that these are violating the sovereignty of individual nation-states. As a result, the legal tools of this framework are too weak and cannot force states to comply with its directives and sentences. This has been the case for the Inter-American Human Rights system and the OAS, more generally, and has only deteriorated the protection of human rights in the region. Similar flaws are found in both the international human rights systems and in the instruments of governance, organization of debate, and decision-making to confront climate change, such as the Kyoto Protocol, the IPCC, or the Paris Agreement (Keohane 2015, 21; O'Lear 2016, 110).

The global governance regime on climate change has achieved very poor results, after long and complex negotiation processes between participating states. The states that emit the most greenhouse gases—the United States and China—have no real incentive nor are there binding legal mechanisms to force them to comply with the agreements established in these international forums. In addition, key nonstate actors, such as large companies, are left out of the focus of these agencies. Further, the institutions that make up this system of governance on climate change do not engage in discussions about the structural causes of climate vulnerability and fair allocation of responsibility between the great winners in the global economic system. In Central America, both in the field of human rights and in the protection of the environment and adaptation and mitigation of the effects of climate change, there is a contradiction between the official declarations of the states in these international forums and the political decisions made by local governments. In the case of Honduras, the government collaborates with international agencies to carry out diagnoses on climate vulnerability while passing legal reforms to facilitate extractivist projects that have a high environmental impact and devastating consequences for entire communities, including the persecution and murder of many of its leaders (*La Prensa* 2013).

CONCLUSION

Repositioning food at the center of life and environmental sustainability, and disputing the notion of food as solely a good to be bought and sold in the market, is one of the most urgent changes needed to ensure both food justice and climate justice in our time (see Rawlinson, this volume). This is an ethical, political, and cultural challenge that demands an extraordinary effort, given the fact that neoliberal capitalist thinking has been successful in normalizing the idea of food as a commodity. That idea currently permeates the governance structures of global trade. Following Shiva's ideas about "Earth Democracy" (2006), a solid democracy can only exist based on active local economies, which emerge from living, participatory cultures, that make possible the exercise of full citizenship rights. This proposal for revitalizing and rescuing democracy implies that we must put a premium on the protection of ecological processes that sustain life and on those fundamental human rights that make up our basic right to life: the human rights to water, food, healthcare, education, and work. This ethical and political goal is against the flow of the current economic system, described by Sassen as one of production of dead land and dead water. Keeping within this framework, I also would add the concept of *dead food*, which I see as designating that which the hegemonic food system produces. *Dead food* is the cheapest food: highly processed, toxic, calorie-rich and low in nutrients. It is the food that makes up the diet of the dispossessed and displaced poor. It is the food that President Trump wants to offer the poor in the United States instead of food stamps (Dewey 2018). It is the food that sickens and produces obesity, the food that kills the most vulnerable.

Feminist food justice makes clear that hunger is not just an undesired effect of the hegemonic food regime, but, rather, the necessary product of the perpetuation of the status quo and its power differentials. Moreover, it is women who, in the great majority of cases, end up being the first to live through and talk about the brutal damage incurred by hunger and environmental destruction in their families and communities. Taking the human right to food as part of a global, minimal ethics, to which the international community has to respond, will show us a path of action quite different from the one that follows on the idea of charity. Helping the needy is not necessarily the result of embracing shared responsibility for harms done in a systematic way over time. The collective duty to guarantee the human right to food, as one that is essential and fundamental in the preservation of the physical, psychological, and moral integrity of human beings, requires action to prevent both land dispossession and accumulation and not just plain acts of charity in cases of emergency and starvation.

Finally, I propose that the fundamental philosophical question in this context is not whether from the global North and its privileged position there is a duty to help, like many philosophers, such as Peter Singer, Onora O'Neill, and others, have proposed. Rather the central question is whether ordinary individuals, stakeholders, and organizations have a duty to do no harm—that is, whether they have the duty to abide by the principle of nonmaleficence, which is a fundamental principle of global coexistence. If we take this question seriously, then we should confront and question the discourse that normalizes and justifies extractivist neoliberalism's socioecological destruction of the global South.

Both climate change and hunger are by-products of the hegemonic economic system, which is inherently violent in the regions of the world—Central America, for one—that are seen as mainly sources of what is understood to be just "raw material." In those regions, the advocates of the system try to rationalize and make acceptable any destruction, in order to perpetuate the process of wealth accumulation. As long as this rhetoric, which disguises destruction and inherent cruelty, continues to be accepted as a legitimate ethical and political position, justice and human rights will continue to be aspirations with little practical relevance for regions like Central America.

NOTES

1. For example, the 1954 U.S. military intervention in Guatemala to overthrow President Jacobo Arbenz and protect the interests of the United Fruit Company; the attacks ordered by Reagan against the Nicaraguan Sandinista government in the 1980s, that used Honduras to establish military bases for those operations; Reagan's financing of El Salvadoran military forces, which fought the Farabundo Martí Liberation Front (FMLN) and the military invasion of Panama in 1989; among other well-known U.S. imperialist actions (McPherson 2016).

2. Approximately 13 percent of the total Central American population is undernourished (Estado de la Región 2015).

3. "Microexpulsions," in Sassen's work, refers to the expulsion of entire small communities caused by massive land acquisition.

4. Referring to Honduran economic and political elites, the Commission indicates that they act in accordance with the strategic interests of those transnational corporations that operate in their country. According to this report, one of the principal material and economic objectives of the coup was to access and control more land. It also says that Honduras's recent history shows that one of the sectors most affected by conflict and exclusion is the rural sector. Agrarian development in the country has been marked by the state using land as a bargaining chip, gifting land as compensation for those who do them a service.

5. In order to learn more about Zelaya's policies and how they were strongly rejected by the politico-economic elites and military that orchestrated the coup, see the analysis done by the Honduran sociologist Leticia Salomón, at https://www.alainet.org/es/active/31381.

6. Amnesty International has shown that trying members of social movements and human rights organizations has created an enormous material and psychological burden for them. This weighs upon them individually as defenders but also on their families and the organizations that they belong to. For many families, these legal processes also foster severe economic crises.

7. Latin America is the most dangerous region in the world for environmental activists and defenders of territories, peasant and indigenous communities, or ecosystems, more generally. *Global Witness* reports: "In 2014, we found 116 cases of killings of land and environmental defenders in 17 countries—on average more than two victims per week and almost double the number of journalists killed in the same year. Around three-quarters of these deaths took place in Central and South America, with South East Asia the second-most affected region. Brazil is again the worst-hit country, followed by Colombia, the Philippines and Honduras" (*Global Witness* 2015).

8. When Oscar Arias was president, the Costa Rican government used anti-communist and antienvironmentalist discourses in order to promote the approval of CAFTA in 2007. In a document known as the "Fear Memo," written by Vice President Kevin Casas and Representative Fernando Sánchez, they proposed a strategy that would convince the greater population that those who opposed CAFTA were communists, linked to Hugo Chávez and Daniel Ortega (Rojas 2010). During the 2017–2018 Costa Rican electoral campaign, two of the principal presidential candidates used violent discourses against these social movements. Juan Diego Castro, of the National Integration Party (*Partido Integración Nacional*, PIN), has referred to ecological activists as "eco-terrorists" (Sequeira 2018), and Fabricio Alvarado, of the evangelical party National Restauration (*Restauración Nacional*, RN), and who won the first round of presidential voting in 2018, calls them "ecólatras" (Partido Restauración Nacional 2017), a play on words between "eco" and "idólatra" ("idolater"), a biblical term whose closest translation might be "false prophet."

Chapter 8

From "Corn Mother" to King Corn

Contested Narratives of Corn in the Era of Climate Change

Deborah Adelman and Shamili Ajgaonkar

"Corn Mother" by Anita Endrezze

Beneath Mexico City, there is a lake
sealed tightly below concrete boulevards
and buildings of blind glass
windows where the pigeons batter their wings
and the cleaning women press damp clothes,
dreaming of the lake beneath the city where skulls
have been crushed into mud and the long paths
out of the palaces, markets where the ripe fruit rotted,
tables where chocolate pots tipped over,
unattended, bone ladles clinking to the floor.

Where are we? Stories above
the lake and the dead Aztecs
who were kinsmen of the Yaquis
in some northern desert way
and I won't pause because history didn't,
if you know your history: you know
that Cortes killed thousands of people,
by sword, hunger, sickness
and all their bones fell into the lake,
the water of floating gardens.

So drill into the sediment
and this is what you'll find:
jade flute music, bamboo combs,
a woman's shy whisper,
small clay statues,
a woman giving birth

in a warm bath,
a hunchbacked old man
touching earth with the palms
of his hands
in his oath to the earth,
royal seals with jaguars,
and jugglers.

Drill deeper into the core:
these are the grasses,
teosinte, Gramineae, Zea mays,
maize, corn;
20,000 years ago the seeds
inherited the hands of women.
They cultivated the shaggy heads,
the sacred ears, so that humans
became the same flesh.

6500 B.C.
They sifted soil over Mexica
and gave corn a family;
maize,
beans,
squash.

Maize journeyed to Ontario, Canada,
Before 1200 A.D.
blue corn
yellow corn
white corn
black corn

Table #1
Corn: endosperm, germ, pericarp, tip cap
16% moisture (rain, sweat, prayers)
72% starch (sun, moon, finger prints)
10% protein (Indian flesh, Corn Mother, the Virgen of Guadalupe)
zinc: good for your immune system
iron: improves your blood, whether full-blood, mestizo, or Other
aluminum, phosphorus, potassium, boron: chant these minerals
like a prayer, with both hands folded over the earth

Blue corn: tortillas, piki (paper bread
you can write on with the hieroglyphics of your teeth),
chaqueque (cornmeal mush),

atole (cornmeal drink),
corn flakes, syrup,
chips for salsa,
muffins, popcorn,
pancakes,
polenta.

Table #2:
Set the plates the color of polished sun
for the three sisters

One loves to eat corn on the cob slathered with butter,
sprinkled with salt.
She props her elbows on the table, leans over the plate,
and grins, corn sticking between her teeth.

One loves to eat spoonfuls of yellow squash.
Later she takes the fried gourd and carves out a door
like the mouth of a woman surprised in a dark window
as a lover plays a jade flute
She hangs the gourd up in a willow,
so that the small brown birds nest
and sleep
warm in the belly of a sister.

And one loves to cook beans
as she sings away the day's complaints:
red, black, white, pinto, kidney, green,
lima, butter, navy, pole, frijole,
spotted, striped:
all snap like Nahuatl vowels

Set the table for the Corn Mother and her family: Alamo
Utton, Curry, Santa Ana, Taos,
Rose, Best, Average, Yellow, White,
Kinsman.

To prepare corn: Boil it in lime
(it dissolves flesh and bone)
and water ancient as language.
steep
overnight
while the moon is
an Aztec calendar
dividing centuries

into the green silk body
of the Virgen of Guadalupe,
her chocoatl sex,
her serpent-skirted hips,
her yellow teosinte heart.
in the morning,
take two dark reeds,
pounded into paper,
and using ink from beans,
write poems about maize,
then throw out
the liquid.

Rinse, discard
the splattered
blood of innocent
cracked kernels.

Drain, wash, drain.
Grind with stone
in a skull bowl.
Grind for 500 years
until the flour is fine
as Indian bones,
and shape into hands,
brown faces, virgins,
and mothers,
small icons of corn women
carrying bags of groceries
In Los Angeles, Guaymas,
Spokane, Portland, Seattle.

In her poem "Corn Mother," Native American (Yaqui) writer Anita Endrezze adds her voice to the polysemous conversation about this extraordinary yet controversial plant that has traveled far from its site of original domestication in Mesoamerica to become the most commonly grown grain in the world. In a journey of millennia that has transformed it from a sustainable subsistence crop to an industrial commodity, corn has taken over much of the landmass of the planet. However, its future is far from certain. The debates central to its continued cultivation—who will grow it, where, in what quantities, for whom, for what purpose and by what farming methods?—encompass key issues of environmental justice. These include indigenous self-determination, dislocation, cultural loss and revitalization, corporate globalization, health issues, genetically modified seeds, and ecological degradation. Furthermore,

more than two-thirds of world corn cultivation utilizes industrial techniques (Warman 2003, 203), and thus the crop is increasingly implicated as a contributor to climate change, since the agricultural sector of the world economy produces up to 13 percent of global greenhouse emissions, second only to the energy sector (World Resources Institute n.d.b).

The story of corn is made up of conflicting narratives told in myriad forms, from pre-Columbian Mesoamerican codices to Monsanto advertising, in government documents, scholarship, political manifestos, and in artistic and literary representations such as Endrezze's "Corn Mother." Narrative matters, because public debates and public policy are shaped by how issues are framed. An indigenous perspective views corn as a symbol of a culture and way of life that has withstood five hundred years of colonization. Conversely, modern agribusiness touts industrial corn as a crowning glory of technological development and scientific prowess. In this chapter, using "Corn Mother" as a map, we argue that the transformation of corn from an indigenous subsistence crop into an industrial commodity has resulted in social and environmental injustices that must be rectified as part of a vision for a just, democratic food system that is resilient and able to respond to the challenges of climate change.

"Corn Mother" opens in modern-day Mexico City, a metropolis of glass windows, office buildings, and congested traffic in the heart of Mesoamerica. The poem quickly delves beneath the surface in an imagined archaeological excavation recollecting the Aztec past. Mexico City was built by the Spanish over the ruins of the Aztec city of Tenochtitlan, on the shores of Lake Texcoco, which the conquistadores eventually drained and filled. Tenochtitlan, center of the Aztec Empire, the largest metropolis of preconquest America, a city of palaces, marketplaces, boulevards, and public gardens built around a series of interconnected lakes, fell to Spain in 1521.

Endrezze reminds us of what lies beneath the modern city: archaeological excavations continue to unearth human bones and artifacts revealing the complex lifestyle of Tenochtitlan. In a few precise and evocative images, Endrezze links past to present, connecting modern daydreaming cleaning women to the Aztec women of Tenochtitlan. Endrezze thus deftly sets the stage to explore the contrast, tension, and interplay between the indigenous and the colonizer, between differing epistemologies, and between tradition and modernity, that reveal the social injustice inherent in the history of corn.

In the fourth stanza, Endrezze introduces another character: the grasses "teosinte, Gramineae, Zea mays, maize, corn." Corn has "inherited the hands of women," she writes. Plant and human are equal participants in this story, and Endrezze establishes the intimate reciprocal relationship between the plant and the people who domesticated it, thus exemplifying Michael Pollan's argument in *The Botany of Desire*: plants and humans engage in a coevolutionary process of mutual impact. We domesticate plants to suit our purposes but fail to recognize that plants also get us to behave in ways that suit their evolutionary bidding. Corn has cleverly mobilized humans to disseminate it as widely as possible, leading to its position of predominance as the largest grain crop in the world, more than a billion tons in 2014–2015 (Food and Agriculture Organization of the United Nations 2015). Wherever corn was introduced, it has played a role in transforming ecology, culture, and economy. This transformation in many cases has led to environmental injustice.

Endrezze's poem contains acute awareness of corn as a shaper of human culture as well as a major ecological player. It portrays corn as both agent and object, and this awareness invites an ecocritical reading of her words. Ecocriticism, a developing field within literary studies, in the words of Cheryl Glotfelty, the field's foundational voice, is described thus: "As a critical stance ... [ecocriticism] has one foot in literature and the other on land; as a theoretical discourse, it negotiates between the human and the nonhuman" (Glotfelty and Fromm 1996, xix). For Glotfelty, literature does not "float above the material world in some aesthetic ether, but, rather, plays a part in an immensely complex global system, in which energy, matter, and ideas interact" (Glotfelty and Fromm 1996, xix). Glotfelty argues that literature and the study of imaginative works of art contribute to environmental thinking in areas of "value, meaning, tradition, point of view, and language" (Glotfelty and Fromm 1996, xix). "Corn Mother," which links corn's long history with its current abundant but degraded state and draws attention to the problems of industrial corn production, is an example of Glotfelty's argument that literature has a role within environmental justice movements. And while "Corn Mother" does not directly reveal what its author envisions for corn's future, an attentive reading of Endrezze's words and images lead us to ask how we might advocate for a just and secure future for corn and its cultivators. Endrezze, by asking us to examine the past, when corn and humans were bound by intricate kin relationships, implicitly asks us to imagine the future and to envision ways to restore and rebalance the reciprocal relationship that existed between corn and humans.

I. INDIGENOUS CORN (CORN MOTHER)

Endrezze's poem first identifies corn as mother, invoking the Mayan creation story in which humans are actually shaped from corn dough, which they viewed as the best building material after attempts using mud and wood failed. It can certainly be said that corn is born of humans since, unlike most grains, it cannot grow wild and cannot exist without deliberate and attentive intervention, as cultivation requires humans to separate the grains from the cob for dispersal. The reciprocal relationship between humans and plants is particularly evident in the case of corn. In Zapotec Science, anthropologist Roberto Gonzalez argues that corn domestication, propagation, and improvement required such an extremely sophisticated level of farming knowledge and human intervention that it can be considered the most remarkable plant breeding accomplishment of all history (2001, 1).

Indigenous peoples across the variety of landscapes and climatic zones developed varieties of corn that were adapted to a wide diversity of ecoregions ranging from wetlands to deserts to tropical rainforests to high altitude plains. Though the history of corn domestication is still uncertain, evidence points to Oaxaca, Mexico, as the region where corn was first cultivated approximately six thousand years ago (Benz 2001, 2105). By the time of contact between Europe and the Americas, corn had traveled some 3,500 miles in either direction from its place of origin, from southern Ontario in the north to the Los Rios region of Chile in the south (Warman 2003, 25).

Indigenous peoples long ago mastered the art of growing local, often in less-than-hospitable terrain but with a sophisticated understanding of plants, land, and soil. The Maya people of the subtropics adopted techniques that allowed for clear-cutting and slash-and-burn farming to fertilize the soil with nutrients like phosphorus from the ash. In swampy lowland areas of the Yucatán, the Maya addressed the challenges of seasonal flooding, low soil fertility, and highwater tables by developing a system of raised fields and canals. Maya farmers dug canals through swamps, piling excess soil onto their fields, raising them by two to four feet to reduce waterlogging. Canals provided irrigation and natural fertilizer. The Maya harvested water plants from the canals and spread them on the fields to further enrich the soil. Irrigation and fertilizing resulted in an extended growing season for crops (Baker 2003, chapter 7, chapter 9). Hopi and Zuni desert farmers perfected dry farming techniques, cultivating species of corn and beans suitable to their parched desert landscapes. Despite twelve inches or less of average yearly rainfall, the Hopi managed to endure and thrive by developing a farming system totally dependent on natural precipitation, through wide spacing and proven depths of planting (Salmon 2012, chapter 4).

Mesoamerican farmers developed the milpa—small fields where corn is the central plant but squash and beans, avocados, tomatoes, chilis, sweet potatoes, jicama, amaranth, and a variety of greens are also included. The milpa mimics nature: companion plantings avoid the soil degradation so common in industrial monocultures, and the plants are environmentally and nutritionally complementary. The milpa is exceptionally sustainable as there are places in Mesoamerica that have been continually cultivated for four thousand years and are still producing (Mann 2005, 199). The biodiversity of the milpa shows an understanding of corn's nutritional value as well as what it lacks: the amino acids lysine and tryptophan, which the body needs to make proteins and niacin. Adding beans to a corn-based diet provides the missing amino acids (Gonzalez 2001, chapter 1, 238).

The milpa is also a sociocultural construct, involving complex interactions and relationships between farmers, crops, and land. As R. Nigh notes in his study of the Maya in the Mexican state of Chiapas, "the making of *milpa* is the central, most sacred act, one which binds together the family, the community, the universe.... [It] forms the core institution of Indian society in Mesoamerica, and its religious and social importance often appear to exceed its nutritional and economic importance" (1976, n.p.).

The original domestication of corn by indigenous famers throughout the Americas resulted in a hugely diverse cultivated plant. The hundreds of varieties of corn that have appeared over nine thousand years of history are a combination of the corn plant's own natural changeability as well as early farmers' willingness to observe and attend to these variations when selecting corn suited local diets as well as local landscapes. Corn allowed the diverse and complex cultures of Mesoamerica, including the Maya, Aztec, Toltec, Zapotec, and Mixtec and Olmec, to thrive. People lived by and for corn, which was integral to all aspects of life from basic subsistence to religion and mythology.

Traditional indigenous cultivation is what Arturo Warman (2003, 203) identifies as one of the two main modes of corn production. The other is the modern industrial mode, and as Warman (2003, 203) argues, these two categories of production have clearly different purposes for growing corn and are based on distinct underlying economic premises. Based on this classification, indigenous corn represents "farming by the poor" while industrial corn is "production by the wealthy" (Warman 2003, 203).

In the opening stanzas of "Corn Mother" Endrezze celebrates the intimate relationship between corn and its indigenous domesticators. However, in the seventh stanza of her poem, her language shifts abruptly in tone and substance. The flowing compound sentences that describe corn's origins and journey throughout the Americas transform into the short staccato of a scientific table that pulls corn apart into its nutritional components. In this dichotomous story, Endrezze now turns her eye to the industrial production of corn. This process began when settlers and colonizers in what is now the United States recognized corn's importance and the suitability of Midwestern soil for growing it. The two-hundred-year process that has followed has converted the native prairies of the region into the "Corn Belt" and has changed corn from food crop to commodity.

II. INDUSTRIAL CORN (KING CORN)

The importance of corn as a crop is clear in any analysis of the food crops that currently feed the world. There are eighty thousand edible plants in the world (Füleky 2016), of which humans have domesticated seven thousand species (Action Group on Erosion, Technology, and Concentration 2017, 19). However, we only actively cultivate some 150 species, and of these, only 4 plants (corn, wheat, rice, and potato) provide half our food calories (Füleky 2016). Though the production values of the three grains are similar (Füleky 2016), unlike rice and wheat, much of the corn harvest is not directly consumed as a human food source. Just looking at U.S. corn values as an example, the National Corn Growers Association (2018, 6) indicates that the two primary uses of corn are as an ingredient in livestock feed (46 percent) and to produce fuel ethanol (30 percent). In the United States today, more than 90 million acres are reserved for corn planting, with an annual harvest of 82.7 million acres. In 2017 the U.S. corn crop yielded 14.6 billion bushels, accounted for 35.5 percent of the world's corn exports, and was worth about $47.5 billion (United States Department of Agriculture Economic Research Service n.d.). But it was not always this way.

Warman (2003, 26) points out that prior to settlement of the prairies by European farmers, the Native people of the Great Plains were primarily hunters, and the region was a marginal corn producer. Technological developments facilitated the industrial scale of corn agriculture in the American Midwest by reframing a relationship between people, plants, and land to a relationship between people and technology. The invention of the steel plow in 1838, and the subsequent invention of the mechanized harvester, the tractor, and other farm implements such as disks and scrapers, changed farming and put the prairie ecosystem on the path to extinction, setting the stage for industrial corn that dominates the landscape in the present.

Traditional indigenous corn production systems are place-based and diverse. Despite the widespread proliferation of industrial agriculture, indigenous and peasant farming practices endure, still feeding 70 percent of the world population (Action Group on Erosion, Technology, and Concentration 2017, 12–14) on 25 percent of agricultural land (GRAIN 2014, 3). Most noteworthy, peasant farmers grow this food using only 10 percent of agriculture's share of fossil fuels. Indigenous and peasant corn farming uses three times less energy than is used to grow industrial corn (Action Group on Erosion, Technology, and Concentration 2017, 35). So, corn cultivation per se is not the cause of problems, but rather, it is specifically the industrial mode of corn production and the industrial use of the corn harvest that are implicated in a variety of social, health, and environmental concerns (Action Group on

Erosion, Technology, and Concentration 2017, 6–47; Wallinga 2009, 258–64; Tegtmeier and Duffy 2004, 4–14). Among these, significantly, is the fact that both the industrial methods of cultivating corn and the industrial uses of the harvest have a significant carbon footprint that contribute to climate change. With the increasing complexity of agricultural machinery, the fuel source changed from renewable food calories (to feed animal and human labor) to nonrenewable fossil fuel calories (to feed the tractors and combines). Today fossil fuels are the basis of the entire agriculture enterprise, providing ingredients and energy to produce the chemical fertilizers and pesticides that are used in corn cultivation. They are the energy source used to dry corn before storage; transport the grain to silos, processing facilities, and markets; and to process the corn kernel into a range of nonfood commodities (Center for Sustainable Systems 2017b). The environmental consequences of relying on fossil fuels range from habitat destruction in mining or drilling sites to water pollution from mining and drilling operations or oceanic transport of oil (Union of Concerned Scientists n.d.). But arguably the atmosphere carries the major brunt of the costs associated with the combustion of fossil fuels (Wallinga 2009, 262–63; Tegtmeier and Duffy 2004, 4–5, 9–10; Working Group I 2013, chapter 6).

As Midwest farmers embraced industrial corn production, they abandoned age-old practices such as crop rotation and fallowing and focused instead on maximizing yields through vast acreages of corn monocultures. This meant that they increasingly relied on chemicals to support crop production. According to the Institution for Mechanical Engineers (2013,13), between 1961 and 1999, use of synthetic nitrogen-based fertilizers increased by 638 percent. Crop yields increased for a while, but eventually the chemical sparkle fizzled, and there has been fallout, such as the well-documented example of eutrophication, which leads to hypoxia and the creation of dead zones in coastal regions like the Gulf of Mexico and Chesapeake Bay (World Resources Institute n.d.a; Wallinga 2009, 258–59; Tegtmeier and Duffy 2004, 5–6). What may be less well known is that nitrogen-based fertilizers are a major contributor to the enhanced greenhouse effect due to nitrous oxide emissions (Working Group I 2013, 475–80).

The United States Energy Information Administration (2011, chapter 4) indicates that agriculture contributes 73 percent of U.S. nitrous oxide emissions, and similarly, in Canada, 77 percent of nitrous oxide emissions can be traced back to agriculture (Environment and Climate Change Canada 2018, 11). Corn in particular, because it is a high nitrogen user, contributes a significant amount of nitrous oxide emissions. In South African agriculture, cereal crops account for 73 percent of national total greenhouse gas (GHG) emissions from application of synthetic fertilizer, and corn accounts for 85 percent of this total (Tongwane et al. 2016, 30). But much of this fertilizer use reflects inefficiency, and as Warman (2003, 205) explains, "There is an inverse relationship between amounts of fertilizer applied and rising yields." Evidence from the U.S. Corn Belt supports this claim, for when first applied, each pound of fertilizer produced an additional twenty-four pounds of grain. However, each subsequent fertilizer application reduced the yield gains until by the fifth fertilizer application the yield gain was less than a pound (Warman 2003, 205–6).

The on-farm emissions from nitrogen fertilizers are a result of volatilization of ammonia and oxides of nitrogen as well as the leaching of nitrate from the application of nitrogen fertilizers (Working Group I 2013, 475–80). Additional upstream GHG emissions occur during the production of these fertilizers. According to LeCompte (2013), globally, ammonia-based nitrogen fertilizer production facilities are responsible for 3 to 5 percent of carbon emissions, without even taking into account the production of natural gas, which is utilized as an ingredient in fertilizer production. Furthermore, LeCompte points out that in the United States alone, such fertilizer production facilities released twenty-five million tons of mostly carbon dioxide (ibid.). Producing and field-applying nitrogen fertilizers use more fossil fuels, on average sixty liters per hectare (Institution for Mechanical Engineers 2013, 13). A 2008 FAO Report (Tenkorang and Lowenberg-DeBoer 2008, 8) suggests that the demand for nitrogen-based fertilizers is expected to increase by some 34 percent to 137.4 million metric tons by 2030. In a more recent article, LeCompte (2013) suggests that this demand could further escalate and that production, especially in the United States, would likely ramp up to meet it due in part to the availability of cheap natural gas.

Another significant way that corn contributes to climate change is through the corn-ethanol link. To reduce GHG emissions, biofuels—with their promise of being carbon neutral—seem like a smart solution and currently some 30 percent of the U.S. corn harvest is used to produce ethanol (National Corn Growers Association 2018, 6). But not all biofuels are created equal, and this is the case with corn-based ethanol. A Duke University study (2009) shows that over a life-cycle analysis, corn-based ethanol only reduces GHG emissions by 20 percent when one liter of gasoline is substituted with one liter of ethanol. The study also finds that the GHG reduction may only be evident after several years of corn production, depending on what the prior land use of the cornfield was. Additionally, the study explains that the reason for this is that industrial corn farming can release 30 to 50 percent of the soil carbon as a result of land-use change. So if the field was initially an unfarmed conservation set-aside that was converted to corn production (a practice promoted by current U.S. federal government efforts to increase biofuel production), the result is an increase in carbon emissions for the first fifty years of corn cultivation for the purposes of producing ethanol (Duke University 2009).

The third link between corn and climate change is via livestock, as 46 percent of the U.S. corn harvest is routed as livestock feed (National Corn Growers Association 2018, 6). The carbon footprint of livestock, especially cattle, is well documented (Center for Sustainable Systems 2017a; Hamerschlag 2011, 5–8; Food and Agriculture Organization of the United Nations 2006b, chapter 3). But, as with the industrial versus indigenous models of corn cultivation, how livestock is raised does matter. It is hard to make a broad generalization about the differences in carbon footprints between pasture versus feedlot cattle, due in part to the geographical location of the cattle operation. For example, as Pelletier et al. (2010, 385) discovered in their comparative analysis of beef production systems, pasture-based operations in U.S. upper midwestern states require growing and harvesting hay for the winter, which carries a carbon footprint that would be absent in pasture operations in warmer climates. Furthermore, while an argument can be made that feedlot beef operations have more efficient feed conversion ratios (Food and Agriculture Organization of the United Nations 2006b, 113; Pelletier et al. 2010, 387–88), as Garnett (2010) argues, feedlot beef facilities "although highly efficient when defined on their own terms (i.e. emissions per kg of output), have nothing to offer in terms of soil efficiency, carbon sequestration, or biodiversity benefits and indeed cause multiple problems such as unsustainable water use, and air and water pollution." The potential for carbon sequestration in pasture soils is due to the high density of grass roots (which enable more underground carbon storage in soil rather than above-ground plant biomass) and lack of tillage (which means that there is minimal physical disturbance of the soil). While more extensive studies about the carbon sequestration of pasture lands in different geographic regions are needed (National Trust 2012, 12–13), according to work by Follett et al. (2001, chapter 16), some 29.5 to 110 million metric tons of carbon could be annually sequestered in grazing lands in the United States. The argument against converting grasslands to agriculture is further underscored when one grasps that total carbon emissions from all U.S. croplands are equivalent to about 1 percent of the soil carbon that is stored in the top four inches of grassland soils (Follett et al. 2001, chapter 3). Furthermore, given that pasture lands are often not suitable to intensive crop production, grass farmers increase food security by making use of marginal land to raise food (National Trust 2012, 3).

The American public is increasingly aware of the pitfalls of industrial corn production. As the popular documentary *Food Inc.*—which has become a staple of U.S. high school curricula—makes clear, the industrial production and consumption of corn creates and spreads illness, waste, and economic and ecological degradation within the United States. As these films and texts such as Michael Pollan's *The Omnivore's Dilemma* and *In Defense of Food* make clear, the high-fructose corn syrup diet of the average American results in overnutrition and illness, including epidemic proportions of childhood obesity. More than a quarter of the forty-five-thousand-odd items in American supermarkets contain corn (Pollan 2006, 19). And in the United States, most meat is also ultimately corn: chickens, turkeys, pigs, and even cows are forced into eating corn, as are, increasingly, carnivores such as salmon (ibid., 18). Corn has a particular carbon structure that can be traced in everything that consumes it. As University of California biologist Todd Dawson notes in a response to Pollan's Omnivore's Dilemma, "Stable isotope analysis of human hair reveals that corn has increased by some 10,000 percent in modern North American diets in just 50 years. We are corn walking" (2009).

We know the dangers of monocultures and the resulting loss of biodiversity (Faber, Rundquist, and Male 2012, 3–10). But we do not yet understand the impact of GMOs, though they pervade corn cultivation in the United States and are documented as having penetrated the landrace varieties of corn so carefully saved and developed by the subsistence agriculture of indigenous Mesoamerica. The introduction of transgenics, should these genes persist, potentially impacts on the genetic diversity and the evolutionary future of corn in its region of origin. The diversity of landraces is of particular import-ance for global food security (Quist and Chapela 2001, 541). And yet, as the playful title of the documentary King Corn suggests, despite our increasing awareness of the folly of our current corn cultivation practices, the crop rules U.S. agriculture and permeates our diets.

III. DIASPORIC CORN (NEOLIBERAL CORN)

In "Corn Mother" the language of science begins in the seventh stanza, but even as it intrudes into the poem, the indigenous origins of corn remain, an insistent voice calling for recognition, albeit in parentheses. The scientific measurement "16% moisture," for example, contrasts with "(rain, sweat, prayers)," invoking indigenous agricultural practices that understood envir-onmental limits, relied on human and animal traction rather than fossil fuels, and maintained a relationship of reverence with the plant. Thus the poem asserts the continued existence of indigenous corn despite the predominance of monocultured industrial corn in the United States and increasingly in Mexico. Through the interplay between indigenous voices and the language of modern science that continues throughout the rest of the poem, "Corn Mother" insists against the erasure and marginalization of the indigenous per-spective that today's corporate cultivation of corn tries to impose.

Current corn production in Mexico has been deeply impacted by trans-national neoliberal policies. In the 1980s the Mexican government began restructuring its economy in accordance with changes demanded by the World Bank, International Monetary Fund, and the U.S. government. These included "privatization of parastatal agencies; the rolling back of safety net programs; liberalization of trade rules and markets; privatization of communal landholdings through earlier agrarian reform programs; and ending tariffs on food imports and small farmer supports, including ending price guarantees on corn, the country's most fundamental subsistence crop" (Brown and Getz 2011, 138).

The North American Free Trade Agreement (NAFTA) of 1994 opened the Mexican market to corn imports from the United States, and small-scale producers could not compete with the cheaper industrial corn, generously subsidized by U.S. agricultural policy. Unable to continue cultivating, small-scale farmers, many of them indigenous, left their land and found jobs in factories in Mexican cities or went to the United States, where many displaced farmers went to work for U.S. agribusiness. By 2002, at least 1.3 million jobs in the Mexican agricultural sector had been lost (Brown and Getz 2011,139). These small-scale producers had been responsible for 25 percent of corn production in Mexico (Barry 1995, 101). Mexico had actually achieved food self-sufficiency in the twentieth century, in great part due to postrevolution land reform that redistributed half of all arable land to peasants, but in the aftermath of NAFTA, Mexico began to import its food, most notably, and of disastrous consequences, its staple crop, corn (Barkin 2006). USDA statistics bear witness to the drastic increase in imports of U.S. corn in the years following NAFTA. In 1993, one year before its implementation, Mexico imported 1,691 MT (metric tons) of corn from the United States. By 2016, that number had gone up to 14,569 MT (IndexMundi n.d.).

In her study of the struggles over transgenic corn in Mexico, Elizabeth Fitting notes that the neoliberal corn regime policies favor "conventional capital-intensive agriculture and the exports of fruits and vegetables to Canada and the United States." In this regime, "maize agriculture, rural development and food security are reduced to questions of profit and market efficiency" (2011, 4). Yet, Fitting notes, small producers have other reasons for growing their crops, other goals and other types of knowledge, which are discounted (2011, 4). David Barkin writes that Mexico's leaders "no longer think twice when they declare it an error to continue cultivating maize in traditional ways; they insist that peasants are inefficient producers who should leave its cultivation to modern producers, capable of eking out much more from each hectare" (2006, 74). Mexican policy began pushing for a shift to irrigated corn from traditional rainfed corn farming and then privileged water rights for high-yield varieties of corn for export. So while in some cases corn production did actually increase, it was not by or for peasant and indigenous farmers and communities. Barkin summarizes the full impact of these changes as financial (the costs of imported corn), a decline in diet quality, damage to ecosystems by mono-cropping, and a sizeable fall in the prices of principal crops grown by peasants (2006, 74).

There are emerging implications for food security in Mexico. These include threats to corn diversity, increasing reliance on imports of the yellow corn that in the United States is intended for cattle rather than human consumption, and changes in diet that have led to greater consumption of industrial foods, including many that are sweetened using high-fructose corn syrup, thus increasing obesity and obesity-related health problems. Furthermore, in rural areas, many people prefer local white corn to imported yellow but are confronted with higher prices for local corn, making it unaffordable (Clark et al. 2012; Mendoza-Cano 2016).

Clark et al. note post-NAFTA changes in food production and consumption, including an increase in soft drinks, snack foods, processed dairy products, and chicken that had been fed with imported yellow corn and soy (2012, 62). They conclude that U.S. food and agricultural exports are "one important way in which U.S. agriculture and trade policy influences Mexico's food system. Because of significant U.S. agribusiness investment in Mexico across the full spectrum of the latter's food supply chain, from production and processing to distribution and retail, the Mexican food system increasingly looks like the industrialized food system of the United States" (2012, abstract). There have also been significant social and cultural impacts as villages became depopulated and family and community structures were fractured by the departure of large numbers of working age men (and increasingly women) (Levine 2011, 35–38).

But neoliberal corn has not actually succeeded in eliminating indigenous corn. In Mexico, corn cultivation by small-scale producers for community sustenance has not disappeared, and surprisingly in spite of predictions, post-NAFTA cultivation of the traditional white corn for local consumption continues (Barkin 2006; Fitting 2010). Barkin reports local efforts throughout rural Mexico, where "the staunch struggle of large parts of its peasantry to continue cultivating maize in spite of a hostile political environment is stark testimony to the complexity of the transitions that the country is enduring" (2006, 74).

The most significant strategy small-scale farmers employ to continue production has been to subsidize farming practices with remittances sent by displaced community members who have immigrated to the United States (Barkin 2006). Those remittances continue to grow, totaling $26.1 billion from January to November 2017, the highest amount ever recorded according to figures released by the Central Bank of Mexico (Gillespie 2018). Elizabeth Fitting, however, in her 2010 study of corn production in the Tehuacan Valley in the state of Puebla (the "Cradle of Corn") warns that nonetheless, the broad migration of youth from villages also results in a disruption in the transmission of knowledge, which does not bode well for raising the next generation of corn farmers (230).

This exodus of Mesoamerican farmers is an integral part of "Corn Mother." The displaced farmers appear in the poem, now having crossed into the United States. They have been transported to the north as part of Endrezze's five-hundred-year "recipe" for preparing corn, really a recipe for colonization. "Boil it in lime," she writes, evoking the ancient practice of nixtamalization (mixing corn with calcium hydroxide for nutritional value). "Steep the corn" in "an Aztec calendar dividing centuries." The liquid, rinsed, discarded, contains the "splattered blood of innocent cracked kernels. ... Grind for 500 years until the flour is fine as Indian bones." This flour that is shaped into:

> Brown faces, virgins,
> And mothers,
> Small icons of corn women
> Carrying bags of groceries
> In Los Angeles, Guaymas,
> Spokane, Portland, Seattle.

These final lines of "Corn Mother" leave us with the image of small, brown women walking the map of the western coast of the United States, from Los Angeles to Seattle, feeding their families not by growing corn but rather by shopping for groceries. They are the dislocated indigenous farmers who have had to find a new niche in the global economy. Perhaps ironically, they are walking the very map of one of the major precolonial indigenous trade routes that followed the long stretch of the Pacific Coast (Dunbar-Ortiz 2014, chapter 1). Five hundred years later, those corn women are Mexican and Central American immigrants, the migrant workers, the itinerant. Shopping in U.S. grocery stores, these corn mothers carry corn in their grocery bags: the refined, industrial, GMO corn that dominates in the American diet. In fact, probably the bags themselves are made out of this corn.

But it is important to see these corn mothers as more than victims. They carry with them the literal seeds as well as the cultural practices that can guide us toward a better future for corn and its cultivators. Their wisdom and tenacity in the face of disruption and dislocation merit careful attention. An example of this can be found in a study by anthropologists Teresa M. Mares and Devon G. Peña (2011) of immigrant and diasporic indigenous communities in Los Angeles, which found that many of these corn farmers, caught in broad global forces that caused them to leave home, continue their cultivation practices in their new communities. The South Central Farmers, an urban farming group of 360 families that existed in Los Angeles from 1992 to 2006, cultivated fourteen acres in a semiabandoned industrial area of warehouses and wrecking yards. Families that included U.S.-born Chicana/os and displaced Mesoamericans of Mixtec, Nahua, Tojolobal, Triqui, Tzeltal, Seri, Yaqui, and Zapotec heritage worked together in a collective space, practicing Mesoamerican agroecology in the middle of a modern urban center. Farmers planted seeds (corn, squash, and beans) that they had brought with them from their Mesoamerican homes, seeds that could be traced back at least five thousand years.

Farming practices at South Central were collective and democratic. Mares and Peña write, "By asserting autonomy over their own food systems through cultivating foods they ate in Mexico, the South Central Farmers preserved both heirloom crop varieties and their own cultural identities" (2011, 208). Beyond producing food, the South Central Farmers example also shows, as Mares and Peña point out, the "production of meaning" (2011, 209). This was evident in the *pochote* trees planted at the farm site. A sacred tree to Mesoamerican peoples, it became a gathering spot where children heard stories told to them by elders. One young Nahua woman stated, "Without our gathering under these trees, the garden cannot be happy. The corn needs the pochote tree to be happy so the corn silk will not wither. Our children learn the ways of our people by making this tree part of their place in the world" (2011, 209). Thus, their "cultivation is tied to a deep sense of place and community identity" (ibid.).

Mares and Peña note that in fact any community in the United States is actually located in a place that once had a deeply rooted, historic native foodway, most of which have been severely weakened or forced to disappear. This point is also made in a 2017 report commissioned by the Seeds of Native Health, a campaign of the Shakopee Mdewakanton Sioux Community to study the impact of the 2018 U.S. Farm Bill on Native Americans. Farm policy in what is now the United States historically worked against these foodways, first by policies that facilitated homesteading and settling on indigenous land and then by "teaching" indigenous people to farm. Policymakers were unable to see that indigenous people had already been "deeply involved in complex agricultural systems … domesticating a wide variety of crops used for feeding our communities and families" (Simms Hipp and Duren 2017, 9). Attempts to impose farming practices familiar to settlers onto indigenous people "led not only to the loss of our rights to be at home on our own traditional lands, but to feeding our people in food systems which had supported us for centuries" (Simms Hipps and Duren 2017, 9). Indigenous people in the United States were disconnected from their own food systems, denied their right and ability to feed themselves, all amounting to a loss of self-determination and self-governance. As Kyle Powys Whyte notes, "violations of food sovereignty are one strategy of colonial societies, such as U.S. settler colonialism, to undermine Indigenous collective continuance in Indigenous people's own homelands" (Whyte 2018, 347).

The increasing obstacles that the neoliberal economic regime imposes on indigenous Mesoamerican corn cultivation is a threat to the collective continuance of indigenous lifestyles and cultures. This threat can be traced historically to the initial European colonization of the region, with the resulting displacement and dispossession continuing to the present. Furthermore, climate change has only intensified this process, as is evident, for example, in the case of Mexico, where already arid and semiarid areas have experienced decreasing precipitation over the past few decades, a trend predicted to worsen (Council on Hemispheric Affairs 2010). This has resulted, according to a UN report based on Mexican government data, in approximately nine hundred thousand people leaving these areas every year since the mid 1990s because they can no longer sustain a living from the land (ibid.). It is here, in the midst of this dislocation, that Endrezze's "Corn Mother" leaves readers. The poem presents a story of injustice but at the same time highlights a history of a more harmonious relationship between food and humans. It is up to readers to not only contemplate the injustice the poem presents but to also consider what alternatives to this story might be possible.

IV. FOOD JUSTICE CORN (DEMOCRATIC CORN)

The current global food system is profit-driven, antidemocratic, and environmentally destructive. The system features overproduction, corporate concentration, unregulated markets and monopolies, monocultures, GMOs, agrofuels, mass global consumption of industrial food, and the phasing out of peasant and family agriculture and local retail (Holt-Giménez 2011, 322–23). The consequences of this model are dire, and nowhere are they more evident than through the careful examination of how this system has impacted on corn cultivation for producers, consumers, and the environment.

As described earlier, industrial corn is implicated in contributing to climate change as a consequence of the heavy reliance on fossil fuels at every step of production, the heavy use of nitrogen-based fertilizers, the conversion of unfarmed conservation set-asides for corn grown for biofuels, and the predominant use of corn as livestock feed or to produce biofuels. But not only does corn contribute to climate change; it is likely that climate change is already affecting corn yields, and the situation could be further exacerbated in the future.

David Lobell and his team from Stanford's Center on Food Security and the Environment analyzed real-time corn production data, in conjunction with daily weather data, for farm fields in the U.S. Midwest. The goal was to look at how crop yields were affected by various stressors and particularly to assess drought sensitivity. Lobell's team discovered that while corn yields improved as a result of the use of no- or low-till systems and advances in genetics that allowed farmers to sow corn more densely, the drought sensitivity in these fields also increased over the last eighteen years. This is likely a consequence of both the increased sowing density, which imposes higher stress on the plants in times of drought, and the fact that the corn seeds have been bred for increased yield under ideal conditions (Lobell et al. 2014, 518–19). Current climate models indicate that, globally, corn yields are likely to decline by 7.4 percent for every degree Celsius rise in temperature (Zhao et al. 2017, 9327). But this research only analyzed the direct effect of rising temperatures and not the other, indirect effects of climate change, like water stress. According to Lobell (2014, 519), at the current rate of drought sensitivity, U.S. corn yields will be even more significantly impacted with declines of as much as 15 percent over the next fifty years. Lobell further notes that if drought sensitivity of corn plants continues to increase, the losses could amount to as much as 30 percent (ibid.).

Opposition to this unsustainable food system is multifaceted and increasing. The strongest opposition comes from the food sovereignty movement, which seeks to dismantle corporate agribusiness's monopoly power. The movement seeks parity, redistributive land reform, community rights to water and seed, regionally based food systems, democratization of the food system, sustainable livelihoods, protection from dumping and overproduction, and the revival of agroecologically managed peasant agriculture to distribute wealth and to cool the planet. Its members comprise food justice and rights-based movements, including the international Via Campesina and the International Planning Committee on Food Sovereignty. The movement considers locally sourced, sustainably produced, culturally appropriate, and democratically controlled food to be a human right (Holt-Giménez 2011, 322–23).

In fact, the most important lessons for establishing a just and democratic future for corn already exist and come from its history and the past practices of its original cultivators. Not only does "Corn Mother" affirm this history, but as a literary text it provides the imagination that we need to create an alternative narrative. To rectify the social and environmental injustices of corn production and build a resilient system that is able to respond to the challenges of climate change we propose the following five principles:

1. Embracing Diversity: In the modern industrial system, a lot of money is devoted to breeding very few crops. Commercial breeders actively cultivate 137 crop species, of which just sixteen account for 86 percent of the world's food production (Action Group on Erosion, Technology, and

Concentration 2017, 19). And just one crop, corn, receives 45 percent of all private research and development spending. The plant-breeding model in industrial agriculture is expensive, as a single genetically modified seed variety can cost $136 million to get to market. (Action Group on Erosion, Technology, and Concentration 2017, 19). Yet, as we have already discussed, there already exists a great diversity of seeds that can grow in a wide variety of conditions, for example, the corn variety developed long ago by the Hopi that can grow in desert conditions. This is a clear example of why protecting existing diversity in corn germplasm is so necessary for the future uncertainties that climate change may bring.

Indigenous corn cultivation valued diversity in seed (fifty-nine landraces of corn) and cropping systems (i.e., milpas). There is movement toward regaining both, evidenced by the growth of organizations that help farmers protect the diversity of corn seed sources, develop locally adapted seed varieties, and participate in the open exchange of seeds. These include CIMMYT (Centro Internacional por Mantenimiento de Maize y Trigo/International Maize and Wheat Improvement Center), which stores over twenty-eight thousand unique seed collections of maize and has provided 50 percent of the improved corn varieties grown in the global South (O'Leary, 2016.); Mother Seeds in Resistance, a "community-based effort to save the native corn of the indigenous Maya peoples of Chiapas" (Schools for Chiapas n.d.); the Maize Genetic Stock Center at the University of Illinois, which serves "the maize research community by collecting, maintaining, and distributing seeds of maize genetic stocks" (Maize Genetics Cooperation Stock Center n.d.); the Open Source Seed Initiative, which is "dedicated to maintaining fair and open access to plant genetic resources worldwide in order to ensure the availability of germplasm to farmers, gardeners, breeders, and communities of this and future generations" (Open Source Seed Initiative n.d.); and The Crop Trust,[1] which among other activities is dedicated to "carefully targeted project work to upgrade and build the capacity of key genebanks around the world" (The Crop Trust, n.d.). This movement recognizes that planning for corn cultivation in the face of climate change lies not just in ex situ seed storage but also requires ongoing *in situ* development of seeds to changing environments. While seed saving through storage is important, it is not sufficient for planning for the future. Environmental conditions change constantly and thus evolution of corn seeds must take place in accordance with actual changes taking place in the changing conditions of actual fields.

Small-scale agriculture can incorporate polyculture, a modern variation of Mesoamerican milpas and Iroquois Three-Sisters companion planting. Regardless of their scale, all farmers can adopt agroforestry, which means farming like an ecosystem, a form of biomimicry, by integrating trees into agricultural landscapes. Trees provide both products (fruit, nuts, oils, resins, latex, medicinal compounds, leaves for food, fodder for livestock, timber, and fuel wood) and essential ecological services (carbon sequestration, groundwater recharge, nitrogen fixation, shelter from wind erosion, and habitats for pollinators).

There must also be diversity in economic systems. Food activist Raj Patel asserts, "A truly democratic food system will need to rewrite the rules of the financial system. That can't happen without naming and confronting capitalism as the enemy of food sovereignty" (2011). Economist Prasannan Parthasarathi (2002) advocates for diversity of ownership, arguing for forms of collective/common ownership for which there are historical precedents in the South Indian practice of property as "share," among other historical examples. Common property would change our relationship to nature, bringing profound changes to how we grow food, and would coexist with individual property (ibid.).

2. Respecting Ecology: In the face of climate change, agriculture that is locally attuned to the environmental conditions is imperative. The necessary respect for ecology is exemplified by Climate Smart Agriculture (CSA), a holistic approach to agriculture defined by the Food and Agriculture Organization of the United Nations as a way to integrate sustainable development goals while simultaneously addressing food security challenges in the face of climate change. Food security and sustainable development are the primary goals of CSA, achievable by adopting three support systems: sustainable increase in agricultural productivity and incomes, adapting and building resilience to climate change, and climate mitigation by reducing agriculture's GHG contributions. CSA emphasizes maintaining ecosystem services and advocating for a landscape approach in which farms are "large enough to produce vital ecosystem services, but small enough to be managed by the people using the land which is producing those services" (Food and Agriculture Organization of the United Nations 2013, 41).

3. Growing Food (not commodities): National Corn Growers Association statistics indicate that less than 10 percent of the 2017 U.S. corn harvest was used as food, and of this only 1.4 percent goes to produce cereal. The remainder is used to produce high-fructose corn syrup (3.2 percent), other sweeteners (2.7 percent), starch (1.6 percent), and beverages (1 percent). The bulk of the corn harvest goes to animal feed (46.3 percent), fuel ethanol (30.1 percent), seed (0.2 percent), or is exported (13.5 percent) (2018, 6). This balance must change if agriculture seeks to feed people. As Patel writes, "Harvests remain strong, and people still go hungry. This

isn't because of population growth—there's enough produced to feed everyone on a Small Planet's diet. But the economics of crop production have increasingly left concerns about human eating in the dust" (2011).

4. Building Relationships: Growing corn as food must be accompanied by the building of relationships of reciprocity and respect. These have been the driving force for traditional indigenous corn cultivation over the millennia: reciprocity and respect between people and corn, between people and landscape, between farmers and seed, and between farmers and consumers. Food justice requires that all of these relationships thrive. Building relationships also means respecting the rights of existing communities and farmers. As Mexican author Armando Bartra writes, people must have "the right to not migrate—the right to stay home" (quoted in Fitting 2011, 5). That is, subsistence farmers and their communities should find it possible to continue their lifestyle in their traditional homelands regardless of whether that lifestyle meets the exigencies of the capitalist economy to produce profit.

5. Imagining Justice: In this chapter, we have used a literary text as a springboard for our discussion. As Glotfelty argues, literature uses language to raise questions of value and meaning. In *Global Appetites: American Power and the Literature of Food*, literary scholar Allison Carruth argues for the importance of literature in efforts to mobilize for food system change. Literary texts that examine the food system have the possibility to "shuttle between social and interpersonal registers and between symbolic and embodied expressions of power" (Carruth 2013, 5). Literature can shift from "macroscopic to intimate scales of representation that can provide an incisive lens on the interactions between local places and global markets that are so central to how communities and corporations produce, exchange and make use of food in the modern period" (ibid., 5–6).

The story that "Corn Mother" tells includes its historic journey from Mesoamerica to Ontario. However, the powerful forces of contemporary corporate globalization in our food systems are its dominant register, as the final images of the poem show us displaced corn mothers now dependent on U.S. supermarkets rather than their own milpas. But the poem is driven by an insistent struggle between visions for corn. This inner tension parallels a process that Carruth (2013) identifies in *Global Appetites*, for, as she notes, globalization also brings with it seeds of opposition to the very power imbalances it promotes. Accordingly, Carruth argues for the role of literature in envisioning a more just food system worldwide. The way we use language can provide the imaginative framework and material structures for the contemporary movement to re-localize food and reconnect producers and consumers ... imaginatively reconnecting farmers and eaters—cities and countrysides ... the literature of food shows us that the endgame of globalization may not be the freemarket that the US has underwritten for decades.... (R)ather it opens the possibility that the outcome of globalization may be a post capitalist system defined by interchanges between regional communities and the global networks that ... circulate the knowledge and resources that advance alternative food movements, from organic agriculture to urban farming. (ibid., 8)

Thus, we can view the final image of Endrezze's poem, while sad, as also hopeful. The displaced corn mothers of the poem are also the South Central Farmers who carry with them into their diaspora not only ancient heirloom seeds but also their patterns of organizing communities built around collective labor and democratic relationships. As Mares and Peña note, there is a "wealth of place-based agroecological ethnobotanical and gastronomical knowledge within Native communities in the US ... but also in diasporic and immigrant communities that have faced parallel histories of colonization, displacement and environmental racism" (2011, 201). Corn has, in fact, long connected the indigenous peoples of the Americas. All people interested in changing the food system have much to learn from indigenous practices, and Mares and Peña advocate for a "relocalization" and "alterNative" viewpoint to "create our own sovereign freedoms through direct organizing and community-based action" (2012, 216).

"Corn Mother" is an example of a literary text that is part of the imaginative framework and vision for a better and more just food future. Food—and the literature of food—provides us a lens through which we can begin to think like ecosystems and see ourselves connected to each other and the planet. And the corn mothers, the actual as well as the literary, show us the way.

NOTE

1. For more information about these organizations, see International Maize and Wheat Improvement Center, https://www.cimmyt.org/maize-from-mexico-to-the-world/\; Mother Seed in Resistance, http://www.schoolsforchiapas.org/advances/sustainable-agriculture/mother-seeds-resistance/; Maize Genetic Stock Center, http://maizecoop.cropsci.uiuc.edu/; Open Source Seed Initiative, https://osseeds.org/about/about/; and The Crop Trust, https://www.croptrust.org/our-work/supporting-crop-conservation/.

Chapter 9

Balancing Food Security and Ecological Resilience in the Age of the Anthropocene

Samantha Noll

Climate change increasingly impacts the resilience of ecosystems and agricultural production. On the one hand, changing weather patterns negatively affect crop yields and thus global food security. Indeed, we live in an age where more than one billion people are going hungry, and this number is expected to rise as climate-induced change continues to displace communities and thus separate them from their means of food production (Internal Displacement Monitoring Centre 2015). In this context, if one accepts a humancentric ethic, then the focus would be on addressing impacts to agricultural production, and thus food security (Borlaug 1997; Navin 2014). On the other hand, ecological resilience is also being impacted by climate change, as species go extinct or migrate due to fluctuating temperatures and shifting weather patterns. This reduction of resilience negatively impacts ecosystem services and the ability of the natural world to support life (Palmer and Larson 2014; Urban 2015). From an environmental holist perspective, then, one could argue that the ethical path would be to focus on reducing negative impacts to species and/or local ecosystems rather than increasing crop yields. Thus, there appears to be a tension between the prioritization of crop yields and the mitigation of ecosystem impacts. While this tension is well established in the agricultural literature (Kirschenmann 2010; Noll 2017a), climate change exacerbates the situation, as agricultural lands are stressed and climate-induced migrations increase already high demands for foodstuffs, thus bringing the conflict to the forefront (Macdonald et al. 2015; Food and Agriculture Organization of the United Nations 2017).

The aim of this chapter is to explore the tension between increasing crop yields and cultivating ecological resilience, in light of climate change, and to provide tools that may be helpful when making management decisions on the ground. Specifically, in the first section of the chapter I introduce readers to the growing problem of human and nonhuman, climate-induced migration and how migration impacts food security. After that, I go on to apply ethical theories prominent in food security (both utilitarian and rights-based) and environmental ethics to the conflict, illustrating how dominant theories fail to resolve the dispute. I end by arguing that insights coming from food sovereignty movements could help resolve the tension, as they challenge agricultural paradigms and provide a blueprint for cultivating ecological resilience, as well as food-crops, in the age of the Anthropocene.[1]

I. HUMAN MIGRATION AND FOOD SECURITY

While humans (and other species) have a long history of migration, climate change increasingly plays a role in population shifts (Gemenne 2012; Gregory 1991). In particular, "climate change impacts continue to be linked to environmental 'push' factors, such as extreme weather events and other slow-onset events," including but not limited to desertification, rising sea levels, and drought (Noll 2017a, 25; Gemenne 2012). For the last thirty years, these environmental push factors have been recognized as among the most troubling ramifications of shifting weather patterns. In fact, Mark Pullin went so far as to argue that "as overwhelming as these migrations (due to civil war and oppressive governments) have become to many destination states and countries, it is forecast that these will be minute to what might take place in the next fifty years due to climate change events" (2017a, 1). In addition, the International Displacement Monitoring Centre claimed that from 1990 to 2000, climate change-related events displaced approximately 22.5 million people (2015). Today the international community largely accepts the position that environmental-induced migration is one of the most problematic ethical issues of the twenty-first century.

Specifically, climate-induced migration is pressing because of its connection to human conflict and global hunger (United Nations High Commissioner for Refugees 2017). Since at least the 1980s, prolonged conflicts were linked to global hunger, as these can be understood as "extreme push factors," or events that forcibly displace people. Furthermore, slow-onset events (such as rising sea levels and desertification) and other climate shocks have been linked to human conflict (Food and Agriculture Organization of the United Nations 2017a). One could argue that climate change is linked to environmental push factors that are, in turn, related to an increase in conflict events and migrations, all of which connect to global hunger. More directly, the World Food Programme (2018a) argued that extreme weather events and "long-term and gradual climate risks" exacerbate the risk of malnutrition and hunger. With 702 million people living in extreme poverty (World Bank 2016) and

793 million people undernourished (Food and Agriculture Organization of the United Nations 2017b), even minor climate changes would cause an increase in hunger worldwide, especially in rural areas that bear the brunt of conflict, migration, and slow-onset events (Food and Agriculture Organization of the United Nations 2017a).

Environmental Effects and Migration

The above analysis primarily focuses on humans. However, the effects of climate-induced push factors are not limited to the human species. Indeed, there is a growing literature on nonhuman environmental migration (Urban 2015; Thomas et al. 2004; Tingley et al. 2009). Like us, other species respond to environmental "push" factors, including extreme weather events and other slow-onset events, by migrating to new areas (Angetter et al. 2011; Palmer and Larson 2014). Additionally, they respond to "pull" factors or features that entice individuals to migrate, such as an abundance of water, food, and/or habitat (Gemenne 2012). In ecology, "this is frequently described as species following their 'ecological niches' or 'climate niches,' which can approximately be defined as the identifiable limits of a species' range or the range in which a species can flourish" (Palmer and Larson 2014, 641). In contrast to annual migrations, climate-induced species migrations are caused by environmental shifts that are not part of (or disrupt) "seasonal" behavioral patterns. As can be seen today, a plethora of species are shifting their ranges in response to environmental push and pull factors (Botkin et al. 2007; Bellard et al. 2012).

Like climate-induced human migration, these movements are troubling as they are correlated with species loss. Environmental stress factors such as habitat destruction, the reduction of wildlife corridors, and food and water scarcities are pushing a wide range of species to the brink of extinction (Bellard et al. 2012; Noll 2017b; Food and Agriculture Organization of the United Nations 2016). In fact, "one influential review predicts that, depending on the rate and magnitude of planetary warming, up to 35% of the world's species could be on the path to climate-driven extinction" (Minteer and Collins 2010, 1801; cf. Thomas et al. 2004). More recently, Urban argued that "if we follow our current, business-as-usual . . . , climate change threatens one in six species (16%)" (2015, 571). While the numbers of extinctions could vary depending on contextual factors, even a relatively small reduction (especially of keystone species) could impact biodiversity levels (Botkin et al. 2007; Bellard et al. 2012; Palmer and Larson 2014) and thus ecosystem resilience. When stressed, ecological processes and structures are maintained by diverse species that perform overlapping and redundant functions (Peterson, Allen, and Holling 1998). As such, they reinforce ecological regeneration and renewal over a wide range of scales.

As biodiversity levels are reduced, ecological processes are thereby threatened, thus negatively impacting ecosystem services (Nelson et al. 2013). This reduction is problematic, as ecosystem benefits include "provisioning services (production of foods, fuels, fibers, water, genetic resources), cultural services (recreation, spiritual and aesthetic satisfaction, scientific information), and regulating services (controlling variability in production, pests and pathogens, environmental hazards, and many key environmental processes)" (Perrings 2010, 2). While this list includes a wide range of activities and services, it is important to note here that several could threaten the processes that agricultural practices are reliant upon (Nelson at al. 2013). A 2015 EPA report stated that climate changes are already negatively impacting our ability to raise food animals, grow crops, and catch fish using the same methods as those used historically (United States Environmental Protection Agency 2015, 1). In short, the loss of biodiversity impacts (1) ecological resilience and the (2) systems that food production is built upon. Beyond food production, as species go extinct or migrate due to fluctuating temperatures and shifting weather patterns, this reduction impacts the ability of the natural world to support life.

The above analysis illustrates how climate-induced migration could harm both human and animal communities.[2] Push and pull factors displace humans, increase instances of conflict, and exacerbate already high levels of global hunger (United Nations High Commissioner for Refugees 2017). Species migration, on the other hand, reduces the resilience of the ecosystems that we rely on for a wide range of services, from cultural to provisioning benefits (Perrings et al. 2010). In this context, it may be difficult to determine priorities, as one weighs the importance of increasing crop yields in order to help ensure food security, against the mitigation of harms to migrating nonhuman species, biodiversity levels, and ecosystems.

With approximately 702 million people living in extreme poverty and 793 million people undernourished, it is relatively easy to accept the position that we need to increase crop yields in order to "feed the world." In fact, according to Marion Guillou, the chief executive of France's National Institute for Agricultural Research, agricultural researchers are mobilized and working to address global hunger by strengthening the productivity of farms, reducing waste, and genetically engineering crops to thrive in changing conditions (Butler 2010). Additionally, Norman Borlaug (1997), the father of the Green Revolution, argued that "in the not too distant future … I predict that many environmentalists will embrace GMOs (and other industrial technologies) as a powerful 'natural' tool to achieve greater environmental protection" and sustainably produce enough food to feed a growing population

(3). These strategies primarily focus on increasing the productivity of land already in production (through the modification of crops or methods of production), while simultaneously better utilizing the food we produce. In the context of agri-food systems, "resilience" is often defined as "maintaining production of sufficient and nutritious food in the face of chronic and acute environmental perturbations" (Bullock et al. 2017, 880).

In contrast, other scholars focus on protecting and/or improving contributions from ecosystem processes and supporting systems, as they are crucial for ensuring the sustainability of food supplies and ecosystem resilience (Bizikova et al. 2016; Chapin 2009). Both providing support to local small-scale farmers (de Bres 2017) and organic production methods (Barnhill et al. 2017) are seen as potential ways to achieve these goals and, thus, to limit negative impacts of agricultural production.[3] The argument is usually constructed as follows: Local food is better for the environment. Therefore, we must "buy local" (de Bres 2017). However, by design, local food systems are often less productive than conventional agriculture, as farmers tend to utilize smaller parcels, especially in urban and suburban areas. This leads supporters of industrial agriculture to draw the conclusion that increasing production to "feed the world" should not be prioritized. Indeed, Fred Kirschenmann (2010) goes so far as to question whether or not feeding the world is the right question, as what we feed the world, how long we can feed the world, and in what context we can feed the world are important factors that also need to be weighed.

Thus there appears to be a tension between increasing yields and supporting ecological resilience. With climate change exacerbating the situation, as agricultural lands are stressed and climate-induced migrations expand demands for foodstuffs, addressing this conflict becomes ever more imperative. The next section of this chapter identifies and explores ethical frameworks guiding the above discussions. Specifically, it provides a detailed analysis of ethical theories' guiding arguments for (1) increasing food security, (2) prioritizing the reduction of environmental impacts, and (3) mitigating animal and/or species loss. While this third position was not explicitly discussed above, impacts to nonhuman others often factor into larger environmental arguments. Yet, as we will see, they are built on markedly distinct ethical foundations. This analysis will also illustrate how (1) proponents of each approach would potentially address the above conflict and (2) the application of dominant theories fails to resolve the dispute. The analysis could prove useful, as producers, policymakers, and other stakeholders determine if they should prioritize food production or ecological resilience. However, before providing a detailed analysis of the values motivating food security arguments, it is imperative to define our terms, or what is meant by food security.

II. FOOD SECURITY AND AN ANALYSIS
OF KEY ETHICAL FRAMEWORKS

The term "food security" was originally coined during international policy and development discussions that occurred during the 1970s (Maxwell 1996). The initial definition primarily focused on food supply, or the ability for people to access resource bundles at stable prices in both national and international contexts. For example, the 1975 World Food Conference report states that food security is the "availability at all times of adequate world food supplies of basic foodstuffs to sustain a steady expansion of food consumption and to offset fluctuations in production and prices" (Maxwell 1996, 156). During the 1980s, the definition expanded to include access at the household and individual level (World Bank 1986), as well as temporal and contextual dynamics of food insecurity (Food and Agriculture Organization of the United Nations 2006a). By the 1996 World Food Summit, food security encompassed a wide range of issues concerning food access, availability, utilization, stability, and risk management, among others. As this brief sketch illustrates, international communities gradually moved away from the position that food insecurity is an issue of crop failure and, instead, began to adopt a more nuanced understanding where obtaining food is dependent on a wide range of social and political forces (Food and Agriculture Organization of the United Nations 2006a; Devereux 2006).

This developmental trend continued, as policymakers and development ethicists turned their attention to the human rights dimension of food security. While the "right to food" is not new, as it was first discussed in 1948 (in the UN Declaration of Human Rights), a rights-based approach came to prominence in the 1990s. Specifically, "in 1996, the formal adoption of the Right to Adequate Food marked a milestone achievement by World Food Summit delegates" (Food and Agriculture Organization of the United Nations 2006a). Today over forty countries recognize their citizens' right to food and, in 2004, the Food and Agriculture Organization of the United Nations (FAO) put together an international working group with the goal of providing a set of guidelines to realize the right to food in the wider context of national food security policy. Thus it appears that there are at least two distinct positions taken up during food security discussions: one that focuses on issues of distribution (access, availability, price stability, etc.) and another that highlights individuals' right to food.

When placed in this context, it is not surprising that scholars adopted the position that solving problems associated with food security is "not only a technical challenge but also a problem of fundamental ethical values and political will" (Lopez-Gunn et al. 2012). In fact, Lopez-Gunn et al. (2012)

have gone so far as to argue that wider utilitarian concerns, or those aimed at utilizing scarce resources so as to bring about the greatest good for the greatest number, need to be balanced with "intangible values." Two prominent ethical frameworks they identified and highlighted are utilitarianism and the rights tradition. Interestingly, they intentionally collapse rights-based concerns with issues of just distribution, and label both utilitarian. While moral considerability certainly plays a role in larger utilitarian-based ethics, both utilitarian and rights-based ethics are unique ethical positions that sometimes provide conflicting recommendations (Rachels and Rachels 2012). Thus, our analysis of the ethical frameworks guiding food security initiatives should include an overview of both.

Utilitarianism and the Rights Tradition

In his analysis of agricultural policy, Thompson argues that utilitarian-based arguments in this context include "the doctrine of allocative efficiency as the norm for effective resolution of conflicts" (1996, 194). This doctrine combines "the a) utilitarian maxim ('right' action is the one that produces the greatest good for the greatest number) and b) the allocative efficiency mandate (that resources should be distributed so that their utility is maximized) in order to bring about the just distribution of goods" (Noll 2017a, 25; cf. Anderson and Leal 1991). For those espousing a utilitarian position, the good of the many outweighs impacts to the few. Thus, for a utilitarian, rights play a limited role in decisions. Instead, the most effective use of resources takes priority.

For example, from this position, one could argue that (1) minimizing food waste (to improve current utility) and (2) increasing yields (to improve future utility) would benefit the greatest number and thus is the ethical thing to do. Arguments defending industrial methods of production (to increase the productivity of farmland) often include a utilitarian component (Thompson and Noll 2015). For example, Norman Borlaug takes it for granted that it is ethically imperative to develop agricultural technologies that could feed "a world of ten billion people" and growing (1997, 4). In this way, utilitarianism at least partially guides those working to achieve food security.

However, food security initiatives can and are also guided by a rights-based ethic. As discussed above, food security is achieved "when all people at all times have physical, social and economic access to sufficient, safe and nutritious food to meet their dietary needs and food preferences for an active and healthy life" (FAO 2002). While this at least implicitly includes the utilitarian goal of maximizing the distribution of resources so as to ensure that all humans have access to food, it is also often framed as a "right to food" or "freedom from want" in global development literature (Lopez-Gunn et al.

2012). According to Lopez-Gunn et al. (2012), "a rights-based approach to development starts from the premise or 'signal' for all global actors of the need to secure the human right to water and sanitation, and the human right to food" (89). This shift moves the ethical conversation beyond the mere distribution of goods. Instead, it is built on a different ethical foundation grounded in the intrinsic value of humans, which entails both direct and indirect duties (Korsgaard 2014). As Beauchamp (2014) argues, while utilitarianism places ethical importance on mental states (such as desires, pleasures, and pains), rights-based approaches value the human themselves. As such, human rights are not tradable and cannot be violated in the name of distribution to benefit the greatest number.

Environmental Ethics

Thus, while food security policies utilize both utilitarian and rights frameworks (Lopez-Gunn 2012), they could provide fundamentally incompatible recommendations. With this being said, however, as food security largely concerns the availability of resources and who has access to these resources, it is understandable that the guiding ethical frameworks in food security are those that can be used to determine what constitutes the just distribution of resources (utilitarianism) and what positive and/or negative duties should guide this distribution (rights approaches). This discussion predominately limits its scope to impacts on humans, as it focuses on food-access or human entitlements to commodity bundles (Devereux 2001). However, philosophers continue to make strong arguments for placing ecosystems, individual animals, and/or entire species into the moral sphere (Norton 1991). For example, deep ecologists, such as Arne Naess (1973), and ecofeminists, such as Karen Warren (2000), support the position that the natural world does not exist solely for the use of humans but has intrinsic value (Norton 1991).

This difference illuminates a larger tension between humancentric concerns and what Lopez-Gunn et al. (2012) call "intangible values," or larger environmental impacts that arise when trying to ensure food security. As Aiken argues, "since agriculture causes environmental damage as a result of growing food to feed people, there seems to be a still to be resolved conflict between human needs and environmental integrity" (1984, 24). Similarly, Vaux (2012) illuminates disparate trade-offs concerning agricultural and environmental uses of land that occur across multiple scales. These trade-offs or conflicts include impacts beyond the human sphere, or those that impinge upon larger ecologies and the nonhuman communities that make up these ecologies. Trade-offs (such as a reduction in biodiversity levels, the disruption of annual migrations, etc.) often prompt arguments to prioritize ecosystem resilience and wider environmental sustainability (Bizikova et al. 2016; Macdonald et al. 2015).

If the ethical sphere is expanded to include ecosystems and/or biotic communities, then wider environmental impacts also gain ethical importance. Such "biocentric" arguments make use of two distinct yet intertwined philosophical frameworks: (1) ethical individualistic approaches and (2) ethical holist approaches. Reed discusses this tension when she argues that "unfortunately, the environmental ethics underlying public policies and public debate are often cast in terms of a dichotomy between ethical holism, preserving nature as self-sustaining ecosystems, versus ethical individualism, protecting the welfare of individual animals" (2008, 278). More generally, since the 1980s, environmental philosophers, such as Callicott (1980) and Jamieson (1998) have been discussing the ways these two approaches are distinct and how they recommend markedly distinct solutions to problems.

The most prominent ethical individualist approaches (concerning nonhuman animals) often share the following basic structure: They begin with the argument that nonhuman others have a specific capability (be that consciousness, the ability to suffer, to lie, etc.) that places them in the ethical sphere (Palmer 2010). After that, the theorists apply specific ethical theories (such as utilitarianism, rights theory, virtue ethics, feminist care ethics, etc.) to ethical questions, modifying them so that they can be used to guide action in human-animal contact zones. While my intention here is not to re-create every ethic in this large and growing literature, if one accepts the basic claim that animals have intrinsic value, then one could argue that we have a duty to help mitigate the animal-focused impacts of climate change. Depending on which individualistic framework one applies, ethical concerns associated with climate change could include issues related to animal suffering (Singer 2009), negative welfare impacts, the inability of nonhuman others to meet their needs or to achieve their *telos* (Rollin 1995), and the like.

In contrast, holist or ecological ethics begin by embracing the following basic starting point: that we should expand the definition of "ethical patient" to include the surrounding biotic communities and the ecosystems they comprise. For example, Aldo Leopold, one of the founders of environmental philosophy, argues that his land ethic "simply enlarges the boundaries of the community to include soils, waters, plants, and animals, or collectively: the land" (1968, 62). More recently, environmental philosophers, such as Arne Naess (1973) and Baird Callicott (1989), expanded Leopold's view into what is now called biocentric egalitarianism or biocentric holism, or the view that inherent value should be extended to all living things, including the biosphere. This position stands in marked contrast to the anthropocentric frameworks guiding food security, which primarily value human lives.

Biocentric individualist approaches and biocentric holist approaches also come into conflict, as placing emphasis on preserving nature as self-sustaining ecosystems can sometimes require that the lives of individuals be forfeited. For example, the overpopulation of a specific species, such as white-tailed deer in New England, may degrade the larger ecosystem to the point where basic functions are compromised. In this situation, the biocentric holist may argue that we need to bring the system back into balance and thus cull, provide contraception, or move some of the deer. Depending on which individual ethic one ascribes to, one could argue that each of the above solutions would be problematic. In the context of utilizing agricultural land to support the larger environment, similar conflicts could arise when deciding to shift production methods to support biodiversity levels, provide wildlife corridors, or provide habitat for a specific species.

The above analysis illustrates three distinct ethical approaches that can be drawn on to potentially address the tension between increasing yields and supporting ecological resilience: (1) human centric ethics used to ground food security arguments, (2) ethical individualist approaches that have been expanded to include nonhuman animals, and (3) holist or ecological ethics that place ecological communities in the ethical sphere. However, each of these ethical frameworks will give us markedly different recommendations concerning which goals should be prioritized. For example, humancentric ethics have been used to support the position that we should prioritize food security, while both environmental ethics support shifting our focus to ensure wider ecological resilience and thus to reduce impacts to ecosystems or nonhuman animals. Within this second category, there is a tension between prioritizing individuals or larger ecological communities, which could also produce different recommendations, depending on which perspectives one adopts.

As climate change continues to reduce the productivity of our already strained agricultural lands and expand demands for foodstuffs, it is imperative that we find a way to balance the need to achieve food security and to maintain ecological sustainability for the long term. With this aim in mind, which ethical framework should be prioritized? It appears that each illuminates important ethical aspects of food production and distribution in light of a changing climate. When we focus on the numbers of people going hungry around the world and recognize that people (including ourselves) have certain rights and responsibilities, it appears that the ethical intuition to help those in need is justified (Singer 2009). Additionally, when we couple the information that ecosystem services and/or communities are being threatened with a larger holistic ethic, the position that we should prioritize reducing impacts to the larger environment also appears to be justified. However, this places us back at the starting point, where the dispute is not readily resolved. In fact, the tension between human-focused ethics, animal ethics, and holistic or eco-logical ethics is well known in the environmental ethics literature (Callicott 1980; Jamieson 1998). Despite over twenty years of scholarly work, the incompatibility of these frameworks has not been resolved. Thus, the eth-ical positions illuminated in the above analysis appear to bring us no closer to addressing the tension between the prioritization of food security and the mitigation of ecological impacts.

III. A NOVEL SOLUTION: FOOD SOVEREIGNTY FRAMEWORKS

In light of this dilemma, decision-makers have two options: (1) they can adopt the position that the impasse is unresolvable, or "agree to disagree," or (2) they can turn to another ethical framework equipped to help them weigh important, yet distinct, ethical components that arise when making difficult decisions. Unlike the food security and ecological positions detailed above, food sovereignty movements are built on claims that food access should be balanced with a wide range of other ethically important issues, from the empowerment of communities, to the mitigation of environmental impacts. For such movements, "food" is more than a commodity that needs to be better distributed; it is intertwined with culture, place, and identity (Murdock and Noll 2015). Desmarais captures this point eloquently when she discusses the significance of La Via Campesina:

> This place-bound identity, that of "people of the land," reflects the belief that they have the right to be on the land. They have the right and obligation to produce food. They have the right to be seen as fulfilling an important function in society at large. They have the right to live in viable communities and the obligation to build community. All of the above form essential parts of their dis-tinct identity. (2008, 138–49)

As this quotation illustrates, food sovereignty movements incorporate several of the ethical frameworks discussed above. For example, they martial rights-based arguments when they include the "*right* of people and countries to define their agricultural policy" as part of the definition of food sovereignty. While not utilitarian, they also incorporate conceptions of "just distribution" when they advocate that food products and production should be organized "according to the needs of local communities, giving priority of production to local consumption" (Schanbacher 2010, 98). Finally, they recognize that a wide range of other issues (beyond individual needs) should be included as part of achieving food sovereignty. According to the Declaration of Nyéléni

(2007), these clearly include but are not limited to ensuring long-term sustainability, environmental health, high levels of biodiversity, and local participation when making decisions.

Even this cursory analysis illustrates how food sovereignty movements utilize an ethical foundation that is flexible enough to weigh a plethora of concerns that arise in the context of food production, rather than myopically focusing on human or ecological-centered impacts. In fact, Murdock and Noll argue that "food sovereignty movements largely accept a more holistic justice paradigm that includes a wide range of social concerns and rights claims [beyond human interests]" (2015, 57). They continue their analysis, arguing that food sovereignty movements "hold broadened conceptions of who or what is an 'ethical patient' to include future generations, ecosystems, and biotic communities. They are community focused, place-based, and seek to address racial and gender injustices" (58). This justice paradigm expands rights-based arguments, and paradigms concerning what constitutes "just distribution," to incorporate wider social and environmental concerns. As such, food sovereignty advocates appear to simultaneously recognize the importance of human rights while extending the moral sphere to encompass the wider environment.

For these reasons, I argue that the justice paradigm at the heart of food sovereignty movements could help resolve the tension between food security and ecological resilience, as it provides an ethical framework useful for cultivating both ecological resilience and food-crops in the age of the Anthropocene. Specifically, the above analysis of food sovereignty movements illuminates a pluralistic ethic at their heart, or a framework that recognizes a wide range of ethical positions and normative values (see, also, the chapter in this volume by Robaey and Timmermann). In contrast to absolute ethics that prioritize a single ethical theory (such as utilitarianism), the strength of pluralistic frameworks (such as the one guiding food sovereignty movements) includes the following: they (1) recognize and value different positions, (2) provide the tools necessary to weigh these against one another, and (3) place the responsibility of coming to a decision on those in the context where the problem exists. Due to these strengths, this approach could potentially help to bring disparate stakeholder groups together, rather than freezing debates, and so nudge community and policy groups toward consensus.

In reply, one could argue that adopting an ethical framework that recognizes competing claims does not address the conflict, as recognizing that there are conflicts does not mean that we have the tools to resolve these adequately. However, this objection presupposes that an ethic should provide the tools necessary to choose between competing claims, regardless of the context where conflict is situated. This is not necessarily the case, however, as pluralistic frameworks are built on the premise that contextual factors often influence which ethical concerns gain prominence. For example, when addressing medical issues, contextual ethics, such as principlism, are regularly used precisely because they capture the nuanced value dimensions of complicated situations (such as during end-of-life care) where stakeholders often hold disparate positions. Principlism, in this context, provides the vocabulary necessary to adequately communicate the values (autonomy, beneficence, etc.) at the heart of the conflicts and frames discussions concerning which values should be prioritized. Rather than providing a single answer to debates, then, the goal of pluralistic ethics is to develop a public language to frame discussion and to help resolve contextual/time sensitive disputes when action is necessary.

When applied to the conflict between prioritizing food security or ecological resilience, I argue that food sovereignty movements provide the vocabulary and flexibility needed to weigh adequately both humancentric and environmental factors. This is due to the fact that they utilize a holistic justice paradigm that provides space for weighing distribution claims and rights-based arguments and broadens the concept of "ethical patient" to include the environment, thus placing ecological concerns on the ethical table, so to speak. During the decision-making process, then, this holistic paradigm ensures that each of these concerns is recognized as having ethical significance. Even if one position is ultimately prioritized over the other, what this does is create the space to have further discussions concerning how negative impacts in that sphere could be mitigated. It also provides the insight necessary for understanding the ethical price that we may pay when one framework is prioritized over another. For example, when utilizing a food sovereignty framework, the choice to sacrifice long-term ecological sustainability for short-term production gains would only occur after a deliberate weighing of the consequences of this action. As such, stakeholders will be pushed to weigh the costs and benefits of the prioritization of food security over ecological resilience or vice versa, thus helping them make a more informed decision.

CONCLUSION

In an age where climate change is increasingly impacting a wide range of human activities and environmental systems, it is necessary to have an ethical framework that can help us weigh the costs of our decisions when there is no "good" answer or perfect fix. From a food sovereignty position, human-centered impacts, such as impeding agricultural production and food security, and ecological impacts, such as reducing biodiversity, undermining ecosystem resilience, and exterminating species, are ethical issues that the community needs to address. In certain circumstances, communities may have to prioritize one over the other to survive, but this does not negate the fact that we should also be working to mitigate harms in the other areas. The seemingly simple act of recognizing the ethical importance of the myriad issues that are encompassed by food sovereignty concepts of justice helps to undermine myopic human-centered food security and agricultural paradigms. It forces decision-makers to weigh the heavy costs of their choices, in particular, and of decision-making, in general, in the age of the Anthropocene.

NOTES

1. The "Anthropocene" is often defined as the current geological epoch, where human beings are conceptualized as a "blind" planetary force, irrespective of reason, that impacts Earth's biodiversity, geology, and weather patterns on a massive scale (Grusin 2017). In contrast to earlier epochs, human activities (such as urbanization, colonization, and resource extraction) are permanently scarring the planet. This led Eugene F. Stoermer to coin the term "Anthropocene" in the early 1980s. However, other scholars, such as chemist Paul J. Crutzen, were responsible for popularizing the term and bringing it to public attention. For more information, see Richard Grusin's (2017) historical sketch of the term in *Anthropocene Feminism*.

2. In fact, as such migrations are the result of climate changes, one could also argue that the migrations themselves are harms, as they force species out of their typical ranges and/or traditional migratory patterns.

3. Negative impacts of industrial production include, but are not limited to, environmental impacts, such as the reduction of biodiversity, and social/political impacts, such as farmer suicide, pesticide exposure, and the "death" of the family farm. To learn more, see Thompson and Noll (2015).

Part III

RESPONSIBILITY AND SOCIAL CHANGE

Chapter 10

Emerging (Food) Technology as an Environmental and Philosophical Issue in the Era of Climate Change

Paul B. Thompson

Climate change intersects with food production in two prominent ways. First, as many commentators have noted, agriculture is a significant source of climate-forcing emissions. Methane from livestock production is the most widely recognized (Ilea 2009; Thompson 2017), but synthetic fertilizers applied to commodity crops are also significant (Snyder et al. 2009). Second, the predicted impacts of climate change include altered rainfall patterns and drought, changes in seasonal ambient temperatures (including changes that will affect seasonal plant growth), and loss of coastal landmass due to seawater rise. Although some regions will experience an increase in the potential for food production, the total global effect of these impacts will present challenges for meeting food needs on a regional basis (Brown and Funk 2008). As such, agricultural scientists have developed a research agenda that emphasizes reduction of greenhouse gas (GHG) emissions, as well as adaptation of agricultural production systems to the conditions that are expected to prevail in the future.

The phrase "emerging technology" designates a large and diverse group of innovations that encompass genetic engineering, synthetic biology, information technology, artificial intelligence, and nanotechnology. Even a succinct attempt at describing these innovations and explaining what makes them novel would become tedious. Thus it must suffice to say that at a general level, they comprise the toolkit that agricultural scientists will draw upon in meeting the twin challenge of reducing emissions while increasing food security, but at the same time, all of them raise the specter of environmental risk. The risks from these diverse types of technology haunt us because humankind has long experience with industrial technologies that have turned out to have unintended and, in some instances, horrific environmental consequences. Asbestos, sulfur mustard, thalidomide, DDT, and nuclear weapons serve as one series of data points, while Love Canal, the Exxon Valdez, Chernobyl, and Superfund point to another. At the same time, it is impossible to imagine sustaining the current global population in the absence of industrial processes, so the known hazards of these processes must be mitigated if life is to be bearable, much less attractive, in the future.

First stabilizing and then reducing GHG emissions is perhaps the most dramatic instance of this necessity, but similar imperatives can be found in every quarter of natural resource utilization, including the production of food. These challenges are not unrelated. Successive reports of the Intergovernmental Panel on Climate Change (IPCC) discuss how changes in rainfall and average temperature and rising sea levels will threaten existing agricultural production systems in parts of the world where poverty and hunger are already preponderant. One measure is predicted impact on crop yields. Although increases may offset decreases in total crop yield (computed on a global basis) through 2029, IPCC estimates that for the period of 2030 to 2049 about a third of the world's cropland will experience yield increases, while three-quarters will see a decrease in yield ranging from 5 percent to 50 percent of harvestable material. Losses in excess of 50 percent of the harvestable crop begin to appear in the projection for 2050–2069, and by the end of the century fully one-quarter of the earth's arable land is projected to lose between 50 percent and 100 percent of the food currently produced. Equally significant is the fact that gains will occur primarily in North America and far northern regions of Asia while declines will occur in Africa and heavily populated parts of southeast Asia and the Indian subcontinent (Working Group II 2014).

What is to be done? A standard answer that has emerged among philosophers is to encourage new consumption habits, such as vegetarianism (see Kenehan this volume). Widespread reduction of meat consumption in wealthy countries can reduce methane emissions that are driving climate change, but this strategy provides little relief to people in regions where yields are expected to be adversely affected. Meeting subsistence and quality of life goals for the global population of human beings implies that emerging technology will be part of the response, as well. For example, drought-tolerant crops have already been developed using gene transfer, and the scientific literature contains many suggestions for alterations to plant phenotypes that could improve the response of crops grown in regions where climate change has an adverse impact on annual rainfall (Mao et al. 2015; Vivek et al. 2017).

Nevertheless, the use of recombinant DNA to modify agricultural crop varieties has been met with substantial resistance. Indeed, it seems clear that opposition to genetically engineered varieties of cotton, soya, and maize has been greatest among people who do not want for enlightenment with respect to the intertwined challenges of environmental protection and meeting the needs of a growing global population. Will the next generation of emerging technologies enjoy support from environmentally minded people, or will nanotechnologies, gene editing, and innovations that combine these tools with the analysis of big data or artificial intelligence be viewed as antithetical to environmental goals? The answer to this question turns on a number of contingent factors. This chapter will focus on some contingencies that are rich with philosophical significance.

I. A TOO-BRIEF ACCOUNT OF THE CURRENT QUANDARY

Genetic engineering of agricultural crops became a protracted environmental controversy during the first decade of the twenty-first century. Although a thorough discussion of the issues that were contested far exceeds the remit of the present chapter, a few highlights of the debate can be noted in the spirit of stage-setting. This section of the chapter will undertake the following tasks:

1. A very succinct discussion of issues that were raised in connection with the first generation of transgenic crops (e.g., so-called GMOs);
2. A discussion of the dominant framing for the controversy that has developed over the last two decades: unknown risks vs. the need to feed the world; and
3. A brief discussion of next-generation technology: nanotechnology, gene editing, gene drives, and synthetic biology.

The account is not to be interpreted as an argument for or against GMOs that were introduced between 1997 and 2017. As I have argued elsewhere, I do not regard extreme views on the risks of genetically engineered crops as especially credible (see Thompson 2015; 2017). Nevertheless, as I have also said, there are important respects in which the social institutionalization of first generation GMO crops is ethically indefensible (Thompson 2014).

GMOs were initially viewed as having both generic or process-based risks as well as hazards that were specific to the particular type of genetic modification being undertaken. Scientists speculated as to whether manipulating genomes might be inherently dangerous, leading to the landmark Asilomar conference in 1977. An initial voluntary moratorium was followed by an era in which the use of recombinant DNA was permitted only under strict biocontainment. By the late 1980s, the scientific consensus had shifted. While it was clear that genes could be manipulated in ways that could introduce known toxins into modified plants and animals or that could pose risks to biodiversity, these were known hazards associated with all forms of plant and animal breeding. Furthermore, toxicity would be evident in plant and animal phenotypes and thus amenable to known forms of testing. The risks posed by agriculture to biodiversity were less well understood but were not unique to GMOs (McHughen 2000).

Specific hazards were identified in connection first with the use of anti-microbial markers in early crop GMOs, but these were no longer in use by 2010. In addition, it was recognized that genes could move (and in fact typically *did* move) from agricultural crops to close relatives in wild plants. Gene flow could be an environmental hazard when the gene construct had the potential to give wild types a competitive advantage over other flora and fauna in their ecological niche. *Disadvantageous* gene constructs would disappear from a population of wild-types rapidly, due to natural selection. Finally, it was recognized that GMOs would not be exempt from a widely observed impact associated with agricultural chemicals: acquired resistance. Plants altered to resist herbicides or to control insects would, by their very existence in agricultural fields, place selection pressure on native organisms in the agroecosystem. Eventually, weedy plants would become resistant to frequently used herbicides, and insects would become resistant to toxins introduced using genetic engineering. But such events were hardly *new* in industrial agriculture. What is more, they were and remain totally unregulated.

The result was inconvenient from both a legal and a public perception standpoint. On the one hand, the risks of GMOs were not different in either kind or degree from those of long-standing methods for introducing genetic novelty, especially when mutation breeding (in use since World War II) is included in the mix. Requiring regulatory review of genetically engineered crops while exempting these previously unregulated techniques was logic-ally inconsistent from a risk-based perspective. On the other hand, lingering uncertainties from the cloud of doubt that formed at Asilomar fueled the fire of environmental and consumer activists hoping to make life difficult for industrial agriculture. Campaigns against GMOs also served the develop-ment of a market for organically produced crops. Some kind of regulatory oversight was needed to assuage public reaction. Former FDA official Henry Miller asserts that the biotech industry played public fears like a flute, cre-ating a regulatory environment where the costs of generating safety data denied publicly funded researchers and small start-up innovators any oppor-tunity to succeed. The result was an oligopoly with only a few large corporate players that can muster the capital needed to move a GMO through the regu-latory system (Miller 1997).

Opponents of biotechnology represented a conglomeration of interests with a number of entirely legitimate concerns. Many revolved around the concen-tration of economic power in the agricultural input industry, and a general left-leaning suspicion of multinational corporations. Others sought to expand regulatory oversight over agriculture well beyond GMOs but saw a focus on biotechnology as the proverbial camel's nose under the tent. The loss of farmer control over production decisions loomed larger and larger, as patents and technology licenses became the framework for this new class of seeds. Virtually none of these socially oriented concerns were open to government intervention in a neoliberal political era. Whether activists were honestly concerned about environment and food safety risks (and some undoubtedly were), activating public fears along these lines was the only political strategy with any chance of slowing dramatic economic concentration in seed production that was occurring on a global basis (Schurman and Munro 2010).

By 2010, casual observers of the biotechnology debate were becoming increasingly concerned about environmental risk and food safety, while more knowledgeable people were focused on troubling socioeconomic trends. Since it is logically impossible to prove absolute safety where any plausible hazard can be maintained, agricultural scientists have countered both speculative risks and known socioeconomic costs by arguing that GMOs are needed to feed a growing world population. The argument is not particularly subtle. Existing GMOs have increased harvestable food and fiber on a per acre basis. The increase in functional or usable yield allows for a growth in total global production while constraining the need to expand the footprint of agriculture into uncultivated lands that serve as habitat for wild plant and animal species. Limiting the expansion of farming into uncropped areas is important to climate ethics because deforestation due to agriculture is responsible for an estimated 80 percent of overall global deforestation (Kissinger et al. 2012), and forests, of course, provide an important sink for carbon. These benefits are alleged to offset what are typically represented as acceptable risks and costs. This has become the dominant response of those who would defend biotechnology and GMOs. Importantly, a largely speculative, unknown risk is counterbalanced by the putatively certain tragedy of widespread future starvation (see Borlaug 2000; Trewavas 2002; Paarlberg 2009). I have called those who push this line of thinking "world-feeders."

At this juncture a new generation of emerging technology is positioned for launch. During the last decade new tools for inserting gene constructs into plant or animal genomes have emerged. The key improvement over the agrobacter, ballistic, and microinjection techniques used for the first generation of GMOs is that genes can be inserted at known loci in the recipient organism. Genes can also be deleted or "turned off" (e.g., the control sequence that enables transcription to RNA is rendered ineffective), a process referred to as a "knockout" (see Chrispeels and Sadava 2003). CRISPR is the most recent and almost certainly the most powerful and widely applicable of such tools, giving rise to an era of "gene editing." This precision is expected to reduce the time and failure rate for gene transformations and is also thought to further reduce the probability of unexpected changes, such as the production of a novel toxin or an unanticipated phenotypic trait (Ledford 2015).

Tools for gene editing will facilitate a number of other emerging technologies. These are summarized in table 10.1, which lists a number of generic innovation types and correlates each type with some of the prominent applications that are envisioned for making changes in food production techniques. The third column of the table describes the primary mode of action for each type of technology, while the fourth column is a rough estimate of when applications can be expected to appear in the food system. Estimates that are accompanied by the term "testing" reflect the time when prototypes are expected to be well enough developed so that risk assessments can be undertaken and data can be collected that would be needed for eventual regulatory approval. The table does not speculate on what types of regulatory approval will actually be required for these emerging technologies. Indeed, the lack of a clear regulatory framework could delay implementation, though without clear regulatory requirements, technology innovators would not necessarily be in violation if they were to introduce some applications with no oversight at all.

Recounting the specific ways in which these forms of emerging technology might serve in a response to climate impacts on agriculture would be a daunting task. As already noted, changes in plant genetics might create crops with drought tolerance or flowering or seed-setting characteristics that are better aligned with shifts in seasonality. Nanotechnologies are being developed as sensors for detecting stress in both plants and animals (Rai and et al. 2012) as well as for filtration in irrigation systems (Prasad et al. 2014). Future uses have yet to be envisioned. What is important to recognize from the perspective of climate ethics is that while all these applications and their attendant benefits are somewhat speculative, an examination of the risks and downside of emerging technology must not lose sight of the way that scientists and engineers have indeed met the burden of providing a rationale that favors development and implementation of their favored innovations. They may not publish their argument in philosophy journals, but this does not mean that the case has not been made. Elsewhere I have called this "the presumptive case," for emerging technology (Thompson 2009b), but the argument is not settled until the risks are also taken into account.

II. EMERGING TECHNOLOGIES AND ENVIRONMENTAL RISKS

Given the history of GMOs and the current regulatory systems that are in place in Europe, North America, and industrialized countries in other regions,

Table 10.1: Emerging Technologies for Future Food Production

Nanotechnology	Ultrathin coatings for fertilizers & pesticides; encapsulation of flavors & food ingredients for aesthetic & nutritional enhancement; nanoparticles for monitoring & more efficient biochemical activity	Exploits material properties including bonding, permeability & biophysics that emerge at nanoscale	Now to 50 years
Synthetic biology	Potential for totally novel organisms; microbes that produce valuable products in contained environments	Building an entire genome, sequence by sequence	Not soon
Gene editing	Insert or delete genes at precise locations; key tool for many other applications	Multiple tools, especially CRISPR	5 years
Gene drives	*In situ* forms of gene modification for response to emerging diseases; lethal drives for control of agricultural pests; removal of invasive species	Move a gene construct through a naturally breeding population	Field testing: 10 years
Biosensors	Monitoring of plant & animal disease vectors; tracing movement of pathogens or pollutants through an ecosystem	Combine nanotechnology with info & gene technologies	Now

Synthetic meat	Substitute for "on the hoof" production of meat products; environmental & food safety impacts are currently unknown	Genetic modification of plant proteins to simulate animal protein; stem cells for building meats *in vitro*	Testing & regulation: 5 years
Farm AI	Tractors & robots that navigate fields, performing mechanical cultivation & weeding tasks without human operators	GPS, visual recognition & navigation adapted from driverless cars	Field testing: 5 years
Genetically engineered food animals	Rapid growth (salmon); disease resistance (gene-edited pigs); possible shifts in nutritional or flavor composition	Microinjection of gene constructs into fertilized egg	Now (but very little) to 20 years
Adult cell animal cloning	Used in conjunction with genetic engineering of animals & cloning of high-value breeding animals	Converting somatic cell into totipotent cell	Now, but expensive

Author's own

we can expect that the suite of technologies summarized in table 10.1 will be the focus of some controversy followed by as yet uncertain regulatory responses. Although the particular structure of the regulatory framework will indeed be crucial, an initial grasp of the environmental ethics can be attained by examining these technologies from the perspective of risk assessment. For present purposes *social choice* can be defined as the application of decision-theoretic approaches (including ethical theories) to problems where society as a whole is viewed as the choice-making agent. Social choice can be a purely theoretical exercise conducted by academics, or it can be an applied practice in real-world decisions. The social choice perspective is most obviously useful in policymaking contexts where a governmental decision is expected to transcend partisan interests, but it can also be used to comparatively evaluate future scenarios that have been generated by technical capabilities. Alternative scenarios generated by climate models are sometimes evaluated in terms of their overall risks and benefits, for example (Stern 2008). Although social choice is philosophically complex (see Sen 2011), the focus of this section is to clarify how value judgments are deployed in risk assessments that have been developed for application in classic cases of governmental policymaking.

The risk assessment framework can be summarized by the following schematic (see figure 10.1). *Hazard identification* is the process of identifying what bad outcomes can occur as a result of adopting one option rather than another. In classic regulatory decision-making, the option under analysis is often whether to permit the use or release of a new product, or whether to adopt rules governing some technical practice (such as generation of electricity using nuclear reactors of a given design). Hazard identification is a largely inductive process of ascertaining the possibility of an adverse outcome based on the current state of the relevant science and estimating its severity. Simply knowing what can go wrong does not provide an estimate of risk, however. Hence *exposure quantification* utilizes a variety of modeling, statistical, and experimental techniques to estimate the probability that a hazard will materialize, given adoption of the option under consideration. Though conceptually simple, both activities can be difficult to accomplish in practice. Some of these difficulties are philosophical and will be taken up below.

Risk analysts will stress a subtle point at this juncture: risk should not be conflated simply with the loss or "badness" of the hazard, should it occur. Risk must also reflect the chance or probability that hazard actually *will* materialize, and this can only be appreciated once the various factors that contribute to a given individual's or group's exposure to the hazard have been taken into account in the exposure quantification phase. Research in the social psychology of decision-making suggests that many people tend to neglect or poorly understand the probabilistic dimension of decision-making (Sunstein 2002), hence there is an argument for discounting the public's estimate of relative risks associated with any given activity or phenomenon. This argument has been made with respect to environmental and food safety risks, especially in connection with genetic modification of food and fiber crops or food animals (Hettlich and Walther 2012).

Having an estimate of risk does not tell a regulator what to do about it. One option is always "nothing": simply accept the risk. Other options include regulatory measures that mitigate the severity of hazards, that compensate losers, or that develop mechanisms to secure consent from those parties that

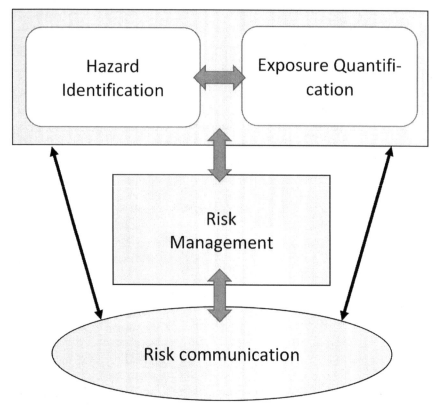

Figure 10.1:   Stages of Risk Assessment
Author's own

will bear risks. The procedure for making a decision about risks is represented by the *risk management* element in the schema. *Cost-benefit analysis* is a pro-cedure developed by economists to allow decision-makers the opportunity to include not only risks (as determined by hazard identification and exposure quantification) but also beneficial elements associated with adopting the option. The key point to notice is that one can make a distinction between *assessing* (or estimating) what the risk is and deciding what to do about it. The decision-making phase is referred to as *risk management*.

Social choice models for decision-making under risk that were propagated in the 1970s and 1980s tended to stop with hazard identification, exposure quantification, and risk management. These models were criticized as lacking a role for public input. In response, *risk communication* was added to the model following an influential U.S. National Research Council study of the

1990s colloquially referred to as "the orange book" (NRC 1996). The role of risk communication within the overall framework of risk assessment and social choice continues to be a topic of confusion, contestation, and continuing debate. Some participants in those debates argue that all the interests that gave rise to controversy over GMOs should be brought into decision-making through the mechanism of risk communication (see, e.g., Wickson 2007; Hartley 2012). On this view, risk communication equips a political decision-maker with a better grasp of what matters to his or her constituents. However, regulators in neoliberal states are more narrowly constrained by the statutes that delimit their authority, which generally specify a restricted class of hazards that can be the basis for regulatory action. In the United States, for example, regulators at the Environmental Protection Agency have authority to review and restrict the human health and environmental impacts of pesticides, while authority for other food safety hazards is lodged at the Food and Drug Administration. The Department of Agriculture can regulate substances or activities that could pose an economic threat *to* agriculture, but not *from* agriculture. Most socioeconomic effects fall entirely outside the scope of the authorizing legislation under which these agencies operate.

Given the perspective of risk assessment-guided social choice and the prevalent approach to technologically generated risks just discussed, one might expect that food safety hazards, poisons, animal health, and ecological hazards would currently be subjected to careful risk assessment and governmental review. This is not, in fact, the case. Even in the wake of controversies over the safety of GMOs, the toxic properties of many foods produced through ordinary plant breeding escape regulatory oversight altogether. Both tomatoes and potatoes are Solanaceae plants that contain toxins called tropane alkaloids, though not in the parts of the plant that we normally eat. Varieties developed through ordinary plant breeding can introduce these toxins into consumable parts of the plant. Hence there is a non-negligible chance that new potato and tomato varieties are food safety hazards (Oksman-Caldentey and Arroo 2000; Smith 2013). Nevertheless, this risk is currently managed entirely through the voluntary efforts of the plant breeding community. Plant breeders understand this hazard and take steps to control it, but conventional plant breeding methods that do not deploy recombinant plant transformation techniques are not subject to oversight by the U.S. Food and Drug Administration, the European Food Safety Authority, or any other national government body (Thompson 2015).

This voluntary system that prevails for plants and animals that are not modified using first-generation rDNA tools sets the stage for a looming debate over emerging technologies and one that has already started in Europe, where regulatory review of GMOs is currently mandatory. If the voluntary system is reliable, review by a governmental agency will only delay and add cost to the development and implementation of a new technology. Although gene editing is potentially quite powerful, many agricultural scientists are confident that they can use this tool safely. They believe, in fact, that the precision afforded by gene editing makes this tool much safer than conventional breeding techniques, where many thousands of genes combine with potential for undesirable results (as in the Solanaceae plants just discussed). Scientists are far less confident about the use of other emerging technologies. Indeed, a group of distinguished biologists have signed a manifesto warning against the development of gene drives, representing a widely shared cautionary attitude that has not been seen since Asilomar (Emerson et al. 2017; Hotchkirch et al. 2018; Min et al. 2018). At the same time, publications *are* appearing that describe how gene drives might be utilized in fairly standard forms of agricultural pest control (Harvey-Samuel et al. 2017; Buchman et al. 2018).

In conclusion, then, the risk assessment framework does provide a logically coherent way to conceptualize hazards from the next generation of agricultural technologies, but one should not draw the further inference that risks will necessarily be well managed. Whether the risks of emerging technologies listed in table 10.1 turn out to be highly significant or largely speculative, as some have said for GMOs, simply characterizing the environmental ethics of emerging technology in terms of risk invites a reprise of the dominant argument that has emerged in response to the political controversy over GMOs. To wit: whatever the risks, we have to eat. Even in the absence of a climate change argument, the necessity of feeding a global population seems to emerge as the ultimate trump card, one that could potentially override virtually *any* level of risk associated with a food production technology. With projected *declines* in the productivity of current systems due to climate change, this argument redoubles its force. Any technology that can be portrayed as a necessity will have a rhetorical advantage against precautionary arguments or questions that can be raised about its safety (Thompson 1984). On this view, if we need gene drives, gene editing, farm AI, or synthetic meats to feed the world in an era of food insecurity brought on by climate change, whatever chances they pose for unwanted and untoward consequences are simply chances that will have to be taken.

III. RESISTING RISK ASSESSMENT, RESISTING RISK

At this point in my argument, the reasonable word limit for my contribution to a multiauthor collection is looming, and the patience of readers is assuredly beginning to fade. It is also the point at which the trajectory for philosophical reflection shatters into a dozen fragments, all of them compelling and each calling forth its own subtleties. On one hand, the presumptions of neo-Malthusian arguments that support any and all manner of tools for increasing food production need to be questioned, a task to which I have devoted considerable effort throughout my career (see especially Thompson 2017). On the other hand, skepticism about the models that predict shortfalls in food availability requires a measured epistemology that can temper the enthusiasms of climate deniers. Neither of these tasks is simple enough to be completed in the closing sections of the present chapter. At the same time, there are additional reasons to resist all manner of emerging technology that have not been given their due in the preceding discussion of risk assessment.

Unfortunately, a catalog of *these* reasons itself precipitates a series of branches and bifurcations that build upon one another. We might start where we began, by noticing the history of unnoticed and unanticipated consequences that have ensued from earlier attempts to solve a pressing problem. Do the sound, heat, and electrical insulating properties of silicate minerals offset the risks of lung cancer and mesothelioma that are now known to accompany the use of asbestos? Aren't we to learn lessons from the dumping by Hooker Chemical at Love Canal, or the contamination of Hinkley, California, drinking water with hexavalent chromium (the case that made Erin Brockovich famous)? Well, certainly we are, but what are the lessons we should learn? Should we learn that private industry will not only conceal environmental risks but will also deploy the tools and defile the reputation of science to do it (Oreskes and Conway 2010)? Or is the lesson here the more general one that Heather Douglas notes with respect to inductive risk, the fact that scientific inferences are always fallible and that a value judgment necessarily determines when you have enough evidence to make a judgment (Douglas 2000)? These questions will point philosophy in significantly different directions. But we might also notice a point that looks political at first glance: the "losers" in these cases are usually people who were already disadvantaged by class, race, gender, or some other marginalizing feature, an observation that Samuel Epstein has documented in connection with the politics of AIDS research (Epstein 1996). And from here we might note that risk is itself positional: as black, as gay, as poor, and as a woman one is fully justified in presuming that one's social position places one within the population that is most likely to suffer from *any* hazard, and *any* mechanism of exposure. Yet none of these features is well reflected in mainstream approaches to risk analysis. IPCC documents hint at such concerns without adequately discussing how they figure as legitimate factors that contribute to risk (Working Group II 2014, 6).

Pursuing any of these threads would be a significant task, and it is the sheer difficulty of these separate tasks, compounded by the obstacles to comprehension that arise when we begin to grasp their multiplicity, that I wish to focus upon in closing. How could we not react with simple resistance?

Isn't this part of what has made a "precautionary approach" so attractive? "Let's just not think about all these formidable problems requiring hard thinking. Let's just oppose emerging technology and stick with the devil that we know." Speaking personally, this strikes me as an eminently *reasonable* posture to take with respect to emerging technologies, though not necessarily correct. My sympathy for it gives rise to one last philosophical puzzle, which is the puzzle I have wished to pose from the outset. It is to ask, how can philosophy acknowledge and respect the eminent reasonableness of simply rejecting emerging technologies, especially given the history of failures that any rational person must recognize in the twenty-first century? What does philosophy owe to this history of failure and to the politics of resistance toward it?

My answer to this question has been foreshadowed by the path I have taken to reach it. Were I to conclude that resistance is adequate, that opposition is called for, it would not have been necessary to take my readers through the history of GMOs nor to describe the logical architecture of risk assessment or its origins in social choice. It would have been sufficient to emphasize the gaps in regulation or recite the hazards without any qualifying comments on their likelihood. Such a posture would raise suspicion (if not hackles) and would incite resistance, especially among those who are primed for it by virtue of their social position. So the reader is alert to the fact that I am not content to align myself with those whose outrage fuels an epistemology of confidence in skepticism. The skepticism that fuels resistance is too sure that things are not as they are found to be in the painstaking methods of hazard identification and exposure quantification. It is not skeptical enough of the certainty that risk assessment can only service a leviathan aligned with the dominant power structure.

But neither am I content to align with the world feeders. I have not taken readers down this path to assure them that science has it right, that risk assessment is the very paradigm of rationality, and that they should simply trust "science" to do the right thing. Hopefully *that* point is clear enough from the exposition that has actually been provided. Instead, philosophy's task is to navigate the Bosporus and Hebrides created by this fragmented and rhizomic landscape of ethical, political, and epistemological intersections. On the one hand, there is a pressing need to explain why resisting risk is very reasonable (and certainly not irrational), especially among groups that have been disadvantaged time and time again and who have learned hard lessons about trusting those who are sure of their dinner. The audience for *this* philosophical task resides primarily within the biological sciences and within the corridors where technologies are developed and risk assessments are conducted. On the other hand, philosophy must also lay the groundwork for inductively listing hazards in a more inclusive manner, and for estimating exposures in a manner that is more sensitive to the probabilities that emerge in populations defined by nuanced characteristics of social and biological position. One concern is that a philosophical community enthused with a politics of resistance and solidarity may not be up to this latter task, even while our scientists are (too slowly, perhaps) becoming more and more receptive to hearing voices that have previously been excluded.

IV. ARE WE THERE YET, DAD?

We have almost reached the word limit and have yet to mention the word "justice." Risk scholars have always understood that there are issues of distributive justice that arise in formulating plans for managing risk. Their thinking owes a debt to welfare economics, where elegant solutions to maximization of welfare have always run afoul of distributive issues (MacLean 1986). Economists have never been sure how to approach the distribution of costs and benefits, but their emphasis on exchange relations undergirds the dominant schools of thought on justice that emerged in the twentieth century. (Surely it would be tedious to rehearse them once again!) In fact, environmental justice emerged largely through activism based on obviously racially skewed distributions of toxic exposure from manufacturing (Cole and Foster 2001). Perhaps I should simply confess my own impatience with the need to find a spidery philosophic rationalization for addressing a situation in which the class of harms to health and well-being that are classed as "environmental" fall so consistently and disproportionately on people who are identified through variables of race, class, and gender.

As other chapters in this book will address in more detail, some of the basic questions in food justice revolve around the way in which we understand food access, food security, and how the emerging discourse of food sovereignty has qualified the way in which hunger and the right to food have been understood for more than half a century (see Noll; Rawlinson; Szende; all in this volume). Technological risks figure into these classic notions of justice in the right to and consumption of food in two principal ways. First, technical infrastructure plays a crucial role in the physical distribution and cost of food, with obvious implications for access, security, and sovereignty. Second, when technology is implicated in causing certain foods to be viewed as low-quality, unsafe, or substandard, everything we know about economic transactions will lead us to expect that poor people will be exposed to the hazards of said foods at much higher rates than people with higher incomes. One might indeed find some cases of actual toxic exposure that fit this model; ongoing scandals in China might be an example (see Sharma and Paradakar 2010). But whether the poor actually *are* exposed to a biological hazard because they cannot afford organic or non-GMO foods would be a hotly contested issue that circles back to the epistemic and political debates that *have* been the focus of this chapter, so far.

There are also some important caveats to observe with respect to justice in the *production* of food. It is abundantly clear that fieldworkers (who tend to be poor and from racially marginalized groups) *are* differentially exposed to technologically induced hazards from agricultural chemicals (Wright 2005). But again we circle back to the beginning. Do the technologies listed in table 10.1 introduce a novel class of hazards or exposure mechanisms that can be expected to increase these risks? Is risk assessment a reasonable strategy for approaching the distribution of risk? This is territory that we have covered already, and mentioning the differential risks borne by fieldworkers is important primarily because it makes the connection between risk assessment and food justice at the level of agricultural production more explicit. But the question of justice also takes us back to the concerns of the world-feeders. They are concerned about two issues that can be seen in the light of food justice. First, there is the obvious matter of justice for future generations, the people who will need the expansion in global food production that world-feeders think these emerging technologies can provide. But second, there are the poor farmers in Africa that, in the words of Robert Paarlberg, are "starved for science." Paarlberg argues that the opposition to GMOs has deprived them of tools that have the potential to lift them from poverty. Access to these new emerging technologies is the form of food justice with which he is most concerned (Paarlberg 2009).

Like Norman Borlaug before him, Paarlberg suggests that rich people should stifle whatever doubts they have about emerging technology and that they should do this because their speculative fears are utterly disproportionate to the actual suffering being endured by poor farmers who would benefit from better tools. This suggestion was the focus of a 30-page treatment in my 2015 book *From Field to Fork: Food Ethics for Everyone*, followed by an additional 20 pages discussing the food safety risks of GMOs. I do not think that the navigational task I have outlined for philosophy above can tread these waters in only a few paragraphs. Suffice it to say that though I disagree with Paarlberg's cheerleading for science, I agree that there are potential applications of gene technology that are compatible with the immediate needs of very poor farmers in Africa and that climate change will probably make their situation even worse. And I have no qualms about eating GMOs myself. Nevertheless, poor African farmers are the victims of injustice so many times over that it is difficult for me to endorse Paarlberg's rebuke to rich Europeans who are keeping biotechnology out of Africa because this is only *one* vector in a complex web of forces. The structural injustice in global food systems is such that opening Africa to biotechnology might only leave poor farmers vulnerable to some new form of exploitation. Resisting biotechnology is plausibly a tactical maneuver in a larger battle on behalf of the poor. But I would also hate to be the person who stood in the way of any poor farmer's access to better means of food production.

CONCLUSION: THE ETHICS OF EMERGING TECHNOLOGY AND NEXT STEPS

The (perhaps) boring conclusion is that emerging food technologies will need to be discussed and debated. Although we will never reach full certainty about the wisdom or justice of adopting them, approaching them through deliberative democracy and discourse ethics is a far cry better than leaving things up to scientized regulatory agencies and the vagaries of the market. Though boring, the conclusion is still urgent. I have indicated a few of the many ways in which climate change threatens existing food production systems and cited the IPCC projections indicating how these impacts will fall disproportionately on poor people. It is also worth underlining the fact that globally, the poor tend to be farmers or to depend on farming for their income (see Thompson 2015), so when climate change affects food production, it is affecting the livelihood of people who are least able to deal with it. I have spent a fair part of my scholarly life attempting to participate in a discourse on GMOs only to see a more deliberative frame of mind overturned by reaction, at one turn, and manipulation by those who have had pecuniary interests in the success or failure of these technologies, at the next. Much of the specific thinking that will need to be done with respect to the emerging technologies listed in table 10.1 will have to be done by people who succeed me.

There is still work to be done in building the institutional setting for reflective discourse on our technological future (Ben-Ari and Or-Chen 2009). I have argued that a logico-ethical framework of risk assessment really does have much to offer for those who are willing to grapple with emerging technology in its details. But this is not to defend interpretations of that framework that ignore the role of value judgments at every stage or that arbitrarily exclude hazards or exposure mechanisms simply because they do not conform to the methodological dictates of established biophysical disciplines. Philosophers can, as John Dewey suggested, serve like liaison officers in the discursive activities that are needed to achieve a greater food justice, both *through* the emergence of new technologies and occasionally by constraining them. But they will have to know more than philosophy to do that. They will need to know more than the average consumer knows about food.

Chapter 11

Fair Agricultural Innovation for a Changing Climate

Zoë Robaey and Cristian Timmermann

Agricultural innovation happens at different scales and through different streams. In the absence of a common global research agenda, decisions on which innovations are brought to existence, and through which methods, are taken with insufficient view on how innovation affects social relations, the environment, and future food production. Mostly, innovations are considered from the standpoint of economic efficiency, particularly in relationship to creating jobs for technology-exporting countries (Zwart, Landeweerd, and van Rooij 2014). Increasingly, however, the realization that innovations cannot be successful on their technical prowess alone calls for a broader investigation (von Schomberg 2015; Stilgoe, Owen, and Macnaghten 2013).

When thinking about the role of agricultural innovations in tackling climate change, one recalls, for instance, promises of biotechnology companies to create crops that can adapt food production to changing climate conditions (Saad 2015). For instance, a 2010 policy brief issued by the International Centre for Trade and Sustainable Development and the International Food & Agricultural Trade Policy Council states, "The core challenge of climate change adaptation and mitigation in agriculture is to produce (i) more food, (ii) more efficiently, (iii) under more volatile production conditions, and (iv) with net reductions in GHG [greenhouse gas] emissions from food production and marketing" (Lybbett and Sumner 2010). These types of manifestos, which tend to assume that innovations are placed in a neutral social environment, ignore crucial ethical considerations, such as historical emissions contributions, importance of heirloom varieties, vast inequalities in purchasing power and scientific capacity, quality of agricultural work, corruption, honesty among seed retailers, and extreme poverty. They also ignore the high diversity of personal motivations and circumstances of actors engaging in innovation.

As extreme weather events are on the rise, it has become clear that we need a broader ethical assessment tool to judge the desirability of agricultural innovation in order to make sure food production becomes resilient to the added environmental and social stress factors caused by climate change (McMichael 2017). Moreover, food is a basic need and its production requires continuous innovation to maintain harvest yields. Given the importance of food production, how are decisions made regarding agricultural innovations?

Typical assessments for new technologies involve risk assessments, environmental impact assessments, socioeconomic assessments, and participatory technology assessments. These are dictated by the legal landscape where the innovation is developed and introduced. Assessments are meant to point to problems with an innovation and to make suggestions to address these issues. The problem with these assessments is that they typically consider issues after an innovation is developed and is about to be introduced, leaving insufficient room for outsiders to shape the technology (Beyleveld and Jianjun 2017). This exclusion raises several issues regarding fairness.

Our aim in this chapter is to address this lack of attention concerning fairness by focusing on three major stages of agricultural innovation: goal setting, research and development, and empowerment strategies.[1] To do this, we analyze two approaches for an ethical assessment of innovation systems: one using the insights from Responsible Research and Innovation (RRI) and the other applying theories of justice (see table 11.1). To compare both perspectives, we show their contributions to addressing five major social challenges we have identified and that are manifest in the agricultural concerns that are worsened by climate change: (i) availability, (ii) accessibility, (iii) participation in science, (iv) arbitration and rectification measures, and (v) long-term sustainability.

By using two distinct ethical approaches (RRI and theories of justice) we formulate an ethical assessment framework that has the capacity to identify a wider set of social justice challenges, and that combines the strengths of both approaches in a single tool. By extending the focus beyond the innovator, our framework places a strong emphasis on issues of empowerment. The benefit of this approach is that the assessment does not stop once the agricultural innovation is delivered to the market; instead, it is taken up by users. Users then become empowered to continue assessing and innovating, thereby reinforcing the ethical assessment and contributing to scientific advancement. Through this dual ethical framework, we build an ethical tool that is better tailored to identify and address the abovementioned social challenges as they arise in agricultural innovations for climate change.

I. WHY IS FAIRNESS A SPECIAL CONCERN FOR INNOVATION IN A CHANGING CLIMATE?

Climate change obliges humanity to speed up the rate of agricultural innovation and to redirect the course of innovation toward addressing new vulnerabilities. However, the necessity to speed up innovation due to climate change is not morally neutral. The countries of the Global North have made a far greater per capita contribution to climate change than the countries of the Global South (McMichael 2017). Yet the effects of climate change vary in different regions of the world. While the harvest yields will increase in some parts of Canada and Russia, areas near river deltas and in the tropics are already suffering major losses due to the salinization of waterways and droughts (Cline 2007). These factors underline the need for a normative assessment of climate change adaptation innovations. While making an invention publicly available can be generally considered as providing a public good, the provision of inventions to adapt to climate change by the Global North has also a reparatory character (Gosseries 2004).[2] The failure of the Global North to provide adequate compensation for the harms asserted by climate change makes the commercialization of climate change adaptation technologies particularly problematic (Biddle 2016).

Nowadays, adaptation is necessary, as climate change mitigation is no longer sufficient due to the failure to curb emissions (McMichael 2017). This raises major global justice issues. While seed companies and biotechnology laboratories in the Global North are developing seeds that will be ready to adapt to the new environmental conditions, the smallholders in the Global South have practiced and developed a variety of farming methods that allow the capture of large amounts of carbon by making effective use of the synergies of different plant associations and plant-animal interactions (Timmermann and Félix 2015a). An excessive delay to take action by the Global North may cause ecological disruptions that will impede the ability of smallholders to use the varieties they know how to use and to stimulate symbiotic relationships. Ultimately, because of these disruptions, smallholders might be obliged to opt for a technology they did not produce, which could lead to technological dependency.

Together, this means that companies in the Global North might be in a position to exploit climate-vulnerable markets by selling climate change adaptation technologies that are not morally neutral, and guidelines need to address this unfair advantage. Nowadays countries of the Global North are not only carrying much less of the burden of climate change compared to countries in the tropical region, but a few countries in the Global North are even benefiting economically by selling agricultural innovation to adapt to the new climatic conditions they created collectively, for example, by marketing varieties that have a higher salinity tolerance or more resistance to droughts.

II. INNOVATION: GOALS, PROCESS, AND EMPOWERMENT

Historically, the idea of innovation has not always been a positive one. Tracing the Western history of the concept since antiquity, Benoît Godin finds that while in today's societies, innovation is seen as good, even as necessary, it was not always the case (2015). In Ancient Greece, concepts akin to innovation were considered the disruption of a working order. He writes, "Innovation is a concept for inducing actions oriented toward practicality" (Godin 2014, 53). Nowadays, innovation is intricately linked to technology.

Innovation is commonly recognized by means of patents. The general rationale for patents is to grant the inventor a right to exclude others from the use of the invention in order to gain an economic advantage as well as the opportunity to recover investments in research and development. Traditionally this approach has been seen as a driver for innovation. Patents, however, bring a number of social problems, such as hindering poorer people's access to the fruits of innovation and fostering a secretive research environment, which is not necessary for stimulating innovation, especially when considering other models such as open innovation (Bartling and Friesike 2014; Gupta et al. 2016; Koepsell 2016). In other words, patents are a tool for controlling access to knowledge about an invention and its functioning and for blocking the possibility of making further modifications to the innovation. These restrictions hinder the ability of the user to take active moral responsibility for the innovation because the patent restrictions limit the user's intervention on the technology itself (Robaey 2016b). Authorization from the patent holder is needed to contribute to the innovation by making further improvements, through the application of local knowledge, or in experimentation to discover new uses.

If an innovation is a practical and technical solution to a problem, then, under the circumstances of a changing climate, access to these innovations and their knowledge should be key. However, when it comes to knowledge, different streams of agricultural innovations present different ways of concentrating, sometimes withholding, and distributing knowledge. In order to be morally responsible for risks of technologies as well as to be able to properly assess them, knowledge is an important condition (Robaey 2016b; van de Poel et al. 2012).

Knowledge is not only about responsibility but also about justice, in several dimensions. For the purpose of our analysis, we distinguish between three components of innovation that raise issues of knowledge, responsibility, and justice and that are found at different stages of innovation: the definition of goals at the beginning, the process of innovating (research and development), and empowerment, after the innovation is delivered to society.

The *goal* of an innovation refers to what we want to achieve with the innovation. If one defines the problem for which a solution is sought, then one also decides for others what the problem entails and how to solve it. We can ask: What problem does an innovation solve? How was it defined and who defined it? And for whom does it solve a problem, that is, who is meant to benefit from this innovation?

The *process* of innovating refers to how we produce, use, and share knowledge. This process needs, as much as possible, to be inclusive, so the system can harvest and integrate ideas from any interested party. Injustice occurs if you are able to meaningfully contribute but are not allowed to (Timmermann and Félix 2015b). The process should therefore consider different types of experts. Ideally, an innovation system should be able to incorporate such findings systematically. In the process of innovation, we ask: Who has access to what knowledge about the agricultural innovation? Is the innovation the result of participatory processes?

The level of *empowerment* that an innovation may stimulate depends on both its design and contractual arrangements. Empowerment implies that an innovation is not finished at the end of the innovation process—it continuously welcomes and encourages user innovation. Therefore, it is crucial that during and after the innovation process, means to participate are facilitated. While readers might be more familiar with stakeholder participation during the process of innovation, its extension beyond this stage is often not considered. Technologies are usually designed with one specific function that links the object to its goal. This can lead to technologies becoming a black box to the user for the sake of efficiency. Yet the contrary is possible: the design and contractual arrangements of an innovation may not only allow the user to use the technology in other ways than was foreseen but actually encourage user experimentation. All in all, empowerment relies on having sufficient access and being able to create a range of action with a given technology (Robaey 2016a).

III. FROM THE FIELD TO THE LABORATORY AND BACK: INNOVATION IN AGRICULTURE

Nature is continuously evolving to adapt to new threats, challenges, and opportunities, as living organisms search for survival and propagation. Agriculture, as the most extensive human intervention in nature, also has to adapt to these changes (Mazoyer and Roudart 2006), which makes innovation mandatory to improving food production and to maintaining current production levels.

In the field, innovations are often not implemented in a strictly prescribed form: many farmers adapt and use innovations to make best use of available resources or meet regulations. For example, much of organic agriculture continues to use the principles of conventional agriculture but replaces fertilizers and pesticides with the components permitted by organic certifiers (Rosset and Altieri 1997). The differences in risk adversity among farmers, together with the existence of crop insurance programs, intellectual property restrictions, type and level of education, and availability of financial resources, affects the choice and usage of innovation. People naturally avoid novel or unfamiliar procedures if they have too much to lose.

For the purpose of this chapter, we differentiate between three emblematic streams of innovation destined to improve crop production and reduce the ecological footprint of agriculture: conventional agriculture, precision agriculture, and agroecology. These three innovation streams differ not only in their research goals but also in their research processes and the way they empower users to keep innovating.

Conventional agriculture is the most propagated form of food production among large-scale farmers. The goal is to increase yields of key staple crops and reduce labor inputs. This farming method is characterized by the use of improved seed varieties, externally produced pesticides and fertilizers, and heavy machinery. Conventional agriculture is also characterized by the use of standardized solutions, or use guides (Robaey 2016b), thereby reducing the risk of losses due to absenteeism or the unavailability of a skilled labor force (Timmermann and Félix 2015b). Little innovation is done on farms themselves, as much of the research and development is outsourced to specialized laboratories and industry and requires biotechnological, chemical, and mechanical knowledge. Knowledge is produced and exchanged in academia, public institutions, private-public partnerships, and industry, but its full access is restricted by the use of intellectual property rights (Robaey 2016b). This applies both to conventionally bred crops and genetically modified ones. This innovation stream often uses controlled test sites or model organisms in the knowledge acquisition process. Typically, user innovation in this stream is limited as indicated in contracts, use guides, and intellectual property law.

Precision agriculture seeks to overcome the shortcomings of conventional agriculture and strives for sustainability by using forefront technology (Lindblom et al. 2017). For instance, sensors and the use of satellites for detailed mapping help avoid the use of excessive amounts of agrochemicals, thereby reducing contamination and the destruction of nontarget organisms

(Gebbers and Adamchuk 2010). In general, innovation is done in specialized industry sectors and research institutes. However, there is a key difference when compared to conventional agriculture. Specifically, the high technologization of agriculture demands a skilled labor force that is able to read the instruments on-site and adjust inputs. As such, the use of information technology allows for the integration of users' data and observations back into the innovation system. Whether the users are delegated to being a mere data collector or an autonomous user of such data depends on the technology design. Different possible scenarios can therefore occur in terms of user innovation.

Agroecology seeks to develop farming systems that are self-sufficient by closing ecological cycles and producing the necessary inputs to allow an ecological intensification of food production. As a principle-based approach, farmers need to learn how to use biodiversity to their advantage, mimic the functioning of local ecosystems for food production, and build long-term synergies between the living organisms of the farm and the surrounding social and natural environment (Altieri, Nicholls, and Montalba 2017; Gomez Echeverri et al. 2017). Farmers gain knowledge as they experiment with plant associations, composting methods, and biological fertilizers and observe how and if these changes contribute to the closing of nutrient cycling, the maintenance of moisture levels, and the improvement of harvests and soils. The knowledge gained on farms is often exchanged among farmers, yet efforts are needed to network farmers with other farmers and ecologists in distant locations to improve knowledge exchange. Here, given that innovations rely on practices and experimentation, user innovation is increased.

Given this brief characterization of the three streams of agricultural innovation, we now move on to analyze how innovations address key social challenges and meet the different criteria of fairness.

IV. WHAT MAKES AN INNOVATION FAIR?

Responsible Research and Innovation

Responsible Research and Innovation (RRI) grew out of a European research agenda, is a concept that has gained traction in academia, industry, and policy (Stilgoe, Owen, and Macnaghten 2013; von Schomberg 2015), and is slowly gaining interests in other parts of the world (Macnaghten et al. 2014). Von Schomberg defines RRI as "a transparent, interactive process by which societal actors and innovators become mutually responsive to each other with a view to the (ethical) acceptability, sustainability and societal desirability of the innovation process and its marketable products (in order to allow a proper embedding of scientific and technological advances in our society)" (2012, 49).

This approach suggests that many social issues can be taken up and addressed during the design phase, before a technology is "released" in society. This is realized through a process centered on the innovator. In RRI, the innovator must carry out a range of activities around the four pillars of RRI: anticipation, inclusion, reflexivity, and responsiveness (Stilgoe, Owen, and Macnaghten 2013). For instance, an innovator must anticipate the broader societal and environmental effects of the innovation. This process needs to include stakeholders to gain a more accurate picture of the possible effects of the invention. After gathering this information, the innovator is invited to reflect on his or her work and should respond to social and environmental concerns. RRI suggests that carrying out these activities will lead to more responsible innovations.

As a process, RRI connects the formulation of goal definition to the process of innovation. The process of RRI and its creation of activities and spaces of inclusion allow for the anticipation of how a technology might impact certain users or groups. In addition, reflection and responsiveness allow for changes to be made to the technology or to the institutions around the technology in order to respond to identified concerns. An example of such change could be in the choice of an affordable material for a design, so that it could be reproduced at low cost. A nontechnical choice could be opting for an open license instead of a patent so that the innovation would be more accessible. In other words, under RRI, an innovation comes to solve a problem *for* a group.

As a concept, we can understand RRI as a notion of forward-looking moral responsibility, that is, moral responsibility to fulfill certain desired outcomes, duties, or virtues (van de Poel 2011). This suggests that a fair innovation according to RRI is the result of participatory processes and a redefinition of goals. However, fairness is not necessarily a goal of RRI in itself, as it will depend on the stakeholders involved. In the same manner, the acceptability, sustainability, and social desirability of the innovation will also be dependent on the extent of participatory activities. Identifying and addressing social challenges is therefore dependent on those who manage the process of participation, how they ask questions, and what space they leave for discussion. Also, the innovator is most often in the private sector or at a university research center, so setting the goals and deciding on the process is necessarily constrained by these settings.

Depending on its depth, any given activity runs the risk of remaining superficial and not actually leading to changes in the goals or design (De Hoop, Pols, and Romijn 2016). Yet by having a starting point for innovation with industrial agendas, RRI "may lead to silencing of critical, 'rogue' voices and outsiders in the debate, due to increased dependency on private sector parties and policy agendas" (Zwart, Landeweerd, and van Rooij 2014, 11). By working closely with industry, RRI gets additional insights and accuracy but may lose its ability to argue for radical shifts in research agendas and marketing practices.

Theories of Justice

Complementing RRI with theories of justice might provide for a further elaboration of the concept of fair innovation. As we will see, being inclusive, responsive, and reflexive and anticipating impact are only part of what constitutes a fair innovation. We need points of reference, or ethical guidelines, that are independent of processes like RRI, in order to guide it. Toward this end, we can identify five dimensions of social justice that affect agricultural innovations. These are distributive justice, commutative justice (i.e., justice in transactions), contributive justice, restorative justice, and intergenerational justice (Timmermann 2017). Table 11.1 summarizes the observations that the two theoretical approaches contribute to the assessment of the five social challenges.

Distributive Justice

Distributive justice is generally concerned with the fair distribution of a good or set of goods. There are different ways we can interpret how distributive justice applies to innovation. One way is to argue that research attention is a good to be distributed, and therefore should be distributed according to principles of justice, for example, by aligning the distribution of research attention to the social goal of reducing suffering. This would demand research attention in proportion to the urgency of the needs of people and the environment. In the context of food and climate change, this translates to doing more research on adapting tropical agriculture to climate change and on developing appropriate technologies to reduce the carbon footprint of agriculture, and to studying methods to capture carbon in farmlands as a climate change mitigation strategy. Conversely, it condemns the spending of large amounts of resources in ornamental plants and minor aesthetic attributes. This could mean focusing more on flood-resistant varieties and less on selecting for shape or color. This dimension of justice provides a base to formulate ethical guidelines for defining the goals of innovation.

Commutative Justice

Also, principles of commutative justice (or justice in transactions) demand that exchanges involve informed consent, avoid causing harm, and are not exploitative or usurious. Market practices such as intentionally deceiving buyers or sellers are condemned. And principles of commutative justice demand that prices should not be set according to what the market will bear but instead to recoup necessary costs and to earn a reasonable profit. For instance, should a flood-resistant crop become extremely necessary, it would be important to have justice in transactions in order to avoid inflated prices or the creation of a black market for counterfeited seeds. This dimension of justice is important in defining ethical guidelines for the goal of innovation, since a socially sensitive design can make sure that innovations do not incorporate superfluous features that inflate prices and thus limit access.

Contributive Justice

The aim of contributive justice is to create the conditions where people are willing and able to contribute to society. To make innovation fair, this notion of justice demands an increase in participation opportunities, as well as more diversified participation opportunities that stand in meaningful and respectful relation to others. If we continue with the example of flood-resistant varieties, contributive justice demands that these varieties not be developed outside of their context and the farmers who plant them. This dimension of justice provides criteria to formulate ethical guidelines for defining how an innovation can empower social groups by providing sufficient access.

Restorative Justice

This idea of justice seeks to restore good social relationships after an injustice or misunderstanding. Innovation, as a social enterprise of considerable magnitude, will inevitably give rise to problems that will demand penalization mechanisms and proper reconciliation measures. Living in a world with common threats, such as pathogens and climate change, requires good relations to be able to work together toward solutions and contention strategies. This dimension of justice is relevant to providing ethical guidelines for the process of innovation, so that future cooperation is not hampered by injustices committed during research and development.

Intergenerational Justice

This last dimension of social justice condemns the decisions of earlier generations that make it difficult for future generations to live a flourishing life. This demands that innovators offer adequate compensation for the destruction of exhaustible resources that the use of their innovations directly or indirectly causes. For instance, a new crop might provide benefits in the near future at the cost of rapid soil erosion. What measures will be taken to ensure the quality of soils for future generations? This dimension of justice can serve as an ethical guideline for thinking about the sustainability goals of innovation.

Application to Social Challenges

For each social challenge (listed below), we can see how RRI and the different dimensions of social justice can help formulate guidelines for fair agricultural innovations in the context of climate change when it comes to the goals, processes, and opportunities for empowerment surrounding these innovations. Table 11.2 summarizes the ethical guidelines proposed for each social challenge and identifies the part of the innovation process to which each one matters.

Availability is linked to the process and the goal of an innovation, mostly because availability is dependent on early decisions in the innovation process. From an RRI perspective, reflexivity can provide the space to make design choices that would increase availability. From the perspective of theories of distributive justice, reflection should create awareness of problems that demand priority for social challenges. The guideline for addressing availability is, therefore: in the definition of the goal and in the process resulting thereof, innovators should think not only about the availability of their innovation, but also about the context and the scope of their innovation, as well as whether it is addressing issues of need. Dealing with climate change requires prioritizing pressing issues such as adaptation or mitigation innovations.

Accessibility is important both at the beginning of innovation, when decisions are made about the design, and toward the end, when strategies are made to improve inclusion and participation to allow empowerment. From the perspective of theories of commutative justice, attention should be paid to ensure just transactions between innovators and farmers. The guideline for addressing accessibility is, therefore, a result of participatory actions before and after the innovation process, which derives from an RRI perspective; innovators and other actors should create a responsive agreement that leads to just transactions. The adoption of agricultural innovations for climate change will depend on how distribution channels are set up.

Participation in science and governance is linked to the process, which, if responsive, will relate to a redefinition of goals. Participation stems from both theories of contributive justice as well as the inclusive and responsive aspects of RRI. This requires including different voices in the process, including traditionally underrepresented ones. The importance of considering these various voices is primordial for fairness—this is a requirement for both participation in innovation governance and inventive endeavors. Here, the guidelines for addressing participation are the inclusion of as many voices as possible, especially from affected areas, the explication of choices made to their consideration in a democratic way, and the creation of opportunities to participate after the innovation is "released" in society.

Arbitration concerns the process of fair innovations. This has to do with the limited range of action of innovators, meaning that not all the decisions are in their hands. Here, from an RRI perspective, responsiveness is not limited to them. Instead, institutional agreements, such as decisions about a global climate fund or how to address issues of restorative justice, must also be responsive. For instance, rising sea levels will affect many countries, which will need a range of innovations to adapt. Agreements regarding those agricultural innovations should look to support those facing imminent threats in order to avoid exploitative sales practices.

Last but not least, *long-term sustainability* is essential to the process of innovation and can also help redefine the goals of innovation. As a guidepost for fair innovation, sustainability requires a process of anticipation from an RRI perspective, where activities are carried out by and with different actors, including innovators, with regard to intergenerational justice issues. This social challenge is inextricably linked to society's realization that we must deal with climate change so as to not overburden future generations.

V. ASSESSING FAIRNESS OF AGRICULTURAL INNOVATION

We see our ethical framework as a procedural approach for fair innovation, incorporating issues of social justice. Here, we briefly apply our framework to the three innovation streams.

Table 11.1: Defining Fairness with RRI and Theories of Justice

5 Key Social Challenges	Responsible Research and Innovation	Theories of Justice
Availability	Reflexivity (self-scrutiny, or institutionalized scrutiny; e.g., social responsibility to assist)	Fair distribution of research attention
Accessibility	Responsiveness (fairness)	Just transactions
Participation in science and governance	Inclusion (a dialogue with diverging voices) Participatory decision-making	As a social mandate to include in innovation processes (open science) Condemns exclusion in democratic processes
Arbitration	Limited to the range of action of innovators Responsiveness (capacity to change)	Everyone needs to commit to principles of social justice to avoid systemic deprivation Address historical injustices
Long-term sustainability	Anticipation (capacity of foresight)	Fair shares for each generation

Authors' own

Table 11.2: Guidelines for Fair Agricultural Innovations

5 Key Social Challenges	Innovation Stage	Guidelines
Availability	Process and goal	- Design choices for availability - Direction of innovation: Does it respond to socially relevant needs?
Accessibility	Goal and empowerment	- Responsive agreements for just transactions
Participation in science and governance	Empowerment	- Inclusion of all actors - Democratic process - Explication of decisions
Arbitration	Process	- Support for those facing imminent threats in order to ensure fair innovations
Long-term sustainability	Process and goal	- Anticipation activities carried out by and with different actors, including innovators, with regard to intergenerational issues

Authors' own

Conventional Agriculture

Availability: Under a proprietary science regime, where market demands set research agendas, research attention may not be granted to the needs of the poor. In agriculture, this means that the regions with the largest numbers of hungry people will continuously remain underserved. Well-funded public research institutes are needed to make technological solutions available and accessible to this group. This is a huge issue for social justice, as conventional agriculture foresees that the objects of innovation have to be acquired, primarily by farmers purchasing these from innovators and suppliers (Thompson 2009a).

Accessibility: Technologies in this stream are sold or licensed under contracts, which limits their access. For instance, in the case of genetically modified seeds, contracts typically dictate the extent of use, often preventing farmers from saving seeds or experimenting (Robaey 2016b). Different choices can be made for accessibility in this stream. They can be licensed under contracts, and farmers can be prevented from saving seeds; another choice is to distribute them for free, allowing wider access. Taking accessibility seriously can empower farmers.

Participation in science and governance: The nature and existence of intellectual property regimes make participation in science and science governance particularly difficult unless the patent holders welcome participation. Intellectual property rights can restrict access to innovation and meaningful participation.

Arbitration: Arbitration is extremely difficult and costly, especially when insufficient knowledge is publicly available. Involved parties will have to come to a consensus and settle disputes. Here, special care needs to be taken so that specialists, such as lawyers and scientists, are not exploiting weaker negotiation partners.

Long-term sustainability: Finally, the weak record conventional agriculture has in internalizing negative externalities makes this form of food production inadequate in terms of long-term sustainability (Tittonell et al. 2016). Innovation has to take into account the full costs of food production, including carbon footprints, fossil fuel dependency, and pollution.

Precision Agriculture

Availability: In terms of availability, many of the sensor and ICT technologies that precision agriculture uses need not be context specific. The challenge lies in social and infrastructural limitations, as these technologies require a skilled labor force (Aubert, Schroeder, and Grimaudo 2012) and easy access to technical service centers.

Accessibility: By relying on vanguard technology, precision agriculture continuously faces struggles with accessibility. Who can purchase and operate these technologies? But also, even if affordable, who owns the data and who has the power to make decisions about it? Access to data has the potential to empower farmers (Fountas et al. 2005) by helping them make better decisions for the management of their farm. However, access and ownership of data can also lead to different corporate decisions by those who collect the data (Bronson and Knezevic 2016). Such corporate decisions could threaten access to certain essential technologies in view of increased profit. For instance, learning about farming practices and behavior can inform industrial decisions on pricing for their services and technologies.

Participation in science and governance: The use of information technologies allows, in principle, a higher level of participation both in scientific work and in governance. However, allowing participation needs to be in the interest of technology developers. As far as participation in the development and governance of equipment goes, we may find the same hurdles as with conventional agriculture, due to intellectual property restrictions.

Arbitration: The case with arbitration is also very similar to the one with conventional agriculture. However, we speculate that as more data produced by precision agriculture becomes publicly available, the more likely it is to be used by civil society and government agencies to make comparisons and assert pressures on farmers.

Long-term sustainability: In terms of long-term sustainability, the very aim of precision agriculture is to use more technology to reduce the environmental footprint. Yet it is a costly variant, making its expansion slow and, for many, a luxury. This may lead to a social justice issue, as richer regions will be able to grasp the benefits of such scientific advancement at a much greater scale than poorer regions.

Agroecology

Availability: Agroecology offers a wide range of innovative solutions that are particularly well suited for the tropical environment, as it draws heavily on the methods and knowledge that indigenous communities have used to build resilient farming systems in these latitudes. Studies that apply agroecological principles to temperate climates and urban settings are much more recent and therefore more uncommon.

Accessibility: While offering innovations that depend largely on local resources, economic incentives to diffuse and test agroecological innovations are insufficient. As a result, most agroecological innovations are underused despite being freely accessible.

Participation in science and governance: As a principle-based approach, agroecology foresees that innovations be adapted to local circumstances and encourages participation in its development. This requires tacit knowledge, the ability to apply principles, and good observation skills (Timmermann and Félix 2015b). Unfortunately, even though farmers' organizations are very large, the modularity of most agroecological farms does not provide a compulsory platform where innovation governance issues are discussed. Also of concern is that nonfarming citizens will rarely be involved.

Arbitration: As agroecology seeks to eliminate the use of agrochemicals and to live in harmony with adjacent ecosystems, it perceives itself as nonintrusive, working toward avoiding annoyances rather than establishing mechanisms to resolve them. By not claiming exclusivity and welcoming a farmer-to-farmer knowledge exchange, agroecologists have treated traditional knowledge as common heritage, a practice that may lead to disputes and over which no commonly agreed-upon arbitration principles exist.

Long-term sustainability: Agroecology strongly embraces long-term sustainability, both socially and environmentally (Altieri, Nicholls, and Montalba 2017). An example of a noteworthy innovation is the use of termites to recover deteriorated soils. By filling small holes with woody scrubs farmers attract termites that forage on the woody amendments, thereby allowing water and air into the lower layers of the soil, which ultimately contributes to soil restoration and thus the ability to grow food again in arid areas (Félix et al. 2018). Here the benefits of the farming systems are fully acknowledged, including the benefits to ecosystem services and farm workers' health.

In sum, each of the three streams of agricultural innovations presents room for improvement to varying degrees concerning fairness. We see this as an opportunity to innovate for social justice, regardless of technological preferences.

CONCLUSION

Climate change presents serious challenges to the environment and food systems. As a result, there is an increasing need for agricultural innovation in the regions that count the highest number of hungry people, which are also the regions most underserved with regard to agricultural innovation. Moreover, the regions with the largest number of hungry people have historically benefited the least from the past liberty to emit greenhouse gases. These issues are morally relevant and require an ethical assessment of agricultural innovations. Due to the dire conditions climate change is creating and their unequal impacts, this ethical assessment needs to address five major social challenges: accessibility, availability, participation in science and governance, arbitration mechanisms, and long-term sustainability. Complicating the ethical assessment is the diversity of agricultural innovation streams: conventional agriculture, precision agriculture, and agroecology.

How do we assess agricultural innovation in light of these social challenges? How can we support addressing the shortcomings of the agricultural innovation systems? We suggest an assessment using a double ethical framework of RRI and theories of justice. The formulated guidelines (table 11.2) address a specific social challenge and a specific component of innovation in relation to its goals, processes, and empowerment.

After a brief and general assessment of each agricultural innovation stream, we have identified the following overarching shortcomings: (1) the need to improve the availability of agricultural innovation to adapt to climate change for the areas where they are most needed; (2) the need to make sure that these innovations are accessible to those who urgently need them and that users are empowered, without neglecting regions most vulnerable to climate change; (3) the need to improve participation in agricultural innovation, especially in the context where those innovations are meant to be used; (4) the need to enforce strong arbitration measures in the innovation system, with special consideration to the problem of commercial exploitation of climate-vulnerable countries; and (5) the need to work toward long-term sustainability by incorporating both climate change adaptation and mitigation strategies.

Further research would help to pinpoint specifically where responsibilities lie for each of these components of innovation and social challenges. For now, the guidelines we suggest can be used either to assess recent innovations and make adjustments or to set up a process with clear guideposts that would result in fairer agricultural innovations. Ultimately, these guidelines aim to redress the unequal balances in access to knowledge, participation in innovation decisions, and the governance of these innovations.

NOTES

1. Acknowledgments: ZR is funded under NWO-MWI project "Inclusive Biobased Innovations," and CT is supported by a postdoctoral fellowship (FONDECYT/ CONICYT No. 3170068).
2. For criticism, see Meyer and Roser (2010).

Chapter 12

Liberal Political Justice, Food Choice, and Environmental Harm

Why Justice Demands We Eat Less Meat

Sarah Kenehan

In this chapter, I seek to explore the tension between limiting food choice and liberal democratic principles of justice. In particular, what we choose to eat is very often a function of our moral autonomy; for some of us, our diets are intimately tied to our conception of the good life, and so protecting the ability to choose what we eat is one way in which our autonomy as moral agents is guaranteed. But our food choices also have consequences: what we eat and how we produce our food could have an enormous cumulative impact on the health of the planet. Perhaps one of the most vivid examples of this impact is the choice to consume animals that were raised on factory farms. There is no debating the environmental costs of intensive animal agriculture (Simon 2013; Food and Agriculture Organization of the United Nations 2006b), and yet, however compelling the reasons, restricting meat consumption in liberal democracies is often thought to be at odds with the aims and values of such societies.

This chapter analyzes this claim by exploring the link between animal agriculture and political injustice. Toward this end, I begin by looking at the possibility of condemning animal agriculture in liberal societies by appealing to comprehensive moral doctrines. While this route surely has the potential to be effective, its political strength is necessarily a function of the moral consensus of the majority, and so the influence of these types of arguments is merely contingent. As such, I develop an alternate route that is rooted in strict principles of liberal political justice, first detailing the environmental costs of animal agriculture and then exploring how the U.S. government participates in the animal food market. Next, I examine exactly how those costs are distributed, highlighting trends that show that the poor—domestically and globally—disproportionately bear the environmental costs of factory farming. Because this burden further contributes to the oppression of these groups, such practices are necessarily the concern of political justice. I apply Rawls's theory of justice as illustrative of these concerns and I argue that government participation in programs that essentially serve to subsidize these harms is contrary to the aims of liberal democratic societies. Thus, it appears that there is strong justification for employing coercive measures (either directly or indirectly) to limit food choice in liberal democracies.

I. CONDEMNING ANIMAL AGRICULTURE IN A LIBERAL DEMOCRACY

Most condemnations of common practices used in industrial animal agriculture are based on the effects these practices have on animals; they focus on animal suffering, animal rights, or the virtue of human compassion (see, for instance, Donovan 1990; Regan 1983; Singer 2009). For many of us, these arguments are compelling, and so we make the personal choices to limit or eliminate animal products from our diets. And, there are even some among us who are so moved by these arguments that they are inspired to lobby on behalf of the animals, to try to convince others to make similar choices, and to try to create change on the political level. Of course, the ability to do these things—to deliberate over and choose a conception of the good life, and then to act from that conception, both privately and publicly—is a function of our autonomous nature. It is the need to protect and preserve this nature, coupled with the acknowledgement that equally autonomous and well-informed individuals may come to radically different conclusions on what constitutes the good life (i.e., reasonable value pluralism) that most strongly grounds calls for political liberalism.

In recognition of value pluralism, most agree that deliberation over constitutional essentials and questions of basic justice should only be debated from the standpoint of public reason, not from the standpoint of one's own conception of the good (Rawls 1993, 214). But for other nonfundamental issues, including the treatment and consumption of animals, the limits of public reason do not strictly apply, which means that values other than political ones can be appealed to when discussing/debating such concerns. In these sorts of matters, citizens can appeal to their own comprehensive moral, religious, or philosophical doctrine to make their case. So, for instance, a citizen is permitted to appeal to moral principles in the public realm that point to the wrongness of inflicting unnecessary suffering in an effort to condemn animal agriculture. Of course, there is no guarantee that other citizens with different and competing views of the good life will find these arguments compelling, and so the political force that such arguments might have toward inspiring change is questionable, as it is largely dependent on political will. This is not to say that public discourse will necessarily result in failure or gridlock, but rather that the success of this method is just as much (perhaps more) a function of the receptivity and open-mindedness of the voting population as it is of compelling and coherent arguments.

Notwithstanding the very serious concerns about animal welfare and the strength of the moral arguments that draw attention to these concerns, it may be that the environmental costs of factory farming provide an important though often unnoticed link to concerns of political justice. In particular, I contend that by focusing on the harmful environmental costs of factory farming, liberal political theorists can coherently argue that there are strong reasons to ban the consumption of intensively produced animal products. And if such a connection can be made, then rethinking the way that we use animals for food will be not simply be a matter of political will, but rather a matter of political justice as well. Of course, in order to defend this claim, I must first detail the sorts of environmental harms that are linked to factory farming; this will be the topic of the following section.

II. THE ENVIRONMENTAL COSTS OF INTENSIVE ANIMAL AGRICULTURE

The Food and Agriculture Organization of the United Nations reports that "the livestock sector emerges as one of the top two or three most significant contributors to the most serious environmental problems, at every scale from local to global" (2006b, xx). Given the enormity of these impacts, it is impossible to catalog all of the environmental harms brought on by factory farming, or to list all of the relevant statistics documenting these harms, in the short space of this chapter allotted to these descriptions. Nonetheless, in this section I will offer a brief sketch of the damages caused by factory farming, starting first with water pollution and land degradation and then exploring the effects of factory farming on global climate change.

Animal Agriculture and Environmental Degradation

Unsurprisingly, raising animals for food requires massive amounts of water; for instance, roughly four hundred gallons of water are required to produce a single egg, four thousand gallons of water are used to produce one hamburger, and three million gallons of water are used to raise a single, half-ton beef steer (Simon 2013).[1] This use of water is surely wasteful in light of the fact that water security is threatened around the globe in both developed and developing nations; in fact, according to the World Health Organization, four out of every ten people live in a state of water insecurity (United Nations n.d.). And while we might be tempted to think that nations like the United States are immune to these problems, we need only to point out that, as of the writing of this chapter, 23.2 percent of the United States is currently in a drought (affecting approximately 62 million people) (National Integrated Drought Information System n.d.).

Concentrated animal feeding operations (CAFOs) also pose a threat to available water in the form of dangerous pollution. Packing tens of thousands of animals into a small space and feeding them a diet of largely unnatural foods aimed at increasing their size in the shortest amount of time creates enormous amounts of waste materials that need to be managed. Specifically, "a typical pig factory farm will produce 7.2 million pounds of manure annually, a typical broiler facility will produce 6.6 million pounds, and a typical cattle feedlot 344 million pounds" (Foer 2009, 90). All together, "farmed animals in the United States produce 130 times as much waste as the human population—roughly 87,000 pounds of shit *per second.* The polluting strength of this shit is 160 times greater than raw municipal sewage" (ibid.). But the sheer amount of waste, while staggering, is not the largest concern: the real problem is that in the United States at least, there is no waste treatment infrastructure for farmed animals. Indeed, there are almost no federal guidelines that regulate waste from these facilities; according to the U.S. GAO (Government Accountability Office), "no federal agency even collects reliable data on factory farms or so much as knows the number of permitted factory farms nationally and therefore cannot 'effectively regulate' them" (Foer 2009, 90). Consequently, it is common industry practice for the waste from these farms to go untreated for disease-causing pathogens, chemicals, pharmaceuticals, heavy metals, or other pollutants (Sierra Club: Michigan Chapter n.d.). Inevitably, be it through runoff, air transport, aerial spraying, flooding, or some other means, the poisons contained in the waste eventually make it to the water sources that people depend on (United States Environmental Protection Agency n.d.). In one North Carolina town surrounded by pig farms, the local Department of Environmental Quality "admits that there are intakes for municipal water systems on area rivers, which means that even if locals aren't using well water, they can still be bathing in, cooking with, and drinking water tainted with hog waste" (Skolnick 2017).

In addition to using and polluting substantial amounts of water, intensive animal agriculture likewise requires vast amounts of land on which to raise animals and to grow the plants that are used to feed them. The Food and Agriculture Organization of the United Nations reports that

> livestock is the world's largest user of land resources, with grazing land and cropland dedicated to the production of feed representing almost 80% of all agricultural land. Feed crops are grown in one-third of total cropland, while the

total land area occupied by pasture is equivalent to 26% of the ice-free terrestrial surface. (n.d.)

Creating space to support this type of farming has resulted in enormous amounts of global deforestation, with one study concluding that as much as 80 percent of deforestation is catalyzed by agricultural needs (Kissinger, Herold, and De Sy 2012, 5). For instance, 70 percent of the previously forested areas of the Amazon are now occupied by pasture, with feed crops covering the remainder of the area (Food and Agriculture Organization of the United Nations 2006b, xxi). Furthermore, 20 percent of the world's pastures and rangeland have been significantly degraded because of overgrazing, compaction, and erosion, all resulting from livestock production (ibid.). In turn, these land changes create a real threat to biodiversity:

> Habitat loss from grazing livestock and feed crops is far and away the most pervasive threat to terrestrial animal species, impacting 86 percent of all mammals, 88 percent of amphibians, and 86 percent of all birds. One in every eight birds, one in every three amphibians, and one in every four mammals is facing an extremely high risk of extinction in the near future. (Machovina, Feeley, and Ripple 2015, 419)

Animal Agriculture and Global Climate Change

In fact, in the United States, agriculture is the primary source of methane emissions (United States Environmental Protection Agency 2018), with animal agriculture (via enteric fermentation and manure management) making up 36 percent of total U.S. methane emissions (ibid). Globally, methane accounts for 16 percent of total GHG emissions (Working Group III 2014, 6). And in 2005, agriculture was the source of 47 percent of total anthropogenic methane emissions (Working Group III 2007, 503), with enteric fermentation and manure management together comprising 43 percent of total non-carbon dioxide emissions from agriculture (ibid). (This specific data was not available in the most recent IPCC report, so data from the previous publication was used.) This proportion may at first seem relatively inconsequential, but in a pound for pound comparison to carbon dioxide, methane has a twenty-five times greater impact in catalyzing climate change, despite the fact that it has a much shorter atmospheric lifespan (United States Environmental Protection Agency 2018). And while these numbers are surely impactful, some studies have nonetheless concluded that they are actually incomplete. In particular, there are many "indirect ways" in which animal agriculture contributes to global climate change (GCC) that are not accounted for in these statistics. These include:

- Burning fossil fuels to produce mineral fertilizers used in feed production;
- Methane produced from the breakdown of fertilizers;
- Land-use changes for feed production and for grazing;
- Land degradation;
- Fossil fuel use during feed and animal production; and
- Fossil fuel use in production and transport of processed and refrigerated animal products (ibid.).

In considering all of these indirect sources, it is estimated that animal agriculture contributes to approximately 18 percent of total anthropogenic GHG emissions (Food and Agriculture Organization of the United Nations 2006b, 112).[2] Clearly then, animal agriculture is a very significant driver of GCC.

Summary

In this section, I offered a tentative description of the environmental problems that are related to factory farming. In the following section, I will show how these harms are directly supported by the U.S. government, an important first step in connecting the environmental harms of factory farming to concerns of liberal political justice.

III. GOVERNMENT INTERFERENCE IN THE ANIMAL PROTEIN MARKET

While the process of producing animal protein is largely unregulated (as detailed above), the U.S. government is heavily involved in the regulation and manipulation of the animal protein market. Consider first the use of checkoff programs: checkoffs are essentially a tax on certain commodities, generating revenue to support marketing and research to increase the sale of that commodity (Simon 2013, 4). The USDA oversees all animal food product checkoff programs and spends approximately $557.5 million every year to promote these products to American consumers (Becker 2008, 1–2). These programs are responsible for the massively successful "Beef: It's What's for Dinner," "Pork: The Other White Meat," and "Milk: It Does a Body Good" campaigns (Becker 2008, 2). The USDA estimates that these programs have led to a $4.6 billion increase in sales; that is, $4.6 billion dollars of animal products were sold over and above what would have otherwise been purchased (Simon 2013, 78).

Government subsidies have likewise influenced the production and consumption of meat in the United States. In total, the U.S. government pays out about $57.3 billion annually in agricultural subsidies, and these payments are awarded to animal food producers by more than thirty times what is granted to fruit and vegetable farmers (Becker 2008, 1). In fact, animal food producers have benefited so much from these programs that, from 1980 to 2008, the inflation-adjusted price of ground beef fell by 53 percent while the costs of fruits rose 46 percent and the costs of vegetables rose 41 percent (Simon 2013, 78; Physicians Committee for Responsible Medicine n.d.; Leonhardt 2009). Expressed differently, nearly 63 percent of U.S. agricultural subsidies benefit animal food producers. Add to this the $2.3 billion for fish subsidies, and the total annual estimated subsidy payment to animal food producers is roughly $8.4 billion (Simon 2013, 80).

And, if the subsidies weren't enough, the government also supports large buyback programs, through which they purchase back already heavily subsidized food products that went unsold:

> In fiscal year 2009, USDA spent more than $623 million to buy dairy products. … In the same year, USDA spent more than $1.4 billion to purchase other agricultural commodities, including at least $793 million for beef, pork, poultry, eggs, and fish, $644 million for fruits and vegetables, $96 million for grains, and $50 million for oils and nuts. USDA also made $319.5 million in "emergency" commodity purchases intended to relieve farm surpluses in 2009, which included large purchases of pork and poultry. (Physicians Committee for Responsible Medicine n.d.)

The cumulative consequence of these various forms of market interference is somewhat predictable: animal products are readily available and promoted, and the costs borne by consumers of animal products are much lower than they would otherwise be. The lower prices and increased availability, in turn, lead to an increased production and consumption of animal products, subsequently increasing the externalized environmental costs that are created by factory farming. Put succinctly, the U.S. government is responsible in more ways than one for the environmental damages listed previously: they consistently fail to properly regulate CAFOs and, through checkoff, subsidy, and buyback programs, they actively promote the purchase and production of environmentally damaging animal food products. Thus, given the connection between the U.S. government and the environmental harms of factory farming, we need to consider how these harms are distributed, since the distribution of these harms will be of direct interest to concerns of political justice. As such, this will be the topic of the following section.

IV. WHO BEARS THE BURDEN OF ENVIRONMENTAL HARMS?

Political justice is oriented toward identifying the rights and freedoms of individuals and the ways in which these rights and freedoms may be threatened. As such, liberal political theorists should be concerned with practices and policies that tend toward political injustice and social inequalities that may threaten political justice (or the possibility of political justice). This means that it is important for us to consider the ways in which the environmental harms of factory farming are distributed, both domestically in the United States and abroad. As before, it would be impossible to list all of the relevant facts and statistics here, so I will only attempt to sketch the larger trends that define these distributions. I'll begin by considering how the costs of factory farming are spread domestically, and then I'll consider the global apportioning of these burdens.

The Distribution of Environmental Harms in the United States

The National Association of Local Boards of Health reports:

> All of the environmental problems with CAFOs have direct impact on human health and welfare for communities that contain large industrial farms .... human health can suffer because of contaminated air and degraded water quality, or from diseases spread from farms. Quality of life can suffer because of odors or insect vectors surrounding farms, and property values can drop, affecting the financial stability of a community. (2010, 2)

Specifically, table 12.1 lists the various CAFO pollutants and the ailments with which they are associated:

While all people living near factory farms are at risk of developing the illnesses listed in table 12.1, the research shows that children are particularly at risk, since they take in 20 to 50 percent more air than adults do (National Association of Local Boards of Health 2010, 5–6). Additionally, the odors produced by these farms can have damaging impacts on physical and mental health:

> CAFO odors can cause severe lifestyle changes for individuals in the surrounding communities and can alter many daily activities. When odors are severe, people may choose to keep their windows closed, even in high temperatures when there is no air conditioning. People also may choose to not let their children play outside and may even keep them home from school. Mental health deterioration and an increased sensitization to smells can also

Table 12.1: CAFO Emissions and Health Risks

CAFO Emissions	Health Risks
Ammonia	Respiratory irritant; chemical burns to the respiratory tract, skin, and eyes; severe cough, chronic lung disease
Hydrogen Sulfide	Inflammation of the moist membranes of the eyes and respiratory tract, olfactory neuron loss, death
Methane	No health risks. It is a greenhouse gas and contributes to climate change.
Particulate Matter	Chronic bronchitis, chronic respiratory symptoms, declines in lung function, organic dust toxic syndrome

Source: National Association of Local Boards of Health. 2010. "Understanding Concentrated Animal Feeding Operations and Their Impact on Communities." Bowling Green, OH: 6.

result from living in close proximity to odors from CAFOs. Odor can cause negative mood states, such as tension, depression, or anger, and possibly neuro-psychiatric abnormalities, such as impaired balance or memory. People who live close to factory farms can develop CAFO-related post traumatic stress disorder, including anxiety about declining quality of life. (National Association of Local Boards of Health 2010, 8)

Further, the plume of odor released from these farms has been found to contain high levels of hydrogen sulfide, and "measures of odor, endotoxin, hydrogen sulfide, and PM_{10} were associated, variously, with increased respiratory difficulty, sore throat, chest tightness, nausea, and eye irritation, whereas hydrogen sulfide and semivolatile particles were linked to reports of feeling stressed, annoyed, nervous, and anxious" (Nicole 2013).

Beyond the health problems that exposure to these pollutants raise, decreases in property value are also serious concerns for individuals living near factory farms. Depending on the type of farm and one's proximity to the farm, property values can decrease from 6.6 percent (three miles from the operation) to 88 percent (one-tenth of a mile from the operation) (National Association of Local Boards of Health 2010, 11). Of course, decreases in property value lead to decreases in tax revenue that is used to support the community, thus adding another layer of harm to the equation (Simon 2013, 84).

Perhaps unsurprisingly, studies suggest that the environmental costs of factory farming in the United States, and the health problems that result, are disproportionately borne by poor communities, especially poor communities of color (Skolnick 2017; Mirabelli et al. 2009; Joint Center for Political and Economic Studies San Joaquin Valley Place Matters Team 2012; Nicole 2013). Indeed, "there is clear evidence of discriminatory impacts by race and class such that counties with larger minority populations, regardless of income, have larger concentrations of hog waste despite controlling for regional difference, urbanization, property values, and labor force attributes" (Edwards and Ladd 2001, 64). And one research team noted, "People of color and the poor living in rural communities lacking the political capacity to resist are said to shoulder the adverse socioeconomic, environmental, or health related effects of swine waste externalities without sharing in the economic benefits brought by industrialized pork production" (Nicole 2013). These trends therefore imply that the poor and persons of color are more likely to contract asthma, bronchitis, and chronic respiratory problems; are more likely to be exposed to zoological diseases and pathogens; are more likely to suffer from depression and fatigue, and are more likely to suffer socioeconomic harms than the relatively well-off white person, simply because of their proximity to factory farms. There is strong evidence that suggests that these sorts of cases can appropriately be categorized as environmental racism and classism.

The Distribution of Environmental Harms Abroad

As noted above, the methane released when raising animals for food is a significant driver of global climate change. As such, we must consider how the burdens of a warming world are being distributed. To begin, consider the following passage from the recent IPCC report on "Impacts, Adaptation, and Vulnerability":

> Differences in vulnerability and exposure arise from non-climatic factors and from multidimensional inequalities often produced by uneven development processes *(very high confidence)*. These differences shape differential risks from climate change. ... People who are socially, economically, culturally, politically, institutionally, or otherwise marginalized are especially vulnerable to climate change and also to some adaptation and mitigation responses *(medium evidence, high agreement)*. This heightened vulnerability is rarely due to a single cause. Rather, it is the product of intersecting social processes that result in inequalities in socioeconomic status and income, as well as in exposure. Such social processes include, for example, discrimination on the basis of gender, class, ethnicity, age, and (dis)ability. (Working Group II 2014, 6)

In fact, over and over in this report, the researchers stress the vulnerability of poor and developing nations, explaining that GCC will have adverse impacts in livelihoods, crop yield, and food security (Working Group II 2014, 7–8); that GCC will exacerbate health problems in already vulnerable populations, increasing the risk of weather-related morbidity and mortality, undernutrition, and food-, water-, and vector-borne diseases (Working Group II 2014, 19–20); that it will increase the displacement of people, especially for communities that lack resources for planned migrations (Working Group II 2014, 20); that it will indirectly increase the risk of violent conflicts by intensifying poverty and economic shocks (Working Group II 2014, 20); and that it will make poverty reduction more difficult while simultaneously exacerbating poverty in most developing countries (Working Group II 2014, 20). In short, the global poor are predicted to bear the largest burden of an increasingly warmer world.

Summary

In this section I outlined the patterns that mark the distribution of the environmental harms caused by factory farming. The most emergent trend is that the poor—both globally and domestically—bear a disproportionate burden of these harms. In light of the massive amount of money that the U.S. government spends to promote animal food products, combined with the fact that it enforces very little by way of substantive environmental regulation of CAFOs, the unavoidable conclusion is that the U.S. government is supporting and perpetuating the injustices of environmental racism and classism described above. In light of this conclusion, we are now nicely situated to think about the ways in which a conception of political justice can respond to this problem; this will be the focus of the following section.

V. LIBERAL POLITICAL JUSTICE AND ANIMAL AGRICULTURE

As detailed above, the costs of animal agriculture are more likely to be borne by the least well off among us, thus creating, or perpetuating, unjust inequalities. Specifically, the poor in the United States are more vulnerable to the environmental risks to which factory farming contributes (and are positioned in ways that make it difficult to avert these risks). And similarly, the global poor will suffer the worst consequences of a warming world, as many will lose their homes, others will find it increasingly difficult to grow food and secure potable water, and even more will be faced with threats to the stability of their public and political infrastructures, including but not limited to their economies (Working Group II 2014). To be clear, this means that the U.S. government's participation in the animal food market helps perpetuate the unjust marginalization of already oppressed segments of our domestic and global societies and likewise threatens the ability of other nations to achieve and maintain democratic stability. These are concerns that would likely be shared among a broad range of theories of liberal political justice.

Of course, as there are many such theories, it would be impractical here to explore how each one is able to capture the injustices instigated and perpetuated by animal agriculture. Instead, to illustrate how such theories can be applied to these injustices, I will analyze these connections from the point of view of Rawls's theory of justice, and I will show that, in this context, we can offer substance and force to our concern for the harms committed by animal agriculture.[3] I'll first consider the domestic harms and then move to a discussion of the international harms.

Animal Agriculture and Justice Between Citizens

Rawls writes that the aim of a liberal democracy is to "realize in the basic institutions the idea of society as a fair system of cooperation between citizens as free and equal" (Rawls 2001, 140). In order for this aim to be accomplished, society must be rooted on a foundation of equality to assure that each citizen can be a fully cooperating member. This equality must be established and ensured by society's institutions, primarily by guaranteeing each citizen the means to be a fully cooperating member of society. Rawls writes, "Only in this way can the basic structure [of society] realize pure pro-cedural background justice from one generation to the next" (ibid.).

One way to ensure citizens the means to become and remain fully cooper-ating members of society is to guarantee that each citizen has those things that are prerequisites for such participation. However, given the fact of rea-sonable pluralism, these prerequisites should not be determined by appealing to any one particular conception of the good; instead, we should think about what citizens need as citizens (Rawls 2001, 151). Rawls explains that two principles of justice assess the basic structure of society according to how it regulates a citizen's share of these prerequisites—what he calls "primary goods"—since these goods enable each citizen to advance his or her own con-ception of the good life.[4] There are some obvious goods related to the natural environment that are required in order to ensure public health, including, for example, potable water, clean air, and a functioning atmosphere, and so these things should be included on the list of primary goods.

Based on the evidence presented previously, it's quite clear that intensive animal agriculture exposes poor communities to serious public health risks. As such, guaranteeing environmental integrity that is directly related to public health should be a function of the policies and institutions of the basic structure in a well-ordered society. To this end, policies that properly manage the environmentally dangerous by-products of factory farms are necessary if the basic structure is to remain "a fair system of cooperation between free and equal citizens from one generation to the next" (Rawls 2001, 136).[5] Similarly, the government should refrain from subsidizing or marketing products that have such serious public health implications, since to do so underwrites the very injustices that inform these health concerns.

Furthermore, social cooperation results in the production of certain (primary) burdens that threaten the long-term health of the natural environment and so threaten the possibility of maintaining just institutions into the future (to the extent that environmental integrity is necessary for this endeavor). For example, air pollution and a degraded atmosphere can be categorized as primary burdens, as they are direct by-products of social cooperation. This categorization makes sense particularly in light of the fact that some social burdens would restrict a citizen's access to those goods that are rooted in environmental integrity (or, more generally, inhibit the possibility of preserving and establishing just institutions in later generations). For these reasons it seems that these social burdens should also be proper objects of control by our social institutions. More specifically, the government should be directly concerned with the environmental harms perpetuated by animal agriculture, as they are surely limiting access to the goods of clean water, viable land, clean air, and physical health of many already socially and politically marginalized communities.[6]

This previous point is underscored by Rawls's claim that the good of self-respect is also a primary good. He writes:

> It is clearly rational for men to secure their self-respect. A sense of their own worth is necessary if they are to pursue their conception of the good with satisfaction and to take pleasure in its fulfillment. Self-respect is not so much a part of any rational plan of life as the sense that one's plan is worth carrying out. Now our self-respect normally depends on the respect of others. Unless we feel that our endeavors are respected by them, it is difficult if not impossible for us to maintain the conviction that our ends are worth advancing. (Rawls 1999, 155–66)

Put succinctly, if the social bases of self-respect are absent or undermined, then individuals may begin to lose their social and political autonomy (Kollar and Santoro 2012), and it stands to reason that this condition is perpetuated or possibly even worsened when the bases of respect are eroded by the government itself, as in the case of the harms that result from intensive animal agriculture in the United States. Add to this situation the fact that these burdens disproportionately affect poor communities and communities of color, and it is not hard to see how all of these harms, including the damage done to self-respect, can cause, perpetuate, and reinforce damaging and unjust social and political inequalities between citizens.

Animal Agriculture and Justice Between Nations

The idea of well-orderedness is pivotal to Rawls's conception of international justice as outlined in the *Law of Peoples*; in his words, a society is well-ordered when it

> is not only designed to advance the good of its members but when it is also effectively regulated by a public conception of justice. That is, it is a society in which (1) everyone accepts and knows that the others accept the same principles of justice, and (2) the basic social institutions generally satisfy and are generally known to satisfy these principles. (Rawls 2002, 4)

Simply, a well-ordered society is one that is regulated by publicly known and accepted principles of justice and in which the institutions and structures of that society reflect those principles. One of the roles of the principles of justice in a well-ordered society is to protect citizens' two higher order interests: their capacity for a sense of justice and their capacity for a conception of the good. Rawls writes, "These capacities enable citizens to fulfill their role as citizens and underwrite their political and civic autonomy. The principles of justice protect citizens' higher order interests" (2002, 92). It is these two powers that ground the freedom and political equality of individual citizens, and without these qualities, persons would not be able to be fully cooperating members of society (Freeman 2003, 295). Together, the exercise of these capacities allows citizens to enjoy the benefits of society; they are integral to a person's abilities to think about and pursue a conception of the good (Kenehan 2015). In short, protecting these capacities is protecting the ability of people to be autonomous creatures, that is, to deliberate over and then pursue their conception of the good life.

So, given the nonarbitrary and morally important nature of well-orderedness, it is important to examine whether the practices and processes that are common to animal agriculture in the United States can threaten this status abroad. In short, if the connections between animal agriculture and global climate change made above are correct, then it is possible that the well-orderedness of some societies may be threatened. In particular, if GCC threatens the ability of some societies to maintain the right sort of public political infrastructures and political culture, the ability to maintain human rights standards, and/or the ability to meet the further requirements of well-ordered liberal democratic or decent societies, then GCC is a threat to well-orderedness (Working Group II 2014; Kenehan 2015). Of course, these impacts will not necessarily threaten a people's well-ordered status in and of themselves, but they might coincide with other threats to well-orderedness and so, cumulatively, threaten this status. And these threats are especially dangerous if they are inflicted on a society that does not have the capacity to adapt.

The Rawlsian framework offers at least one important international principle of justice that can help us think about these harms: the duty to assist. Specifically, each well-ordered state has an international duty of justice to assist in the establishment and maintenance of well-orderedness. In Rawls's words: "Peoples have a duty to assist other peoples living in unfavorable conditions that prevent their having a just or decent political and social regime" (2002, 37). Rawls envisions this principle being employed so as to help societies move out of burdenedness and into a state of well-orderedness. This principle can also be applied proactively in response to threats to well-orderedness so as to protect already well-ordered societies from slipping into burdenedness (Kenehan 2015). This means, then, that if a particular action or practice will likely have devastating effects with regard to well-orderedness, then the action or practice is unjust. This conclusion holds so long as that particular activity is itself not pivotal to the well-orderedness of the nation engaging in the harmful practice. So, in returning to the case at hand, we now have strong reasons grounded in concerns of international justice to reconsider the practice of intensively raising animals for food. Namely, to the extent that intensively raising animals for food is not necessary to our own well-orderedness, and so long as it contributes to dangerous GCC, the consequences of which have the potential to threaten the well-orderedness of other nations, then we have an obligation of justice to minimize our use of this practice.

Summary

In this section, I considered the environmental harms that result from factory farming within the framework of Rawls's theory of justice. The purpose of this analysis was twofold: first, to illustrate the broader claim that theories of liberal political justice can capture the environmental harms that are caused by factory farming; second, and more specifically, to argue that, from the Rawlsian perspective, the environmental costs of intensively raising animals for food raise serious concerns of political justice. Consequently, this argument provides us with the groundwork for regulating food choice in the context of liberal democracies.

VI. LIBERAL POLITICAL JUSTICE AND ANIMAL AGRICULTURE: SOME CONCLUSIONS

In light of the above examination, we are now equipped to revisit the practice of animal agriculture within the confines of liberal political justice. In particular, in the context of the Rawlsian ideal of liberal political justice, the concept of primary goods and the principle of assistance can orient us in articulating and responding to the justice concerns that arise from intensive animal agriculture. But first, it is important to note that the tradition of raising animals for food, intensively or otherwise, is not essential to well-orderedness, at least for the vast majority of us. The emissions and environmental harms generated via animal agriculture in industrialized parts of the world are, to borrow phrasing from Henry Shue, "luxury" in their nature (Shue 2010c): we do not need to consume animal products to survive or flourish as individuals (i.e., they are not implied by a list of primary goods), and the availability of such products is not a necessary component of well-orderedness.[7] This is not to say that animal agriculture is not important economically—it surely is—but it is unlikely that the stability of the economy depends on animal agriculture as an industry. To the contrary, it has been shown that animal agriculture actually poses a threat to social and political equality domestically and to well-orderedness abroad, given the substantial environmental and climate harms to which it contributes.

As such, the demands of justice would dictate that we engage in real and substantive mitigation efforts with regard to our consumption of unnecessary goods and services that contribute to the abovenamed harms. Specifically, if we are concerned with establishing justice between citizens, then liberal political justice demands, at a minimum, that the government refrain from both subsidizing animal food products and from promoting their consumption. It likewise means that the government should be working to protect the interests that affected communities have in clean air and clean water, as these are necessary conditions of social and political equality. With regard to concerns of global justice, the duty to assist demands that we engage in serious efforts to mitigate our contributions to GCC, which likely poses a serious threat to the well-orderedness of the least well-off nations. And since animal agriculture is responsible for an estimated 18 percent of total global anthropogenic GHG emissions (Food and Agriculture Organization of the United Nations 2006a, 112), and is itself not necessary to our well-ordered status, the conclusion that the United States has strong obligations to refrain from both subsidizing and promoting animal agriculture is further reinforced.[8]

To be clear, it follows that government participation in subsidy, checkoff, and other such programs in the animal protein market is contrary to the aims of liberal democratic societies. Furthermore, these conclusions offer strong reasons for the government to disincentivize the consumption of animal products via taxes, mandated price increases, stronger and more costly regulations, and the like. And finally, given that the harms of animal agriculture are so severe from the point of view of liberal political justice, there is even justification for eliminating the practice of animal agriculture altogether. That is, protecting the political equality of citizens and protecting the well-orderedness of other nations jointly offer strong political justification for limiting food choice in a liberal democracy.

CONCLUSION

In this chapter I explored the tension that exists between limiting food choice and the aims and values of liberal democracies. I showed that appeals to comprehensive moral doctrines to condemn this practice may be fruitful but only if they represent the majority moral consensus. Nonetheless, given the relationship between animal agriculture and the harmful environmental and climate damages that result, I argued that we can condemn animal agriculture on principles of strict political justice. Specifically, so long as these harms threaten justice between citizens by creating unnecessary public health risks, by exposing vulnerable communities to the ills of air and water pollution, and by eroding bases for self-respect, and so long as GCC threatens the abilities of some nations to establish and maintain well-orderedness, then we have strong obligations of justice to abstain from intensively raising animals for food. We can thus conclude that it is fundamentally unjust for the U.S. government to subsidize the production and promote the consumption of animal products. Moreover, taking these obligations seriously means that there are very strong reasons of justice to limit the production and consumption of animal products entirely.

NOTES

1. Compare these numbers to the amount of water that it takes to grow the equivalent amount of plant proteins: "Pound for pound, it takes one hundred times more water to produce animal protein than grain protein" (Simon 2013, 119).

2. This adds up to a 9 percent contribution to global anthropogenic carbon dioxide emissions, 35–40 percent of global methane emissions, 65 percent of global nitrous oxide emissions, and 64 percent of global ammonia emissions (Food and Agriculture Organization of the United Nations 2006b, 112–14).

3. This is not an arbitrary choice, as the liberalism theorized by Rawls is likely representative of (or at least exerts influence on) mainstream and contemporary liberalism. It's my belief that most viable theories of liberal political justice will be able to capture and respond to these environmental harms in substantive ways. For instance Martha Nussbaum's capabilities approach to justice would likewise be directive in thinking substantively about environmental harms (Nussbaum 2000). However, exploring all of these theories and their applications in this context is beyond the scope of this chapter.

4. Rawls's two principles of justice are: "(a) Each person has the same indefeasible claim to a fully adequate scheme of equal basic liberties, which scheme is compatible with the same scheme of liberties for all; and (b) Social and economic inequalities are to satisfy two conditions: first, they are to be attached to offices and positions open to all under conditions of fair equality of opportunity; and second, they are to be to the greatest benefit of the least-advantaged members of society (the difference principle)" (Rawls 2001, 42–43).

5. Of course, it could be that there are alternative ways of providing public health to citizens that would not require protecting environmental integrity, but this is unlikely, given the dependence that exists between human health and environmental health. Put differently, it is not clear that there are any substitutes for things like clean air and a functioning atmosphere that would produce the same public health goods.

6. Indeed, many of the regulatory agencies in the United States, such as the EPA, FDA, USDA, and others are aware of these disparities, though little has been done to attenuate them.

7. This may not be the case for all nations everywhere. In extreme climates, or hard to reach geographical areas, some peoples may have no other choice than to rely on farmed animals as a food source, for example, in places where plant-based foods cannot be grown or where the obstacles to importing plant-based foods may be so great as to make it impractical. In these instances, to restrict this practice might actually threaten their ability to remain well-ordered. These sorts of emissions would be necessary, and so justified. Even so, the vast majority of the communities in the United States very likely do not fall into this category.

8. Indeed, the IPCC has recommended plant-based diets as one GCC mitigation option (Working Group III 2014, 838).

Chapter 13

Comparing Apples and Oranges

Ethical Food Choice at the Grocery Store

John Nolt and Annette Mendola

You are shopping at a grocery store. As you consider each item, you probably ask some mundane practical questions: Is this fresh? Is it nutritious? Will I enjoy it? Can I afford it? How much time and effort would go into its preparation? If you are buying for others as well as yourself, further questions may arise: What dietary needs do they have? Will everyone enjoy it? If not, who may feel left out?

And as an ethical and well-informed person, you may ask some broader questions as well: What was destroyed, damaged, or polluted to grow, harvest, and transport this food? What toxic materials were used? Is there residue still present in the soil? In waterways? In the product? How many steps of processing were there, and how much transportation in between? How much water was used? How is the food packaged and what problems does the packaging cause? What were the working conditions of those who produced it? Did the food's production enhance or degrade human relationships? What animals were killed or made to suffer? How much did the production, packaging, and transportation involved in this item's appearance on the shelf contribute to global climate change?

Or maybe not. Who has the time, the knowledge, the patience, to consider all this? Three daunting problems face the ethical food shopper: (1) to organize this welter of concerns into simpler, yet not simplistic, criteria of selection, (2) to use these criteria to make rational, ethical decisions, even though not enough information is available and even though the various considerations are often incommensurable, and (3) to do all of this in real time, without overtaxing your intellect, emotions, or food budget.

This chapter considers all three problems. Regarding the first, we recommend organizing the ethical concerns—which are not, of course, the only concerns—around a single principle, the principle of non-harm, and we describe its application. That, however, requires some general knowledge of the various harms that occur along the food supply chain. We then discuss the twin problems of insufficient information and incomparability. That discussion takes us very briefly into decision theory. But reliance on abstract theory would only increase the cognitive burden on the food shopper. We therefore conclude by discussing some practical principles for assessing harm and some characteristic virtues that promote ethical food buying.

Our topic is food choice at the grocery store—food that is to be prepared and eaten in the home by oneself and one's family or friends. Similar considerations apply to food bought by individuals at restaurants or by institutions that serve meals, but that is beyond the scope of our discussion.

We do not mean to suggest that buying food at the grocery store is ideal. It isn't, but for most of us it is unavoidable. In our experience, the most enjoyable and wholesome food is grown organically by you or by people with whom you can have a face-to-face conversation. Food co-ops and farmers' markets are excellent sources. Yet the opportunity to enjoy such food, though common throughout history, is rare today. Everyone now consumes much that is produced by unknown others who may give more thought to the appearance of wholesomeness than to wholesomeness itself.

I. ORGANIZING AND ANALYZING ETHICAL CONSIDERATIONS

The Principle of Non-Harm

The ethical framework that we recommend is a simple imperative: when buying food, *do no unjustified harm*. This *principle of non-harm* is fundamental, because (as is explained in the next section) our contemporary food system, while a source of vital benefits, also causes innumerable harms.

To harm something is to reduce its welfare. Though we naturally think first of human welfare, all living things, even microorganisms, can be healthy or unhealthy and hence have some degree of welfare. All living things can therefore be harmed. It does not follow, however, that all living things are *morally considerable*—that is, that they all ought to figure into our ethical decision making (Nolt 2006). Which beings ought to matter ethically is highly controversial.

All ethical traditions, both religious and nonreligious, accept some version of the principle of non-harm, but their conceptions of moral considerability differ widely. In *anthropocentric* conceptions, only the welfare of humans matters morally. Harm to humans can take many forms, including impoverishment, bereavement, homelessness, suffering, disease, injury, and death.

Sentiocentric ethics regard the welfare of all and only sentient beings (those capable of enjoying and suffering or pleasure and pain) as morally significant. Sentient animals can be harmed in some, but not all, of the ways that humans can. All, for example, can suffer pain, and all can be harmed by injury, disease, or death. Social animals may, in addition, suffer from the loss of companions, mates, parents, or offspring.

Biocentric ethics are broader still. They hold that even nonsentient organisms—such as (we presume) insects, plants, bacteria, or fungi—can be harmed by injury, disease, and death, and that such harms have some moral significance. Moderate biocentric views regard the welfare of individual nonsentient organisms as minuscule and hence practically negligible in moral deliberations. But they maintain, nevertheless, that large populations of such organisms can have considerable moral significance, not merely because of their ecological importance to sentient animals (including humans), but also because their aggregate welfare itself may be great enough to make a moral difference. Ours is such a view (Nolt 2015b, chapter 6).

We do not, however, expect the reader to agree. Our central line of reasoning in this chapter (the line concerning climate change) requires only an anthropocentric understanding of the principle of non-harm. We do, however, comment from time to time on the richness of moral vision introduced by more inclusive sentiocentic or biocentric perspectives.

Still, that central line of reasoning depends on an unconventional assumption—namely, that the principle of non-harm has a very long temporal scope. In particular, we assume that a harm of a given kind (say, the killing of a person) is equally morally significant whether it occurs today or thousands of years from now. The case for this *assumption of temporal invariance* is explained elsewhere (Nolt 2015b, 94–101; Nolt 2016). Temporal invariance is, in our view, crucial to an adequate conception of the ethics of anthropogenic climate change; for, as is explained in the next section, the harms of today's greenhouse gas (GHG) emissions occur continually through millennia. That matters for food choice at the grocery store because, like many aspects of the global economy, our food system contributes substantially to those temporally distant harms.

The principle of non-harm forbids only *unjustified* harm. Justified harm is often tragic, but it is not morally wrong. The obvious justification for eating is that it is necessary for life. But that doesn't, of course, justify eating anything we please. Cannibalism, to take a crude and obvious example, is—except, perhaps, in the most awful of circumstances—unjustifiable. More to the point, there is a growing planet-wide debate over when, if at all, eating sentient nonhumans (usually animals that are hunted or raised for meat) can be justified. But, as is explained in the next section, many of the harms of contemporary food systems are not just to those we eat but to other humans or other living things. Such harms, too, require moral justification.

There are two reasonable and widely accepted justifications for harm: (1) to fulfill an overriding moral imperative, and (2) to either avoid a greater harm or produce a greater good. The first sort of justification is characteristic of deontological ethics, the second of consequentialist ethics.

Deontological ethics posit a system of rules, often understood by a legal analogy as moral laws. These "laws" always include some form of the principle, often formulated as a *right* of non-harm—for example, the right to life. In theory, the rules may be deemed morally inviolable, but in practice conflicts arise among them; thus, even without malfeasance, some rules are inevitably broken. Conflicts are usually resolved by assuming that a rule may be overridden, and hence temporarily suspended, by a weightier rule. Suppose, for example, that an animal rights advocate happens into a situation in which the only way to avoid starvation is to kill and eat animals. Then, if (as is standard in deontological ethics) the animal rights advocate affirms a right of self-preservation, she or he may infer that this right overrides the animals' right of non-harm. The human's right of self-preservation is thus the human's moral justification for the harm. The overriding rule must, of course, be especially weighty—as self-preservation is generally assumed to be. Mere preference or impulse would not suffice.

According to consequentialist ethics, harm can be justified only if it prevents greater harm or produces greater benefit. Ethical consequentialists understand harm and benefit as decrease or increase in *total* welfare—the welfare of all morally considerable beings affected by the action. Thus, for example, to feed her family, an impoverished mother may take a job that impairs her health, reasoning that the harm she suffers is outweighed by the benefits to her family. This justification is adequate, on a consequentialist ethic, only if the benefits to the family really are greater.

Unjustified Harm in the Food System

However we understand the principle of non-harm and however we justify particular harms, the principle itself is the centerpiece of our ethical analysis because contemporary food systems cause great harm. Eating is, and has always been, a morally equivocal action. It keeps us alive, but it also requires killing—even if all we eat are plants, for vegetarianism merely reduces, but does not eliminate, killing. Merely tilling a plot of land kills countless insects, worms, and other tiny creatures that live in the soil, and often also mice, voles, moles, or other sentient animals that burrow there. Then comes the battle to protect the growing crops from "pests." All growers, even organic farmers, struggle with blight, weeds, marauding animals, and destructive insects. Harvest, too, may require killing.

Yet we grant that these actions are morally justified. Deontology typically takes the right of human self-preservation to be weightier than any imperative of non-harm to animals or other life forms. Consequentialism, similarly, even when not entirely anthropocentric, accounts human welfare more valuable than that of any nonhuman and hence concludes that the greater good is served by the killing of nonhumans when that is necessary for keeping people from starving.

It is obvious that we should not allow people to starve. But starvation is not usually the issue in grocery shopping. Much of the "food" sold in grocery stores is junk, and people would be healthier without it. And some nutritious food is produced at the cost of avoidable harm. For example, most of the meat sold in commercial grocery stores comes from factory farms, where animals, treated as mere economic means, suffer through short and miserable lives. These operations are impossible to justify, given even minimal moral consideration for these animals. Since meat is not essential to human health or welfare and can also be produced more humanely, factory farms inflict great harms for benefits (dietary protein, taste satisfaction) that can be obtained by far less harmful means (see Singer 1990, chapter 3; and Regan 2004, chapter 9).

Other aspects of the current food system cause harms that are difficult to justify as well: the poor treatment of many workers; the use of insecticides, fungicides, and herbicides that may do harm beyond their intended targets; wasteful and unnecessary packaging; the conversion of habitat—most worryingly tropical rainforests, the richest assemblages of life on the planet—to food production; the depletion of freshwater supplies; and so on.[1] But perhaps the greatest among the food system's harms are those it inflicts via GHG emissions.

Food's Carbon Footprint

The global food system runs on fossil fuels. The farm machinery that is used to grow and harvest crops burns fossil fuels, as do the forms of transport that bring the food to consumers. From the growing operation to the processor, from the processor to the packager, from the packager to the distributor, and from the distributor to the grocery store, the food we eat is transported mainly by diesel-burning trucks. Sometimes there are fewer steps of transportation, but supply chains for heavily processed products tend to have many more. Transportation's carbon footprint depends directly on the distance traveled; hence the fewer transportation steps (that is, the less distance from farm to grocery store) the better. Fossil energy also powers food processing and the refrigeration for food storage. According to the Intergovernmental Panel on Climate Change, the agriculture, forestry and other land use (AFOLU) sector and the transport sector of the global economy produce, respectively, about 24 and 14 percent of direct anthropogenic GHG emissions (Working Groups I, II, and III 2015, 47: figure 1.7).[2]

Some of these emissions are morally justified. The planet's human population is so large that we cannot all be fed without mechanized agriculture, and in many places there is no practical alternative to fossil-fueled farm machinery and fossil-fueled transport. Of course, rapid conversion of these systems to alternative energy sources is, and ought to be, a global priority. But for now, we have no choice but to continue using some fossil fuels.

Still, that does not justify using them wastefully. Some uses of fossil fuels for food provision are definitely not morally justifiable. Virtually no one needs heavily processed foods—which are, in any case, generally less healthful than whole, fresh foods. And virtually no one needs to consume food from thousands of miles away, with its high transportation costs and exorbitant GHG emissions. (There are exceptions, of course. Poor people who live in food deserts—often in inner cities, where the only available food is heavily processed and packaged—may have no choice but to buy heavily processed food. People in famine-stricken areas may have no choice but to accept food from far away. And, as Mark C. Navin has argued, developed nations and their citizens may sometimes have moral obligations of beneficence, repair, or fairness to buy food from people in less developed nations [2014]. We can admit such exceptions and still maintain that less transportation is better and ought to be preferred in nonexceptional cases.)

All GHG emissions take their toll. The effects of climate change already cause hundreds of thousands of deaths annually.[3] Even at current mortality rates, as John Broome has noted, climate change will cause tens of millions of deaths by 2100 (Broome 2012, 33). Yet these rates continue to increase. Of course, millions, perhaps billions, would die, if mechanized agriculture were eliminated. But we are not suggesting anything like that. What we are suggesting is resisting the purchase of food that causes morally unnecessary harm—food, for example, whose production involves the destruction of forests, excessive resource consumption, heavy processing, or much long-distance transportation.

If that suggestion seems extreme, it may be because the harms of climate change are underappreciated. They are, in fact, unprecedented in ways that pose significant challenges to human understanding. For one thing, responsibility, though great, is diffuse. Some individuals, corporations, or nations are more responsible for the harms than others, but *all* are responsible to some degree. The CO_2 that an individual emits or whose emission the individual promotes by having made purchases, is, of course, both a tiny fraction of and inseparable from the total. It blends with the CO_2 from all other sources, and it is the mix that produces the harm. Yet the magnitude of the harm is so sensitive to total carbon emissions, and cumulatively so great that even a small change in GHG emissions can make a morally significant difference.

Each CO_2 molecule that is added to the atmosphere can on its own absorb infrared radiation from the earth's surface and so contribute, however minutely, to the rise of atmospheric temperature. Though many other variables affect temperature, advancing or retarding the rate of increase, physical laws dictate that, absent these other variables, global temperature increases continuously with atmospheric carbon. How much the planet will warm depends almost entirely on humanity's cumulative total carbon emissions and very little on their rate and timing (Stocker 2013; Allen et al. 2009). Harm to human and nonhuman life, moreover, increases continuously with increasing temperature. Since temperature increases continuously with increasing emissions, and harm increases continuously with increasing temperature, it follows that harm increases directly and continuously—hence quite sensitively—with carbon emissions (Nolt 2018). Small carbon inputs matter.

The harms of climate change are, moreover, not simply one-off. They occur repeatedly over a very long time and hence are cumulatively enormous. Atmospheric carbon remains elevated for centuries after emission, heating the planet all the while (Archer et al. 2009, 117). And a variety of feedbacks, nearly all of them positive, ensure that temperatures remain elevated for *millennia* beyond that (Archer et al. 2009; Zeebe 2013). Thus, emissions during the historically brief fossil fuel era will likely cause a vast array of harms during the coming millennia—harms cumulatively so enormous that even small carbon emissions may eventually yield morally significant quantities of harm (Nolt 2011; 2013; 2015; 2018). Adaptation, mitigation, or geoengineering can lessen this harm, but all become more difficult and expensive the longer we wait, and they inflict harms of their own. We are, often without justification, passing these costs and problems on to our successors. So we have weighty moral reasons not to buy unnecessary food (or anything else) that has a large carbon footprint.

The only greenhouse gas we have so far mentioned is CO_2, but others, particularly methane, make significant contributions to anthropogenic climate change. Methane emissions are indisputably important. They have a much higher warming potential in the short term than equal quantities of CO_2; and agriculture, especially animal agriculture, is responsible for a significant portion of them. We nevertheless emphasize CO_2, for two reasons. First, methane is emitted in smaller quantities than CO_2 and hence is responsible for much less of the anthropogenic warming (about 16 percent for methane vs. about 76 percent for CO_2) (Working Groups I, II, and III 2015, 87–88: Box 3.2; and 46: figure 1.6). Second, atmospheric levels of CO_2 remain elevated after emission much longer than do methane levels; they are thus predomin-antly responsible for the *long-term* harms of climate change. Serious harms that accumulate over long time spans are likely to be large enough in total to account for much, if not most, of the moral significance of anthropogenic climate change.

But will a given purchase really increase total harm over the long term— say, over the next thousand years? There is no way to be sure. Let us suppose not. Deontologists remind us, nevertheless, that we ought to do the right thing (follow the moral law) whether it makes any difference or not. Refusing to buy products with high carbon footprints could still be right because such purchases increase the *likelihood* of harm. Or it could still be right because if we act morally, our example can encourage others to act morally as well and multiply the effect of our actions. Even if individually we can't make any difference, it is certain that collectively many people can, and that is good reason (by both deontological and consequentialist reasoning) to act as part of that collective (Schwenkenbecher 2012).

Moreover, though it is often assumed that individual purchases make no difference, that has never been shown. Given the sensitivity of harm to carbon inputs explained above, and the huge amount of harm over wide stretches of time, it is quite possible that small individual acts do matter. Even if what you buy this day makes no difference, it may well be that your choices this year, or over a lifetime, do (Nolt 2011; 2013; 2018; Hiller 2011).

We have so far argued that food choice at the grocery store is potentially harmful in many ways and that, since not all harm can be avoided, the ethical food shopper should try to avoid purchases that promote especially harmful practices. The shopper should, therefore, compare the consequences of purchases made; and so, for the most part, the justification of choices ought to be consequentialist in form. The next section offers an example and then discusses some of the difficulties and complications that arise when we make the effort.

II. DECISION MAKING IN THEORY

Comparing Apples and Oranges: An Example

How do you make less harmful choices? Consider a simplified example. On your grocery list is the item "fresh fruit." Suppose you live in the United States, say, along the East Coast and somewhere north of Georgia, and it is winter, so fresh, local fruit is not available. It's a small store, and the only fresh fruits available there within your budget are apples and oranges. The quality of both seems good. Often stores and suppliers provide no information on where the fruit comes from, but sometimes they do. Suppose that here they do. You see that the apples are organic and they come from Washington State. The oranges are from Florida. Since the carbon footprints of the production of apples and of oranges are probably similar, but transportation from Washington burns more fossil fuel, the overall carbon footprint of the oranges is probably somewhat smaller.

Technicalities can, however, complicate such judgments. Weber and Matthews argue, for example, that by far the largest GHG emissions associated with food occur in production (83 percent) and that transportation accounts for only a small fraction (11 percent) (Weber and Matthews 2008, figure 2). The upshot, as they see it, is that

> dietary shift can be a more effective means of lowering an average household's food-related climate footprint than "buying local." Shifting less than one day per week's-worth of calories from red meat and dairy products to chicken, fish, eggs, or a vegetable-based diet achieves more GHG reduction than buying all locally sourced food. (Weber and Matthews 2008, 3508)

That point is both sound and important. But the percentages mentioned are themselves skewed by red meat and dairy products, whose production generates very high GHG emissions. For fruits and vegetables, emissions in the production phase are generally much smaller, so transportation emissions comprise a greater percentage of the total. When the choice is between apples and oranges, whose production emissions are presumably similar, transportation emissions can reasonably be the deciding factor. These emissions may not be terribly large, but because of the extremely long-term harms of climate change, every emissions reduction matters.

Carbon footprint, however, is only one of many considerations that may reasonably affect your decision. The apples are organic, which suggests that their production is less harmful to people and other living things and that they are less likely to contain pesticide residues than the oranges. Both fruits are excellent sources of many nutrients, but an orange has much more vitamin C than an apple. Your taste preferences and those of others you may be buying for matter, too, in part because they determine who will eat what. The list could go on, but we'll stop there.

You could, of course, buy no fruit at all. That might do the least harm to others—if you then did not spend the money instead on something else that is harmful. But it would deprive you (and any others for whom you may be buying) of fresh fruit for some time. Since fruits and vegetables are essential to a healthful diet, there is moral justification for buying them. Let's suppose for the sake of the example that that justification is adequate.

The considerations mentioned so far include expense, apparent quality, carbon footprint, nutrition, organic versus nonorganic production, and taste. You might, then, reason as follows: The apples and oranges are similar in price and apparent quality, and you and your family like both. But the oranges are superior in both carbon footprint and nutrition. The apples have the edge, though, on the organic versus nonorganic criterion. Of the six criteria, the oranges are better in two, the apples are better in one, and they are tied (or we can't tell the difference) in the other three.

That doesn't automatically mean you should buy the oranges. Some categories may be more important than others. But superiority in a plurality of the criteria is generally a useful heuristic that tends to produce more good decisions than bad ones when the relative importance of the criteria is unclear.

Ignorance and Incomparability

In practice, the relative importance of the criteria is often unclear for either, and usually both, of two reasons. The first reason, ignorance, is obvious. We don't know how much harm, for example, the nonorganic production of the oranges does relative to the amount of harm done by the greater carbon footprint of the apples. Moreover, because we buy only tiny amounts of fruit relative to the huge amounts that are grown and shipped, we don't know how, if at all, our buying habits are related to the harm. In these and other ways our ignorance is vast.

The second reason for confusion about the relative importance of our choice criteria is *not* obvious. It is that some ethically relevant values are genuinely incomparable with others. Incomparability is value difference without superiority or inferiority. Two values are incomparable if neither is greater than nor less than nor equal to the other. They are just different. This is one of the things people mean when they criticize a comparison by saying, "That's like comparing apples and oranges."

Often, though not always, incomparability is a result of the simultaneous use of various value criteria. Usually some of the criteria favor one choice and others favor another. There still may be a best choice if enough of the criteria favor one of the choices strongly enough. But there needn't be. Several choices may be unexcelled, yet none of them better than any of the others.

Incomparability has nothing to do with ignorance. It persists even if we know all the relevant facts. It has to do with the comparison structure of the values themselves. Where there is incomparability, values are merely partially ordered, rather than being linearly ordered, which is how we tend to conceive them. Some *are* better than others, but some are neither better nor worse than some others, but simply different.

Some economists like to think of the value of a thing as its price—or assumed price. Since prices are numbers and numbers are linearly ordered, that gives them a neat linear value system, but it distorts more fundamental values in all sorts of ways (Nolt 2015b, 75–79). We advocate choosing food, not strictly according to price, but also in accord with the principle of non-harm. This does not mean that harm provides a common currency by which all purchases can be compared. Even if, godlike, we knew every consequence of our actions and every harm down to the last detail, we might still not be able to determine a best choice, because harms themselves are to some extent incomparable. It may be better for a person to be hurt or ill than to die, but there is no precise, factual answer to such questions as these: How much better? How many illnesses would it be worth causing to prevent one death?

We are not, of course, denying that there are better or worse choices. A partial ordering is not a lack of ordering. Our point is merely that ethical choice, even at the grocery store, is more complicated than is commonly realized. We want to be realistic about the difficulties, but we still need to find ways of acting ethically.

There are some generally applicable principles that, while not providing assurance that our choices are right, tend to help. If one choice has better consequences than the alternatives by all relevant criteria, then it is the best choice. A value that has better consequences than the others by *most* of the criteria is *likely* to be the best choice. If we lack information to choose between *A* and *B*, or recognize that their consequences are incomparable in value, we may nevertheless find them better or worse than the potential consequences of other choices. If others are better, we can eliminate both. If others are worse, we can eliminate the others. In the end, we may wind up with a pool of uneliminated options. At that point there may be no reason not to choose by whatever nonethical criteria seem relevant.

Yet even this much thinking is probably too much for the harried shopper, who may ask, "Do I really need to worry about all of this? After all, most people don't shop ethically, and if they don't, then what I do can hardly matter."

But that line of thought can leave everyone without hope. If many people think this way, their belief in their own inefficacy becomes self-fulfilling prophecy. This is what decision theorists call a collective action problem. Everyone waits for someone else to act, and, as a result, no one acts. Such thinking can make big problems (and climate change is the biggest of all) unsolvable.

Dale Jamieson has argued that, paradoxically, the most practical way to produce good consequences when faced with such a collective action problem is *not* to consider what others are doing. It is to cultivate relevant virtues, or habits of character, and stick to them regardless of what others do or fail to do (Jamieson 2007). Jamieson suggests that, widely adopted, this practice would accomplish precisely what consequentialism is aiming for—supporting the general welfare of morally considerable beings—but by avoiding convoluted consequentialist thinking! This approach can also be endorsed by those who favor deontological moral reasoning. We are more apt to fulfill our duties and respect the rights of others by bolstering a set of traits that make moral choices habitual and familiar than we are by entertaining questions about competing obligations.

III. DECISION MAKING IN PRACTICE

When trying to make ethically sound decisions at the grocery store, it is strenuous and inefficient to think in terms of competing duties (*à la* deontology) or calculations of relative harms (*à la* consequentialism). It's not that these theories are wrong or never useful. In fact, virtues may be understood as habits arising from the continual intention either to fulfill one's duty or to choose actions that tend to decrease harms and increase benefits for those affected by our actions. However, direct use of consequentialism or deontology to approach practical, complex decisions is generally too cumbersome to produce useful answers in real time. Jamieson is therefore right: the best approach to ethical decision making *in vivo* is to work on developing character traits that incline us toward ethical choices.

This approach has several advantages. As Jamieson suggests, it gets us out of the gridlock of the collective action problem, since each person, in trying to become virtuous, is not apt to get sidetracked by worrying whether others' actions are making his or hers worth the effort. It's also a practical, sustainable approach. Reflecting on and practicing virtues also helps us keep focused on the goal of our actions—in this case ethical food choices. Human beings, with our limited, distractive brains, tend to focus on particulars and lose sight of our goal. This tendency may be inevitable; but focusing attention on cultivating certain habits—not just habits of shopping, but habits of character—can help reorient us to what really matters.

Which moral habits help to make ethical food choices? Here are some to which we aspire.

Nonviolence

We have noted that a principle of non-harm is common to many religious and moral traditions. The virtue that best embodies this principle is *nonviolence*. In the United States, that term is associated primarily with the civil rights activism of Martin Luther King Jr., but his thinking was strongly influenced by what Mahatma Gandhi called *ahimsa*, a Sanskrit term that denotes non-injury or non-harm. Gandhi understood *ahimsa* as a character trait encompassing nonviolence in thought, word, and deed. He also understood it biocentrically. "In its negative form," he wrote, *ahimsa* "means not injuring any living being, whether by body or mind. ... In its positive form *Ahimsa* means the largest love, the greatest charity" (Gandhi 1986, 212).

That, of course, is an extremely lofty ethical ideal—so lofty as to be unattainable in practice. Gandhi himself never claimed to have attained it, though he made a supreme effort. The more moderate goal of living less harmfully, however, is within everyone's grasp.

To practice this virtue is to transcend, insofar as you can, a self-centered perspective, regarding yourself as only one among others (other people, at least, perhaps other animals, and maybe even all other living beings). Gandhi held that to do so was to achieve a clearer vision of truth—a truth that he identified with God (Gandhi 1948, 615–16).

Ask: *Do my choices reflect concern for the welfare of others?*

Integrity

Integrity involves acting consistently on one's moral commitments, even when it's uncomfortable to do so. It requires honesty about what you can do and your willingness to do it, neither underestimating nor overestimating your capacity for action. On the one hand, it is tempting to dismiss tasks that are unfamiliar, difficult, or inconvenient as impossible. Often, we actually *do* have the time or money to prepare more of our meals from basic ingredients, but we have to make the effort to do it. On the other hand, it's also tempting to get overly idealistic, to leave the market with a sense of righteousness and string bags full of picturesque produce that then go to waste for lack of time, skill, or motivation to prepare. Regularly buying a refrigerator full of vegetables you don't use and eating guiltily at the nearest Burger King doesn't help reach the goal of making ethical food choices. Stretching your abilities is part of moral growth, but fooling yourself (and berating yourself) is not.

Ask: *Am I honestly living up to my own ethical standards?*

Courage

A virtue that is closely related to integrity is courage. Courage may not sound like something one needs to go to the grocery store, but it will sound familiar to those who have put meals on a table for picky family members or struggled with their own cravings. It will ring true, too, for those who are trying to cultivate good habits only to have their choices scrutinized or sabotaged by their dining companions. Food is a powerful social connector, so unconventional food choices can be surprisingly controversial, even when you're just eating your own lunch! Real and imagined criticism and ridicule can keep us from moral growth.

Of course, courage to act on one's own commitments is not license to judge someone else's. It's fine to be open, even enthusiastic, about your values and choices, but preaching is usually counterproductive. Likewise, use others' example as inspiration, but be aware that their circumstances are different from your own.

Ask: *Am I facing the challenge of doing the right thing?*

Discernment

Discernment, in this context, means placing appropriate weight on competing duties in a situation. Discerning people have a sense of when to compromise and when to insist on a course of action. They try to do the right thing for the right reasons and to use the right amount of effort for the situation at hand. Being discerning about food choices involves resisting single-issue choices. For example, being scrupulous about being vegan but buying mostly food that is highly processed and packaged likely causes more harm than buying mostly food that is produced locally, with low processing and packaging costs, and that includes some humanely farmed meat. Discernment means keeping the overall goal of non-harm in mind, and reorienting ourselves to that goal when, inevitably, we get caught up in one desideratum or another.

The virtue of hospitality may be seen as part of discernment. If you're buying and preparing food for others, you will probably feel torn at some point between staying true to "your" set of ethical food choices and meeting their needs, tastes, or values. Often a little creativity and flexibility can accommodate everyone, but sometimes there are no options available to suit all and sundry. It is a virtue to recognize those times when it is appropriate to compromise one set of desiderata (e.g., ethical food choices) in order to foster another (e.g., community, relationships).

Ask: *Do I have my priorities straight in this situation?*

Resilience

When it comes to avoiding harm, what we do on a regular basis is more important than what we do occasionally. Rather than nursing unrealistic expectations, start where you are, with the habits you currently have, and think critically about the changes you can make. Setbacks are normal; don't give up just because it's difficult. Take on more ambitious habits when you are ready. In the quest to eat without causing unnecessary harm, as with so many other important goals, perfection is the enemy of progress. Don't let the impossibility of eating without causing *any* harm paralyze you.

Resilience includes the flexibility to accommodate changing circumstances without losing sight of ethical priority. Over the course of your life, you'll have a new child or a new medical condition or you'll move to a new area or you'll have a change in salary. A product or practice that you had been relying on will suddenly be out of reach. New information will become available about the impact of different foods and methods of production. Be flexible, when appropriate, about *how* you make ethical food choices. Even when circumstances change, and shopping and cooking habits must change, the overall goal—causing no unjustified harm—remains the same.

Ask: *Am I keeping at it even though I can't do this work perfectly?*

Joy

A danger of cultivating earnest virtues like those above is that doing so can threaten simple enjoyment of the good things in life. As important as these virtues are, it is also important to nurture delight and satisfaction in buying, preparing, and eating food. For one thing, there's very little external motivation or reinforcement to make ethical food choices. If we don't find pleasure and meaning in this set of tasks, we'll stop. Moreover, we all learn from each other, and people who emanate a sense of purpose and good cheer are more inspiring than those who dourly (or smugly) perform their duties.

Finally, part of living well is relishing life, and eating is one of life's most fundamental pleasures. Simply enjoying one's food is a virtue. Gratitude for the abundance that we live with contributes to joy. So does a relaxed, curious, adventurous palate. If you can cultivate flexible tastes in food, you will enjoy more of what is available more of the time, especially when someone else is feeding you. Likewise, helping your children learn to like many different foods and being aware of the impact food choices have on them and the world, is a gift. Eating is an opportunity to celebrate life.

Ask: *Having considered all the facts, am I able to be at peace with my choices and enjoy my food?*

Food Choices and Living Ethically

The goal of making ethical food choices is one part of a larger goal: living an ethical life. Not everyone can raise their own produce, make their own tofu, slaughter their own chickens—and not everyone should. Some of us live in dense urban environments, some of us lack interest or talent with food, and some of us have pressing, time-consuming responsibilities that can't be ignored. There is much other good work that needs to be done; ethical food choices cannot be the top moral priority for everyone. In similar vein, though global climate change is the factor that has the greatest impact on all living things and therefore must be considered when making ethical food choices, there are many other ethically important factors to consider, and each of us is in a different position to respond to these multiple, competing factors. All of us must consider the impact of food choices within the scope of who we are and where we are in our lives.

It is true that ethical food choices are often costly, in money, time, effort, or all of these. (Not always. But when the ethical choice is easy, fast, and cheap, we usually don't need to try hard to make it.) Recognition of this fact is perhaps the first step in making ethical food choices. Accordingly, when someone else's labor contributes to feeding you, your living ethically involves recognizing what it costs them to prepare food ethically and being prepared to share those costs. This may mean paying small-scale and organic farmers and ethical businesses more, it may mean washing more dishes than you'd like to help minimize packaging, it may mean cheerfully eating yet another turnip dish because that's what the farmers' market or CSA has provided. If you are the person who buys and prepares food, expect it to take longer, cost more money, and be … interesting sometimes. Cut yourself a little slack, and remind others by your own example to be curious, engaged, and understanding about the learning curve.

Developing the above virtues—habits of character—promotes the development of virtuous habits of shopping. It is impossible to say in the abstract which criteria for ethical food choices are most important. Cultivating the habits outlined above should help make practical ethical decisions possible in real life, in real time. Consider your resources and limitations. What matters most right now? Are there people you are feeding who have particular, pressing needs? Is your budget particularly constrained at this time in your life? Are you living in a time or place where certain items are particularly inaccessible? Alternatively, is there a budding resource (a new farmers' market, perhaps, or a new friend who can teach you to bake, or a proposed ordinance that would allow city dwellers to keep chickens) that you can support that will flourish if it gets off the ground now? There are no hard and fast rules of practice, save the goal of thinking, trying, learning, reaching—and doing so with joy.

NOTES

1. Much of the water demand is, incidentally, for grain crops that feed livestock. On average, meat production requires about eight times more water per calorie than does production of plant-based food (Fox and Fimeche 2013, 10).

2. Transportation of food, of course, accounts for only a fraction of total contribution of transport, but it is, no doubt, a substantial fraction. AFOLU includes forest and peat fires, but forest fires are often set deliberately to clear land for agriculture.

3. Three recent estimates and/or projections for annual morality rate from climate change are: Development Assistance Research Associates (DARA) (2012), 400,000 current, 700,000 by 2030; WHO (2014) 250,000 per year by 2030–2050 (selected causes); Springman et al. (2016) greater than 500,000 merely from reduction in food availability by 2050.

Chapter 14

From Food Consumers to Food Citizens

Reconceptualizing Environmentally Conscious Food Decision-Making

Rachel A. Ankeny

In recent years, there has been increased popular attention to making ethical food choices (for a summary on key issues in food ethics, see Ankeny 2012) and scrutiny of the various ways in which people make such choices. A key focus has been ethical consumerism, for instance, choosing to avoid or boycott certain products or types of products or actively seeking out various products that align with our preferred values. Buying local to create economic benefits for those within our own communities or favoring humanely produced foodstuffs because of concerns about animal welfare, to provide just two examples, are often claimed to be markers of ethical food decision-making. However, there has been relatively less focus among food studies scholars and consumers alike on the complexities associated with food choices related to reducing environmental effects or seeking to stem climate change, despite the fact that food seems to be a domain in which we can actually have impacts, given that we have numerous options for food choice and exercise them on a daily basis.

This chapter explores the practical and conceptual difficulties faced by those who wish to make what they view as environmentally conscious food choices, as well as by those who wish to encourage consideration of such issues.[1] First, I discuss the complexities associated with the usual proxy measures utilized to make environmentally conscious food choices, including food miles and local and green foods. Deeper conceptual impediments to promoting such food choices also are outlined, drawing on scholarship from environmental ethics and science and technology studies. Although focusing on ethical choices may be an effective and compelling strategy with regard to decisions where specific types of humans or nonhuman animals are directly affected (say, farmers and producers in one's own community by decisions to buy locally, or nonhuman animals by choices that favor more humane production methods), it is much more difficult to use ethical consumerism to motivate environmentally conscious food decisions for both pragmatic and conceptual reasons.

I then argue that the dominance of ethical consumerism as the frame within which food choices are conceptualized has created tensions in association with making environmentally conscious food choices. The typical emphasis on "voting with your fork" reinforces neoliberal tendencies to view ethical decisions as a matter of individual choice as evidenced by market trends that somehow will lead to beneficial changes in the broader food system. Thus efforts and initiatives that harness people's roles as food citizens are more likely to be effective with regard to climate change for several reasons: first, the idea of a food citizen forces people to consider the collective good and shared values when making food decisions, including with regard to the environment. Second, food citizenship avoids the classic ethical conundrums about difficulties associated with duties to distant others by clearly focusing attention simultaneously on the local and the broader environment. Finally, the collective causal effects of broader policy decisions made or supported by us as food citizens are more clearly connected to environmental impacts (and potentially easier to quantify and evaluate) than individual market-based decisions.

I. WHY OUR USUAL CONCEPTS ARE NOT USEFUL

This section explores a series of key product categories often equated with or utilized as proxies for reduction of environmental impacts of food choices, including food miles, local, and green products. It should be noted at the start that many people attempting to make ethical food choices rely heavily on labeling, despite the well-recognized limitations of such systems, particularly given that most labels associated with environmental impacts are not formally regulated. Hence as will be argued, these sorts of proxy terms, including "food miles," "local," and "green" have a problematic status for those trying to make environmentally friendly food choices.

A common approach used by many people to make what they consider to be environmentally conscious food choices is to select those products that have traveled fewer food miles. The term "food miles" originated in the 1990s and is attributed to the UK academic Tim Lang. It typically refers to the distance that food is transported from the time of its production until it reaches the consumer. As one scholar writes, "The 'food miles' concept has arguably captured the public imagination more than any other term when it comes to debates about sustainable consumption ... largely a result of the apparent simplicity of its application" (Maye 2011, 158). Many contend that there have been considerable increases in recent years in the number of miles traveled by food products because of rapidly increasing global trade, changes in food supply chain patterns (such as consolidation of packaging and supply depots, especially in larger supermarket chains), and the increase of nonlocally produced processed and packaged foods (for an example of a calculation of additional environmental costs hidden in the average UK food basket, see Pretty et al. 2005). However, as will be discussed, practical applications of this concept are far from simple, and attempts to devise formulae or algorithms to calculate food miles as well as measure their actual environmental effects have been plagued with difficulties.

Following its introduction, the concept of "food miles" subsequently was expanded in scholarly literature (e.g., Paxton 2011) to include any ecological impacts created by all processes associated with the product not only during production, but also including storage, delivery, purchase, and so on. Thus the expanded definition includes everything from miles traveled by consumers to reach the grocery store to the energy expanded to prepare food for long-distance transport and extended shelf life. Therefore it has been noted that even in its early incarnations, the food miles concept as used in scholarship included attention to environmental justice issues in parallel to what we now would term "lifecycle analyses" (Coffman 2012). In contrast, more popular literature tends to rely on a simplified notion related primarily to travel distance of the product for it to reach the consumer, and it uses a set distance, such as the "100-mile diet" (Smith and MacKinnon 2007).

It is clearly the case that use of the food miles concept has made it much more obvious how complex and often inefficient our food system is; hence the concept can be used as the general basis of campaigns for more sustainable agricultural practices and systems of food supply. In addition, food miles have come to be used as a measure of environmental impact, and particularly of carbon footprint and contribution to global warming. Major supermarket chains such as Tesco in the United Kingdom have attempted to use labels to indicate food miles traveled or carbon footprint equivalencies, but these schemes have had difficulties due to lack of standardized measurement systems and problems with breaking down the components of processed foods. Thus, many remain concerned that use of food miles as a metric is problematic and continues to be prone to oversimplification when applied, and particularly when utilized in a consumer context (Van Passel 2010).

Also, although food miles provide an intuitive shorthand, empirical research on the concept often has produced unexpected results; for instance, as a study in New Zealand showed, food produced in more energy efficient or temperate settings and then transported used less energy on average than food produced in hothouses (Saunders, Barber, and Taylor 2006). Other studies have shown that distance alone is not an adequate criterion for gauging the sustainability of food products (Schmitt et al. 2017). Finally, a study (Coley, Howard, and Winter 2011) of two contrasting food distribution systems in the United Kingdom compared the carbon emissions that resulted from a large-scale vegetable box scheme to those resulting from customers traveling to a local farm shop: if a shopper drives more than 6.7 kilometers round-trip to purchase organic vegetables, the shopper's carbon emissions are likely to be greater than the emissions from the vegetable box scheme, even though it involves cold storage, packing, transport to a regional hub, and transport to the customer's doorstep. Thus mode of transport and type of system matters as much or more than distance itself.

Parallel to the rise of the food miles concept, choosing to buy local foods has gained in popularity for a variety of reasons that range from supporting the local economy and the desire to build relationships with local producers or retailers based on understanding and trust, to buying what is freshest or cheaper. Eating local also is often used as a way to reduce food miles and decrease negative environmental impacts; however, many studies have shown that the equation of these two concepts is not valid (for a general discussion, see Born and Purcell 2006). For instance, research in the United States (Weber and Matthews 2008) revealed that the bulk of emissions associated with food occur during the production phase (83 percent) rather than transportation (11 percent, of which delivery from producer to retailer contributed only 4 percent) of the average U.S. household's carbon footprint associated with food consumption. Others have noted that always buying locally can result in adverse effects, for instance, due to increased needs to store food to sell in the off-season to meet demand (Smith et al. 2005) or to inefficient growth in hothouses (Garnett 2003).

More generally, local foods might not in fact be locally produced, as the definition of "local" differs radically depending on context, experience, and location. For instance, many participants in our qualitative research in Australia comment to us that something produced within the country should count as local, likely in part because of the extremely long distances between major cities and some agricultural locales. Even if a product is labeled and marketed as local, it may be composed of ingredients that have traveled long distances, if it is processed or produced locally. In summary, equating the category of local food to that of reduced food miles has been argued to inappropriately underemphasize other values and meanings associated with the concept of "local" and people's decisions to eat locally, particularly their desires to reintegrate food production and consumption within the context of place (Schnell 2013). Thus, as Claire C. Hinrichs (2000) puts it, focus on the local might well result in "a conflation of spatial relations for social ones" (301), creating romanticized and elitist illusions of connectedness rather than real, sustainable communities.

Furthermore, the validity of the rationale associated with eating "local" needs to be carefully assessed within the particular context of particular consumption decisions; for instance, Gwendolyn Blue (2009) notes that the turn toward local eating has been embedded in the strong resurgence of neoliberal forms of governance and helps to reinforce these problematic institutions, a point to which we will return. What is critical is that context clearly matters, and any equation of buying local and seeking to have positive environmental impacts is extremely fragile and may well be associated more with broader trends to use consumerist models to displace responsibilities away from governments and onto individuals as purchasers.

Finally, being a "locavore" has become a sort of identity claim for those seeking to be ethical food consumers, particularly in today's "foodie" culture (Johnston and Baumann 2009). Thus, the term may well be used more as a social or status signifier than as an indicator of the underlying values associated with "eating local," particularly given the variable definitions of the term "local" as well as the diverse motivations to pursue it, as is the case with many of the other labels and behaviors associated with key categories related to ethical consumption. As seen in our qualitative research, even those who try generally to eat "locally" make exceptions for a variety of reasons, including taste preferences, convenience, price, and occasion; for instance, some report buying local (and perhaps organic, free-range, and so on) when having people over for dinner or for what they view as products that are more important to buy locally, such as fresh fruit and vegetables. In addition, identity claims in this domain are only available to those who can make decisions to purchase (or avoid) certain sorts of products, and hence they again prioritize consumerist approaches, in contrast to a more democratic approach such as food citizenship, to be discussed below.

Another category of products commonly associated with buying decisions intended to have a positive impact (or at least to reduce negative impacts) on the environment are "green" foods. Many skeptics note that the green category is not well defined legally, and few regulations or even voluntary certification schemes exist for labeling in most locales (as compared for example to organic labeling); hence there is an increasing amount of "greenwashing" of products particularly through labeling claims with little evidence of their environmental impacts (Littler 2009a; 2009b). Organic foods are also favored by some because they are thought to have fewer detrimental environmental effects than more conventional agricultural methods, but in our research, organics are thought to be of high quality and have higher nutritional value (particularly for children) by those who tend to purchase them, hence underscoring the complexities associated with environmentally positive food choices. Yet others argue that dietary shifts can be a more effective means of lowering an average household's food-related climate footprint than "buying local" or other shorthand formulae. For instance, one study (Weber and Matthews 2008) showed that changing from red meat and dairy products to chicken, fish, eggs, or a vegetable-based diet, for less than one day per week's worth of calories, achieves more greenhouse gas (GHG) reduction than buying all locally sourced food.

Finally, and perhaps not surprisingly given all of these complexities, empirical research reveals that consumers are not particularly motivated to avoid (or buy) products because of their potential impacts on the environment; for instance, in the UK, preference surveys indicated that 21.5 percent of people would avoid buying New Zealand products because of "food miles" or the "long distance it travels," whereas in revealed preference surveys in supermarkets, only 3.6 percent indicated that they had consciously chosen British products because such produce was "less harmful for the environment" (Kemp et al. 2010, 504). Our qualitative research in Australia echoes this result, with few participants who buy local indicating that they do so because of environmental effects and with "food miles" generally not being raised as an ethical issue associated with food choice or a consideration when purchasing decisions are made.

II. CONCEPTUAL ISSUES ASSOCIATED WITH ENVIRONMENTALLY CONSCIOUS FOOD CHOICES

Based on the practical difficulties associated with using food choices as noted above, perhaps it is not surprising that many consumers in fact do not tend to use their purchasing and consumption decisions as ways to limit effects on the environment. However, as this section shows, there are several key deeper issues that also can be argued to interfere with people's abilities to use food choices in this way.

First, drawing on claims previously put forward by Alastair Iles (2005), food miles could be viewed as a way to bridge gaps created by things that are not materially present and to attempt to create discourses in what otherwise would be empty spaces. However, as Iles claims, there are few ways in which laypeople are supported in any efforts to calculate food miles or similar, given the complexities associated with developing these metrics. Interestingly, a study of labeling in terms of food miles (Caputo et al. 2013) supports the idea that this category has become a proxy for something else beyond (or different from) environmental impact, inasmuch as consumers preferred labels in terms of time and number of kilometers traveled rather than carbon dioxide emissions. The preference for time and distance traveled might well indicate that these consumers are buying local to support their local economy or express connection to their local community, rather than for environmentally related reasons.

However, most importantly, drawing on Iles (2005, after Banach et al. 2002), I contend that food miles are lacking in meaning, as they in fact represent a (failed) attempt to create a type of "missing object." "Missing objects" are any form of representations, practices, or artefacts that in some sense "stand in" for something that cannot be easily or directly experienced or envisioned. Therefore, these sorts of representations permit people to consider or speak about various issues to which they previously had limited or no access, and little or no direct experience, so long as interpretive conventions, shared standards of proof, preferred evidential forms, and criteria are developed to determine collectively what the missing objects mean.[2] On the positive side, if successful, such terms or representations can allow people to engage socially, conceptually, and otherwise, and to consider potentials for change. They can serve as a sort of translation mechanism, particularly to allow information or knowledge that previously was only held by experts to be accessed by lay actors; think, for instance, of the use of a graph or chart summarizing a complex scientific phenomenon (an apt example, as the original concept comes out of science education scholarship). However, on the negative side, some missing objects can appear to fill a gap without actually allowing access to or development of the underlying concepts and values that they help to bridge, and thus cannot be used as the basis of persuasive arguments. I argue that more generally, a range of proxy categories that might be thought to be useful ways to reduce environmental impact such as "local" and "green," together with "food miles," are ineffectual missing objects at least in their current forms (Iles [2005] has a series of positive suggestions about what might need to occur to make "food miles" more effective). Thus, the concept and terminology fail to motivate people to scrutinize their purchasing and consumption patterns or to seek change from producers, retailers, and policymakers. Thus, in a sense, the rhetorical power of these sorts of ethical food categories has the opposite effect of what might be intended: in their plasticity (and particularly as they have come to be used as unregulated categories in marketing and retailing), they have come to lose power and hence undermine the very values that they might be seen as furthering.

An additional issue relating to making environmentally conscious choices is that many people have difficulties translating their desires to be environmentally friendly into specific types of food behaviors because of the lack of a concrete "moral other" directly affected by individual choices. It is clear that other types of food choices in part or whole hinge on the effects that they have on identifiable moral others, such as humans (say, the economic benefits to local farmers by decisions to buy locally) or nonhuman animals (by choices that favor more humane production methods). However, as has been noted in a variety of contexts within environmental ethics, the preservation of collective entities such as species, ecosystems, populations, and so on is a major concern for many environmentalists, even though these entities are not sentient or otherwise subjects-of-a life in the usual moral sense (for a discussion of these issues within environmental ethics more generally, see Brennan and Lo 2016). Making "environmentally conscious" food choices when the "environment" is difficult to define or envision thus is unsurprisingly problematic for many.

In addition, as has been more generally noted with reference to climate change, motivating people to act presents deep practical problems in part due to the dispersed nature of GHG emissions, together with the fact that those who are responsible for these emissions are uncoordinated and largely unregulated. Furthermore as argued by the philosopher Stephen Gardiner (2006; cf. his 2011), current generations do not have strong incentives to act, as future generations will carry the brunt of the impacts of climate change. In addition, some scholars have argued that the term "sustainability" has come to mean very different things and carries with it different symbolic meanings for different groups, reflecting very different interests (e.g., Redclift 2005), ranging from a biologically based concept to an economic or social understanding of what it means to be sustainable. Similar to what was argued above with reference to "local" and other terms associated with ethical consumption, this sort of ambiguity again results in the creation of a failed missing object, one that is signaled by the term (in this case "sustainability") but the basis of which is weak and uncompelling, given that metrics and evidence for it are hotly debated and relatively inaccessible, particularly for laypersons.

III. FROM FOOD CONSUMERISM TO CITIZENSHIP?

It has become extremely popular to focus on ways in which our food choices can make a difference, such as through socially responsible purchasing and preferential consumerism (sometimes called "buycotts") or boycotts (e.g., Stolle, Hooghe, and Micheletti 2005; Blue 2010). According to this approach, the typical emphasis on "voting with your fork," that is, using purchasing as a way to express values, encourages choices that in turn will be reflected in market patterns that somehow will lead to beneficial changes in the broader food system; if we buy (or avoid) certain products, it will send a signal to those producing them about the changes that we wish to see happen. Some scholars even use "political consumerism" as a term to indicate that people's purchasing preferences can have political effects (e.g., Micheletti 2003; de Tavernier 2012).

However, as numerous critics have argued, ethical consumption more generally can be seen as reinforcing neoliberal tendencies by transferring responsibilities to individuals as consumers and focusing attention away from collective action and acknowledgment of governmental responsibility for meeting social needs, especially with regard to fundamental needs (such as food and water) and broader crises that require larger-scale action (such as climate change) (Clarke et al. 2007; Blue 2009; Littler 2009b). Focusing on individual choice, and thus on individuals as the locus for action, allows us to ignore structural inequalities and consumption practices in the modern food system (e.g., see Guthman 2008). In addition, emphasizing "ethical consumerism" is highly problematic because it relies on an illusory set of shared values or beliefs, particularly given the multiplicity of ways in which many of the key categories are interpreted, as discussed above. Consumerism also is not open to all, and it disenfranchises those in lower socioeconomic groups, which are often correlated with other more marginalized demographic groups.

Thus I contend that efforts and initiatives that harness people's roles as food citizens are more likely to be effective with regard to climate change, as will be argued below: first, the idea of a food citizen forces people to consider the collective good and shared values when making food decisions, including with regard to the environment. It allows more involvement of diverse actors who might otherwise be excluded by a more consumer-based approach. Second, food citizenship avoids the classic ethical conundrums about difficulties associated with duties to the environment or to a vague larger whole by clearly focusing attention simultaneously on the local, the broader, and even the global environment. Third, the collective causal effects of broader policy decisions made or supported by us as food citizens are more clearly connected to environmental impacts (and potentially easier to quantify and evaluate) than individual market-based decisions. As has been argued with reference to the need to shift from viewing people as "green consumers" to considering them as "green citizens," such a move reinforces a more holistic and broader approach to consumption and environmentally related issues (e.g., Prothero, McDonagh, and Dobscha 2010). Finally, drawing on arguments by Neva Hassanein (2003) with reference to food democracy and sustainability, food citizenship is necessary, because having more positive effects on the environment does not merely involve scientific approaches but also fundamentally requires resolution of our value conflicts.

What is food citizenship? Jennifer L. Wilkins defines food citizenship as "the practice of engaging in food-related behaviors that support, rather than threaten, the development of a democratic, socially and economically just, and environmentally sustainable food system" (2005, 269). Thus everyone has (or should have) an interest in creating conditions that allow and foster the development and maintenance of democratic and socially and economically just food systems (see Wilkins 2005 for related discussions), which may well cross traditional boundaries of cities, states or provinces, and nations, and not align directly with being a formal "citizen." Of course, the difficulties associated with acting as a responsible food citizen lie in the details about what counts as just, what other factors should be included in our ideal system (and in particular how we incorporate environmental sustainability), and how we measure such outcomes and weigh them in relation to other desired outcomes.

It is critical to note that consumer and citizen discourses often are incommensurable (Sagoff 1988), as consumerist discourse typically narrows the conversation to those matters that directly affect individuals as evidenced through their purchasing decisions, attributing to them relatively passive roles (Welsh and McRae 1998). In contrast, a discourse rooted in concepts of democracy and citizenship views the public as entitled (and even obligated) to participate in discussions about common purposes and the greater good with regard to food. Although the literature on food citizenship has burgeoned in recent years (e.g., Welsh and McRae 1998; Lang 1999, to highlight a few early contributions), most scholars focus on how to reform what some have termed the "capitalist system of production, distribution, consumption, and commercialization" (Siniscalchi and Counihan 2014, 6), and thus tie food citizenship to local food plans, farmers' markets, community gardens, and so on (but cf. Carruthers Den Hoed 2016, linking hunting to food citizenship). This literature often fails to engage with the larger domains in which food citizenship can have effects, well beyond even the corporate food system and traditional agriculture.

The broader idea of a "food citizen" requires people to consider what our collective good is; in this way it permits more focus on shared values, in concert with needing to consider how to create a society that allows all to pursue a good life (Soper 2004). This approach allows us to avoid the consumerist model, where many ways of expressing ethical values via food purchasing and choices are not open to everyone, and particularly not to socially and economically marginalized groups. In these models, those with the financial or social capital to buy supposedly "ethical" products that will have positive effects on the environment (or reduce negative effects) are the only ones positioned to act, particularly given the relatively high cost of products associated with these values (e.g., green and organic products) and the fact that the practices associated with such purchases (such as patronizing farmers' markets to buy local foodstuffs) typically require time not always available to those in lower socioeconomic and other marginalized groups.

A second advantage to stressing food citizenship as a cornerstone of environmental consciousness is that it avoids the classic ethical conundrums about difficulties associated with duties to the environment or to a vague larger whole by clearly focusing attention simultaneously on the local, the broader, and even the global environment. Participating in policy, regula-tory, and related decisions as food citizens may well be most effective at the local level, but these types of activities can contribute to broader policy and regulation, say, at a regional or national level. Hence the line between actions and outcomes is more defined, causally clearer, and thus likely to be more motivating. In turn, the causal effects of broader policy decisions made or supported by us as food citizens participating in a collective can be more clearly connected to environmental impacts (and potentially easier to quan-tify and evaluate) than individual market-based decisions relying on vague and plastic categories such as "food miles" or "local." Consider, for instance, policy-based efforts to limit food waste or to eliminate plastic grocery bags, which have clear targets and can result in measurable outcomes in relation to which a community can assess and modify behaviors as needed on an ongoing basis.

Because the uncertainties associated with how we can act with regard to food in ways that will benefit (and not further endanger) the environment require considerable exploration and debate, the key aim of those who wish to foster more public engagement with environmentally responsible choices and consumption (of food and otherwise) should be not just to encourage the exchange of opinions or the gathering of purchasing preferences but to priori-tize discussion about arguments and reasons associated with the values that people hold about these issues. As previously argued (Ankeny 2016), such approaches are likely to be best supported by a deliberative system for food policy that seeks to articulate evidence, values, and trade-offs; that fosters participation in decision-making; and that thus generates food policy that is legitimate. As detailed in the deliberative democracy literature (see review in Ankeny 2016) but also explored with regard to food and sustainability (e.g., Hassanein 2008), ongoing discussion and deliberation allows citizens to clarify issues and values and thus make better decisions for themselves and others. To have a strong democracy, we must recognize and promote the public good beyond our individual interests, and deliberative engagement promotes these types of values. In turn, if policy is grounded in deliberation, consensus, and compromise aligned with the broader goal of fostering good for the whole, those policies are much more legitimate and also more likely to be effective.

Finally, fostering food citizenship is simply necessary because questions about environmental impact and how we can have less adverse impacts as a result of our food-related activities are not simply scientific questions but ones that are undergirded by conflicts over values that require reflections. We need to consider how we want to define key concepts including "sustain-ability" in social and political terms and be open to the fact that our collective understanding of such concepts will evolve over time (see Hassanein 2003). Thus, as we all have a stake in these problems, we also must all make contributions to devising solutions.

Of course there are clear obstacles to thinking and acting as a food citizen: many would point to large-scale problems in the food system as it currently stands (e.g., O'Kane 2016), particularly its corporate structures, problems accessing accurate information about food, and the limitations imposed by current food policies that may well be difficult to overcome especially given some of the inherent conflicts between an industry seeking to make a profit and societal norms relating to human and environmental health. There also is a range of pragmatic issues relating to limits on people's capacities to engage as food citizens; for example, scholars have found that action is most likely only when people are at life stages that allow them the time and energy to participate (e.g., Kriflik 2006). However, I contend that increasing engagement by people in food-related policymaking—be they eaters, farmers, or even those involved in the food industry—is likely to lead to reflection that should help to create change over time that will improve our environment and also our democratic society.

CONCLUSION

In sum, even if it is clear that many of us share the goal of being more ethically conscious about our food choices, and particularly with regard to effects on the environment, our shorthand approaches of using concepts and categories such as "food miles" or "local" have been failing us in multiple ways. Rethinking our strategies by turning away from consumerism and the reigning neoliberal emphasis on individual decision-making, and instead encouraging participation by all as food citizens, is likely to be more productive and effective. Furthermore, reflecting on our underlying values associated with food choices and their impacts will allow us to pursue even deeper goals such as ensuring food security, including equal access to nourishing, culturally appropriate, sustainable, secure, and safe food, in part by forcing us to engage with and interrogate the existing food system, including our dominant production and consumption methods (Heldke 2009). Such approaches can allow us or even force us to question our choices and how we make them, to cultivate more popular awareness of alternatives without relying on vacuous terms co-opted by industry or other interest groups, and to examine our moral relationships with others, including with the environment. We need a food system that is governed by food citizens that are reflective and active in inclusive and democratic decision-making processes, and that in turn allows us to consider the environmental implications of our choices and actions.

NOTES

1. Research contributing to this publication was funded by the Australian Research Council Discovery Projects Scheme (DP110105062, "What Shall We Have for Tea? Toward a New Discourse of Food Ethics in Contemporary Australia"). I am also grateful to our research participants, Ms. Liza Huston for administrative support throughout the project, Dr. Heather Bray for her collaboration on the research, and the editors of this book for their helpful feedback on an earlier version of the chapter.

2. Thus, there are some similarities between the notion of "missing objects" as used here and Susan Leigh Star and Jim Griesemer's 1989 idea of "boundary objects" (objects that are plastic enough to be used by different communities in different ways, but also are robust in their identities to allow coherence across different social worlds), inasmuch as both serve as translation mechanisms, at least when the missing objects are effective. However, I have used "missing objects" here because of the explicit nature of the use of the objects as stand-ins or proxies in this domain, and because there is the potential for a representation not to work in the case of missing objects, whereas boundary objects assume effective translation is occurring.

References

Action Group on Erosion, Technology, and Concentration. 2017. "Who Will Feed Us? The Industrial Food Chain vs. the Peasant Food Web." 3rd edition. http://www.etcgroup.org/sites/www.etcgroup.org/files/files/etc-whowillfeedus-english-webshare.pdf.

Adams, Carol. 1995. *Neither Man nor Beast: Feminism and the Defense of Animals*. New York: Continuum.

Adams, Carol. 2015. *The Sexual Politics of Meat: A Feminist Vegetarian Critical Theory*. London: Bloomsbury Press.

Agencia AFP. 2017, October 18. "Cambio climático amenaza áreas de cultivo de café en Latinoamérica." *El Financiero*.

Agyeman, Julian. 2013. *Introducing Just Sustainabilities: Policy, Planning, and Practice*. Chicago: University of Chicago Press.

Agyeman, Julian and Jesse McEntee. 2014. "Moving the Field of Food Justice Forward Through the Lens of Urban Political Ecology." *Geography Compass* 8, no. 3: 211–20.

Ahmed, Azam, Matt Richtel, and Andrew Jacobs. 2018, March 20. "In Nafta Talks, US Tries to Limit Junk Food Warning Labels." *New York Times*. https://www.nytimes.com/2018/03/20/world/americas/nafta-food-labels-obesity.html.

Aiken, William. 1984. "Value Conflicts in Agriculture." *Agriculture and Human Values* 1, no. 1: 24–27.

Alavanja, Michael C. R. 2009. "Pesticides Use and Exposure Extensive Worldwide." *Reviews on Environmental Health* 24, no. 4: 303–9.

Alkon, Alison and Julian Agyeman. 2011. *Cultivating Food Justice*. Cambridge, MA: MIT Press.

Allen, Myles, David J. Frame, Chris Huntingford, Chris D. Jones, Jason A. Lowe, Malte Meinshausen, and Nicolai Meinshausen. 2009. "Warming Caused by Cumulative Carbon Emissions Towards the Trillionth Tonne." *Nature* 458: 1163–66.

Allen, Patricia and Carolyn Sachs. 2007. "Women and Food Chains: The Gendered Politics of Food." *International Journal of Sociology of Food and Agriculture* 15, no. 1 (April): 1–23.

Altieri, Miguel A., Clara I. Nicholls, and Rene Montalba. 2017. "Technological Approaches to Sustainable Agriculture at a Crossroads: An Agroecological Perspective." *Sustainability* 9, no. 3: 349.

Amnesty International. 2015, November 12. "China: Torture and Forced Confession Rampant Amid Systematic Trampling of Lawyers' Rights." Amnesty International. https://www.amnesty.org/en/latest/news/2015/11/china-torture-forced-confession/.

Amnesty International. 2017, July. "Honduras: Submission the United Nations Human Rights Committee." Amnesty International. Accessed January 15, 2018. https://www.amnesty.org/es/documents/amr37/6417/2017/en/.

Anderson, Kip and Keegan Kuhn. 2015. *Cowspiracy: The Sustainability Secret.* http://www.cowspiracy.com/.

Anderson, Terry L. and Donald R. Leal. 1991. "Going with the Flow: Expanding the Role of Water Markets." In *Ethics and Agriculture*, edited by Charles Blatz, 384–93. Moscow: University of Idaho Press.

Angetter, Lea-Su, Stefan Lötters, and Dennis Rödder. 2011. "Climate Niche Shift in Invasive Species: The Case of the Brown Anole." *Biological Journal of the Linnean Society* 104, no. 4: 943–54.

Ankeny, Rachel A. 2012. "Ethics of Food." In *Handbook of Food History*, edited by Jeffrey Pilcher, 461–80. Oxford: Oxford University Press.

Ankeny, Rachel A. 2016. "Inviting Everyone to the Table: Strategies for More Effective and Legitimate Food Policy via Deliberative Approaches." *Journal of Social Philosophy* 47, no. 1: 10–24.

AP. 2010, May 10. "Planet's Biodiversity Said Under New Threat." https://www.cbsnews.com/news/planets-biodiversity-said-under-new-threat/.

AP. 2018, April 27. "Smithfield Foods Pork-Production Division Hit with $50M Jury Award Over Noises, Smells." *Fox Business News.* https://www.foxbusiness.com/markets/smithfield-foods-pork-production-division-hit-with-50m-jury-award-over-noises-smells.

Archer, David, Michael Eby, Victor Brovkin, Andy Ridgwell, Long Cao, Uwe Mikolajewicz, and Ken Caldeira et al. 2009. "Atmospheric Lifetime of Fossil Fuel Carbon Dioxide." *Annual Review of Earth and Planetary Sciences* 37: 117–34.

Arnold, Denis and Keith Bustos. 2007. "Business, Ethics, and Global Climate Change." *Business and Professional Ethics Journal* 24, no. 1–2: 103–30.

Aubert, Benoit A., Andreas Schroeder, and Jonathan Grimaudo. 2012. "IT as Enabler of Sustainable Farming: An Empirical Analysis of Farmers' Adoption Decision of Precision Agriculture Technology." *Decision Support Systems* 54, no. 1: 510–20.

Baker, Jeffrey Lee. 2003. "Maya Wetlands: Ecology and Pre-Hispanic Utilization of Wetlands in Northwestern Belize." PhD diss., University of Arizona. http://arizona.openrepository.com/arizona/bitstream/10150/237812/3/azu_td_3089896_sip1_m.pdf.

Banach, M., N. Brown, C. Carroll, N. Gillespie, D. Glaser, R. Hall, and A. Ryu. 2002. "Constituting 'Missing Objects' in Learning Conversations." In *Keeping Learning*

Complex: The Proceedings of the Fifth International Conference of the Learning Sciences, edited by P. Bell, R. Stevens, and T. Satwicz, 606–10. ICLS. Mahwah, NJ: Erlbaum.

Barker, Charlene, Francois Aderson, Rachel Goodman, and Effat Hussain. 2012, June. "Unshared Bounty." American Civil Liberties Union and NYU Law School, Racial Justice Project. http://www.racialjusticeproject.com/wp-content/uploads/sites/30/2012/06/NYLS-Food-Deserts-Report.pdf.

Barkin, David. 2006. "The Reconstruction of a Modern Mexican Peasantry." *Journal of Peasant Studies* 30, no. 1 (August): 73–90.

Barnett, Jon and W. Neil Adger. 2007. "Climate Change, Human Security and Violent Conflict." *Political Geography* 26, no. 6: 639–55.

Barnhill, Anne, Mark Budolfson, and Tyler Doggett. 2017. "Alternatives to Industrial Plant Agriculture." In *Food, Ethics, and Society: An Introductory Text with Readings*, edited by Anne Barnhill, Mark Budolfson, and Tyler Doggett, 459–80. New York: Oxford University Press.

Barry, Tom. 1995. *Zapata's Revenge: Free Trade and the Farm Crisis in Mexico.* Boston: South End Press.

Bartling, Sönke and Sascha Friesike. 2014. *Opening Science: The Evolving Guide on How the Internet is Changing Research, Collaboration and Scholarly Publishing.* Cham: Springer.

Beauchamp, Tom L. 2014. "Rights Theory and Animal Rights." In *The Oxford Handbook of Animal Ethics*, edited by Tom L. Beauchamp and R. G. Frey, 198–228. Oxford: Oxford University Press.

Beaulac, Julie, Elizabeth Kristjansson, and Steven Cummins. 2009. "A Systematic Review of Food Deserts: 1966–2007." *Preventing Chronic Disease* 6: 1–10.

Becker, Geoffrey S. 2008. "CRS Report for Congress: Federal Farm Promotion ('Check-Off') Programs." Congressional Research Service.

Beitz, Charles. 1973. *Political Theory and International Relations.* Princeton, NJ: Princeton University Press.

Bellard, Céline, Cleo Bertelsmeier, Paul Leadley, Wilfried Thuiller, and Franck Courchamp. 2012. "Impacts of Climate Change on the Future of Biodiversity." *Ecology Letters* 15, no. 4: 365–77.

Ben-Ari, A. and K. Or-Chen. 2009. "Integrating Competing Conceptions of Risk: A Call for Future Direction of Research." *Journal of Risk Research* 12: 865–77.

Bennett, T. M. B., N. G. Maynard, P. Cochran, R. Gough, K. Lynn, J. Maldonado, G. Voggesser et al. 2014. "Indigenous Peoples, Lands, and Resources." In *Climate Change Impacts in the United States: The Third National Climate Assessment*, edited by J. M. Melillo, Terese (T. C.) Richmond, and G. W. Yohe, 297–317. U.S. Global Change Research Program. doi:10.7930/J09G5JR1.

Benz, Bruce F. 2001. "Archaeological Evidence of Teosinte Domestication from Guilá Naquitz, Oaxaca." *Proceedings of the National Academy of Sciences* 98, no. 4 (February 13): 2104–6.

Beyleveld, Deryck and Li Jianjun. 2017. "Inclusive Governance Over Agricultural Biotechnology: Risk Assessment and Public Participation." *Law, Innovation and Technology* 9, no. 2: 301–17.

Biddle, Justin B. 2016. "Intellectual Property Rights and Global Climate Change: Toward Resolving an Apparent Dilemma." *Ethics, Policy & Environment* 19, no. 3: 301–19.

Bitmann, Mark. 2011, April 26. "Who Protects the Animals?" *New York Times.*

Bizikova, Livia, Stephen Tyler, Marcus Moench, Marius Keller, and Daniella Echeverria. 2016. "Climate Resilience and Food Security in Central America: A Practical Framework." *Climate and Development* 8, no. 5: 397–412.

Black, Christina, Georgia Ntani, Ross Kenny, Tannaze Tinati, Megan Jarman, Wendy Lawrence, Mary Barker et al. 2012. "Variety and Quality of Healthy Foods Differ According to Neighbourhood Deprivation." *Health & Place* 18: 1292–99.

Blake, Michael. 2002. "Distributive Justice, State Coercion, and Autonomy." *Philosophy and Public Affairs* 30, no. 3: 257–96.

Blue, Gwendolyn. 2009. "On the Politics and Possibilities of Locavores: Situating Food Sovereignty in the Turn from Government to Governance." *Politics and Culture* 2, no. 2: 68–79.

Blue, Gwendolyn. 2010. "Food, Publics, Science." *Public Understanding of Science* 19, no. 2: 147–54.

Borlaug, Norman E. 1997. "Feeding a World of 10 Billion People: The Miracle Ahead." *Biotechnology & Biotechnological Equipment* 11, no. 3: 3–13.

Born, Branden and Mark Purcell. 2006. "Avoiding the Local Trap: Scale and Food Systems in Planning Research." *Journal of Planning Education and Research* 26, no. 2: 195–207.

Boserup, Esther. 1983. "The Impact of Scarcity and Plenty on Development." In *Hunger and History: The Impact of Changing Food Production and Consumption Patterns on Society*, edited by Robert I. Rotberg and Theodore K. Rabb, 185–209. Cambridge: Cambridge University Press.

Botkin, Daniel B., Henrik Saxe, Miguel B. Araújo, Richard Betts, Richard H. W. Bradshaw, Tomas Cedhagen, Peter Chesson et al. 2007. "Forecasting the Effects of Global Warming on Biodiversity." *BioScience* 57, no. 3: 227–36.

Bradley, Katharine and Ryan E. Galt. 2014. "Practicing Food Justice at Dig Deep Farms & Produce, East Bay Area, California: Self-Determination as a Guiding Value and Intersections with Foodie Logics." *Local Environment* 19: 172–86.

Braudel, Fernand. 1981. *The Structures of Everyday Life, Vol. I, Civilization and Capitalism, 15th–18th Century*. Translated by Siân Reynolds. New York: Harper and Row.

Brecha, Bob. 2016, June 25. "Can Free Trade Agreements Be Consistent with Climate Change Mitigation?" *Huffington Post.*

Brennan, Andrew and Yeuk-Sze Lo. 2016. "Environmental Ethics." In *The Stanford Encyclopedia of Philosophy* (Winter 2016), edited by Edward N. Zalta. Accessed on June 26, 2018. https://plato.stanford.edu/archives/win2016/entries/ethics-environmental/.

Broad, Garrett M. 2016. "Animal Production, Ag-Gag Laws, and the Social Production of Ignorance: Exploring the Role of Storytelling." *Environmental Communication* 10, no. 1: 43–61.

Bronson, Kelly and Irena Knezevic. 2016. "Big Data in Food and Agriculture." *Big Data & Society* 3, no. 1: 1–5.

Broome, John. 2012. *Climate Matters: Ethics in a Warming World.* New York: W. W. Norton.

Brown, Molly E. and Christopher C. Funk. 2008. "Food Security under Climate Change." *Science* 319: 580–81.

Brown, Sandy and Christy Getz. 2011. "Farmworker Food Insecurity and the Production of Hunger in California." In *Cultivating Food Justice: Race, Class, and Sustainability*, edited by Alison Hope Alkon and Julia Agyeman, 121–46. Cambridge, MA: MIT Press.

Brownell, Kelly D. and Kenneth E. Warner. 2009. "The Perils of Ignoring History: Big Tobacco Played Dirty and Millions Died. How Similar Is Big Food?" *Milbank Quarterly* 87, no. 1: 259–94.

Brunsma, D. L., D. Overfelt, and J. S. Picou. 2007. *The Sociology of Katrina.* Lanham, MD: Rowman & Littlefield.

Buchman, Anna, John M. Marshall, Dennis Ostrovski, Ting Yang, and Omar S. Akbari. 2018. "Synthetically Engineered Medea Gene Drive System in the Worldwide Crop Pest Drosophila suzukii." *Proceedings of the National Academy of Sciences.* doi:201713139.

Bullard, Robert. 1990. *Dumping in Dixie.* Boulder, CO: Westview Press.

Bullard, Robert. 1999, July. "Environmental Justice: An Interview with Robert Bullard." Interview by Errol Schweizer. *Earth First! Journal.* Accessed May 21, 2018. https://www.ejnet.org/ej/bullard.html.

Bullock, James M., Kiran L. Dhanjal-Adams, Alice Milne, Tom H. Oliver, Lindsay C. Todman, Andrew P. Whitmore, and Richard F. Pywell. 2017. "Resilience and Food Security: Rethinking an Ecological Concept." *Journal of Ecology* 105, no. 4: 880–84.

Butler, Declan. 2010. "What It Will Take to Feed the World." *Nature* 464, no. 7291: 969.

Cabnal, Lorena. 2015, February 6. "De las opresiones a las emancipaciones: mujeres indígenas en defensa del territorio cuerpo-tierra." *Pueblos: Revista de Información y Debate.*

Cadieux, K. V. and Rachel Slocum. 2015. "What Does It Mean to Do Food Justice?" *Journal of Political Ecology* 22: 1–26.

Calder, Todd. 2010. "Shared Responsibility, Global Structural Injustice, and Restitution." *Social Theory and Practice* 36, no. 2: 263–90.

Callicott, J. Baird. 1980. "Animal Liberation: A Triangular Affair." *Environmental Ethics* 2, no. 4: 311–38.

Callicott, J. Baird. 1989. *In Defense of the Land Ethic.* Albany, NY: SUNY Press.

Caney, Simon. 2006. "Cosmopolitan Justice and Institutional Design: An Egalitarian Liberal Conception of Global Governance." *Social Theory and Practice* 32, no. 4: 725–56.

Caney, Simon. 2010. "Cosmopolitan Justice, Responsibility, and Global Climate Change." In *Climate Ethics: Essential Readings*, edited by Stephen M. Gardiner,

Simon Caney, Dale Jamieson, and Henry Shue, 122–45. Oxford: Oxford University Press.

Cannon, Geoffrey. 1987. *The Politics of Food*. London: Century Hutchinson.

Caputo, Vincenzina, Achilleas Vassilopoulos, Rodolfo M. Nayga Jr., and Maurizio Canavari. 2013. "Welfare Effects of Food Mile Labels." *Journal of Consumer Affairs* 47, no. 2: 311–27.

Carruth, Allison. 2013. *Global Appetites: American Power and the Literature of Food*. New York: Cambridge University Press.

Carruthers Den Hoed, R. 2016. "Hipster Hunters and the Discursive Politics of Food Hunting in Canada." In *How Canadians Communicate VI: Food Promotion, Consumption, Controversy*, edited by C. Elliott, 203–28. Edmonton: University of Athabasca Press.

CEHPRODEC (Centro Hondureño de Promoción para el Desarrollo Comunitario). 2017, May. "Informe del Observatorio de Bienes Naturales y Derechos Humanos." CEHPRODEC and Diakonia, Desarrollo y Paz y Trocaire, May 2017. Accessed November 21, 2017. http://www.cehprodec.org/files/Informe_OBNDH_2017.pdf.

Center for Sustainable Systems. 2017a. *Carbon Footprint Factsheet*. Ann Arbor: University of Michigan.

Center for Sustainable Systems. 2017b. *U.S. Food System Factsheet*. Ann Arbor: University of Michigan.

Challinor, A. J., J. Watson, David B. Lobell, S. M. Howden, D. R. Smith, and N. Chhetri. 2014. "A Meta-Analysis of Crop Yield Under Climate Change and Adaptation." *Nature Climate Change* 4: 287–91.

Chapin III, F. Stuart. 2009. "Managing Ecosystems Sustainably: The Key Role of Resilience." In *Principles of Ecosystem Stewardship*, edited by F. Stuart Chapin III, Gary Kofinas, and Carl Folke, 29–53. New York: Springer.

Charles, Nickie and Marion Kerr. 1988. *Women, Food, and Families*. Manchester: Manchester University Press.

Chayes, Sarah. 2017. *When Corruption Is Operating the System: The Case of Honduras*. Washington, DC: Carnegie Endowment for International Peace.

Chrispeels, Martin J. and D. E. Sadava. 2003. *Plants, Genes and Crop Biotechnology*. Sudbury, MA: Jones & Bartlett.

Clark, Sarah E., Corinna Hawkes, Sophia M. E. Murphy, Karen A. Hansen-Kuhn, and David Wallinga. 2012. "Exporting Obesity: U.S. Farm and Trade Policy and the Transformation of the Mexican Consumer Food Environment." *International Journal of Occupational and Environmental Health* 18, no. 1 (January–March): 53–65. doi:10.1179/1077352512Z.0000000007.

Clarke, Nick, Clive Barnett, Paul Cloke, and Alice Malpass. 2007. "Globalising the Consumer: Doing Politics in an Ethical Register." *Political Geography* 26, no. 3: 231–49.

Cleveland Clinic. 2017, March 28. "Poor Diet Linked to Half of Heart Disease, Stroke, Diabetes Deaths." Accessed March 2018. https://health.clevelandclinic.org/poor-diet-linked-to-half-of-heart-disease-stroke-diabetes-deaths/.

The Climate Reality Project. 2013, October 23. "The Human Impact of Climate Change: Personal Stories from U.S. and Mexico." https://www.climaterealityproject. org/video/human-impact-climate-change-personal-stories-us-and-mexico.

Climate Stories Project. 2018. "Africa Climate Stories: Fatoumata Diallo, Kayes, Mali." Accessed May 21, 2018. http://www.climatestoriesproject.org/ africaclimatestories.html.

Cline, William R. 2007. *Global Warming and Agriculture: Impact Estimates by Country*. Washington, DC: Center for Global Development.

Coffman, Jennifer E. 2012. "Food Miles." In *Encyclopedia of Global Warming and Climate Change,* edited by S. George Philander, 574. Thousand Oaks, CA: Sage.

Cohen, G. A. 2008. *Rescuing Justice and Equality*. Cambridge, MA: Harvard University Press.

Cohen, James. 2017. "Capitalist Transformation, Social Violence and Transnational Migration: The Obama-Clinton Legacy in Central America in Macro-Sociological and Strategic Perspective." *Revue de recherche en civilisation américaine* [online]. http://journals.openedition.org/rrca/853.

Cole, Luke W. and Sheila R. Foster. 2001. *From the Ground Up: Environmental Racism and the Rise of the Environmental Justice Movement*. New York: New York University Press.

Coley, David, Mark Howard, and Michael Winter. 2011. "Food Miles: Time for a Rethink?" *British Food Journal* 113: 919–34.

Comisión de Verdad sobre el Golpe de Estado. 2012, October. "Sin verdad no hay justicia." Plataforma de Derechos Humanos. Accessed April 3, 2014. https://ccrjustice.org/sites/default/files/attach/2015/01/TrueCommission_Report_ Spanish_10_12.pdf.

Council on Hemispheric Affairs. 2010. "Climate Migration in Latin America: A Future 'Flood of Refugees' to the North?" Last modified February 22, 2010. http:// www.coha.org/climate-migration-in-latin-america-part-1/.

Crenshaw, Kimberlé. 1991. "Mapping the Margins: Intersectionality, Identity Politics, and Violence against Women of Color," *Stanford Law Review* 43, no. 6 (July): 1241–99.

The Crop Trust. n.d. "Supporting Crop Conservation." https://www.croptrust.org/ our-work/supporting-crop-conservation/.

CRP (Center for Responsive Politics). 2016. "Poultry & Eggs: Money to Congress." Accessed March 2, 2018. https://www.opensecrets.org/industries/summary.php?in d=A05&recipdetail=A&sortorder=U&mem=Y&cycle=2016.

Cummins, Steven and Sally Macintyre. 2002. "A Systematic Study of an Urban Foodscape: The Price and Availability of Food in Greater Glasgow." *Urban Studies* 39, no. 11: 2115–30.

Daly, Herman E. 1996. *Beyond Growth*. Boston, MA: Beacon Press.

D'Angelo, Chris. 2018, April 1. "This Paleontologist Discovered 'The Find of a Lifetime' in the Area Trump Cut from Bear's Ears." Mother Jones. https://www. motherjones.com/environment/2018/04/this-paleontologist-discovered-a-fossil-find-of-a-lifetime-in-the-area-trump-cut-from-bears-ears/.

Dawson, Todd. 2009, September 10. "Respondent, 'Pollan's Public Interest Prediction.'" *UC Berkeley News.* https://www.berkeley.edu/news/berkeleyan/2009/09/10_pollan.shtml.

De Bres, Helena. 2017. "Local Food: The Moral Case." In *Food, Ethics, and Society: An Introductory Text with Readings,* edited by Anne Barnhill, Mark Budolfson, and Tyler Doggett, 495–510. New York: Oxford University Press.

De Hoop, Evelien, Auke Pols, and Henny Romijn. 2016. "Limits to Responsible Innovation." *Journal of Responsible Innovation* 3, no. 2: 110–34.

De Schutter, Olivier. 2009, November 18. "The Right to Food and the Political Economy of Hunger." Twenty-Sixth McDougall Memorial Lecture Opening of the Thirty-Sixth Session of the FAO Conference. Rome: FAO.

De Tavernier, Johan. 2012. "Food Citizenship: Is There a Duty for Responsible Consumption?" *Journal of Agricultural and Environmental Ethics* 25, no. 6: 895–907.

Declaration of Nyéléni. 2007, February 27. "Declaration of the Forum for Food Sovereignty." Nyéléni Village, Sélingué, Mali. Accessed May 17, 2018. https://nyeleni.org/spip.php?article290.

Desmarais, Annette. 2008. "The Power of Peasants: Reflections on the Meanings of La Vía Campesina." *Journal of Rural Studies* 24, no. 2: 138–49.

Development Assistance Research Associates (DARA). 2012. *Climate Vulnerability Monitor.* 2nd edition. Accessed January 16, 2018. http://daraint.org/climate-vulnerability-monitor/climate-vulnerability-monitor-2012/report/.

Devereux, Stephen. 2001. "Sen's Entitlement Approach: Critiques and Counter-Critiques." *Oxford Development Studies* 29, no. 3: 245–63.

Devereux, Stephen. 2006. "Desk Review: Distinguishing Between Chronic and Transitory Food Insecurity in Emergency Needs Assessments." Rome: Institute of Development Studies/World Food Programme.

Dewey, Caitlin. 2018, February 12. "Trump Wants to Slash Food Stamps and Replace Them with a 'Blue Apron-Type' Program." *Washington Post.*

Dieterle, J. M. 2015a. "Food Deserts and Lockean Property." In *Just Food*, edited by J. M. Dieterle, 39–56. Lanham, MD: Rowman & Littlefield.

Dieterle, J. M., ed. 2015b. *Just Food: Philosophy, Justice, and Food.* London: Rowman & Littlefield.

Director International Affairs and Trade. 2007. "Foreign Assistance: Various Challenges Limit the Efficiency and Effectiveness of US Food Aid." Washington, DC: Committee of Foreign Affairs, Subcommittee on Africa and Global Health, House of Representatives.

Domonoske, Camila. 2016, September 13. "50 Years Ago, Sugar Industry Quietly Paid Scientists to Point Blame at Fat." NPR. https://www.npr.org/sections/thetwo-way/2016/09/13/493739074/50-years-ago-sugar-industry-quietly-paid-scientists-to-point-blame-at-fat.

Doney, Scott C. 2010. "The Growing Human Footprint on Coastal and Open-Ocean Biogeochemistry." *Science* 328, no. 5985: 1512–16.

Donovan, Josephine. 1990. "Animal Rights and Feminist Theory." *Signs: A Journal of Women and Culture in Society* 15: 350–75.

Douglas, Heather. 2000. "Inductive Risk and Values in Science." *Philosophy of Science* 67: 559–79.

Duke University. 2009, March 11. "Corn-for-Ethanol's Carbon Footprint Critiqued." *ScienceDaily*. https://www.sciencedaily.com/releases/2009/03/090302183321.htm.

Dunbar-Ortiz, Roxanne. 2014. *An Indigenous People's History of the United States*. Boston: Beacon Press.

Eakin, Hallie, Hans-George Bohle, Anne-Marie Izac, Anette Reenberg, Peter Gregory, and Laura Pereira. 2010. "Food, Violence, and Human Rights." In *Food Security and Global Environmental Change*, edited by John Ingram, Polly Ericksen, and Diana Liverman, 245–71. London: Earthscan.

Eckersley, Robyn. 2016. "Responsibility for Climate Change as a Structural Injustice." In *The Oxford Handbook of Environmental Political Theory,* edited by T. Gabrielson, C. Hall, J. M. Meyer, and D. Schlosberg, 346–62. Oxford: Oxford University Press.

Edelman, Marc and Andrés León. 2014. "Ciclos de acaparamiento de tierras en Centroamérica: Un argumento a favor de historizar y un estudio de caso del Bajo Aguán, Honduras." *Anuario de Estudios Centroamericanos* 2014, no. 40: 195–228.

Edwards, Bob and A. E. Ladd. 2001. "Race, Class, Political Capacity, and the Spatial Distribution of Swine Waste in North Carolina, 1982–1997." *North Carolina Geographer* 9: 51–70.

EJNET. "Environmental Justice/Environmental Racism." Accessed May 21, 2018. https://www.ejnet.org/ej/.

Elliott, Kevin. 2011. *Is a Little Pollution Good for You?* Oxford: Oxford University Press.

Elver, Hilal, Special Rapporteur on Right to Food. 2016, August 3. "Report of the Special Rapporteur on the Right to Food." United Nations. Accessed December 5, 2017. http://www.un.org/ga/search/view_doc.asp?symbol=A/71/282&Submit=Search&Lang=E.

Emerson, Claudia, Stephanie James, Katherine Littler, and Filippo (Fil) Randazzo. 2017. "Principles for Gene Drive Research." *Science* 358: 1135–36.

Endrezze, Anita. 2002. "Corn Mother." In *The Sweet Breathing of Plants: Women Writing on the Green World*, edited by Linda Hogan and Brenda Patterson, 66–70. Reprint edition. New York: North Point Press.

Environment and Climate Change Canada. 2018. "National Inventory Report 1990–2016—Greenhouse Gas Sources and Sinks in Canada: Executive Summary." Gatineau, QC: Environment and Climate Change Canada. https://www.canada.ca/en/environment-climate-change/services/climate-change/greenhouse-gas-emissions/sources-sinks-executive-summary-2018.html#agriculture.

Environmental Equity Workgroup. 1992, June. "Environmental Equity: Reducing Risk for All Communities." Policy, Planning, and Evaluation. U.S. Environmental Protection Agency. Accessed May 21, 2018. https://nepis.epa.gov/Exe/ZyPURL.cgi?Dockey=40000JLA.txt.

EPA (United States Environmental Protection Agency). n.d. "Global Greenhouse Gas Emissions Data." Accessed March 9, 2018. https://www.epa.gov/ghgemissions/global-greenhouse-gas-emissions-data.

Epstein, Samuel. 1996. *Impure Science.* Berkeley: University of California Press.

Ericksen, Polly J. 2008. "Conceptualizing Food Systems for Global Environmental Change Research." *Global Environmental Change* 18, no. 1: 234–45.

Ericksen, Polly, Beth Stewart, Jane Dixon, David Barling, Philip Loring, Molly Anderson, and John Ingram. 2010. "The Value of a Food System Approach." In *Food Security and Global Environmental Change*, edited by John Ingram, Polly Ericksen, and Diana Liverman, 25–45. London: Earthscan.

Ericksen, Polly, Beth Stewart, Siri Eriksen, Petra Tschakert, Rachel Sabates-Wheeler, Jim Hansen, and Philip Thornton. 2010. "Adapting Food Systems." In *Food Security and Global Environmental Change*, edited by John Ingram, Polly Ericksen, and Diana Liverman, 115–43. London: Earthscan.

Estado de la Región. 2015. "Quinto Informe Estado de la Región: Seguridad Alimentaria y Nutricional en Centroamérica." CONARE. Programa Estado de la Nación. https://estadonacion.or.cr/files/biblioteca_virtual/centroamerica/005/Panorama-Social/Seguridad_Alimentaria.pdf.

Estado de la Región. 2018. "Estadísticas de Centroamérica 2017." CONARE. Programa Estado de la Nación. Accessed January 18, 2018. https://www.estadisticascentroamerica2017.estadonacion.or.cr/.

Evans, Lloyd T. 1998. *Feeding the Ten Billion.* Cambridge: Cambridge University Press.

Faber, Daniel. 1992. "Imperialism, Revolution, and the Ecological Crisis of Central America." *Latin American Perspectives* 19, no. 1: 17–44.

Faber, Scott, Soren Rundquist, and Tim Male. 2012. *Plowed Under: How Crop Subsidies Contribute to Massive Habitat Losses.* Washington, DC: Environmental Working Group. https://static.ewg.org/pdf/plowed_under.pdf?_ga=2.54910307.919886267.1525012317-1315168105.1522827949.

FAO. Also see Food and Agriculture Organization of the United Nations.

FAO. 2013. "Programa Regional de Seguridad Alimentaria para Centroamérica. Centroamérica en cifras. Datos de seguridad alimentaria para Centroamérica." FAO and PRESANCA.

FAO. 2017. *The Future of Food and Agriculture: Trends and Challenges.* Rome: FAO. Accessed March 2018. http://www.fao.org/3/a-i6583e.pdf.

Félix, Georges F., Cathy Clermont-Dauphin, Edmond Hien, Jeroen C. J. Groot, Aurélien Penche, Bernard G. Barthès, Raphaël J. Manlay et al. 2018. "Ramial Wood Amendments (Piliostigma reticulatum) Mitigate Degradation of Tropical Soils but Do Not Replenish Nutrient Exports." *Land Degradation & Development.* doi:10.1002/ldr.3033.

Fiber-Ostrow, Pamela and Jarret S. Lovell. 2016. "Behind a Veil of Secrecy: Animal Abuse, Factory Farms, and Ag-Gag Legislation." *Contemporary Justice Review* 19, no. 2: 230–49.

Fischer, Gunter, Mahendra Shah, and Harrij van Velthuizen. 2002. *Climate Change and Agricultural Vulnerability: A Special Report Prepared as a Contribution to the World Summit on Sustainable Development.* Laxenburg, Austria: International Institute for Applied Systems Analysis.

Fitting, Elizabeth. 2011. *The Struggle for Maize: Campesinos, Workers, and Transgenic Corn in the Mexican Countryside.* Durham, NC: Duke University Press.

Foer, Jonathan Safran. 2009. *Eating Animals*. New York: Little, Brown and Company.

Follett, Ronald F., John M. Kimble, and Rattan Lal. 2001. *The Potential of U.S. Grazing Lands to Sequester Carbon and Mitigate the Greenhouse Effect*. Boca Raton, FL: Lewis Publishers.

Fontas, Jeffrey P. 2010. "The Bush Administration Torture Policy: Origins and Consequences." *Inquiries* 2, no. 8. http://www.inquiriesjournal.com/a?id=276.

Food and Agriculture Organization of the United Nations. n.d. "Animal Production." Accessed February 4, 2018. http://www.fao.org/animal-production/en/.

Food and Agriculture Organization of the United Nations. 2002. *The State of Food Insecurity in the World 2001*. Rome: Food and Agriculture Organization of the United Nations Viale delle Terme di Caracalla. http://www.fao.org/docrep/005/y7352e/y7352e00.htm.

Food and Agriculture Organization of the United Nations. 2006a. "Food Security." Accessed May 15, 2018. http://www.fao.org/forestry/13128-0e6f36f27e0091055bec28ebe830f46b3.pdf.

Food and Agriculture Organization of the United Nations. 2006b. "Livestock's Long Shadow: Environmental Issues and Options." http://www.fao.org/docrep/010/a0701e/a0701e.pdf.

Food and Agriculture Organization of the United Nations. 2013. "Climate-Smart Agriculture Sourcebook." http://www.fao.org/3/a-i3325e.pdf.

Food and Agriculture Organization of the United Nations. 2015. "FAO Statistical Pocketbook: World Food and Agriculture." http://www.fao.org/3/a-i4691e.pdf.

Food and Agriculture Organization of the United Nations. 2016. "Consequences of Climate Change." Accessed May 14, 2018. http://www.fao.org/docrep/015/i2498e/i2498e03.pdf.

Food and Agriculture Organization of the United Nations. 2017a. "Conflict, Migration and Food Security: The Role of Agriculture and Rural Development." Accessed May 15, 2018. http://www.fao.org/3/a-i7896e.pdf.

Food and Agriculture Organization of the United Nations. 2017b. "SOFI 2017—The State of Food Security and Nutrition in the World." Accessed May 14, 2018. http://www.fao.org/state-of-food-security-nutrition/en/.

Food Inc. 2008. Directed by Robert Kenner. New York: Magnolia Pictures.

Ford, James D. 2009. "Vulnerability of Inuit Food Systems to Food Insecurity as a Consequence of Climate Change: A Case Study from Igloolik, Nunavut." *Regional Environmental Change* 9: 83–100.

Foucault, Michel. (1975) 1995. *Discipline and Punish*. Translated by Alan Sheridan. New York: Vintage Books.

Fountas, S., S. Blackmore, D. Ess, S. Hawkins, G. Blumhoff, J. Lowenberg-Deboer, and C. G. Sorensen. 2005. "Farmer Experience with Precision Agriculture in Denmark and the US Eastern Corn Belt." *Precision Agriculture* 6, no. 2: 121–41.

Fox, Tim and Ceng Fimeche. 2013. "Global Food: Waste Not, Want Not." Institution of Mechanical Engineers. Accessed February 21, 2018. https://www.imeche.org/docs/default-source/default-document-library/global-food---waste-not-want-not.pdf?sfvrsn=0.

Fraser, Nancy. 1997. *Justice Interruptus*. New York: Routledge.

Fraser, Nancy. 1998. "Social Justice in the Age of Identity Politics: Redistribution, Recognition, and Participation." *The Tanner Lectures on Human Values* 19. doi:http://dx.doi.org/10.4135/9781446218112.n2.

Fraser, Nancy. 2000. "Rethinking Recognition." *New Left Review* 3: 107–20.

Fraser, Nancy. 2001. "Recognition without Ethics?" *Theory, Culture, and Society* 18: 21–42.

Freeman, Andrea. 2007. "Fast Food: Oppression through Poor Nutrition." *California Law Review* 95: 2221–22.

Freeman, Samuel. 2003. "Congruence and the Good of Justice." In *The Cambridge Companion to Rawls*, edited by Samuel Freeman, 277–315. Cambridge: Cambridge University Press.

Fricker, Mirada. 2007. *Epistemic Injustice.* Cambridge: Oxford University Press.

Friedman, Uri. 2014, May 29. "Two-Thirds of Obese People Now Live in Developing Countries." *The Atlantic.* https://www.theatlantic.com/international/archive/2014/05/two-thirds-of-the-worlds-obese-people-now-live-in-developing-countries/371834/.

Füleky, György. 2016. "Cultivated Plants Primarily as Food Sources." In *Encyclopedia of Life Support Systems*. Paris: UNESCO. http://www.eolss.net/sample-./c10/E5-02.pdf.

Funk, Cary and Brian Kennedy. 2016, October 4. "Public Views on Climate Change and Climate Scientists." Pew Research Center. http://www.pewinternet.org/2016/10/04/public-views-on-climate-change-and-climate-scientists/.

Gaard, Greta. 2015. "Ecofeminism and Climate Change." *Women's Studies International Forum* 49. https://www.academia.edu/11875214/Ecofeminism_and_Climate_Change.

Gaard, Greta. 2017. "Feminism and Environmental Justice." In *Handbook of Environmental Justice*, edited by Jay Chakraborty and Gordon Walker, 74–88. New York: Routledge.

GAIN (Global Alliance for Health). n.d. Accessed November 2017. https://www.gainhealth.org/.

Gandhi, M. K. 1948. *Gandhi's Autobiography: The Story of My Experiments with Truth.* Washington, DC: Public Affairs Press.

Gandhi, M. K. 1986. "On *Ahimsa*: Reply to Lala Lajpat Rai." In *The Moral and Political Writings of Mahatma Gandhi.* Vol. II. Edited by Raghavan Iyer. Oxford: Clarendon Press.

Gardiner, Stephen. 2006. "A Perfect Moral Storm: Climate Change, Intergenerational Ethics, and the Problem of Corruption." *Environmental Values* 15: 397–413.

Gardiner, Stephen. 2010. "A Perfect Moral Storm: Climate Change, Intergenerational Ethics, and the Problem of Moral Corruption." In *Climate Ethics: Essential Readings*, edited by Stephen M. Gardiner, Simon Caney, Dale Jamieson, and Henry Shue, 87–98. Oxford: Oxford University Press.

Gardiner, Stephen. 2011. *A Perfect Moral Storm: The Ethical Tragedy of Climate Change.* Oxford: Oxford University Press.

Garfin, G., G. Franco, H. Blanco, A. Comrie, P. Gonzalez, T. Piechota, R. Smyth, and R. Waskom. 2014. "Southwest." In *Climate Change Impacts in the United*

States: The Third National Climate Assessment, edited by J. M. Melillo, Terese (T. C.) Richmond, and G. W. Yohe, 462–86. Washington, DC: U.S. Government Printing Office.

Garnett, Tara. 2003. *Wise Moves: Exploring the Relationship between Food, Transport and Co_2*. Hoxton, UK: Transport 2000.

Garnett, Tara. 2010. "Intensive versus Extensive Livestock Systems and Greenhouse Gas Emissions." FCRN Briefing Paper. Last modified January 2010. https://fcrn.org.uk/sites/default/files/FCRN_int_vs_ext_livestock.pdf.

Gebbers, Robin and Viacheslav I. Adamchuk. 2010. "Precision Agriculture and Food Security." *Science* 327, no. 5967: 828–31.

Geist, Helmut. 2017. *The Causes and Progression of Desertification*. London: Routledge.

Gemenne, Francois. 2012. "Environmental Migration." In *An Introduction to International Migration Studies: European Perspectives*, edited by Marco Martiniello and Jan Rath, 237–58. Stockholm: Amsterdam University Press.

Gerber, P. J., H. Steinfeld, B. Henderson, A. Mottet, C. Opio, J. Dijkman, A. Falcucci, and G. Tempio. 2013. "Tackling Climate Change through Livestock: A Global Assessment of Emissions and Mitigation Opportunities." Rome: Food and Agriculture Organization of the United Nations (FAO). Accessed May 15, 2018. http://www.fao.org/docrep/018/i3437e/i3437e.pdf.

Gilbert, Natasha. 2012, October 31. "One-Third of Our Greenhouse Gas Emissions Come from Agriculture." *Nature News*. https://doi.org/10.1038/nature.2012.11708.

Gillespie, Patrick. 2018, January 3. "Mexicans in U.S. Send Cash Home in Record Numbers." CNN Money. http://money.cnn.com/2018/01/02/news/economy/mexico-remittances/index.html.

Gilson, Erinn. 2014. "Vote with Your Fork? Responsibility for Food Justice." *Social Philosophy Today* 30: 113–30.

Gilson, Erinn. 2015. "Vulnerability, Relationality, Dependency: Feminist Conceptual Resources for Food Justice." *International Journal of Feminist Approaches to Bioethics* 8, no. 2 (Fall): 10–46.

Global Witness. 2015, April. "How Many More? 2014's Deadly Environment: The Killing and Intimidation of Environmental and Land Activists, with a Spotlight on Honduras."

Glotfelty, Cheryl and Harold Fromm. 1996. "Introduction: Literary Studies in an Age of Environmental Crisis." In *The Ecocriticism Reader,* edited by Cheryl Glotfelty and Harold Fromm, xv–xxxvii. Athens: University of Georgia Press.

Godfray, H. Charles, John R. Beddington, Ian R. Crute, Lawrence Haddad, David Lawrence, James F. Muir, Jules Pretty et al. 2010. "Food Security: The Challenge of Feeding 9 Billion People." *Science* 327: 812–18.

Godin, Benoît. 2014. "The Vocabulary of Innovation: A Lexicon." *Project on the Intellectual History of Innovation Working Paper* 20.

Godin, Benoît. 2015. *Innovation Contested: The Idea of Innovation over the Centuries*. New York and Oxon: Routledge.

Gody, Maria. 2016. "Sugar Shocked? The Rest of Food Industry Pays for Lots of Research, Too." NPR, September 14, 2016. https://www.npr.org/sections/

thesalt/2016/09/14/493957290/not-just-sugar-food-industry-s-influence-on-health-research.

Gomez Echeverri, Luis Fernando, Leonardo Ríos Osorio, and María Luisa Eschenhagen Durán. 2017. "Propuesta de unos principios generales para la ciencia de la agroecología: una reflexión." *Revista Lasallista de Investigación* 14, no. 2: 212–19.

Gonzalez, Carmen G. 2004. "Trade Liberalization, Food Security, and the Environment: The Neoliberal Threat to Sustainable Rural Development." *Transnational Law and Contemporary Problems* 14, no. 2: 419–98.

Gonzalez, Roberto J. 2001. *Zapotec Science: Farming and Food in the Northern Sierra of Oaxaca.* Austin: University of Texas Press.

Goodman, David and Michael Redclift. 1991. *Refashioning Nature.* London: Routledge.

Gortmacher, Stephen L., David Levy, Robert Carter, Patricia L. Mabry, Diane T. Finegood, Terry Huang, Tim Marsh, and Marjorie L. Moody. 2011. "Changing the Future of Obesity: Science, Policy, and Action." *Lancet* 37, no. 9793: 838–47.

Gosseries, Axel. 2004. "Historical Emissions and Free-Riding." *Ethical Perspectives* 11, no. 1: 36–60.

Gottlieb, Robert and Andy Fisher. 2000. "Community Food Security and Environmental Justice: Converging Paths towards Social Justice and Sustainable Communities." *Race Poverty and Environment* 7: 18–20.

Gottlieb, Robert and Anupama Joshi. 2010. *Food Justice.* Cambridge, MA: MIT Press.

GRAIN. 2014. "Hungry for Land: Small Farmers Feed the World with Less than a Quarter of All Farmland." https://www.grain.org/article/entries/4929-hungry-for-land-small-farmers-feed-the-world-with-less-than-a-quarter-of-all-farmland.

Grauel, K. and K. J. Chambers. 2014. "Food Deserts and Migrant Farmworkers: Assessing Food Access in Oregon's Willamette Valley." *Journal of Ethnobiology* 34, no. 2: 228–50.

Gregory, James. 1991. *American Exodus: The Dust Bowl Migration and the Okie Culture in California.* New York: Oxford University Press.

Gross, Samuel R. 2015, July 24. "The Staggering Number of Wrongful Convictions in America." *Washington Post.*

Gruen, Lori and Clement Loo. 2014. "Climate Change and Food Justice." In *Canned Heat,* edited by Marcello Di Paolo and Gianfranco Pellegrino, 179–92. New York: Routledge.

Grusin, Richard, ed. 2017. *Anthropocene Feminism.* Minneapolis: University of Minnesota Press.

Gu, Hallie and Naveen Thukral. 2018, January 25. "Soy Source: Brazil's Share of Soybean Exports to China Hits Record." *Reuters.* Accessed May 15, 2018. https://www.reuters.com/article/us-china-economy-trade-soybeans/soy-source-brazils-share-of-soybean-exports-to-china-hits-record-idUSKBN1FE111.

Gupta, Anil K., Anamika R. Dey, Chintan Shinde, Hiranmay Mahanta, Chetan Patel, Ramesh Patel, Nirmal Sahay et al. 2016. "Theory of Open Inclusive Innovation for Reciprocal, Responsive and Respectful Outcomes: Coping Creatively with Climatic and Institutional Risks." *Journal of Open Innovation: Technology, Market, and Complexity* 2, no. 16: 1–15.

Guthman, Julie. 2008. "Neoliberalism and the Making of Food Politics in California." *Geoforum* 39, no. 3: 1171–83.

Hamerschlag, Kari. 2011. "Meat Eater's Guide to Climate Change + Health." Washington, DC: Environmental Working Group. https://www.ewg.org/meateatersguide/a-meat-eaters-guide-to-climate-change-health-what-you-eat-matters/.

Hanafi, Elyes. 2017. "The Spa-cial Formation Theory: Transcending the Race-Class Binary in Environmental Justice Literature." *Antipode* 49, no. 2: 397–415.

Hartley, J. 2012. *Communication, Cultural and Media Studies: The Key Concepts*. New York: Routledge.

Harvey, David. 2004. "The New Imperialism: Accumulation by Dispossession." *Socialist Register* 40: 63–87.

Harvey-Samuel, Tim, Thomas Ant, and Luke Alphey. 2017. "Towards the Genetic Control of Invasive Species." *Biological Invasions* 19: 1683–1703.

Hassanein, Neva. 2003. "Practicing Food Democracy: A Pragmatic Politics of Transformation." *Journal of Rural Studies* 19, no. 1: 77–86.

Hassanein, Neva. 2008. "Locating Food Democracy: Theoretical and Practical Ingredients." *Journal of Hunger and Environmental Nutrition* 3, no. 2-3: 286–308.

Hegel, G. W. F. (1807) 1977. *Phenomenology of Spirit*. Translated by A. V. Miller. New York: Oxford University Press.

Heldke, Lisa M. 2009. "Food Security: Three Conceptions of Access—Charity, Rights, and Coresponsibility." In *Society, Culture, and Ethics*, edited by Lynn Walter, 213–25. Santa Barbara, CA: Praeger.

Hendrickson, Deja, Chery Smith, and Nicole Eikenberry. 2006. "Fruit and Vegetable Access in Four Low-Income Food Deserts Communities in Minnesota." *Agriculture and Human Values* 23: 371–83.

Hettlich, Peter, and Simone Walther. 2012, "Bleak Prospects for Research in GMP in Switzerland." *European Journal of Risk Regulation* 3, no. 3: 361–71.

Hill, Alex B. 2017. "Critical Inquiry into Detroit's 'Food Desert' Metaphor." *Food and Foodways* 25, no. 3: 228–46.

Hiller, Avram. 2011. "Climate Change and Individual Responsibility." *Monist* 94, no. 3: 349–68.

Hinrichs, Claire C. 2000. "Embeddedness and Local Food Systems: Notes on Two Types of Direct Agricultural Market." *Journal of Rural Studies* 16, no. 3: 295–303.

Holt-Giménez, Eric. 2009. "From Food Crisis to Food Sovereignty: The Challenge of Social Movements" *Monthly Review* 61, no. 3: 142–56.

Holt-Giménez, Eric. 2011. "Food Security, Food Justice, or Food Sovereignty." In *Cultivating Food Justice: Race, Class, and Sustainability*, edited by Alison Hope Alkon and Julia Agyeman, 309–30. Cambridge, MA: MIT Press.

Hotchkirch, Axel, Joscha Beninde, Marietta Fischer, André Krahner, Cosima Lindemann, Daniela Matenaar, Katja Rohde et al. 2018. "License to Kill?—Disease Eradication Programs May Not Be in Line with the Convention on Biological Diversity." *Conservation Letters* 11, no. 1: 1–6.

Ilea, R. C. 2009. "Intensive Livestock Farming: Global Trends, Increased Environmental Concerns, and Ethical Solutions." *Journal of Agricultural and Environmental Ethics* 22, no. 2: 153–67.

Iles, Alastair. 2005. "Learning in Sustainable Agriculture: Food Miles and Missing Objects." *Environmental Values* 14, no. 2: 163–83.

Imbach, Pablo, Megan Beadsley, Claudia Bouroncle, Claudia Medellin, Peter Läderach, Hugo Hidalgo, and Eric Alfaro et al. 2017. "Climate Change, Ecosystems and Smallholder Agriculture in Central America: An Introduction to the Special Issue." *Climate Change* 141, no. 1: 1–12.

Imhoff, Daniel. 2012. "Overhauling the Farm Bill: The Real Beneficiaries of Subsidies." *The Atlantic*. https://www.theatlantic.com/health/archive/2012/03/overhauling-the-farm-bill-the-real-beneficiaries-of-subsidies/254422/.

IndexMundi. n.d. "Mexico Corn Imports by Year." Accessed June 15, 2018. https://www.indexmundi.com/agriculture/?country=mx&commodity=corn&graph=imports.

The Innocence Project. n.d. "False Confessions or Admissions." Accessed March 17, 2018. https://www.innocenceproject.org/causes/false-confessions-admissions/.

Institution for Mechanical Engineers. 2013. "Global Food: Waste Not, Want Not." https://www.imeche.org/docs/default-source/default-document-library/global-food---waste-not-want-not.pdf?sfvrsn=0.

Interamerican Commission on Human Rights (IACHR). 2016, March 4. CIDH repudia asesinato de Berta Cáceres en Honduras. Accessed March 6, 2016. http://www.oas.org/es/cidh/prensa/comunicados/2016/024.asp.

Internal Displacement Monitoring Centre. 2015. "Global Estimates 2015: People Displaced by Disasters." Accessed May 14, 2018. http://www.internal-displacement.org/library/publications/2015/global-estimates-2015-people-displaced-by-disasters/.

Jamieson, Dale. 1998. "Animal Liberation Is an Environmental Ethic." *Environmental Values* 7, no. 1: 41–57.

Jamieson, Dale. 2007. "When Utilitarians Should Be Virtue Ethicists." *Utilitas* 19, no. 2: 160–83.

Jamieson, Dale. 2014. *Reason in a Dark Time.* Cambridge: Oxford University Press.

Jayawickrama, Janaca. 2018, February 24. "Humanitarian Aid System Is a Continuation of the Colonial Project." *Al Jazeera*. https://www.aljazeera.com/indepth/opinion/humanitarian-aid-system-continuation-colonial-project-180224092528042.html.

Jernigan, Gray. 2015. "What to Do When State Regulation Stinks." *Waterkeeper Alliance* 11, no. 2. https://waterkeeper.org/magazine/summer-2015-3/what-to-do-when-state-regulation-stinks/.

Johnston, Josée and Shyon Baumann. 2009. *Foodies: Democracy and Distinction in the Gourmet Foodscape.* New York: Routledge.

Joint Center for Political and Economic Studies San Joaquin Valley Place Matters Team. 2012. "Place Matters for Health in the San Joaquin Valley: Ensuring Opportunities for Good Health for All: A Report on Health Inequities in the San Joaquin Valley." Washington, DC.

Kemp, Katherine, Andrea Insch, David K. Holdsworth, and John G. Knight. 2010. "Food Miles: Do UK Consumers Really Care?" *Food Policy* 35, no. 6: 504–11.

Kenehan, Sarah. 2015. "In Defense of the Duty to Assist: A Response to Critics on the Viability of a Rawlsian Approach to Climate Change." *Critical Review of International Social and Political Philosophy* 18, no. 3: 308–27.

Keohane, Robert. 2015. "The Global Politics of Climate Change: Challenge for Political Science." *American Political Science Association* 48, no. 1: 19–26.

Kessler, David. 2009. *The End of Overeating.* New York: Simon and Schuster.

Kilmer, Richard L. 1986. "Vertical Integration in Agricultural and Food Marketing." *American Journal of Agricultural Economics* 68, no. 5: 1155–60. https://doi.org/10.2307/1241867.

King Corn. 2007. Directed by Aaron Woolf. London: Mosaic Films.

Kirschenmann, Frederick L. 2010. "Can Organic Farming Feed the World? And Is That the Right Question?" In *Cultivating an Ecological Conscience: Essays from a Farmer Philosopher,* edited by Constance L. Falk, 141–52. Lexington: University of Kentucky Press.

Kissinger, Gabrielle, Martin Herold, and Veronique De Sy. 2012. *Drivers of Deforestation and Forest Degradation: A Synthesis Report for REDD+ Policymakers*. Vancouver: Lexeme Consulting.

Klein, Naomi. 2014. *This Changes Everything*. New York: Simon and Schuster.

Koepsell, David. 2016. *Scientific Integrity and Research Ethics: An Approach from the Ethos of Science*. Cham: Springer.

Kollar, Eszter and Daniele Santoro. 2012. "Not by Bread Alone: Inequality, Relative Depravation, and Self Respect." *Philosophical Topics* 40, no. 1: 79–96.

Koneswaran, Gowri and Danielle Nierenberg. 2008. "Global Farm Animal Production and Global Warming: Impacting and Mitigating Climate Change." *Environmental Health Perspectives, National Library of Medicine, National Institutes of Health*. https://www.ncbi.nlm.nih.gov/pmc/articles/PMC2367646/.

Korsgaard, Christine. 2014. "Interacting with Animals: A Kantian Account." In *The Oxford Handbook of Animal Ethics*, edited by Tom L. Beauchamp and R. G. Frey, 91–119. Oxford: Oxford University Press.

Kortetmäki, Teea and Markku Oksanen. 2016. "Food Systems and Climate Engineering: A Plate Full of Risks or Promises?" In *Climate Justice and Geoengineering*, edited by C. J. Preston, 121–35. New York: Rowman & Littlefield.

Kortetmäki, Teea and Tiina Silvasti. 2017. "Charitable Food Aid in a Nordic Welfare State: A Case for Environmental and Social Injustice." In *The Ecosocial Transition of Societies: The Contribution of Social Work and Social Policy*, edited by A.-L. Matthies and K. Närhi, 219–33. London: Routledge.

Korthals, Michiel. 2012. "Two Evils in Food Country: Hunger and Lack of Representation." In *The Philosophy of Food*, edited by David M. Kaplan, 103–21. Berkeley: University of California Press.

Kriflik, Lynda. 2006. "Consumer Citizenship: Acting to Minimize Environmental Health Risks Related to the Food System." *Appetite* 46, no. 3: 270–79.

Kuhnlein, H. V. 1996. "Dietary Change and Traditional Food Systems of Indigenous Peoples." *Journal of Nutrition Annual Review* 16: 417–42.

Kutz, Christopher. 2007. *Complicity: Ethics and Law for a Collective Age.* Cambridge: Cambridge University Press.

La Via Campesina. n.d. "International Peasant Movement." Accessed January 2018. https://viacampesina.org/en/.

Lakhani, Nina. 2017, February 28. "Berta Cáceres Court Papers Show Murder Suspects' Links to US-Trained Elite Troops." *Guardian.*

Landry, Alysa. 2015. "Not Alone in the Dark: Navajo Nation's Lack of Electricity Problem." *Indian Country Today.* https://indiancountrymedianetwork.com/news/native-news/not-alone-in-the-dark-navajo-nations-lack-of-electricity-problem/.

Lang, T. 1999. "Food Policy for the 21st Century: Can It Be Both Radical and Reasonable?" In *For Hunger-Proof Cities: Sustainable Urban Food Systems,* edited by M. Koc, R. MacRae, L. Mougeot, and J. Welsh, 216–24. Ottawa: IDRC Books.

Laughland, Oliver. 2016, February 17. "Donald Trump and the Central Park Five: The Racially Charged Rise of a Demagogue." *Guardian.*

LeClair, Mark S. and Anna-Maria Aksan. 2014. "Redefining the Food Desert: Combining GIS with Direct Observation to Measure Food Access." *Agriculture and Human Values* 31: 537–47.

LeCompte, Celeste. 2013. "Fertilizer Plants Spring Up to Take Advantage of U.S.'s Cheap Natural Gas." *Scientific American.* Last modified on April 25, 2013. https://www.scientificamerican.com/article/fertilizer-plants-grow-thanks-to-cheap-natural-gas/.

Ledford, Heidi. 2015. "CRISPR, the Disrupter." *Nature* 522: 20–24.

Lee, Wendy Lynne. 2010. *Contemporary Feminist Theory and Activism.* Peterborough, ON: Broadview Press.

Lee, Wendy Lynne. 2016. *Eco-Nihilism: The Philosophical Geopolitics of the Climate Change Apocalypse.* Lanham, MD: Lexington Press.

Leiserowitz, Anthony, Edward Maibach, Connie Roser-Renouf, Seth Rosenthal, Matthew Cutler, and John Kotcher. 2017, October. "Climate Change in the American Mind: October 2017." Yale University and George Mason University. New Haven, CT: Yale Program on Climate Change Communication. http://climatecommunication.yale.edu/wp-content/uploads/2017/11/Climate-Change-American-Mind-October-2017.pdf.

Leonhardt, David. 2009, May 20. "What's Wrong with This Chart?" *New York Times.* https://economix.blogs.nytimes.com/2009/05/20/whats-wrong-with-this-chart/.

Leopold, Aldo. 1968. *A Sand County Almanac.* New York: Ballantine Books.

Levine, Elaine. 2011. "The Effects of Large-Scale Emigration on Mexico." *Voices of Mexico* 92 (Winter): 35–38. http://www.revistascisan.unam.mx/Voices/no92.php.

Lilliston, Ben. 2016, September. "The Climate Cost of Free Trade." Institute for Agriculture and Trade Policy. Accessed November 4, 2017. https://www.iatp.org/files/2016_09_06_ClimateCostFreeTrade.pdf.

Lindblom, Jessica, Christina Lundström, Magnus Ljung, and Anders Jonsson. 2017. "Promoting Sustainable Intensification in Precision Agriculture: Review of Decision Support Systems Development and Strategies." *Precision Agriculture* 18, no. 3: 309–31.

Littler, Jo. 2009a. "Good Housekeeping: Green Products and Consumer Activism." In *Community Activism*, edited by Sarah Banet-Weiser and Roopali Mukherjee, 76–92. New York: New York University Press.

Littler, Jo. 2009b. *Radical Consumption: Shopping for Change in Contemporary Culture.* Buckingham, UK: Open University Press, 2009.

Liverman, Diana and Kamal Kapadia. 2010. "Food Systems and the Global Environment: An Overview." In *Food Security and Global Environmental Change*, edited by John Ingram, Polly Ericksen, and Diana Liverman, 3–24. London: Earthscan.

Lobell, David B., Michael J. Roberts, Wolfram Schlenker, Noah Braun, Bertis B. Little, Roderick M. Rejesus, and Graeme L. Hammer. 2014. "Greater Sensitivity to Drought Accompanies Maize Yield Increase in the U.S. Midwest." *Science* 344, no. 6183 (May 2): 516–19. doi:10.1126/science.1251423.

Lobell, David B., Wolfram Schlenker, and Justin Costa-Roberts. 2011. "Climate Trends and Global Crop Production Since 1980." *Science* 333: 616–20.

Loo, Clement. 2014. "Towards a More Participative Definition of Food Justice." *Journal of Agricultural and Environmental Ethics* 27: 787–809.

Lopez-Gunn, Elena, Lucia De Stefano, and M. Ramón Llamas. 2012. "The Role of Ethics in Water and Food Security: Balancing Utilitarian and Intangible Values." *Water Policy* 14, no. S1: 89.

Lybbett, Travis and Daniel Sumner. 2010. *Agricultural Technologies for Climate Change Mitigation and Adaptation in Developing Countries: Policy Options for Innovation and Technology Diffusion.* Geneva and Washington, DC: International Centre for Trade and Sustainable Development (ICTSD) and International Food & Agricultural Trade Policy Council.

Macdonald, David W., Eva M. Raebel, and Ruth E. Feber. 2015. "Farming and Wildlife: A Perspective on a Shared Future." In *Wildlife Conservation on Farmland*, edited by D.W. Macdonald and R. E. Feber, 1–20. Oxford: Oxford University Press.

Machovina, Brian, Kenneth J. Feeley, and William J. Ripple. 2015. "Biodiversity Conservation: The Key Is Reducing Meat Consumption." *Science of the Total Environment* 536: 419–31.

MacIntyre, Alasdair. 1999. *Dependent Rational Animals.* Chicago: Open Court.

MacLean, Douglas. 1986. "Social Values and the Distribution of Risk." In *Values at Risk*, edited by D. MacLean, 75–93. Totowa, NJ: Rowman & Littlefield.

Macnaghten, Phil, Richard Owen, Jack Stilgoe, Brian Wynne, A. Azevedo, A. De Campos, Jason Chilvers et al. 2014. "Responsible Innovation across Borders: Tensions, Paradoxes and Possibilities." *Journal of Responsible Innovation* 1, no. 2: 191–99.

Magrin, Graciela, and José Marengo. "Central and South America. 2014." In *Climate Change 2014: Impacts, Adaptation, and Vulnerability. Part B, Regional Aspects. Contribution of Working Group II to the Fifth Assessment Report of the Intergovernmental Panel on Climate Change*, edited by Barros, V. R. et al., 1499–1566. Cambridge: Cambridge University Press.

Main, Alexander. 2010. "A New Chapter of Engagement: Obama and the Honduran Coup." *NACLA Report on the Americas* 43, no. 1: 15–21.

Maize Genetics Cooperation Stock Center. n.d. http://maizecoop.cropsci.uiuc.edu/.

Mann, Charles C. 2005. *1491: New Revelations of the Americas before Columbus.* New York: Alfred A. Knopf.

Mao, Hude, Hongwei Wang, Shengxue Liu, Zhigang Li, Xiaohong Yang, Jianbing Yan, Jiansheng Li et al. 2015. "A Transposable Element in a NAC Gene Is Associated with Drought Tolerance in Maize Seedlings." *Nature Communications* 6: 8326.

Mares, Teresa M. and Devon G. Peña. 2012. "Environmental and Food Justice: Toward Local, Slow, and Deep Food Systems." In *Cultivating Food Justice: Race, Class, and Sustainability*, edited by Alison Hope Alkon and Julia Agyeman, 197–219. Cambridge, MA: MIT Press.

Margolioth, Yoram. 2012. "Assessing Moral Claims in International Climate Negotiations." *Washington and Lee Journal of Energy, Climate, and the Environment* 3, no. 1: 43–79.

Mark, P. 2017. "Environmental Disruption: Push/Pull Factors, Human Migration, and Homeland Security." *Journal of Political Sciences & Public Affairs* 5, no. 2. doi:10.4172/2332-0761.1000264.

Marsden, Terry. 1997. "Creating Space for Food: The Distinctiveness of Recent Agrarian Development." In *Globalising Food: Agrarian Questions and Global Restructuring*, edited by David Goodman and Michael Watts, 169–91. London: Routledge.

Maxwell, Simon. 1996. "Food Security: A Post-Modern Perspective." *Food Policy* 21, no. 2: 155–70.

Maye, Damien. 2011. "Food Miles." In *Green Consumerism: An A-to-Z Guide*, edited by Juliana Mansvelt and Paul Robbins, 158–59. Thousand Oaks, CA: Sage.

Mazoyer, Marcel and Laurence Roudart. 2006. *A History of World Agriculture: From the Neolithic Age to the Current Crisis.* New York: Monthly Review Press.

McHughen, Alan. 2000. *Pandora's Picnic Basket.* New York: Oxford University Press.

McKeon, Nora. 2015. "La Via Campesina: The 'Peasants' Way' to Changing the System, not the Climate." *Journal of World-Systems Research* 21, no. 2: 241–49.

McMichael, Anthony. 2017. *Climate Change and the Health of Nations.* Oxford: Oxford University Press.

McPherson, Alan. 2016. *A Short History of U.S. Interventions in Latin America and the Caribbean.* Sussex, UK: Wiley Blackwell.

McWilliams, James E. 2009. *Just Food.* New York: Little, Brown and Company.

Mendoza-Cano, Oliver, Ramón Alberto Sánchez-Piña, Álvaro Jesús González-Ibarra, Efrén Murillo-Zamora, and Cynthia Monique Nava-Garibaldi. 2016. "Health Impacts from Corn Production Pre-and Post-NAFTA Trade Agreement (1986–2013)." *International Journal of Environmental Research and Public Health* 13, no. 7 (July): 709. doi:10.3390/ijerph13070709.

Meyer, Lukas H. and Dominic Roser. 2010. "Climate Justice and Historical Emissions." *Critical Review of International Social and Political Philosophy* 13, no. 1: 229–53.

Micheletti, M. 2003. *Political Virtue and Shopping*. New York: Palgrave.

Miller, David. 2007. *National Responsibility and Global Justice*. Oxford: Oxford University Press.

Miller, Henry I. 1997. *Policy Controversy in Biotechnology*. Austin, TX: R. G. Landes Co.

Mills, Charles W. 2005. "'Ideal' Theory as Ideology." *Hypatia* 20, no. 3 (Summer): 165–84.

Min, John, Andrea L. Smidler, Devora Najjar, and Kevin M. Esvelt. 2018. "Harnessing Gene Drive." *Journal of Responsible Innovation* 5, no. sup1 (2018): S40–65

Minteer, Ben A. and James P. Collins. 2010. "Move It or Lose It? The Ecological Ethics of Relocating Species under Climate Change." *Ecological Applications* 20, no. 7: 1801–4.

Mirabelli, Maria C., Steve Wing, Stephen W. Marshall, and Timothy C. Wilcosky. 2009. "Race, Poverty, and Potential Exposure of Middle-School Students to Air." *Environmental Health Perspectives* 114, no. 4: 591–96.

Misselhorn, Alison, Hallie Eakin, Stephen Devereux, Scott Drimie, Siwa Misangi, Elisabeth Simelton, and Mark Stafford Smith. 2010. "Vulnerability to What?" In *Food Security and Global Environmental Change*, edited by John Ingram, Polly Ericksen, and Diana Liverman, 87–114. London: Earthscan.

Moellendorf, Darrel. 2014. *The Moral Challenge of Dangerous Climate Change*. Cambridge: Cambridge University Press.

Montanari, Massimo. 2006. *Food Is Culture*. New York: Columbia University Press.

Moore, Margaret. 2013. "Place-Related Attachments and Global Distributive Justice." *Journal of Global Ethics* 9, no. 2: 215–26.

Moragues-Faus, Ana. 2017. "Problematising Justice Definitions in Public Food Security Debates: Towards Global and Participative Food Justices." *Geoforum* 84: 95–106.

Mortimore, Michael. 2005. "Dryland Development: Success Stories from West Africa." *Environment* 47, no. 1: 8–21.

Moss, Michael. 2015. "The Extraordinary Science of Addictive Junk Food." In *Expanding Addiction: Critical Essays*, edited by Robert Granfield and Craig Reinarman, 127–40. New York: Routledge.

Mowforth, Martin. 2014. *The Violence of Development*. London: Pluto Press.

Murdock, Esme and Samantha Noll. 2015. "Beyond Access: Integrating Food Security and Food Sovereignty Models for Justice." In *Know Your Food: Food Ethics and Innovation*, edited by Helena Rocklinberg and Per Sandin. Netherlands: Wageningen Academic Publishers. https://doi.org/10.3920/978-90-8686-813-1_49.

Murphy, Joseph. 2009, October. "Environment and Imperialism: Why Colonialism Still Matters." SRI Papers, no. 20. Sustainability Research Institute Papers. https://www.see.leeds.ac.uk/fileadmin/Documents/research/sri/workingpapers/SRIPs-20_01.pdf

Myers, Samuel S., Matthew R. Smith, Sarah Guth, Christopher D. Golden, Bapu Vaitla, Nathaniel D. Mueller, Alan D. Dangour, and Peter Huybers. 2017. "Climate Change and Global Food Systems: Potential Impacts on Food Security and Undernutrition." *Annual Review of Public Health* 38: 259–77.

Nadal, Alejandro and Timothy Wise. 2005. "Los costos ambientales de la liberalización agrícola." In *Globalización y Medio Ambiente: Lecciones desde las Américas*, edited by Hernán Blanco, Luciana Togeiro, and Kevin Gallagher, 49–92. Santiago: RIDES-GDAE.

Naess, Arne. 1973. "The Shallow and the Deep, Long-Range Ecology Movement." *Inquiry* 16: 95–100.

Nagel, Thomas. 1977. "Poverty and Food: Why Charity Is Not Enough." In *Food Policy: The Responsibility of the United States in the Life and Death Choices*, edited by Peter Brown and Henry Shue, 54–62. New York: The Free Press.

National Association of Local Boards of Health. 2010. "Understanding Concentrated Animal Feeding Operations and Their Impact on Communities." Bowling Green, OH.

National Corn Growers Association. 2018. *World of Corn 2018*. Chesterfield, MO: National Corn Growers Association. http://www.worldofcorn.com/pdf/NCGA_WOC2018.pdf.

National Integrated Drought Information System. n.d. "Where Is Drought This Week?" Drought.gov US Drought" Portal. Accessed February 12, 2018. https://www.drought.gov/drought/.

National Trust. 2012. *What's Your Beef?* Swindon, UK: National Trust. http://www.campaignforrealfarming.org/wp-content/uploads/2012/06/NT-report-Whats-your-beef.pdf.

Navin, Mark C. 2014. "Local Food and International Ethics." *Journal of Agricultural and Environmental Ethics* 27, no. 3: 349–68.

Nelson, Erik, Peter Kareiva, Mary Ruckelshaus, Katie Arkema, Gary Geller, Evan Girvetz, Dave Goodrich et al. 2013. "Climate Change's Impact on Key Ecosystem Services and the Human Well-Being They Support in the US." *Frontiers in Ecology and the Environment* 11 (November): 483–93.

Nestle, Marion. 2007. *Food Politics*. Berkeley: University of California Press.

Neuhäuser, Christian. 2014. "Structural Injustice and the Distribution of Forward-Looking Responsibility." *Midwest Studies in Philosophy* 38, no. 1: 232–51.

New York Times. 2018, March 3. "Honduras Police Arrest Executive in Killing of Berta Cáceres, Indigenous Activist." *New York Times*.

Newkirk II, Van. 2018, February 28. "Trump's EPA Concludes Environmental Racism Is Real." *The Atlantic*. https://www.theatlantic.com/politics/archive/2018/02/the-trump-administration-finds-that-environmental-racism-is-real/554315/.

Nicole, Wendee. 2013. "CAFOs and Environmental Justice: The Case of North Carolina." *Environmental Health Perspectives* 121, no. 6 (June): 182–89. https://ehp.niehs.nih.gov/121-a182/.

Nicolopoulou-Stamati, Polyxeni, Sotirios Maipas, Chrysanthi Kotampasi, Panagiotis Stamatis, and Luc Hens. 2016. "Chemical Pesticides and Human Health: The Urgent Need for a New Concept in Agriculture." *Frontiers in Public Health* 4, no. 148. doi:10.3389/fpubh.2016.00148.

Nigh, Ronald B. 1976. "Evolutionary Ecology of Maya Agriculture in Highland Chiapas, Mexico." PhD diss., Stanford University. Ann Arbor, MI: University Microfilms.

Nijdam, Durk, Trudy Rood, and Henk Westhoek. 2012. "The Price of Protein: Review of Land Use and Carbon Footprints from Life Cycle Assessments of Animal Food Products and Their Substitutes." *Food Policy* 37, no. 6: 760–70.

Noll, Samantha. 2017a. "Climate Induced Migration: A Pragmatic Strategy for Wildlife Conservation on Farmland." *Pragmatism Today* 8, no. 2: 24–40.

Noll, Samantha. 2017b. "Non-Human Climate Refugees: The Role of Agriculture for Ecological Resilience for a Changing Climate." *Eursafe News* 19, no. 1: 10–12.

Nolt, John. 1995. *Down to Earth: Toward a Philosophy of Nonviolent Living.* Washburn, TN: Earth Knows Publications.

Nolt, John. 2006. "The Move from *Good* to *Ought* in Environmental Ethics." *Environmental Ethics* 28, no. 4 (Winter): 355–74.

Nolt, John. 2011. "How Harmful Are the Average American's Greenhouse Gas Emissions?" *Ethics, Policy and Environment* 14, no. 1: 3–10.

Nolt, John. 2013. "Replies to Critics of 'How Harmful Are the Average American's Greenhouse Gas Emissions?'" *Ethics, Policy and Environment* 16, no. 1: 111–19.

Nolt, John. 2015a. "Casualties as a Moral Measure of Climate Change." *Climatic Change* 130, no. 3: 347–58.

Nolt, John. 2015b. *Environmental Ethics for the Long Term: An Introduction.* New York: Routledge.

Nolt, John. 2016. "Future Generations in Environmental Ethics." In *Oxford Handbook of Environmental Ethics*, edited by Stephen Gardiner and Allen Thompson, 344–54. New York: Oxford University Press.

Nolt, John. 2018. "Cumulative Harm as a Function of Carbon Emissions." In *Climate Change and Its Impacts: Risks and Inequalities,* edited by Colleen Murphy, Paolo Gardoni, and Robert McKim. New York: Springer.

Norton, Bryan G. 1991. *Toward Unity among Environmentalists.* New York: Oxford University Press.

Nozick, Robert. 1974. *Anarchy, State, and Utopia.* New York: Basic Books, Inc.

NRC (National Research Council). 1996. *Understanding Risk: Informing Decisions in a Democratic Society.* Washington, DC: National Academy Press.

Nussbaum, Martha. 2000. *Women and Human Development: The Capabilities Approach.* Cambridge: Cambridge University Press.

OECD. 2016. "Figure 7.21 Agricultural Patents by Country." *Innovation, Agricultural Productivity and Sustainability in the United States.* OECD Food and Agricultural Reviews. Paris: OECD Publishing.

OHCHR (Office of the United Nations High Commissioner for Human Rights). 2000. "Special Rapporteur on the Right to Food." http://www.ohchr.org/EN/Issues/Food/Pages/FoodIndex.aspx.

O'Kane, Gabrielle. 2016. "A Moveable Feast: Exploring Barriers and Enablers to Food Citizenship." *Appetite* 105, October 1: 674–87.

Oksman-Caldentey, K. M. and R. Arroo. 2000. "Regulation of Tropane Alkaloid Metabolism in Plants and Plant Cell Cultures." In *Metabolic Engineering of Plant Secondary Metabolism*, edited by R. Verpoorte and A. W. Alfermann, 253–81. Dordrecht, NL: Springer.

O'Lear, Shannon. 2016. "Geopolitics and Climate Science: The Case of the Missing Embodied Carbon." In *Reframing Climate Change: Constructing Ecological Geopolitics*, edited by Shannon O'Lear and Simon Dalby, 100–117. New York: Routledge.

O'Leary, Matthew. 2016. "Maize: From Mexico to the World." CIMMYT. https://www.cimmyt.org/maize-from-mexico-to-the-world/.

Oosterveer, Peter and David A. Sonnenfeld. 2012. *Food, Globalization and Sustainability*. London: Routledge.

Open Source Seed Initiative. n.d. "Why Open Source Seed." https://osseeds.org/about/about/.

Oreskes, Naomi and Erik M. Conway. 2010. *Merchants of Doubt.* New York: Bloomsbury.

Orford, Anne. 2015. "Food Security, Free Trade, and the Battler for the State." *Journal of International Law and International Relations* 11, no. 2: 1–67.

Organic Trade Association. 2017, May 24. "Robust Organic Sector Stays on Upward Climb, Posts New Records in U.S. Sales." https://www.ota.com/news/press-releases/19681.

Oxfam International. 2015, May 19. "160 millonarios en El Salvador acumulan riqueza equivalente al 87% de la producción nacional." Sala de Prensa Oxfam. Accessed November 30, 2017. https://www.oxfam.org/es/sala-de-prensa/notas-de-prensa/2015-05-19/160-millonarios-en-el-salvador-acumulan-riqueza.

OXFAM, Land Rights Now and Defensoras Madre Tierra. 2017. "Hechos y circunstancias alrededor del asesinato de Berta Cáceres Flores. En la búsqueda de los autores intelectuales". Tegucigalpa: OXFAM. Land Rights Now.

Paarlberg, Robert. 2009. *Starved for Science.* Cambridge, MA: Harvard University Press.

Paerl, Hans W. and Jef Huisman. 2008. "Blooms Like it Hot." *Science* 320, no. 5872: 57–58.

Page, Edward. 2012. "Give It Up for Climate Change: A Defense of the Beneficiary Pays Principle." *International Theory* 4, no. 2: 300–330.

Palmer, Clare. 2010. *Animal Ethics in Context*. New York: Columbia University Press.

Palmer, Clare and Brendon M. H. Larson. 2014. "Should We Move the Whitebark Pine? Assisted Migration, Ethics and Global Environmental Change." *Environmental Values* 23, no. 6: 641–62.

Parekh, Serena. 2011. "Getting to the Root of Gender Inequality: Structural Injustice and Political Responsibility." *Hypatia* 26, no. 4: 672–89.

Parfit, Derik. 1984. *Reason and Persons.* Cambridge: Oxford University Press.

Parks, Bradley C. and J. Timmons Roberts. 2010. "Climate Change, Social Theory and Justice." *Theory, Culture and Society* 27, no. 2-3: 134–66.

Parry, M. L., C. Rosenzweig, A. Iglesias, M. Livermore, and G. Fischer. 2004. "Effects of Climate Change on Global Food Production Under SRES Emissions and Socio-Economic Scenarios." *Global Environmental Change* 14: 53–67.

Parthasarathi, Prasannan. 2002. "Toward Property as Share: Ownership, Community and the Environment." In *Sustainable Planet: Solutions for the Twenty-first Century*, edited by Juliet B. Schor and Betsy Taylor, 141–53. Boston: Beacon Press.

Partido Restauración Nacional. 2017. "Plan de Gobierno 2018–2022."

Passidomo, Catarina. 2014. "Whose Right to (Farm) the City? Race and Food-Justice Activism in Post-Katrina New Orleans." *Agricultural and Human Values* 31: 385–96.

Patel, Raj. 2011. "Why Hunger Is Still with Us." *The Nation*. https://www.thenation.com/article/why-hunger-still-us/.

Patel, Raj. 2012. *Stuffed and Starved*. London: Portobello Books Ltd.

Paxton, Angela. 2011. *The Food Miles Report: The Dangers of Long-Distance Food Transport*. 2nd edition. London: Sustain: The Alliance for Better Food and Farming. Accessed on June 26, 2018. https://www.sustainweb.org/publications/the_food_miles_report/.

Pelletier, Nathan, Rich Pirog, and Rebecca Rasmussen. 2010. "Comparative Life Cycle Impacts of Three Beef Production Strategies in the Upper Mid-Western United States." *Agricultural Systems* 103: 380–89. doi:10.1016/j.agsy.2010.03.009.

Pellow, David. 2016. "Toward a Critical Environmental Justice Studies: Black Lives Matter as an Environmental Justice Challenge." *Du Bois Review* 12, no. 2: 1–16.

Pelto, Gretel H. and Pertti J. Pelto. 1983. "Diet and Delocalization: Dietary Changes since 1750." In *Hunger and History: The Impact of Changing Food Production and Consumption Patterns on Society*, edited by Robert I. Rotberg and Theodore K. Rabb, 309–30. Cambridge: Cambridge University Press.

Perlroth, Nicole. 2017, February 11. "Spyware's Odd Targets: Backers of Mexico's Soda Tax." *New York Times*. https://www.nytimes.com/2017/02/11/technology/hack-mexico-soda-tax-advocates.html.

Perrings, Charles. 2010. *Biodiversity, Ecosystem Services, and Climate Change: The Economic Problem (English)*. Environment Department Papers (120): Environmental Economic Series. Washington, DC: World Bank. http://documents.worldbank.org/curated/en/241621468149401563/Biodiversity-ecosystem-services-and-climate-change-the-economic-problem.

Perrings, C., S. Naeem, F. Ahrestani, D. E. Bunker, P. Burkill, G. Canziani, T. Elmqvist et al. 2010. "Ecosystem Services for 2020." *Science* 330, no. 6002: 323–24.

Peterson, Garry, Craig Allen, and C. S. Holling. 1998. "Ecological Resilience, Biodiversity, and Scale." *Nebraska Cooperative Fish and Wildlife Research Unit—Staff Publications* 1, no. 6: 6–18.

The Pew Charitable Trust. 2008, April 29. "Putting Meat on the Table." A Report of the Pew Commission on Industrial Farm Animal Production. The Pew Charitable Trusts and Johns Hopkins Bloomberg School of Public Health.

Pew Research Center. 2015, December 9. "The American Middle Class Is Losing Ground." http://www.pewsocialtrends.org/2015/12/09/the-american-middle-class-is-losing-ground/.

Phippen, J. Weston. 2018, February 2. "Bears Ears Officially Opens to Oil and Gas." *Outside*. https://www.outsideonline.com/2278981/its-d-day-bears-ears.

Physicians Committee for Responsible Medicine. n.d. "Agriculture and Health Policies in Conflict: How Food Subsidies Tax Our Health." Accessed February 16, 2018. http://www.pcrm.org/health/reports/agriculture-and-health-policies-unhealthful-foods.

Plumwood, Val. 1993. *Feminism and the Mastery of Nature*. New York: Routledge.

Pollan, Michael. 2001. *The Botany of Desire.* New York: Random House.

Pollan, Michael. 2007. *The Omnivore's Dilemma.* New York: Penguin Press.

Pollan, Michael. 2008. *In Defense of Food.* London: Penguin Press.

Pollan, Michael. 2009. *Food Rules.* New York: Penguin.

Posner, Eric A. and David Weisbach. 2010. *Climate Change Justice.* Princeton, NJ: Princeton University Press.

Powell, James Lawrence. 2015. "Climate Scientists Virtually Unanimous Anthropogenic Global Warming Is True." *Bulletin of Science, Technology, and Society* 35, no. 5-6: 121–24.

Prasad, Ram, Vivek Kumar, and Kumar Suranjit Prasad. 2014. "Nanotechnology in Sustainable Agriculture: Present Concerns and Future Aspects." *African Journal of Biotechnology* 13: 705–13.

La Prensa. 2013, August 15. Redacción, "Aprueban nueva ley minera en Honduras." *La Prensa.* http://www.laprensa.hn/honduras/tegucigalpa/331330-98/aprueban-nueva-ley-minera-en-honduras.

Pretty, Jules N., A. S. Ball, T. Lang, and J. I. L. Morison. 2005. "Farm Costs and Food Miles: An Assessment of the Full Cost of the UK Weekly Food Basket." *Food Policy* 30: 1–19.

Prothero, Andrea, Pierre McDonagh, and Susan Dobscha. 2010. "Is Green the New Black? Reflections on a Green Commodity Discourse." *Journal of Macromarketing* 30, no. 2: 147–59.

Pullin, Mark. 2017. "Environmental Disruption: Push/Pull Factors, Human Migration, and Homeland Security." *Journal of Political Science & Public Affairs*, no. 5: 264.

Quist, David and Ignacio H. Chapela. 2001. "Transgenic DNA Introgressed into Traditional Maize Landraces in Oaxaca, Mexico." *Nature* 414 (November 29): 541–43. doi:10.1038/35107068.

Rachels, Stuart and James Rachels. 2012. *The Elements of Moral Philosophy.* 7th edition. New York: McGraw-Hill.

Rai, Vineeta, Sefali Acharya, and Nrisingha Dey. 2012. "Implications of Nanobiosensors in Agriculture." *Journal of Biomaterials and Nanobiotechnology* 3: 315–24.

Raponi, Sandra. 2017. "A Defense of the Human Right to Adequate Food." *Res Publica* 23: 99–115.

Rawlani, Amireeta K. and Benjamin K. Sovacool. 2011. "Building Responsiveness to Climate Change through Community Based Adaptation in Bangladesh." *Mitigation and Adaptation Strategies for Global Change* 16: 845–63.

Rawlinson, Mary C. 2016a. *Just Life.* New York: Columbia University Press.

Rawlinson, Mary C. 2016b. "Women's Work: Ethics, Home Cooking, and the Sexual Politics of Food." In *Routledge Handbook of Food Ethics*, edited by Mary C. Rawlinson and Caleb Ward, 61–71. London: Routledge.

Rawls, John. 1993. *Political Liberalism.* New York: Columbia University Press.

Rawls, John. 1999. *A Theory of Justice, Revised Edition.* Cambridge, MA: The Belknap Press of Harvard University Press.

Rawls, John. 2001. *Justice as Fairness: A Restatement.* Edited by Erin Kelly. Cambridge, MA: The Belknap Press of Harvard University Press.

Rawls, John. 2002. *The Law of Peoples*. Cambridge, MA: Harvard University Press.

Redclift, Michael. 2005. "Sustainable Development (1987–2005): An Oxymoron Comes of Age." *Sustainable Development* 13, no. 4: 212–27.

Reed, Christine M. 2008. "Wild Horse Protection Policies: Environmental and Animal Ethics in Transition." *International Journal of Public Administration* 31, no. 3: 277–86.

Regan, Tom. 1983. *The Case for Animal Rights*. Berkeley: University of California Press.

Regan, Tom. 2004. *The Case for Animal Rights*. Berkeley: University of California Press.

Reiheld, Alison. 2016. "Hungry Because of Change: Food, Vulnerability, and Climate." In *The Routledge Handbook of Food Ethics*, edited by Mary C. Rawlinson and Caleb Ward, 201–10. London: Routledge.

Reyer, Christopher P. O., Sophie Adams, Torsten Albrecht, Florent Baarsch, Alice Boit, Nella Canales Trujillo, and Matti Cartsburg et al. 2015. "Climate Change Impacts in Latin America and the Caribbean and Their Implications for Development." *Regional Environmental Change* 17, no. 6: 1601–21.

Rice, Doyle. 2018, February 13. "Miami Could Be under Water in Your Kid's Lifetime as Sea Level Accelerates." *USA Today*.

Robaey, Zoë. 2016a. "Gone with the Wind: Conceiving of Moral Responsibility in the Case of GMO Contamination." *Science and Engineering Ethics* 22, no. 3: 889–906.

Robaey, Zoë. 2016b. "Transferring Moral Responsibility for Technological Hazards: The Case of GMOs in Agriculture." *Journal of Agricultural and Environmental Ethics* 29, no. 5: 767–86.

Robeyns, Ingrid. 2008. "Ideal Theory in Theory and Practice." *Social Theory and Practice* 34, no. 3 (July): 341–62.

Rodas, Rosario. 2015, April 7. "El capital de 206 guatemaltecos equivale al 56% del PIB." *Nómada*.

Rojas, Nathalia. 2010, September 8. "A tres años de que Universidad divulgó estrategia del Sí al TLC: Impunidad por el Memorando del Miedo." *Semanario Universidad*.

Rollin, Bernard. 1995. *Farm Animal Welfare: School, Biological, and Research Issues*. Ames: Iowa State University Press.

Rosset, Peter M. and Miguel A. Altieri. 1997. "Agroecology versus Input Substitution: A Fundamental Contradiction of Sustainable Agriculture." *Society & Natural Resources* 10, no. 3: 283–95.

Rothstein, Richard. 2017. *The Color of Law*. New York: W.W. Norton and Company.

Saab, Anne. 2015. "Climate-Ready Seeds and Patent Rights: A Question of Climate (in) Justice?" *Global Jurist* 15, no. 2: 219–35.

Saad, Lydia. 2015, March 25. "U.S. Views on Climate Change Stable after Extreme Winter." News Alert. Gallup. http://news.gallup.com/poll/182150/views-climate-change-stable-extreme-winter.aspx.

Sabatini, Christopher and Jimena Galindo. 2017, July 25. "Why is Latin America the Most Dangerous Region in the World for Women?" *World Politics Review*.

Sachs, Carolyn and Anouk Patel-Campillo. 2014. "Feminist Food Justice: Crafting a New Vision." *Feminist Studies* 40, no. 2: 396–410.

Sage, Colin. 2014. "The Transition Movement and Food Sovereignty: From Local Resilience to Global Engagement in Food System Transformation." *Journal of Consumer Culture* 14: 254–75.

Sagoff, Marc. 1988. *Economy of the Earth.* Cambridge: Cambridge University Press.

Salmon, Enrique. 2012. *Eating the Landscape: American Indian Stewards of Food and Resilience.* First Peoples: New Directions in Indigenous Studies. 2nd edition. Tucson: University of Arizona Press.

Sansoucy, R. "Livestock—A Driving Force for Food Security and Sustainable Development." *Feed Resource Group.* http://www.fao.org/docrep/v8180t/v8180t07.htm.

Santelices-Spikin, Andrea and Jorge Rojas-Hernández. 2016. "Climate Change in Latin America. Inequality, Conflict and Social Movements of Adaptation." *Latin American Perspectives* 43, no. 4: 4–11.

Sassen, Saskia. 2014. *Expulsions. Brutality and Complexity in the Global Economy.* Cambridge, MA: Harvard University Press.

Saunders, Caroline, Andrew Barber, and Greg Taylor. 2006. "Food Miles: Comparative Energy/Emissions Performance of New Zealand's Agricultural Industry." Lincoln, NZ: Agribusiness & Economics Research Institute, Lincoln University. Accessed on June 26, 2018. https://ucanr.edu/datastoreFiles/608-324.pdf.

Sbicca, Joshua. 2012. "Growing Food Justice by Planting an Anti-Oppressive Foundation: Opportunities and Obstacles for a Budding Social Movement." *Agriculture and Human Values* 29: 455–66.

Schanbacher, William D. 2010. *The Politics of Food: The Global Conflict between Food Security and Food.* Santa Barbara, CA: Praeger Security International.

Schlosberg, David. 2007. *Defining Environmental Justice.* Oxford: Oxford University Press.

Schlosberg, David. 2004. "Reconceiving Environmental Justice: Global Movements and Political Theories." In *Environmental Values in a Globalizing World: Nature, Justice and Governance,* edited by Ian Lowe and Jouni Paavola, 102–22. New York: Routledge.

Schlosberg, David and Lisette B. Collins. 2014. "From Environmental to Climate Justice: Climate Change and the Discourse of Environmental Justice?" *WIREs Climate Change* 5: 359–74.

Schlosser, Eric. 2001. *Fast Food Nation.* New York: Houlton-Mifflin.

Schmidhuber, Josef and Francesco N. Tubiello. 2007. "Global Food Security under Climate Change." *Proceedings of the National Academy of Sciences of the United States of America* 104: 19703–8.

Schmitt, Emilia, Francesca Galli, Davide Menozzi, Damian Maye, Jean-Marc Touzard, Andrea Marescotti, Johan Six, and Gianluca Brunori. 2017. "Comparing the Sustainability of Local and Global Food Products in Europe." *Journal of Cleaner Production* 165: 346–59.

Schneider, M. and S. Sharma. 2014. *China's Pork Miracle? Agribusiness and Development in China's Pork Industry.* Accessed February 8, 2018. https://www. iatp.org/sites/default/files/2017-05/2017_05_03_PorkReport_f_web.pdf.

Schnell, Steven M. 2013. "Food Miles, Local Eating, and Community Supported Agriculture: Putting Local Food in Its Place." *Agriculture and Human Values* 30: 615–28.

Schools for Chiapas. n.d. "Mother Seeds in Resistance." https://schoolsforchiapas. org/advances/sustainable-agriculture/mother-seeds-resistance/.

Schoonover, Thomas and Ebba Schoonover. 1991. "Statistics for an Understanding of Foreign Intrusions into Central America from the 1820s to 1930. Part III." *Anuario de Estudios Cen-troamericanos* 17, no. 2: 77–119.

Schurman, Rachel and William A. Munro. 2010. *Fighting for the Future of Food: Activists versus Agribusiness in the Struggle over Biotechnology.* Minneapolis: University of Minnesota Press.

Schwenkenbecher, Anne. 2012. "Is There an Obligation to Reduce One's Individual Carbon Footprint?" *Critical Review of International Social and Political Philosophy* 17: 168–88.

Scoville, J. Michael. 2015. "Framing Food Justice." In *Just Food: Philosophy, Justice, and Food,* edited by J. M. Dieterle, 3–20. London: Rowman & Littlefield.

Sen, Amartya. 1981. *Poverty and Famine.* Oxford: Oxford University Press.

Sen, Amartya. 2006. "What Do We Want from a Theory of Justice?" *The Journal of Philosophy* 103, no. 5 (May): 215–38.

Sen, Amartya. 2011. *The Idea of Justice.* Cambridge, MA: Harvard University Press.

Sequeira, Aarón. 2018, January 16. "Juan Diego Castro combatiría a 'ecoterroristas' y explotaría oro y petróleo." *La Nación.*

Shah, Anup. 2007. "Global Issues: Food Aid." Accessed June 10, 2018. http://www. globalissues.org/article/748/food-aid#Typesoffoodaid.

Sharma, Kirti and Manish Paradakar. 2010. "The Melamine Adulteration Scandal." *Food Security* 2: 97–107.

Sharma, Shefali. 2017, December 19. "The Meaty Side of Climate Change." Minneapolis: Institute for Agricultural and Trade Policy. https://www.iatp.org/ blog/201712/meaty-side-climate-change.

Shepherd, Benjamin. 2012. "Thinking Critically about Food Security." *Security Dialogue* 43, no. 3: 195–212.

Sherwin, Susan and Katie Stockdale. 2017. "Whither Bioethics Now? The Promise of Relational Theory." *International Journal of Feminist Approaches to Bioethics* 10, no. 1: 7–29.

Shiva, Vandana. 1994. "Women, Ecology and Health: Rebuilding Connections." In *Close to Home. Women Reconnect Ecology, Health and Development,* edited by Vandana Shiva, 1–9. New York: Earthscan.

Shiva, Vandana. 2006. *Earth Democracy.* London: Zed Books.

Shrader-Frechette, Kristin. 2002. *Environmental Justice.* Oxford: Oxford University Press.

Shue, Henry. 2010a. "Global Environment and International Inequality." In *Climate Ethics: Essential Readings*, edited by Stephen M. Gardiner, Simon Caney, Dale Jamieson, and Henry Shue, 101–11. Oxford: Oxford University Press.

Shue, Henry. 2010b. "Deadly Delays, Saving Opportunities: Creating a More Dangerous World?" In *Climate Ethics: Essential Readings*, edited by Stephen M. Gardiner, Simon Caney, Dale Jamieson, and Henry Shue, 146–62. Oxford: Oxford University Press.

Shue, Henry. 2010c. "Subsistence Emissions and Luxury Emissions." In *Climate Ethics: Essential Readings*, edited by Stephen M. Gardiner, Simon Caney, Dale Jamieson, and Henry Shue, 200–14. Oxford: Oxford University Press.

Sierra Club: Michigan Chapter. n.d. "Why Are CAFOs Bad?" Accessed February 12, 2018. https://www.sierraclub.org/michigan/why-are-cafos-bad#pollutants.

Simms Hipp, Janie and Colby C. Duren. 2017. *Regaining Our Future: An Assessment of Risks and Opportunities for Native Communities in the 2018 Farm Bill*. Prior Lake, MN: Seeds of Native Health. http://seedsofnativehealth.org/wp-content/uploads/2017/06/Farm-Bill-Report_WEB.pdf.

Simon, David R. 2013. *Meatonomics*. San Francisco: Conari Press.

Sinclair, Upton. (1906) 2016. *The Jungle*. Stilwell, KS: Digireads.com.

Singer, Peter. 1972. "Famine, Affluence, and Morality." *Philosophy and Public Affairs* 1 (Spring): 229–43.

Singer, Peter. 1990. *Animal Liberation*. Revised edition. New York: Avon Books.

Singer, Peter. 2002. *One World*. New Haven, CT: Yale University Press.

Singer, Peter. 2009. *Animal Liberation*. New York: Harper Collins.

Siniscalchi, V. and C. Counihan. 2014. "Ethnography and Food Activism." In *Food Activism: Agency, Democracy and Economy*, edited by C. Counihan and V. Siniscalchi, 1–14. London: Bloomsbury.

Skolnick, Adam. 2017, February 23. "The CAFO Industry's Impact on Environment and Public Health." *Sierra*. https://www.sierraclub.org/sierra/2017-2-march-april/feature/cafo-industrys-impact-environment-and-public-health.

Slocum, Rachel and Kirsten Valentine Cadieux. 2015. "Notes on the Practice of Food Justice in the U.S.: Understanding and Confronting Trauma and Inequity." *Journal of Political Ecology* 22: 27–52.

Smiley, Marion. 2017. "Collective Responsibility." *The Stanford Encyclopedia of Philosophy* (Summer 2017), edited by Edward N. Zalta. https://plato.stanford.edu/archives/sum2017/entries/collective-responsibility/.

Smith, Alisa and J. B. MacKinnon. 2007. *Plenty*. New York: Harmony Books.

Smith, Alison, Paul Watkiss, Geoff Tweddle, Alan McKinnon, Mike Browne, Alistair Hunt, and Colin Treleven et al. 2005. "The Validity of Food Miles as an Indicator of Sustainable Development." London: UK DEFRA. Accessed on June 27, 2018. http://library.uniteddiversity.coop/Food/DEFRA_Food_Miles_Report.pdf.

Smith, K. Annabelle. 2013. "Why the Tomato Was Feared in Europe for More Than 200 Years." *Smithsonian Magazine*. Accessed July 3, 2017. https://www.smithsonianmag.com/arts-culture/why-the-tomato-was-feared-in-europe-for-more-than-200-years-863735/.

Smithfield Foods: 2014 Sustainability and Financial Report. https://www.smithfieldfoods.com/integrated-report/2014/international-operations.

Smithfield Foods. 2018, January. "Press Release: Smithfield Foods and Farm Fresh Join Forces to Donate Nearly 120,000 Pounds of Protein to Local Food Bank." https://www.smithfieldfoods.com/newsroom/press-releases-and-news/smithfield-foods-and-farm-fresh-join-forces-to-donate-nearly-120000-pounds-of-protein-to-three-local-food-banks.

Smoyer-Tomic, Karen E., John C. Spence, and Carl Amrhein. 2006. "Food Deserts in the Prairies? Supermarket Accessibility and Neighborhood Need in Edmonton, Canada." *Professional Geographer* 58, no. 3: 307–26.

Snyder, C. S., T. W. Bruulsma, T. L. Jensen, and P. E. Fixen. 2009. "Review of Greenhouse Gas Emissions from Crop Production Systems and Fertilizer Management Effects." *Agriculture, Ecosystems and Environment* 133: 247–66.

Solomon, Ilana. 2016, October 6. "Trade Deals and the Paris Climate Agreement." *State of the Planet*. Earth Institute, Columbia University. Accessed May 3, 2018. http://blogs.ei.columbia.edu/2016/10/06/its-time-to-align-trade-deals-with-the-paris-climate-agreement/.

Soper, Kate. 2004. "Rethinking the 'Good Life': The Consumer as Citizen." *Capitalism, Nature, Socialism* 15, no. 3: 111–17.

Springman, Marco, Daniel Mason-D'Croz, Sherman Robinson, Tara Garnett, H. Charles J. Godfray, Douglas Gollin, and Mike Rayner et al. 2016. "Global and Regional Health Effects of Future Food Production under Climate Change: A Modeling Study." *Lancet* 387: 1937–46.

Stanford, Victoria. 2015, July 31. "Aid Dependency: The Damage of Donation." July 31. https://www.twigh.org/twigh-blog-archives/2015/7/31/aid-dependency-the-damage-of-donation.

Star, Susan Leigh and James Griesemer. 1989. "Institutional Ecology, 'Translations' and Boundary Objects: Amateurs and Professionals in Berkeley's Museum of Vertebrate Zoology, 1907–39." *Social Studies of Science* 19, no. 3: 387–420.

Steinfeld, Henning, Pierre Gerber, Tom Wassenaar, Vincent Castel, Mauricio Rosales, and Cees De Haan. 2006. *Livestock's Long Shadow*. Rome: FAO.

Stern, Nicholas. 2008. "The Stern Review on the Economics of Climate Change." Accessed July 9, 2017. http://webarchive.nationalarchives.gov.uk/20080910140413/http://www.hm-treasury.gov.uk/independent_reviews/stern_review_economics_climate_change/sternreview_index.cfm.

Stilgoe, Jack, Richard Owen, and Phil Macnaghten. 2013. "Developing a Framework for Responsible Innovation." *Research Policy* 42, no. 9:1568–80.

Stocker, Thomas F. 2013. "The Closing Door of Climate Targets." *Science* 339: 280–82.

Stolle, Dietlind, Marc Hooghe, and Michele Micheletti. 2005. "Politics in the Supermarket: Political Consumerism as a Form of Political Participation." *International Political Science Review* 26: 245–69.

Sunstein, Cass. 2002. *Risk and Reason: Safety, Law and the Environment.* New York: Cambridge University Press.

Swinburn, Boyd A., Gary Sacks, Kevin D. Hall, Klim McPherson, Diane T. Finegood, and Marjorie L. Moody. 2011. "The Global Obesity Pandemic: Shaped by Global Drivers and Local Environments." *Lancet* 37, no. 9703: 804–14.

Symonds, Julian. (1972) 1992. *Bloody Murders*. London: Penguin.

Szende, Jennifer. 2015. "Food Deserts, Justice, and the Distributive Paradigm." In *Just Food*, edited by J. M. Dieterle, 57–68. Lanham, MD: Rowman & Littlefield.

Takeuchi, Shinichi. 2014. *Confronting Land and Property Problems for Peace*. New York: Routledge.

Talbot, John. 1997. "Where Does Your Coffee Dollar Go? The Division of Income and Surplus along the Coffee Commodity Chain." *Studies in Comparative International Development (SCID)* 32, no. 1: 56–91.

Tammelleo, Steve. 2015. "Food Policy, Mexican Migration and Collective Responsibility." In *Just Food,* edited by J. M. Dieterle, 101–18. London: Rowman & Littlefield.

Tanentzap, Andrew, Anthony Lamb, Susan Walker, and Andrew Farmer. 2015. "Resolving Conflicts between Agriculture and the Natural Environment." *PLoS Biology* 13, no. 9: 1–13.

Taylor, Charles. 1994. *Multiculturalism*. Princeton, NJ: Princeton University Press.

Tegtmeier, Erin M. and Michael D. Duffy. 2004. "External Costs of Agricultural Production in the United States." *International Journal of Agricultural Sustainability* 2, no. 1: 1–20. doi:10.1080/14735903.2004.9684563.

Tenkorang, Frank and James Lowenberg-DeBoer. 2008. "Forecasting Long-Term Global Fertilizer Demand." *Nutrient Cycling in Agroecosystems* 83, no. 3 (March): 1–17. doi:10.1007/s10705-008-9214-y.

Terminski, Bogumil. 2015. *Development-Induced Displacement and Resettlement*. Stuttgart: Ibidem-Verlag.

Tessman, Lisa. 2010. "Idealizing Morality." *Hypatia* 25, no. 4 (Fall): 797–824.

Thomas, Chris D., Alison Cameron, Rhys E. Green, Michel Bakkenes, Linda J. Beaumont, Yvonne C. Collingham, Barend F. N. Erasmus et al. 2004. "Extinction Risk from Climate Change." *Nature* 427, no. 6970: 145–48.

Thompson, Derik 2014. "Where Does Obesity Come From?" *The Atlantic*, Jan 14, 2014. https://www.theatlantic.com/business/archive/2014/01/where-does-obesity-come-from/283060/

Thompson, Krissah. 2010, October 20. "Native American Farmers Celebrate Settlement in USDA Discrimination Case." *Washington Post*. http://www.washingtonpost.com/wp-dyn/content/article/2010/10/20/AR2010102006171.html.

Thompson, Paul B. 1984. "Need and Safety: The Nuclear Power Debate." *Environmental Ethics* 6, no. 1: 57–69.

Thompson, Paul B. 1996. "Pragmatism and Policy: The Case of Water." In *Environmental Pragmatism*, edited by E. Light and A. Katz, 187–209. New York: Routledge.

Thompson, Paul B. 2009a. "Philosophy of Agricultural Technology." In *Philosophy of Technology and Engineering Sciences*, edited by Anthonie Meijers, 1257–73. Amsterdam: Elsevier.

Thompson, Paul B. 2009b. "The Presumptive Case for Nanotechnology." In *Nanotechnology & Society: Current and Emerging Ethical Issues,* edited by F. Allhoff and P. Lin, 39–54. Dordrecht, NL: Springer.

Thompson, Paul B. 2014. "The GMO Quandary and What It Means for Social Philosophy." *Social Philosophy Today* 30: 7–27.

Thompson, Paul B. 2015. *From Field to Fork: Food Ethics for Everyone.* New York: Oxford University Press.

Thompson, Paul B. 2017. *The Spirit of the Soil: Agriculture and Environmental Ethics.* 2nd edition. New York: Routledge.

Thompson, Paul and Samantha Noll. 2015. "Agriculture Ethics." In *Ethics, Science, Technology, and Engineering: An International Resource.* 2nd edition, edited by J. Britt Holbrook and Carl Mitcham, 35–42. Independence, MO: Cengage Press.

Thow, Anne Marie and Corinna Hawkes. 2009. "The Implications of Trade Liberalization for Diet and Health: A Case Study from Central America." *Globalization and Health* 5, no. 5. doi:10.1186/1744-8603-5-5.

Timmermann, Cristian. 2017, October 16. "Agricultural Innovation and Its Five Dimensions of Social Justice." Book manuscript overview presented at T. C. Beirne School of Law Seminar, University of Queensland, Brisbane, Australia.

Timmermann, Cristian and Georges F. Félix. 2015a. "Adapting Food Production to Climate Change: An Inclusive Approach." In *Climate Change and Human Rights: The 2015 Paris Conference and the Task of Protecting People on a Warming Planet,* edited by Marcello Di Paola and Daanika Kamal. Durham, UK: Global Policy.

Timmermann, Cristian and Georges F. Félix. 2015b. "Agroecology as a Vehicle for Contributive Justice." *Agriculture and Human Values* 32, no. 3: 523–38.

Tingley, Morgan W., William B. Monahan, Steven R. Beissinger, and Craig Moritz. 2009. "Birds Track Their Grinnellian Niche through a Century of Climate Change." *Proceedings of the National Academy of Sciences* 106(Supplement 2): 19637–43.

Tittonell, Pablo, Laurens Klerkx, Frederic Baudron, Georges F. Félix, Andrea Ruggia, Dirk van Apeldoorn, Santiago Dogliotti, Paul Mapfumo, and Walter A.H. Rossing. 2016. "Ecological Intensification: Local Innovation to Address Global Challenges." *Sustainable Agriculture Reviews* 19: 1–34.

Tongwane, Mphethe, Thandile Mdlambuzi, Mokhele Moeletsi, Mitsuru Tsubo, Vuyo Mliswa, and Lunga Grootboom. 2016. "Greenhouse Gas Emissions from Different Crop Production and Management Practices in South Africa." *Environmental Development* 19: 23–35. doi:10.1016/j.envdev.2016.06.004.

Treuhaft, Sarah and Allison Karpyn. 2010. "The Grocery Gap: Who Has Food and Why it Matters." The Food Trust. Accessed March 2018. http://thefoodtrust.org/uploads/media_items/grocerygap.original.pdf.

Trewavas, Antony. 2002. "Malthus Foiled Again and Again." *Nature* 418: 668–70.

Tribes Uniting to Protect Bears Ears. n.d. http://bearsearscoalition.org/about-the-coalition/tribal-statements-of-support/.

Tsosie, Rebecca. 2007. "Indigenous Peoples and Environmental Justice: The Impact of Climate Change." *University of Colorado Law Review* 78: 1625–78.

UN General Assembly. 1948, December 10. "Universal Declaration of Human Rights." http://www.refworld.org/docid/3ae6b3712c.html.

UN General Assembly. 1966, December 16. "International Covenant on Economic, Social and Cultural Rights." http://www.ohchr.org/EN/ProfessionalInterest/Pages/CESCR.aspx.

UNCAT (United Nations Committee Against Torture). 2016. "Review of Saudi Arabia." 57th Session of the United Nations Committee Against Torture. https://www.ohchr.org/en/NewsEvents/Pages/DisplayNews.aspx?NewsID=19837&LangID=E.

UNCCD. 1994, June 17. "Convention Text." *United Nations Convention to Combat Desertification.* Accessed May 8, 2018. https://www.unccd.int/sites/default/files/relevant-links/2017-01/UNCCD_Convention_ENG_0.pdf.

Union of Concerned Scientists. n.d. "The Hidden Costs of Fossil Fuels." Accessed June 15, 2018. https://www.ucsusa.org/clean-energy/coal-and-other-fossil-fuels/hidden-cost-of-fossils#.WyfS7Kknbdc.

United Nations. n.d. "Water." Accessed March 1, 2018. http://www.un.org/en/sections/issues-depth/water/.

United Nations Framework Convention on Climate Change. n.d.a. "History of the Convention: Essential Background." Accessed on May 30, 2018. https://unfccc.int/process/the-convention/history-of-the-convention#eq-1.

United Nations Framework Convention on Climate Change. n.d.b. "The Paris Agreement: Essential Elements." Accessed on May 30, 2018. https://unfccc.int/process-and-meetings/the-paris-agreement/the-paris-agreement.

United Nations High Commissioner for Refugees. 2017. "Global Trends: Forced Displacement in 2016." Accessed May 14, 2018. http://www.unhcr.org/statistics/unhcrstats/5943e8a34/global-trends-forced-displacement-2016.html.

United States Department of Agriculture Economic Research Service. n.d. "Background." Accessed June 15, 2018. https://www.ers.usda.gov/topics/crops/corn-and-other-feedgrains/background/.

United States Energy Information Administration. 2011 "Emissions of Greenhouse Gases in the United States." Accessed June 15, 2018. https://www.eia.gov/environment/emissions/ghg_report/ghg_nitrous.php.

United States Environmental Protection Agency. Also see EPA.

United States Environmental Protection Agency. n.d. "Overview of Greenhouse Gases: Methane Emissions." Accessed March 18, 2017. https://www.epa.gov/ghgemissions/overview-greenhouse-gases.

United States Environmental Protection Agency. 2015. "Climate Impacts on Agriculture and Food Supply." Overviews and Factsheets. Accessed May 15, 2018. https://19january2017snapshot.epa.gov/climate-impacts/climate-impacts-agriculture-and-food-supply_.html.

United States Environmental Protection Agency. 2018. "Greenhouse Gas Emissions: Overview of Greenhouse Gases." Accessed August 25, 2018. https://www.epa.gov/ghgemissions/overview-greenhouse-gases#methane.

Urban, Mark C. 2015. "Accelerating Extinction Risk from Climate Change." *Science* 348, no. 6234: 571–73.

USDA. (United States Department of Agriculture). 2017, May 18. "Food Access Research Atlas." https://www.ers.usda.gov/data-products/food-access-research-atlas/go-to-the-atlas/.

Valentini, Laura. 2012. "Ideal vs. Non-Ideal Theory: A Conceptual Map." *Philosophy Compass* 7, no. 9: 654–64.

Valkila, Jouni and Anja Nygren. 2009. "Impacts of Fair Trade Certification on Coffee Farmers, Cooperatives, and Laborers in Nicaragua." *Agriculture and Human Values* 27, no. 3: 321–33.

Van de Poel, Ibo. 2011. "The Relation between Forward-Looking and Backward-Looking Responsibility." In *Moral Responsibility*, edited by Nicole Vincent, Ibo van de Poel, and Jeroen van den Hoven, 37–52. Dordrecht, NL: Springer.

Van de Poel, Ibo, Jessica Nihlén Fahlquist, Neelke Doorn, Sjoerd Zwart, and Lamber Royakkers. 2012. "The Problem of Many Hands: Climate Change as an Example." *Science and Engineering Ethics* 18, no. 1: 49–67.

Van Passel, Steven. 2010. "Food Miles to Sustainability: A Revision." *Sustainable Development* 21: 1–17.

Vanloqueren, Gaetan and Phillipe V. Baret. 2009. "How Agricultural Research Systems Shape a Technological Regime that Develops Genetic Engineering but Locks Out Agroecological Innovations." *Research Policy* 38: 971–83.

Vaux, Henry. 2012. "Water for Agriculture and the Environment: The Ultimate Trade-Off." *Water Policy* 14, no. S1: 136.

Vermeulen, Sonja J., Bruce M. Campbell, and John S. I. Ingram. 2012. "Climate Change and Food Systems." *Annual Review of Environment and Resources* 37: 195–222.

Vivek, B. S., Girish Kumar Krishna, V. Vengadessan, R. Babu, P. H. Zaidi, Le Quy Kha, S. S. Mandal et al. 2017. "Use of Genomic Estimated Breeding Values Results in Rapid Genetic Gains for Drought Tolerance in Maize." *Plant Genome* 10. doi:10.3835/plantgenome2016.07.0070.

Von Braun, Joachim. 2007, December. "The World Food Situation. New Driving Forces and Required Actions." International Food Policy Research Institute. doi:10.2499/0896295303.

Von Schomberg, René. 2012. "Prospects for Technology Assessment in a Framework of Responsible Research and Innovation." In *Technikfolgen abschätzen lehren*, edited by Marc Dusseldorp and Richard Beecroft, 39–61. Wiesbaden: VS Verlag für Sozialwissenschaften.

Von Schomberg, René. 2015. "Responsible Innovation: The New Paradigm for Science, Technology and Innovation Policy." In *Responsible Innovation: Neue Impulse für die Technikfolgenabschätzung*, edited by A. Bogner, M. Decker, and M. Sotoudeh, 47–70. Baden-Baden: Nomos.

Wahlberg, Katarina. 2008, January. "Food Aid for the Hungry?" *Global Policy Forum*. https://www.globalpolicy.org/component/content/article/217-hunger/46251-food-aid-for-the-hungry.html.

Walker, Renee E., R. Christopher Keane, and G. Jessica Burke. 2010. "Disparities and Access to Healthy Food in the United States: A Review of Food Deserts Literature." *Health & Place* 16: 876–84.

Wallinga, David. 2009. "Food System: How Healthy Is It?" *Journal of Hunger & Environmental Nutrition* 4, no. 3-4 (July): 251–81. doi:10.1080/19320240903336977.

Walzer, Michael. 1983. *Spheres of Justice*. New York: Basic Books.

Warman, Arturo. 2003. *Corn and Capitalism: How a Botanical Bastard Grew to Global Dominance*. Chapel Hill: University of North Carolina Press.

Warren, Karen. 2000. *Ecofeminist Philosophy*. Lanham, MD: Rowman & Littlefield.

Weatherspoon, Dave, James Oehmke, Assa Dembele, Marcus Coleman, Thasanee Satimanon, and Lorraine Weatherspoon. 2013. "Price and Expenditure Elasticities for Fresh Fruits in an Urban Food Desert." *Urban Studies* 50, no. 1: 88–106.

Webb, Patrick, Christine Caiafa, and Shelley Walton. 2017, October 18. "Making Food Aid Fit-for-Purpose in the 21st Century." http://journals.sagepub.com/doi/full/10.1177/0379572117726422.

Weber, Christopher. L. and H. Scott Matthews. 2008. "Food-Miles and the Relative Climate Impacts of Food Choices in the United States." *Environmental Science and Technology* 42, no. 10: 3508–13.

Welsh, Jennifer and Rod MacRae. 1998. "Food Citizenship and Community Food Security: Lessons from Toronto, Canada." *Canadian Journal of Development Studies* 19, no. 4: 237–55.

Werkheiser, Ian, Shakara Tyler, and Paul B. Thompson. 2015. "Food Sovereignty: Two Conceptions of Food Justice." In *Just Food*, edited by J. M. Dierterle, 71–86. Lanham, MD: Rowman & Littlefield.

Whelan, Amanda, Neil Wrigley, Daniel Warm, and Elizabeth Cannings. 2002. "Life in a 'Food Desert.'" *Urban Studies* 39, no. 11: 2083–2100.

Whyte, Kyle Powys. 2018. "Food Sovereignty, Justice and Indigenous Peoples: An Essay on Settler Colonialism and Collective Continuance." In *The Oxford Handbook of Food Ethics*, edited by Anne Barnhill, Tyler Doggett, and Mark Budolfson, 345–66. New York: Oxford University Press.

Wickson, Fern. 2007. "From Risk to Uncertainty in the Regulation of GMOs: Social Theory and Australian Practice." *New Genetics and Society* 26: 325–39.

Wilkins, Jennifer. 2005. "Eating Right Here: Moving from Consumer to Food Citizen." *Agriculture and Human Values* 22, no. 3: 269–73.

Working Group I to the Fifth Assessment Report of the Intergovernmental Panel on Climate Change. 2013. *Climate Change 2013: The Physical Science Basis*. New York: Cambridge University Press.

Working Groups I, II, and III to the Fifth Assessment Report of the Intergovernmental Panel on Climate Change. 2015. *Climate Change 2014: Synthesis Report*. Geneva, CH: IPCC.

Working Group II to the Fifth Assessment Report of the Intergovernmental Panel on Climate Change. 2014. *Climate Change 2014: Impacts, Adaptation, and Vulnerability*. New York: Cambridge University Press.

Working Group III to the Fourth Assessment Report of the Intergovernmental Panel on Climate Change. 2007. *Climate Change 2007: Mitigation of Climate Change*. Cambridge, MA: Cambridge University Press.

Working Group III to the Fifth Assessment Report of the Intergovernmental Panel on Climate Change. 2014. *Climate Change 2014: Mitigation of Climate Change.* New York: Cambridge University Press.

World Atlas. 2017, April 25. "Top Pesticide Consuming Countries in the World." https://www.worldatlas.com/articles/top-pesticide-consuming-countries-of-the-world.html

World Bank. 1986. "World Development Report 1986." New York: Oxford University Press. https://openknowledge.worldbank.org/bitstream/handle/10986/5969/WDR%201986%20-%20English.pdf?sequence=1.

World Bank. 2016. "Development Goals in an Era of Demographic Change." Washington DC: The World Bank. http://pubdocs.worldbank.org/en/503001444058224597/Global-Monitoring-Report-2015.pdf.

The World Bank data. 2017. Accessed September 9, 2018. https://data.worldbank.org/indicator/TX.VAL.FOOD.ZS.UN?view=map&year=2015&year_high_desc=true.

The World Bank. 2018. "Overview." Accessed May 14, 2018. http://www.worldbank.org/en/topic/poverty/overview.

World Factbook. 2015. Accessed September 9, 2018. U.S. Central Intelligence Agency. https://www.cia.gov/library/publications/download/download-2015/index.html.

World Food Program USA. n.d. "Types of Food WFP Delivers." https://www.wfpusa.org/about-wfp-usa/what-wfp-delivers/.

World Food Programme. 2018a. "Climate Impacts on Food Security: United Nations World Food Programme—Fighting Hunger Worldwide." Accessed May 14, 2018. https://www.wfp.org/climate-change/climate-impacts.

World Food Programme. 2018b. "Zero Hunger." Accessed April 2018. http://www.wfp.org/hunger/causes.

World Health Organization (WHO). 2014. "Quantitative Risk Assessment of the Effects of Climate Change on Selected Causes of Death, 2030s and 2050s." Accessed January 16, 2018. http://www.who.int/globalchange/publications/quantitative-risk-assessment/en/.

World Health Organization (WHO). 2017, October 18. "Obesity and Overweight." Fact Sheet. http://www.who.int/news-room/fact-sheets/detail/obesity-and-overweight.

World Resources Institute. n.d.a. "About Eutrophication." Accessed June 15, 2018. http://www.wri.org/our-work/project/eutrophication-and-hypoxia/about-eutrophication.

World Resources Institute. n.d.b. "Everything You Need to Know About Agricultural Emissions." Accessed June 15, 2018. http://www.wri.org/blog/2014/05/everything-you-need-know-about-agricultural-emissions.

Wright, Angus. 2005. *The Death of Ramón González: The Modern Agricultural Dilemma.* 2nd edition. Austin: University of Texas Press.

Wrigley, Neil. 2002. "'Food Deserts' in British Cities: Policy Context and Research Priorities." *Urban Studies* 39, no. 11: 2029–40.

Wrock, Rebecca Kristen. 2016. "Ignorance Is Bliss: Self-Regulation and Ag-Gag Laws in the American Meat Industry." *Contemporary Justice Review* 19, no. 2: 267–79.

Yaggi, Marc. 2017, December 6. "Problems Persist after Smithfield Sells Out to Shuanghui; Future Remains Uncertain." *Huffington Post*. https://www. huffingtonpost.com/marc-yaggi/problems-persist-after-sm_b_4617980.html.

Yagoub, Mimi. 2016, February 11. "Why Does Latin America Have the World's Highest Female Murder Rates?" *Insight Crime*.

Young, Iris Marion. 1986. "The Ideal Community and the Politics of Difference." *Social Theory and Practice* 12: 1–26.

Young, Iris Marion. 1990. *Justice and the Politics of Difference*. Princeton, NJ: Princeton University Press.

Young, Iris Marion. 2006. "Responsibility and Global Justice: A Social Connection Model." *Social Philosophy and Policy* 23, no. 1: 102–30.

Young, Iris Marion. 2011. *Responsibility for Justice*. New York: Oxford University Press.

Zack, Naomi. 2017. "Starting from Injustice: Justice, Applicative Justice, and Injustice Theory." *The Harvard Review of Philosophy* 24: 79–95.

Zaino, Caitlin. 2008. "Sticky Sticker Situation: Food Miles, Carbon Labelling and Development." *International Centre for Trade and Sustainable Development*, no. 2. Accessed on June 26, 2018. http://ictsd.org/i/news/bioresreview/12095/.

Zeebe, Richard. 2013. "Time-Dependent Climate Sensitivity and the Legacy of Anthropogenic Greenhouse Gas Emissions." *Proceedings of the National Academy of Science* 110, no. 34: 13739–44.

Zhao, Chuang, Bing Liu, Shilong Piao, Xuhui Wang, David B. Lobell, Yao Huang, and Mengtian Huang et al. 2017. "Temperature Increase Reduces Global Yields of Major Crops in Four Independent Estimates." *Proceedings of the National Academy of Sciences* 114, no. 35 (August 29): 9326–31. doi:10.1073/pnas.1701762114.

Zwart, Hub, Laurens Landeweerd, and Arjan van Rooij. 2014. "Adapt or Perish? Assessing the Recent Shift in the European Research Funding Arena from 'ELSA' to 'RRI.'" *Life Sciences, Society and Policy* 10: 11.

Index

About the Contributors

Deborah Adelman is a professor of English at the College of DuPage in Glen Ellyn, Illinois. Her work includes essays, fiction, reviews, and books on youth in Moscow during the era of perestroika. Her recent work explores the intersection of the humanities and ecology, with a particular interest in the role of ecocriticism and ecocinema in college curricula. Recent articles include an examination of Bed-Stuy as a food desert in *Do the Right Thing* and an analysis of the representation of nomadic peoples in feature films. She is co-founder and co-director of the Community Education Farm at the College of DuPage, an experiential and service learning site for students and community members.

Shamili Ajgaonkar is a professor of biology at the College of DuPage in Glen Ellyn, Illinois. Her primary work is teaching and curriculum development. In addition to teaching biology and environmental science in various modes of delivery, including traditional classroom, online, field-based, and interdisciplinary seminars, she has developed environmental science courses for local, national, and international settings. Recently she co-wrote a lab manual for teaching environmental biology. She is co-founder and co-director of the Community Education Farm at the College of DuPage, an experiential and service learning site that engages students in addressing food security issues. In her teaching practice she is deeply committed to advancing ecoliteracy. She believes education should help harness our creative abilities to learn to live on a crowded planet and encourages students to critically analyze the meaning and place of ecological systems in human society and explore creative solutions to solve the pressing environmental challenges.

Rachel A. Ankeny is a professor in the School of Humanities and associate dean (research) in the Faculty of Arts at the University of Adelaide, Australia. She is an interdisciplinary teacher and scholar whose areas of expertise cross three fields: history/philosophy of science, bioethics and science policy, and food studies. She is well-recognized as a scholar who can translate academic findings in ways that are relevant for stakeholders in a range of sectors and the broader community. She holds competitive grants from the Australian Research Council on several topics, including food ethics, the history of genetic modification science and activism in Australia, and perceptions of animal welfare among red meat consumers.

Gabriela Arguedas-Ramírez is an associate professor of philosophy and women's studies at the Universidad de Costa Rica, where she teaches bioethics and feminist topics. She holds a professional doctorate in pharmacy, a master's degree in bioethics, and is currently finishing a PhD in cultural studies, working on the issues of hunger, justice and subjectivity in Central America. She has published articles about the ethics of genetic patents, obstetric power/violence, ecofeminism, religious fundamentalism, and sexual rights. She is the author of *Situación de los Derechos Humanos de Poblaciones Históricamente Discriminadas en Costa Rica* (2013). In 2015, as part of an alliance between the Center for Justice and International Law (CEJIL) and the Women's Studies Research Center (CIEM) at the University of Costa Rica, she presented the results of her research on obstetric violence in Costa Rica, in a thematic audience for the Inter-American Commission on Human Rights. She is currently working with Dr. Steven Miles, professor emeritus at the University of Minnesota, on the Spanish translation of his book, *Doctors Who Torture: The Pursuit of Justice.*

Anita Endrezze is a writer and artist living in Washington State. She is the author of a recent book of short stories, *Butterfly Moon.* She also has written two chapbooks as well as earlier books of poetry. A new book of poems, *Enigma*, is forthcoming. She is of European and Native American (Yaqui, Maya, Lower Pima) heritage.

Erinn Gilson is an associate professor of philosophy at Skidmore College, Saratoga Springs, New York, and, prior to that, taught at the University of North Florida from 2010 to 2018. She teaches about and researches a diverse range of topics in ethics, social and political philosophy, and feminist theory, with particular interest in food justice, racial justice, and sexual justice, and a focus on the concept of vulnerability. Her publications include *The Ethics of Vulnerability* (2014), "Vote with Your Fork?: Responsibility for Food Justice," in *Social Philosophy Today* (2014); "Food and Choice," in *The Encyclopedia of Food and Agriculture Ethics*, edited by David Kaplan and Paul B. Thompson (2013); "Vulnerability, Relationality, and Dependency: Feminist Conceptual Resources for Food Justice," in the *International Journal of Feminist Approaches to Bioethics* (2015); and "Beyond Bounded Selves and Places: The Relational Making of Vulnerability and Security," in the *Journal of the British Society for Phenomenology* (2018).

Sarah Kenehan is an associate professor in the Department of Philosophy and Religious Studies at Marywood University in Scranton, Pennsylvania. She earned her PhD in 2010 from Karl Franzens University of Graz in Austria, with specializations in liberal political philosophy (esp. Rawls), international justice, and climate justice. She currently teaches and writes in various areas of ethics and social and political philosophy, including climate justice, Rawls, and animal ethics. Her recent work has appeared in *Climate Justice and Historical Emissions*, edited by L. Meyer and P. Sanklecha (2017); and *The Ethics of Animal Experimentation: Working Towards a Paradigm Change*, edited by K. Herrmann and K. Jayne (2018).

Teea Kortetmäki (PhD) is a postdoctoral researcher at the University of Tampere. Her areas of interest include environmental and food justice, sustainable food systems, and environmental critical theory. Her recent publications include "Reification of Nonhuman Nature," in *Environmental Values*, and two co-authored book chapters on food justice: "Charitable Food Aid in a Nordic Welfare State: A Case for Environmental and Social Injustice," in *The Ecosocial Transition of Societies*; and "Food Systems and Climate Engineering: A Plate Full of Risks or Promises?" in *Climate Justice and Geoengineering*. Currently Kortetmäki studies the obstacles to sustainability transformation in the regional food systems in Finland.

Wendy Lynne Lee is a professor of philosophy at Bloomsburg University of Pennsylvania, where she has taught for over 25 years. Her primary objectives have long been to realize a philosophically informed life both professionally and personally as a citizen dissident. She is deeply committed to teaching and writing as an engaged philosopher, especially with respect to environmental, feminist, social and economic justice, and animal rights issues. Lee has published about 45 scholarly essays in her areas of expertise: philosophy of language (particularly later Wittgenstein), philosophy of mind/brain, feminist theory, theory of sexual identity, post-Marxian theory, nonhuman animal welfare, ecological aesthetics, aesthetic phenomenology, and philosophy of ecology. She was a founding member of the Shale Justice Coalition, ran for lieutenant governor on the 2014 Pennsylvania Green Party ticket, and was vice president of the National Community Rights Network, a branch of the Community Environmental Legal Defense Fund. She's a lifelong vegetarian and has shared her home with a number of rescue animals. She writes an incendiary current issues blog called *The Wrench*. Her most recent book is *Eco-Nihilism: The Philosophical Geopolitics of the Climate Change Apocalypse* (2017). She is now hard at work drafting *This Is Environmental Ethics*. Lee has most recently been involved in the struggle to defend academic freedom against resurgent white nationalist repression courtesy of the profoundly authoritarian and corrupt administration of Donald Trump.

Clement Loo is assistant professor of environmental studies at the University of Minnesota, Morris, and a member of the advisory council of the Association for the Advancement of Sustainability in Higher Education (AASHE). His research focuses on identifying strategies to ensure that marginalized communities are adequately and appropriately included in interventions intended to improve food access. In particular, he is interested in considering how community-academic partnerships might play a role in adapting food systems to climate change or addressing the global obesity crisis.

Joan McGregor is a professor of philosophy in the School of Historical, Philosophical, and Religious Studies at Arizona State University, senior scholar with the School of Sustainability, and a fellow at ASU's Institute for Humanities Research. McGregor's current research interests are focused on moral and legal questions in sustainability and, in particular, food systems and sustainability. She has collaborated with scientists and engineers, worked on the ethics of emerging technologies and concerns to indigenous peoples, among other issues, and published widely in jurisprudence and bioethics. McGregor was co-director of three NEH summer institutes on sustainability: "Fierce Green Fire: Aldo Leopold and the Foundations of Environmental Ethics," "Rethinking the Land Ethic: Humanities and Sustainability," and, in 2016, "Extending the Land Ethic."

Dr. **Samantha Noll** is an assistant professor in the School of Politics, Philosophy, and Public Affairs (PPPA) at Washington State University. She is also the bioethicist affiliated with the Functional Genomics Initiative, which marshals genome editing to control disease in livestock and feed a growing population. Noll's research and teaching focuses on ethical and philosophical topics in food and agriculture. In particular, she publishes widely on topics such as how values impact consumer uptake of agricultural products, local food movements, and the application of genomics technology. Noll contributes to the fields of bioethics (ethics of biotechnology), philosophy of food, and environmental philosophy.

John Nolt and **Annette Mendola**, both philosophers, are a married couple. Together they grow and prepare much of their food at home but also buy from grocery stores, farmers' markets, and a local food co-op. John is a Distinguished Service professor in philosophy at the University of Tennessee and a research fellow in the Energy and Environmental Policy Program at the Howard H. Baker Jr. Center for Public Policy. He specializes in philosophical logic, formal value theory, environmental ethics, and climate ethics and has written or edited seven books, most recently *Environmental Ethics for the Long Term* (2015). Annette is the director of the Division of Clinical Ethics at the University of Tennessee Medical Center and an assistant professor of clinical ethics at the Graduate School of Medicine at the University of Tennessee, Knoxville. She has written or contributed to several articles on practical ethics in medicine and everyday life.

Mary C. Rawlinson is a professor and the director of graduate studies in the Department of Philosophy and an affiliated faculty in art history and women's and gender studies at Stony Brook University in New York. Rawlinson's publications include *Just Life: Bioethics and the Future of Sexual Difference* (2016), *Engaging the World: Thinking after Irigaray* (2016), *The Routledge Handbook of Food Ethics* (2016), *Labor and Global Justice* (2014), *Global Food, Global Justice* (2015), *Thinking with Irigaray* (2011), and *Derrida and Feminism* (1997), as well as articles on Hegel, Proust, literature and ethics, bioethics, and contemporary French philosophy. Rawlinson was the founding editor of *IJFAB: International Journal of Feminist Approaches to Bioethics* (2006–2016) and co-founder and co-director of the Irigaray Circle (2007–2017). Currently, she is a senior visiting research fellow at the Institute for Advanced Studies, University College, London.

Zoë Robaey is a postdoctoral researcher working on inclusive biobased innovations within the IBIS project at Delft University of Technology. After completing her PhD in ethics of technology on moral responsibility for the uncertain risks of GMOs, she worked in technology assessment for new biotechnologies at the Rathenau Institute. Through her work in applied ethics, Zoë brings together her previous experience from public policy, science and technology studies, and biology.

Jennifer Szende is an assistant professor of philosophy at McMaster University. She completed her PhD at Queen's University, Canada, in political philosophy, focusing on human rights and justice in international relations. She completed postdoctoral fellowships at the Centre de Recherche en Éthique at l'Université de Montréal and at the University of Guelph, Canada. Her work has appeared in the *Journal of Global Ethics*; the *Encyclopedia of Global Justice*, edited by Deen Chatterjee; and the volume *Just Food: Philosophy, Justice and Food*, edited by J. M. Dieterle. Her current work brings the insights of feminist theory and relational autonomy to bear on questions of environmental political theory.

Paul B. Thompson is the W. K. Kellogg professor of agricultural, food and community ethics at Michigan State University, where he is also a professor in the departments of philosophy, of community sustainability, and of agricultural, food and resources economics. Thompson has been publishing philosophical studies of emerging technology in the food system for over thirty years, with work appearing in scientific journals including *Plant Pathology, The Journal of Animal Science, Poultry Science, Agriculture and Human Values*, and *Reproduction, Fertility and Development.* His work on gene technology has been translated into French, German, Chinese, Japanese, and Arabic. A second edition of his book *The Spirit of the Soil: Agriculture and Environmental Ethics* appeared in 2017. Thompson's work is supported financially by AgBioResearch at Michigan State and the U.S. Department of Agriculture Hatch Project Number MICL02324.

Cristian Timmermann, PhD, studied philosophy and political science at the Ludwig-Maximilian University, Germany, and Wageningen University, The Netherlands. He is currently a postdoctoral researcher at the Universidad de Chile, after holding research positions at the Universidad Nacional Autónoma de México and the Ben-Gurion University of the Negev, Israel, and shorter academic stays in Manchester, Geneva, Rome, Salzburg and Brisbane. His research areas are agricultural ethics, global justice, science policy, resource governance and property theories. His work has been published in, among other journals, *Agriculture and Human Values, Science and Engineering Ethics, Journal of Agricultural and Environmental Ethics, Agroecology and Sustainable Food Systems*, and *Social Justice Research.*